Alexandre Vatimbella

I0464412

CONTRASTS

DYLIC

© 2016 DYLIC - Vatimbella

Foreword

I do not know if the photography is an art, a technique, a simple testimony of the time when a cliché is taken or all this at the same time.

On the other hand, I know that a photographer, whatever happens, disguises the reality by giving at a short-lived moment the impression of eternity, persuading the existence of a more or less congealed world.

It is moreover always the reality of the photographer, the one that he creates, by his choice of subject, his setting and his decision to rest at some point to the trigger of his device.

Thus a photo is always a unique work even if, at the same moment, thousands of photographers are in the same place, pressing on the triggers of their devices all at the same time.

What makes all the difference, it's the eye of the photographer.

It is moreover how we recognize a good photographer from a bad one. Not by the technical quality of a cliché. In this 21st century, it is often easier "to nail the shot" than to miss it with all the technology which contains a camera, with all which allows us to retouch it if we wish to.

So, from now on, it's not any more simply the fashion photo or the cliché that is used as a medium to an advertising which are "enhanced" and "enhanced again" to reach a perfect image but it is made in all the domains.

But a photo also has to see with magic.

It's deeper than what it shows at first sight. It doesn't tell a story but so many stories as there are of people who are going to look at it. Of course, there is a scene immortalized by the objective of the device. But there is all that we want to see in this scene, all that it evokes, a whole reality which collides with our imagination.

Each sees in a photo its own vision of the scene presented while sharing the reality which this one shows.

It's the reason why it appreciates solo but also in society.

To look at photos together is a social activity which share with enjoyment and pleasure all the women, the men and the children of the planet.

The photo, in spite of the moving picture which definitively invaded our everyday life and which plunges us into a world connected continuously, continues to amaze us.

To open a book of photos or a family photo album, it is these short-lived moments caught by the eye of the photographer through the objective of its camera that provoke in us this interest, this attraction, even memories, which never a moving picture can give.

That is why the photography will disappear not for a while...

Alexandre Vatimbella

Avant-propos

Je ne sais si la photographie est un art, une technique, un simple témoignage de l'époque où un cliché a été pris ou tout cela à la fois.

En revanche, je sais que photographe, quoiqu'il arrive, travestit la réalité en donnant à un instant éphémère l'impression de l'éternité, faisant croire à l'existence d'un monde plus ou moins figé.

Il s'agit d'ailleurs toujours de la réalité du photographe, de celle qu'il crée, par son choix de sujet, son cadrage et sa décision d'appuyer à un instant donné sur le déclencheur de son appareil.

Une photo est donc toujours une œuvre unique même si, au même moment, se trouvent des milliers de photographes au même endroit et appuyant sur les déclencheurs de leurs appareils tous en même temps.

Ce qui fait toute la différence, c'est l'œil du photographe.

C'est d'ailleurs à cela que l'on reconnait un bon photographe, d'un mauvais.

Et non pas dans la qualité technique d'un cliché en ce XXI° siècle où il est souvent plus facile de "réussir" une photo que de la rater avec toute la technologie que contient un appareil photo, avec tout ce qui permet ensuite de la retoucher si on le souhaite.

Ainsi, désormais, ce n'est plus simplement la photo de mode ou le cliché qui sert de support à une publicité qui sont "travaillés" et "retravaillés" pour parvenir une image parfaite mais cela se fait dans tous les domaines.

Mais une photo a aussi à voir avec la magie.

Elle est bien plus profonde que ce qu'elle montre de prime abord. Elle ne raconte pas une histoire mais autant d'histoires qu'il y a de personnes qui vont la regarder. Bien sûr, il y a la scène immortalisée par l'objectif de l'appareil. Mais il y a tout ce que l'on veut voir dans cette scène, tout ce que cela évoque, toute une réalité qui s'entrechoque avec nos imaginaires. Chacun voit dans une photo sa propre vision de la scène présentée tout en partageant le réel que celle-ci montre.

C'est la raison pour laquelle elle s'apprécie en solitaire mais aussi en société.

Regarder des photos ensemble est une activité sociale que partagent avec joie et plaisir tous les femmes, les hommes et les enfants de la planète.

La photo, malgré l'image animée qui a définitivement envahi notre quotidien et qui nous plonge dans un monde connecté en continu, continue de nous émerveiller.

Ouvrir un livre de photos ou un album photos familial, ce sont ces instants éphémères attrapés par l'œil du photographe à travers l'objectif de son appareil photo qui provoquent en nous cet intérêt, cet attrait, voire des souvenirs, que jamais une image animée ne pourra donner.

C'est pourquoi la photographie ne disparaîtra pas de sitôt...

Alexandre Vatimbella

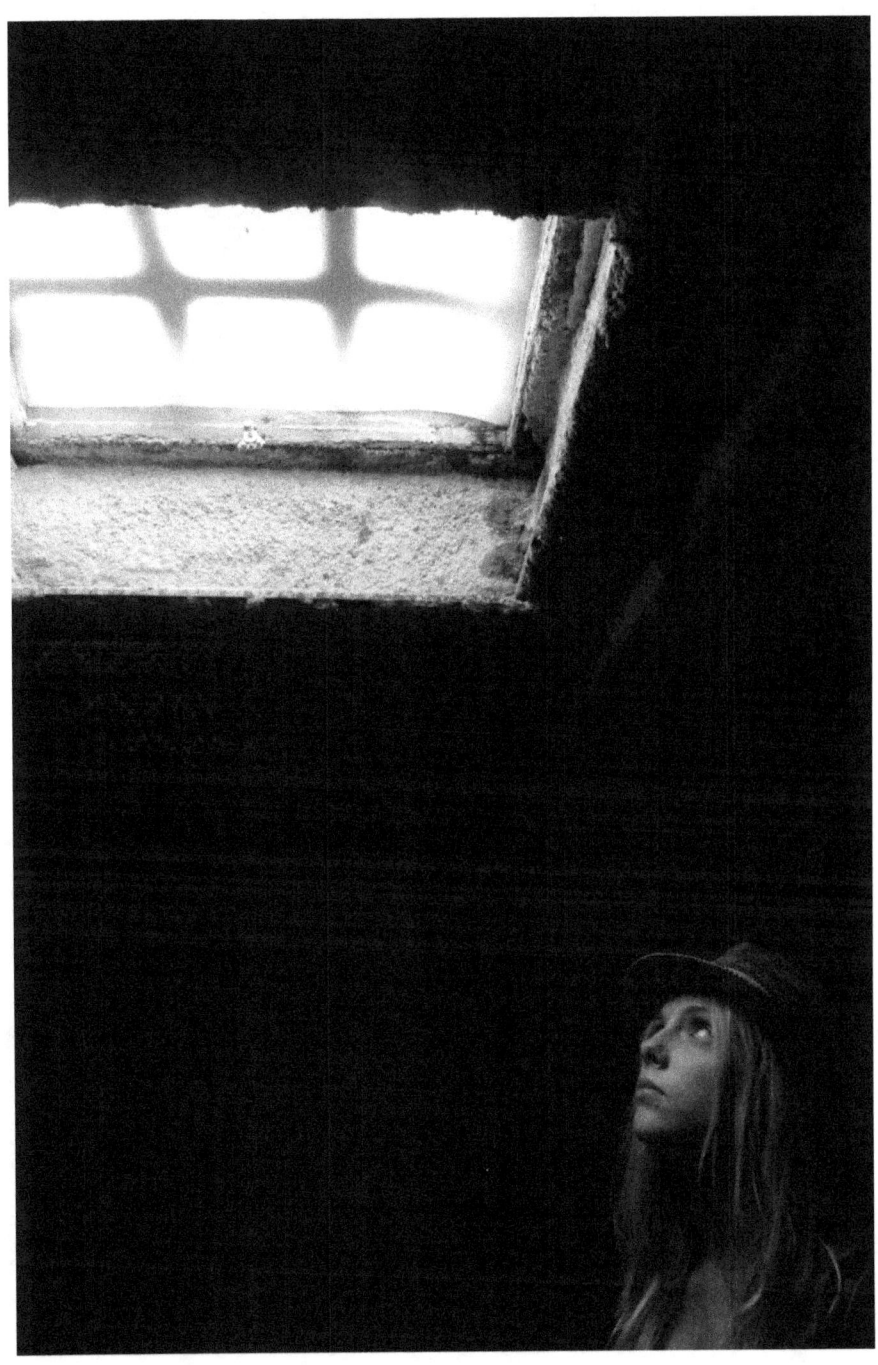

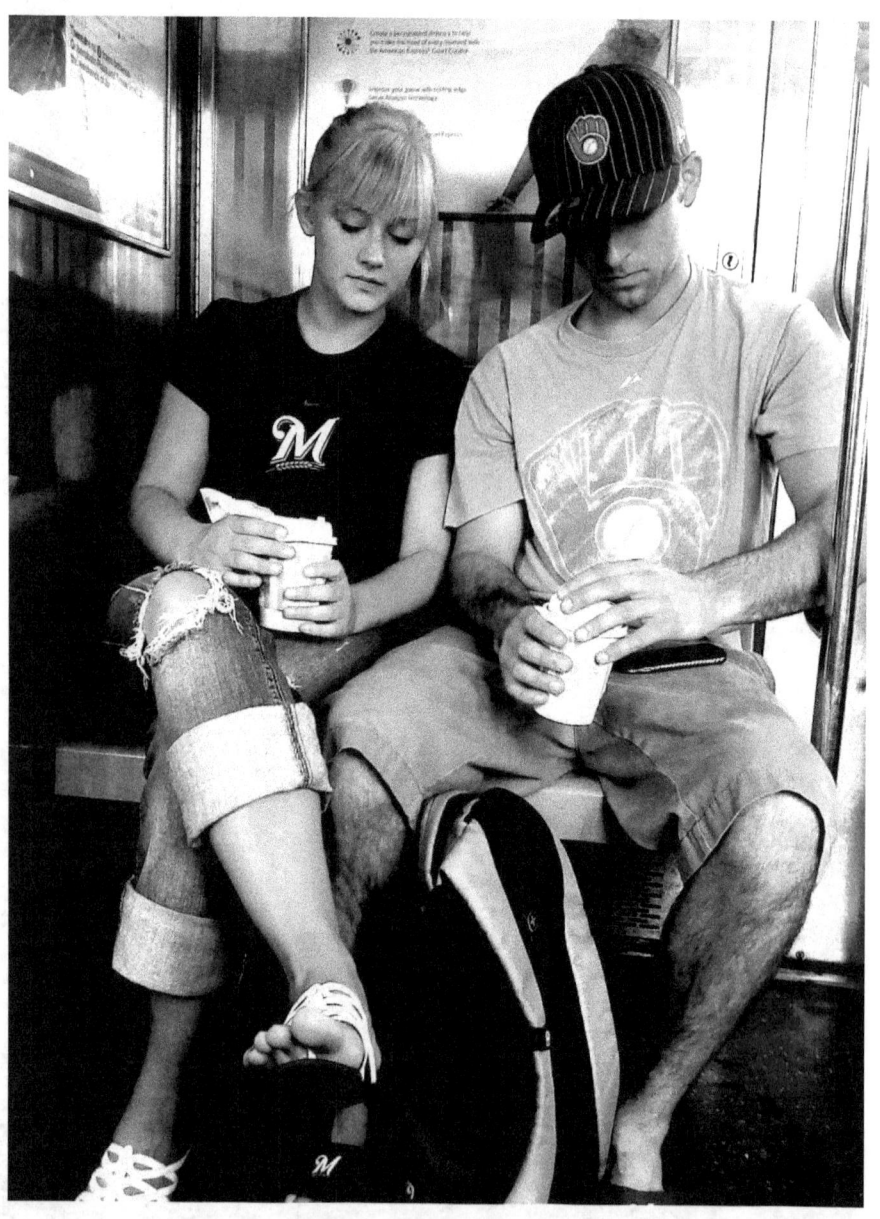

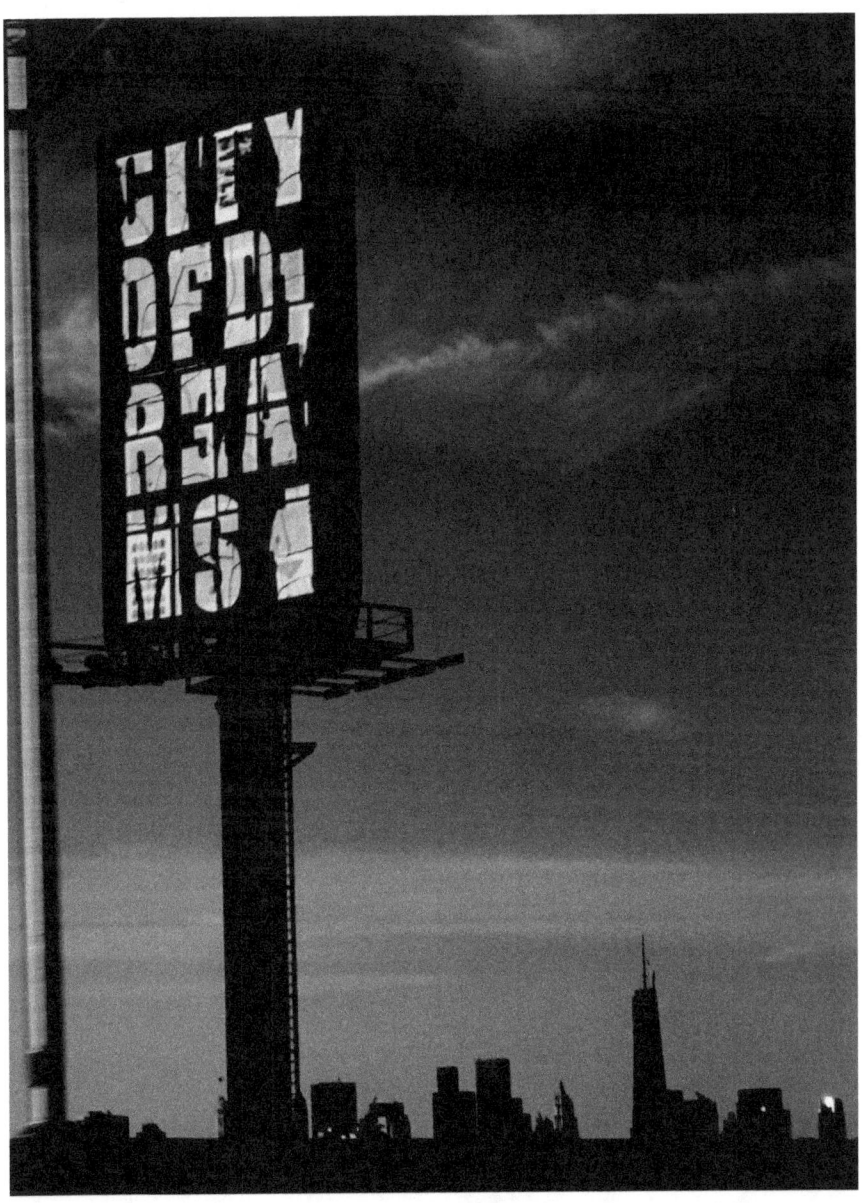

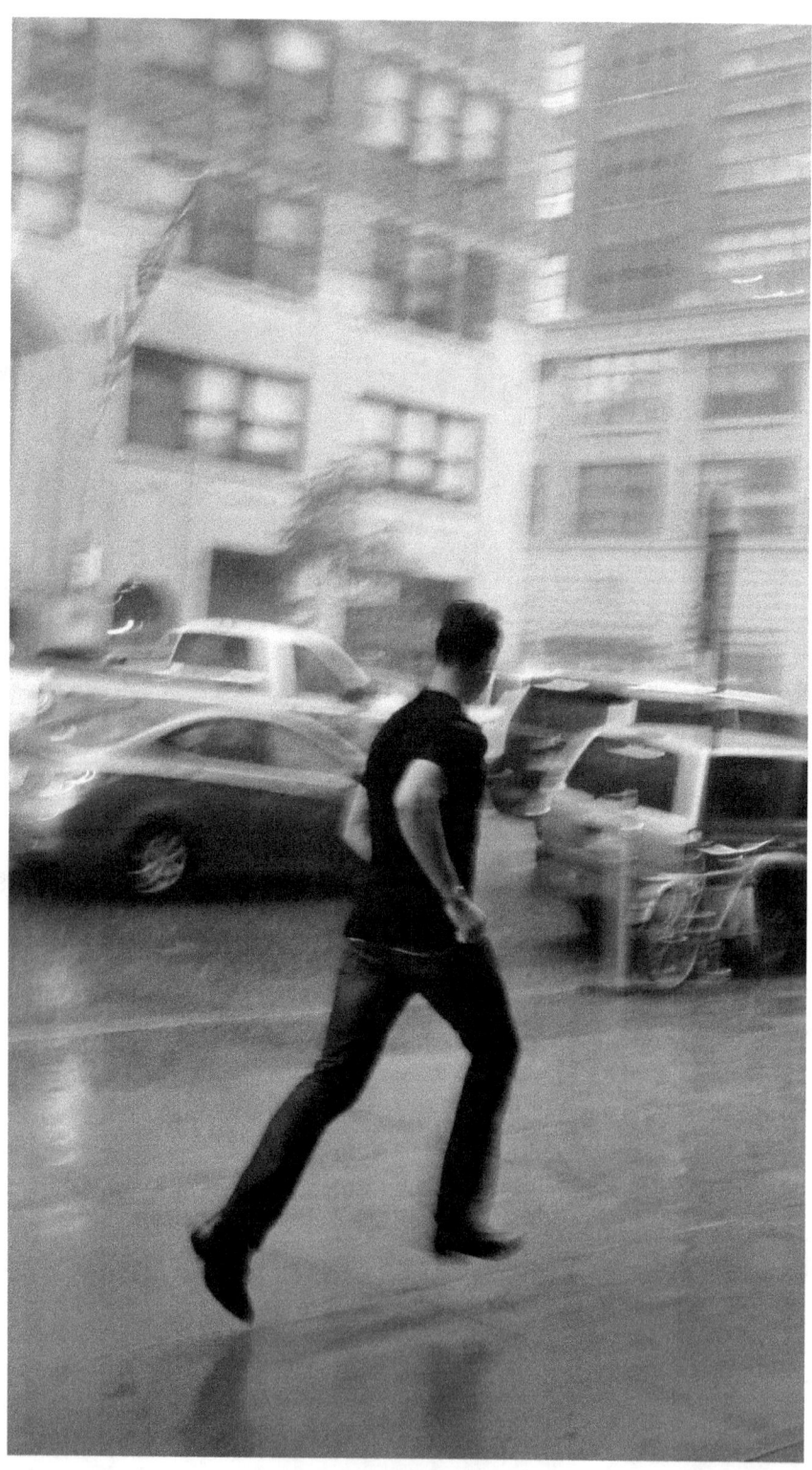

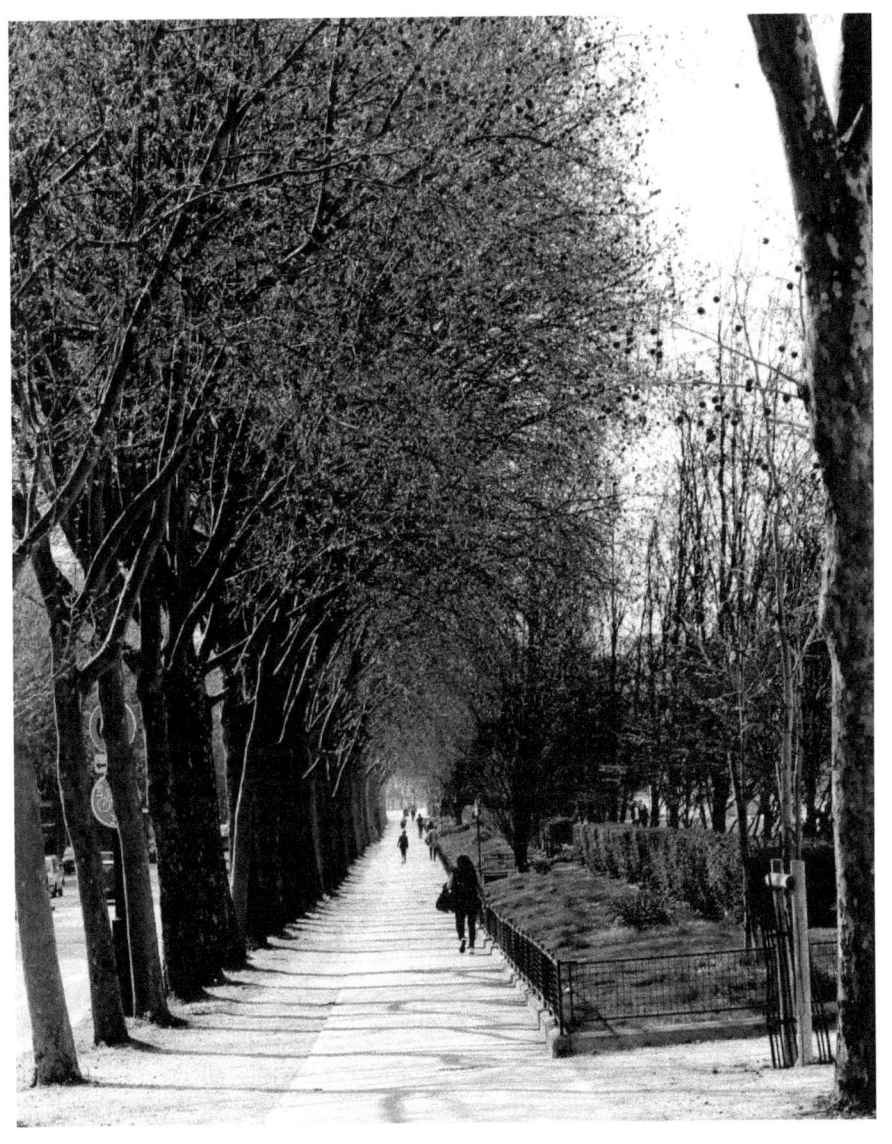

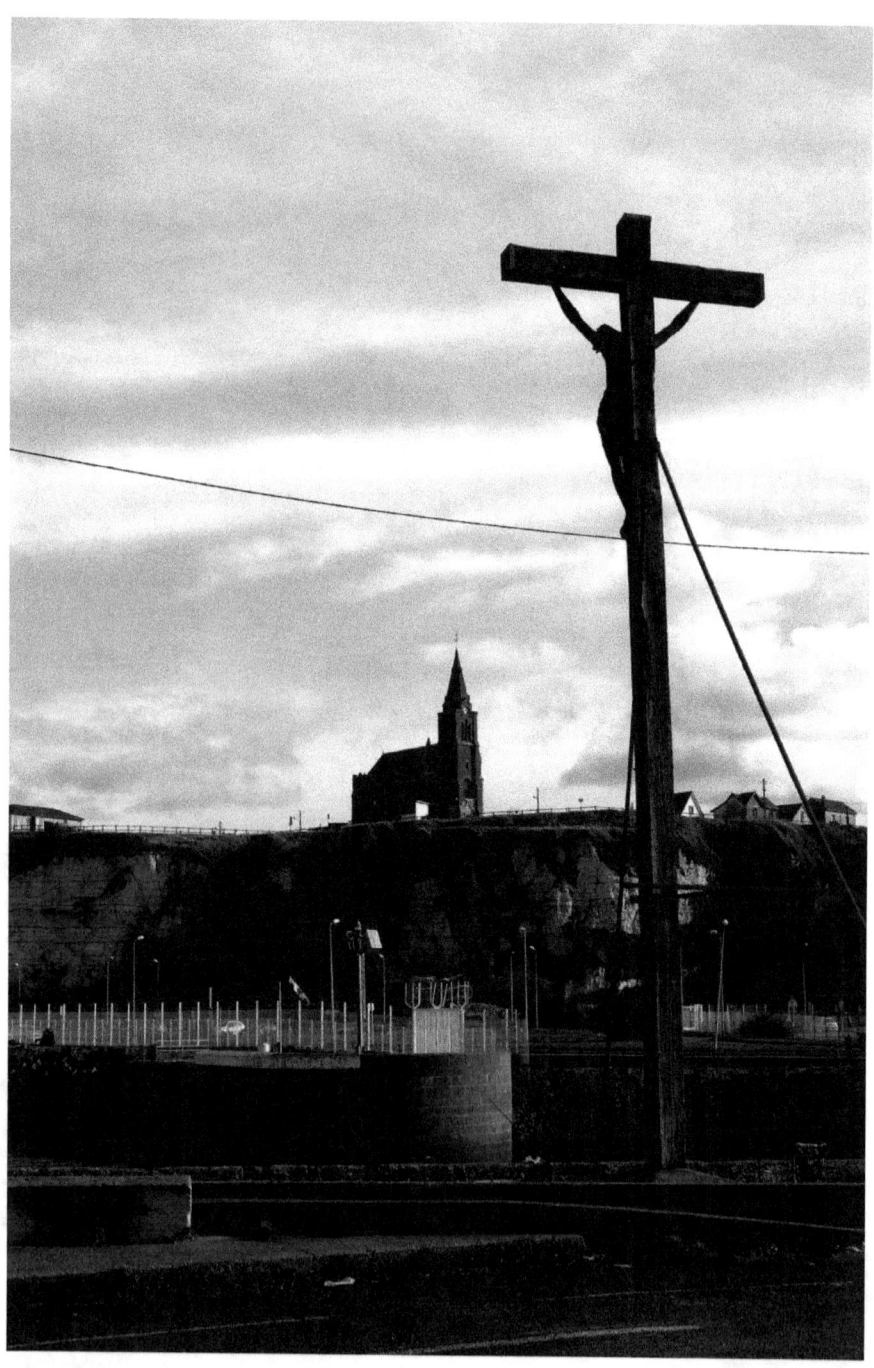

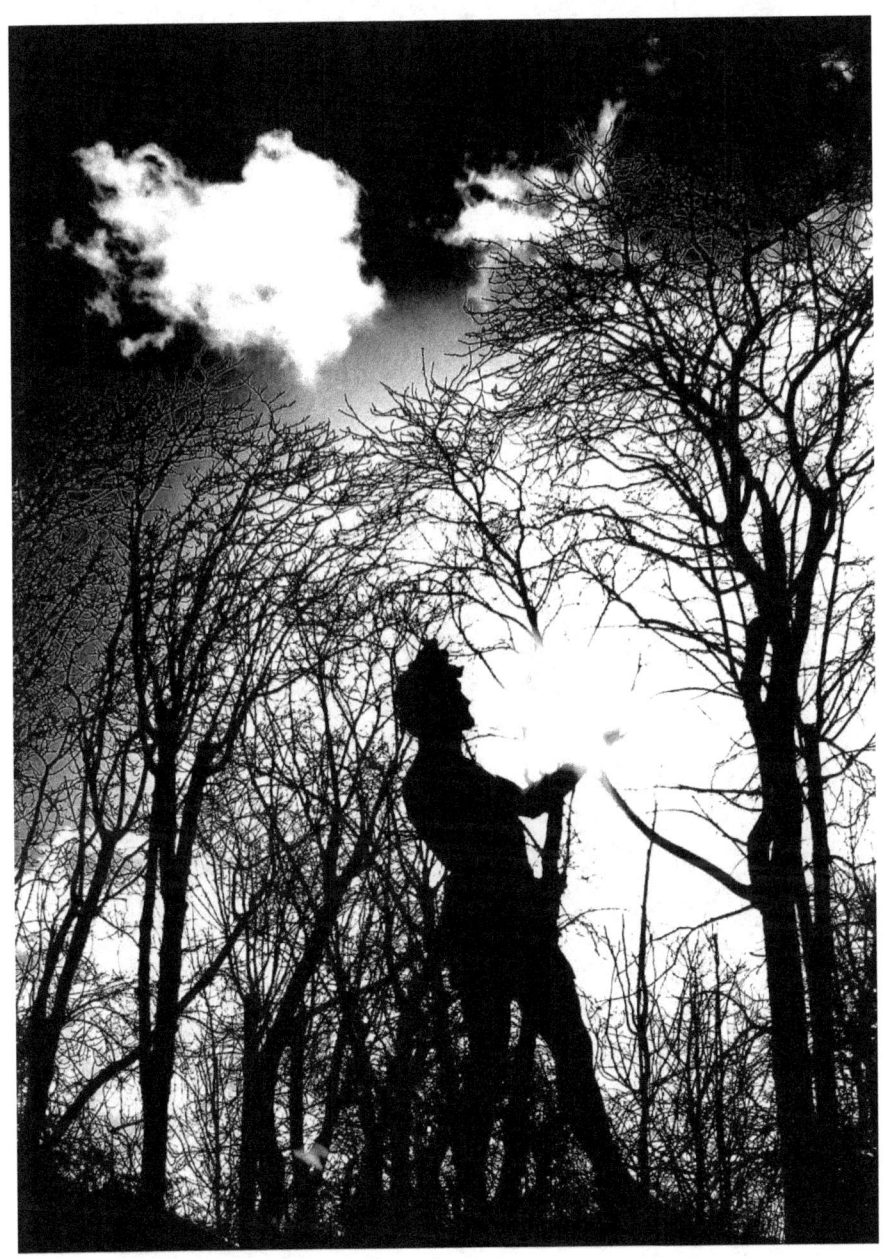

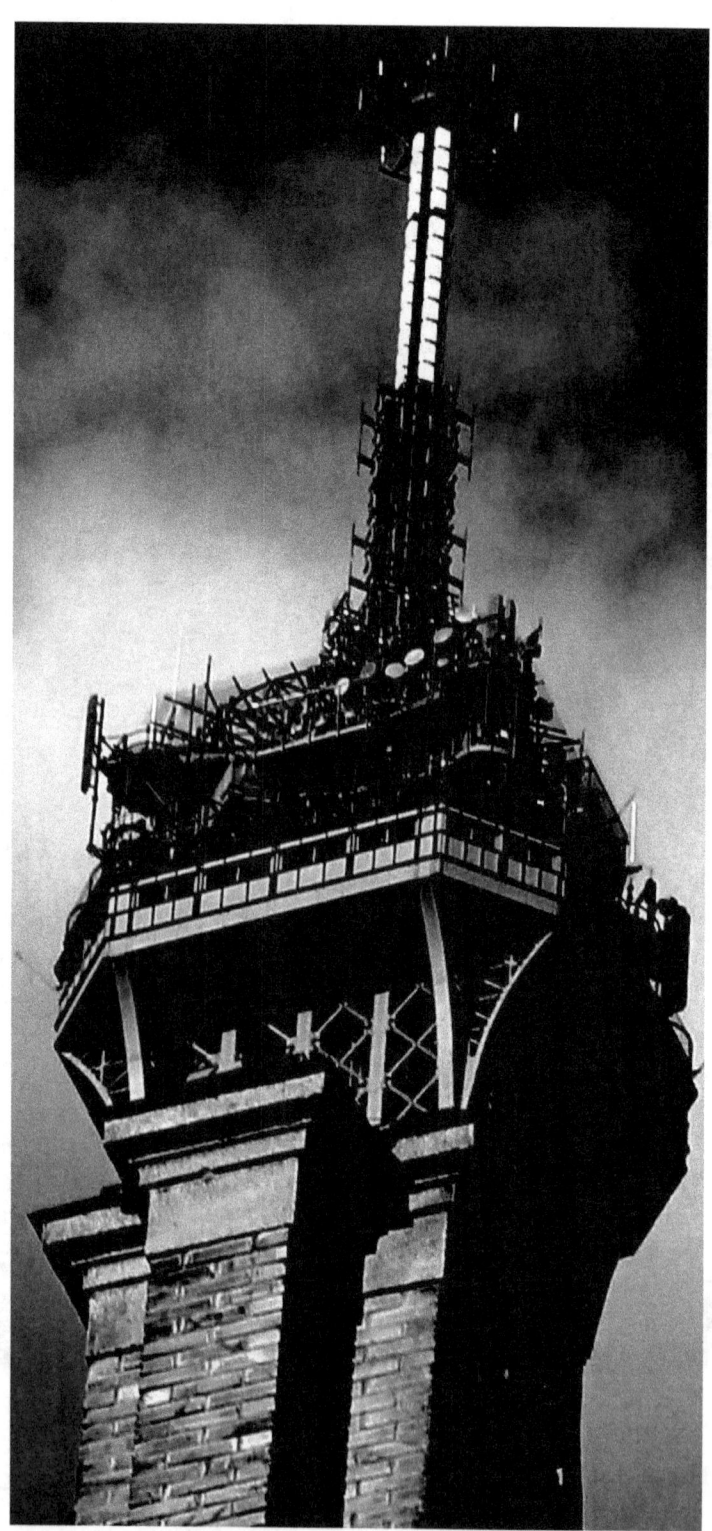

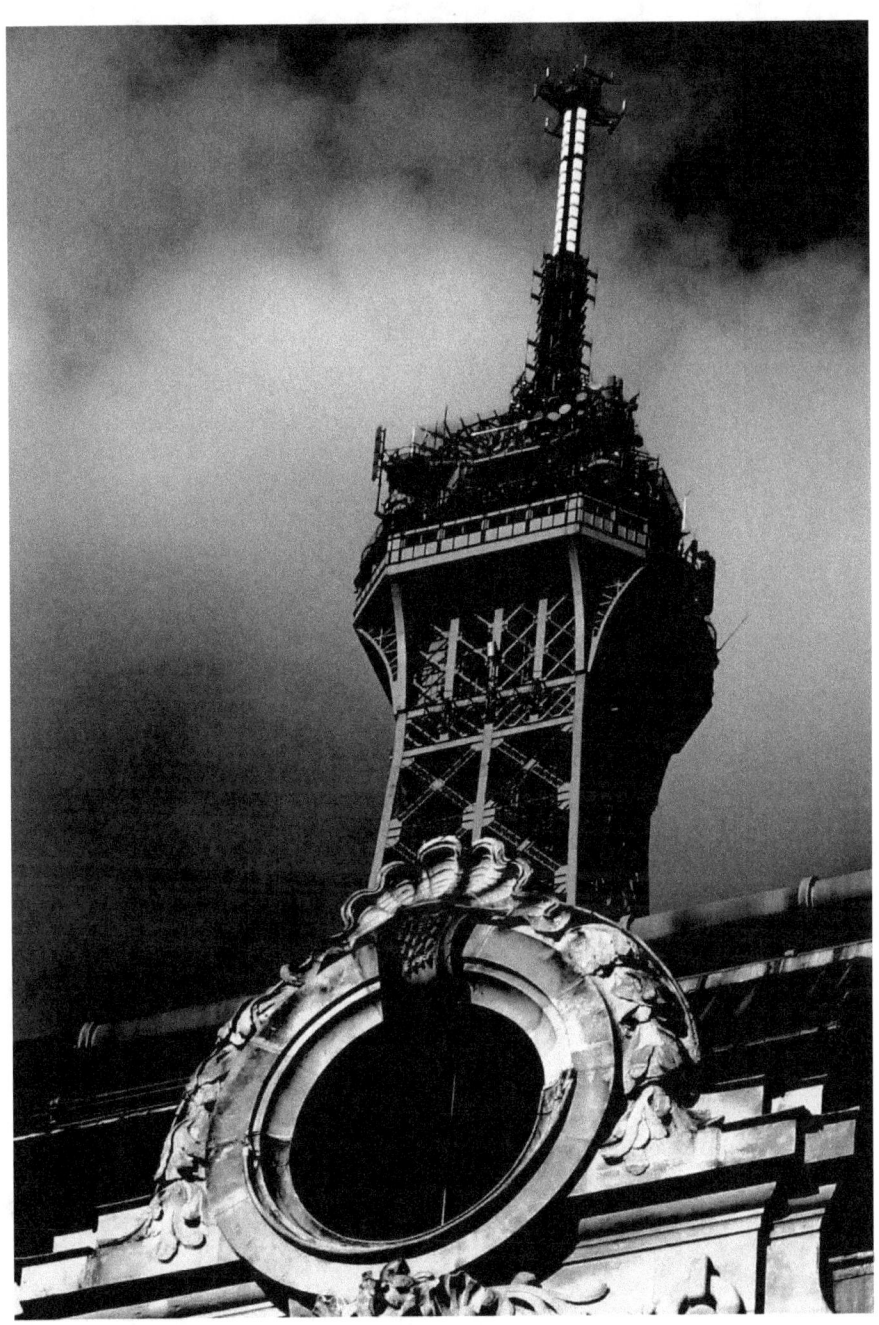

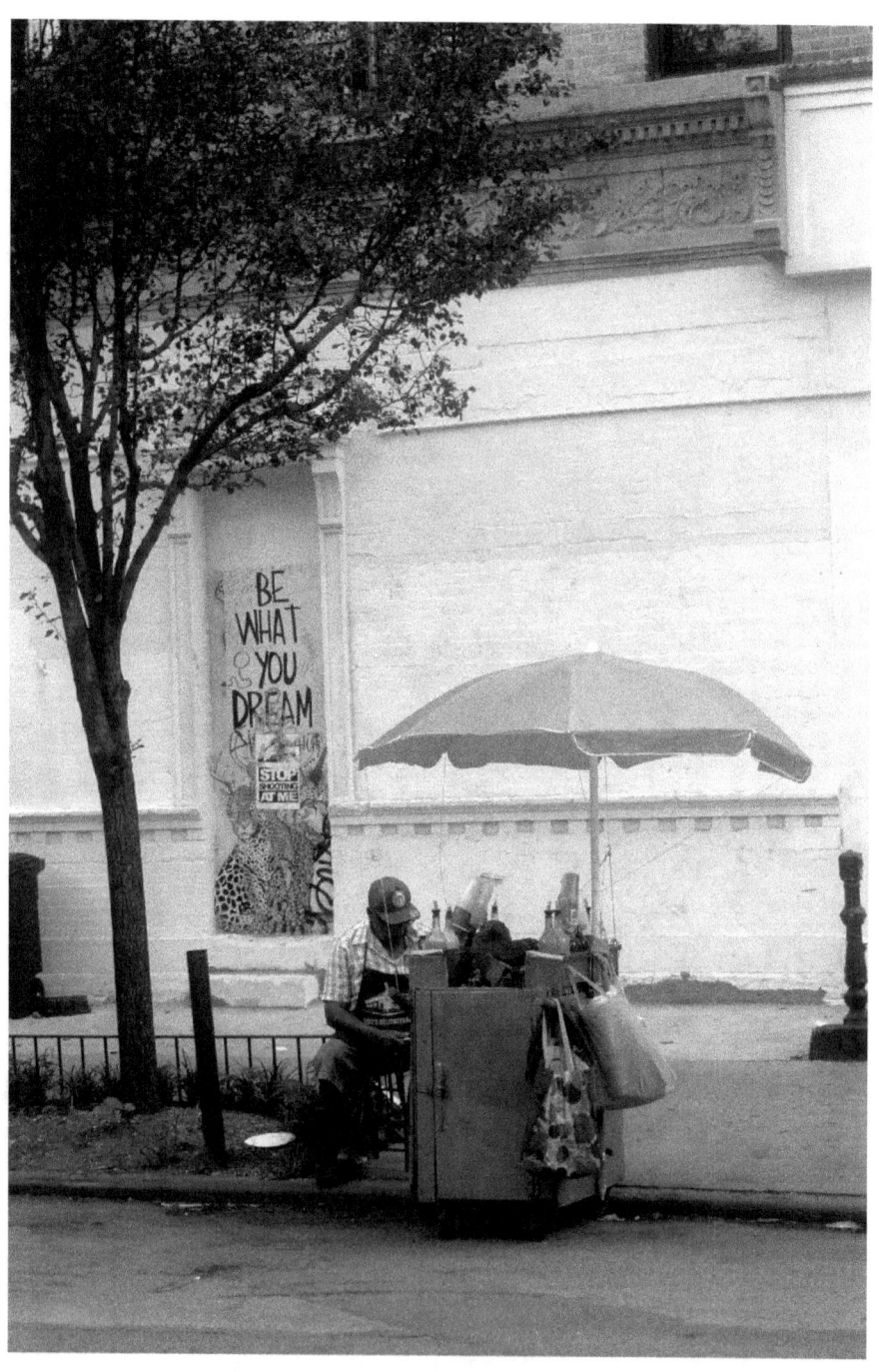

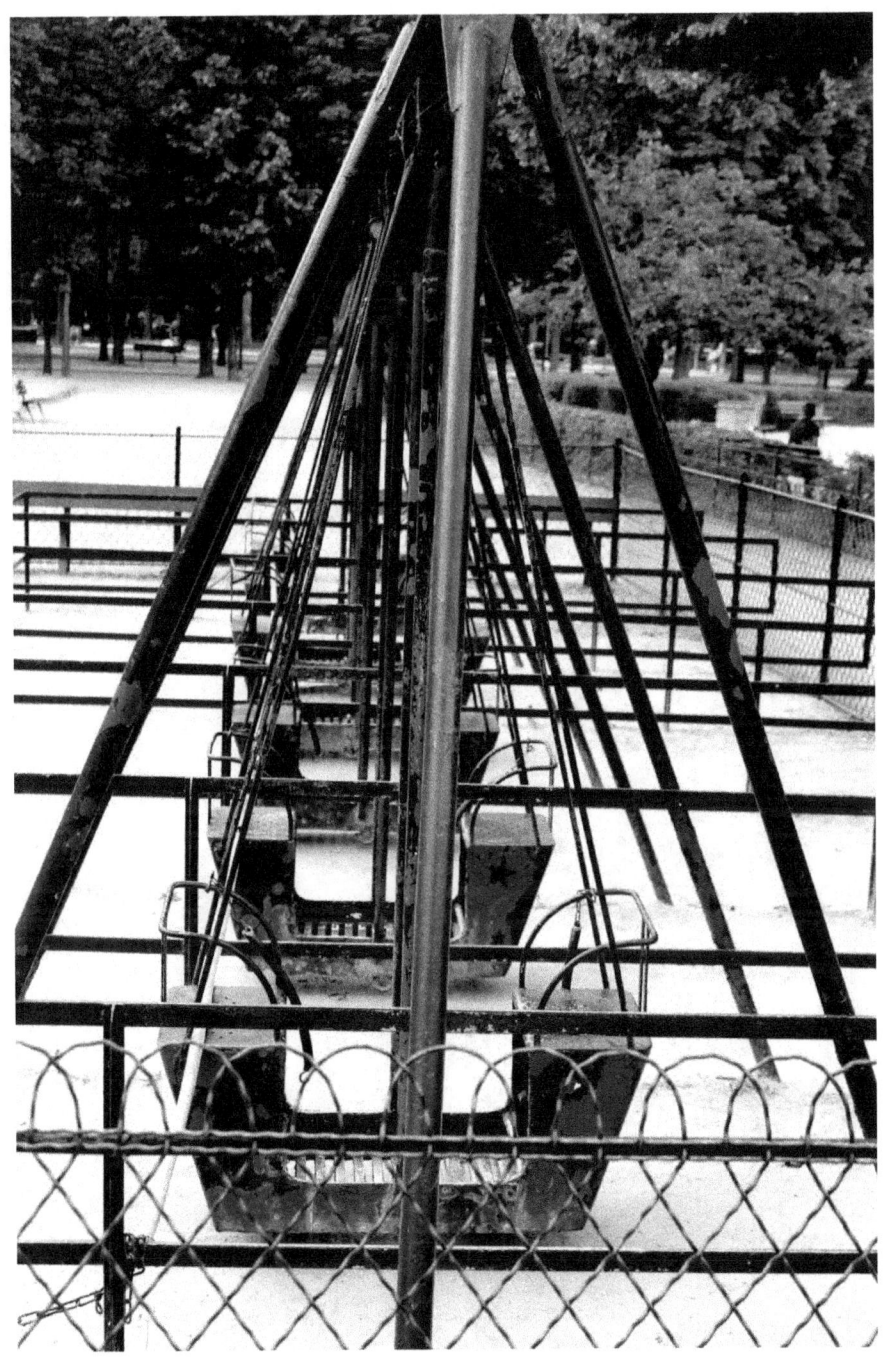

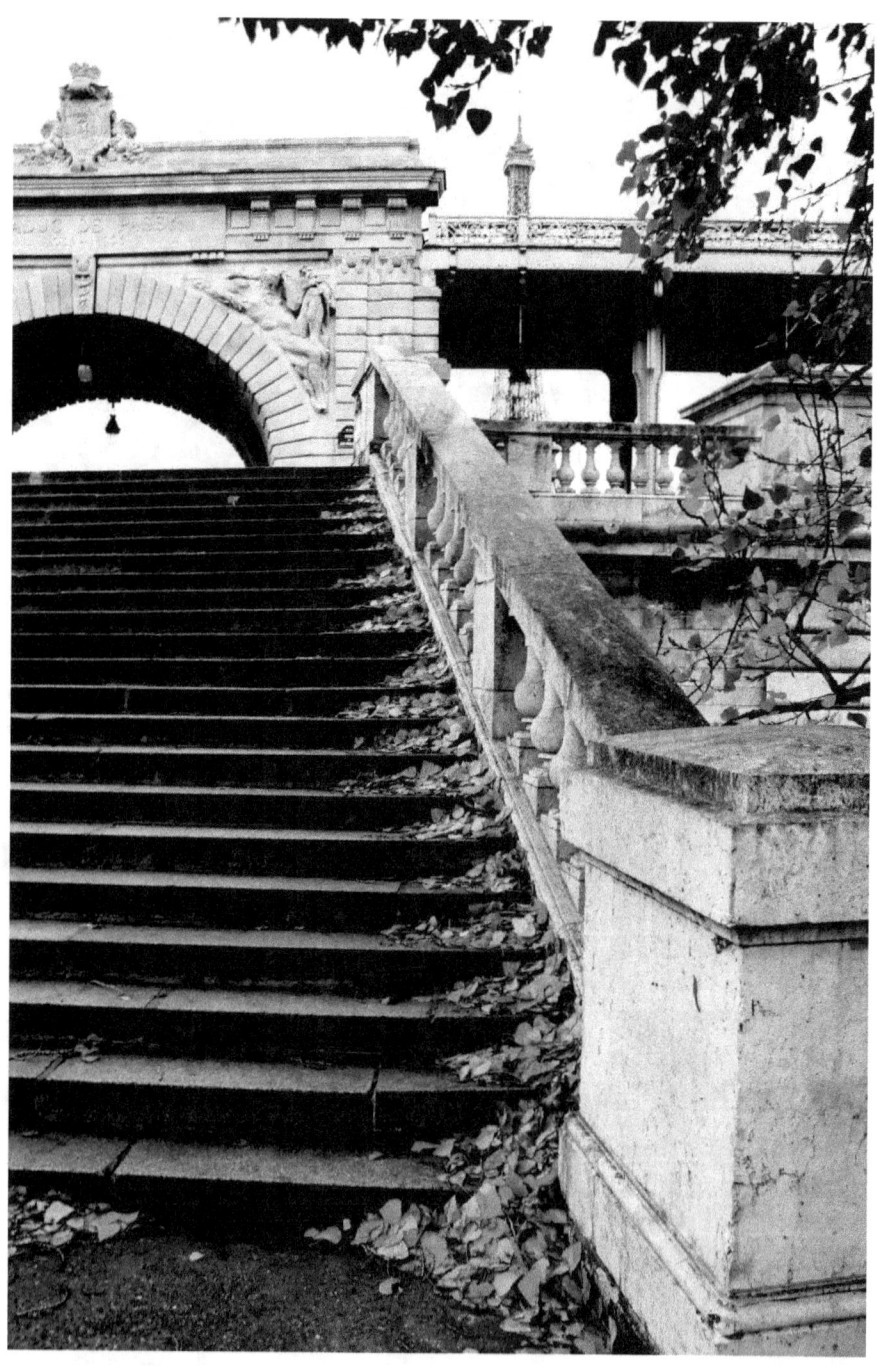

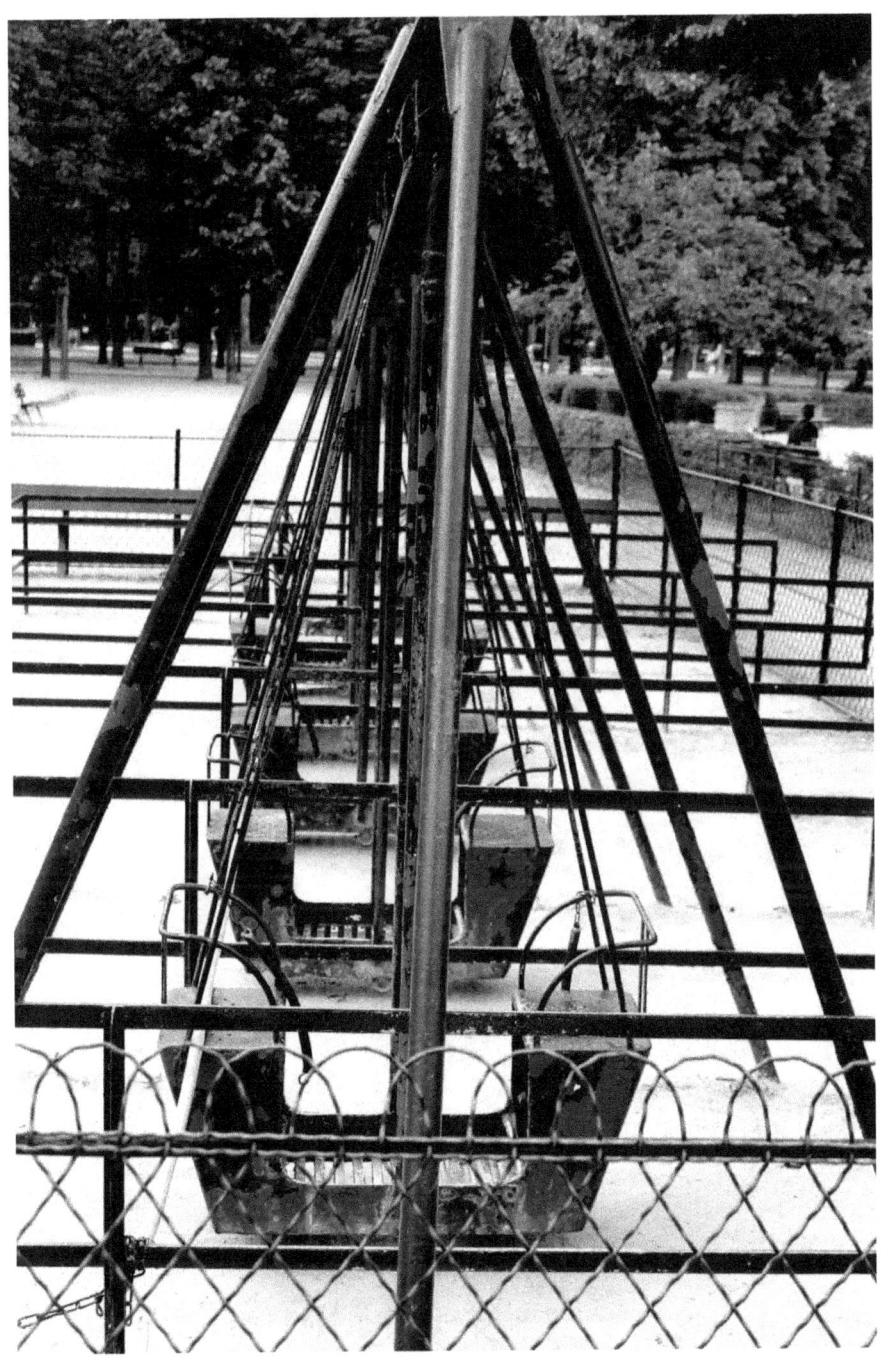

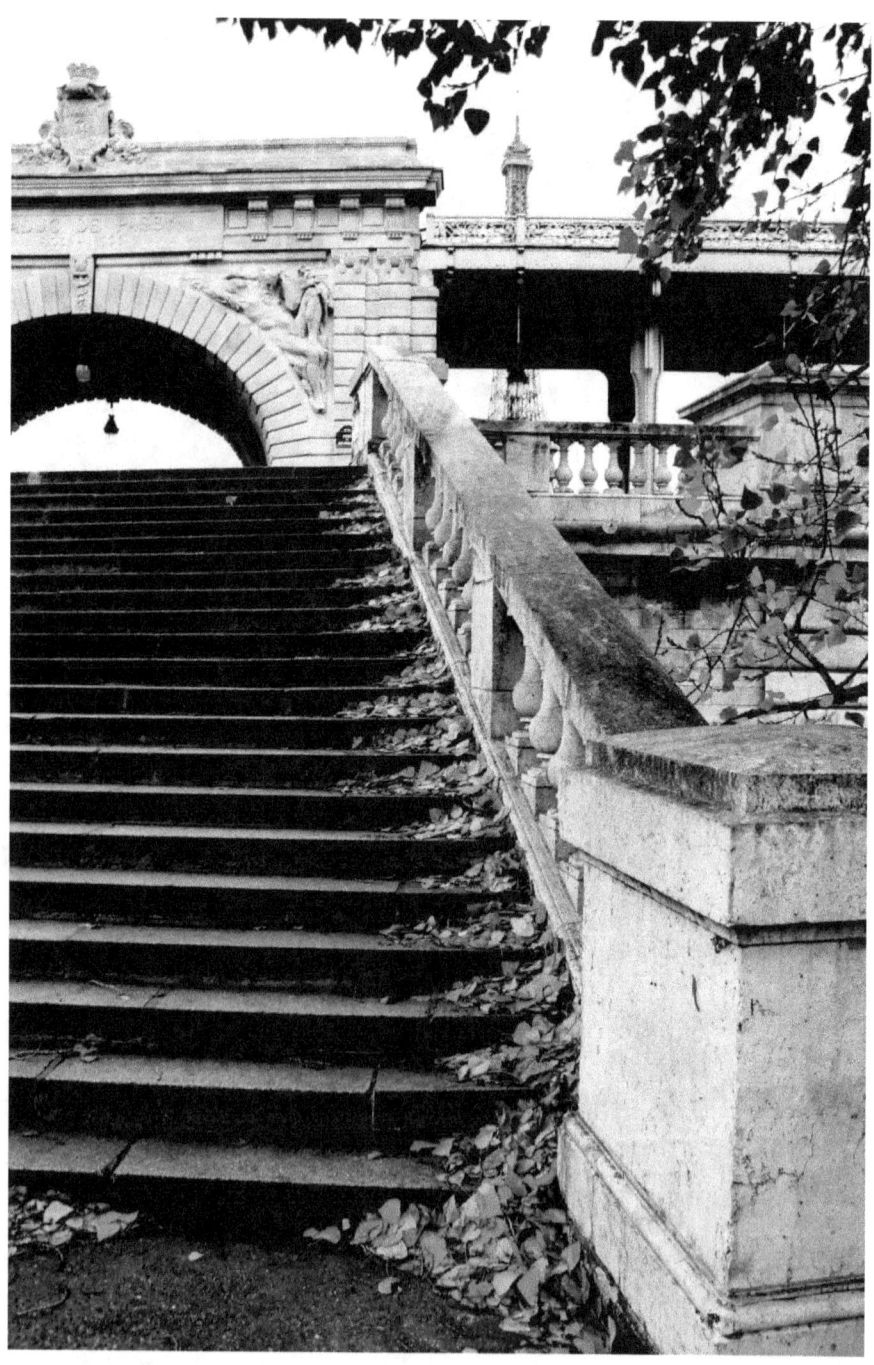

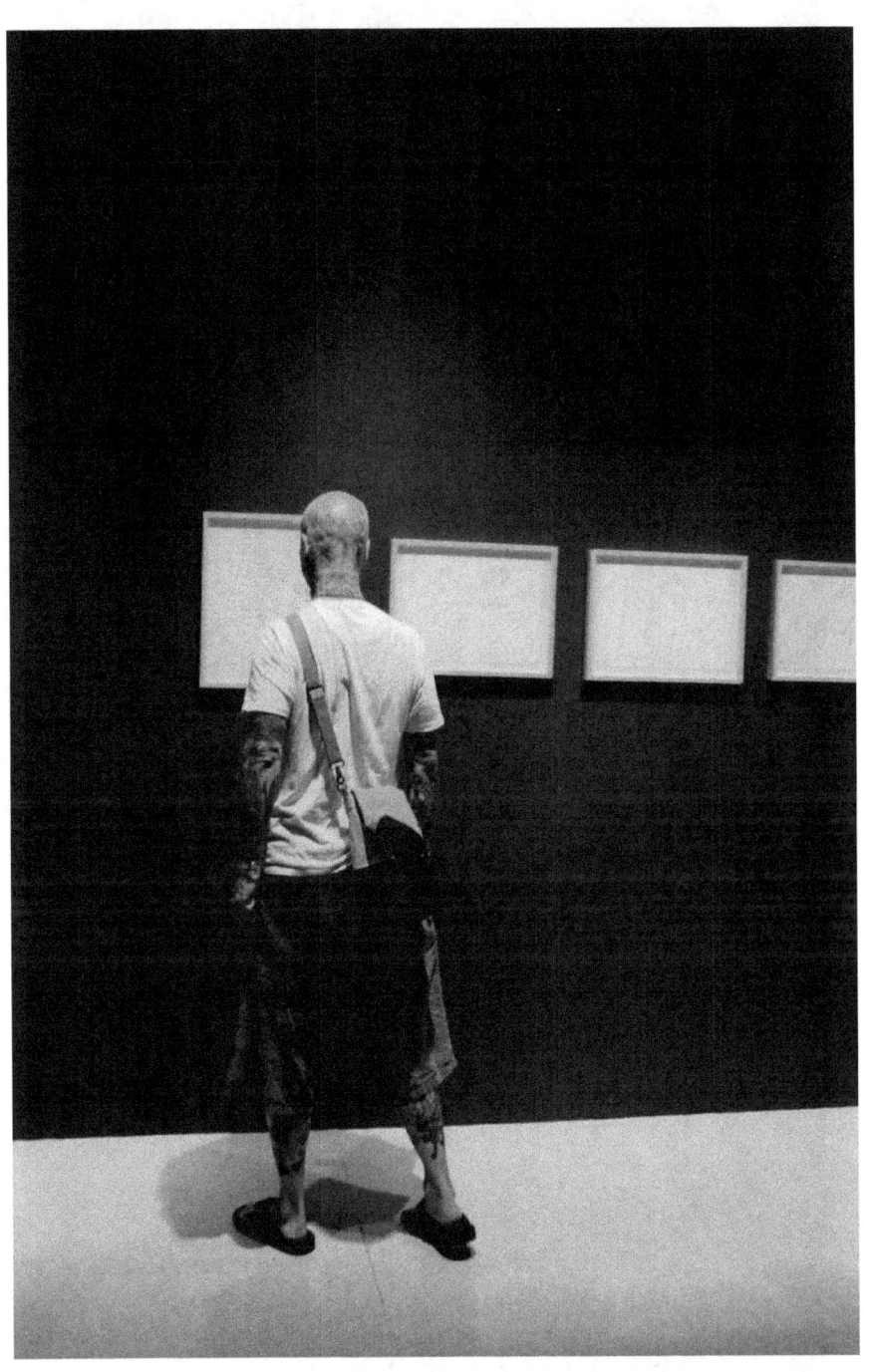

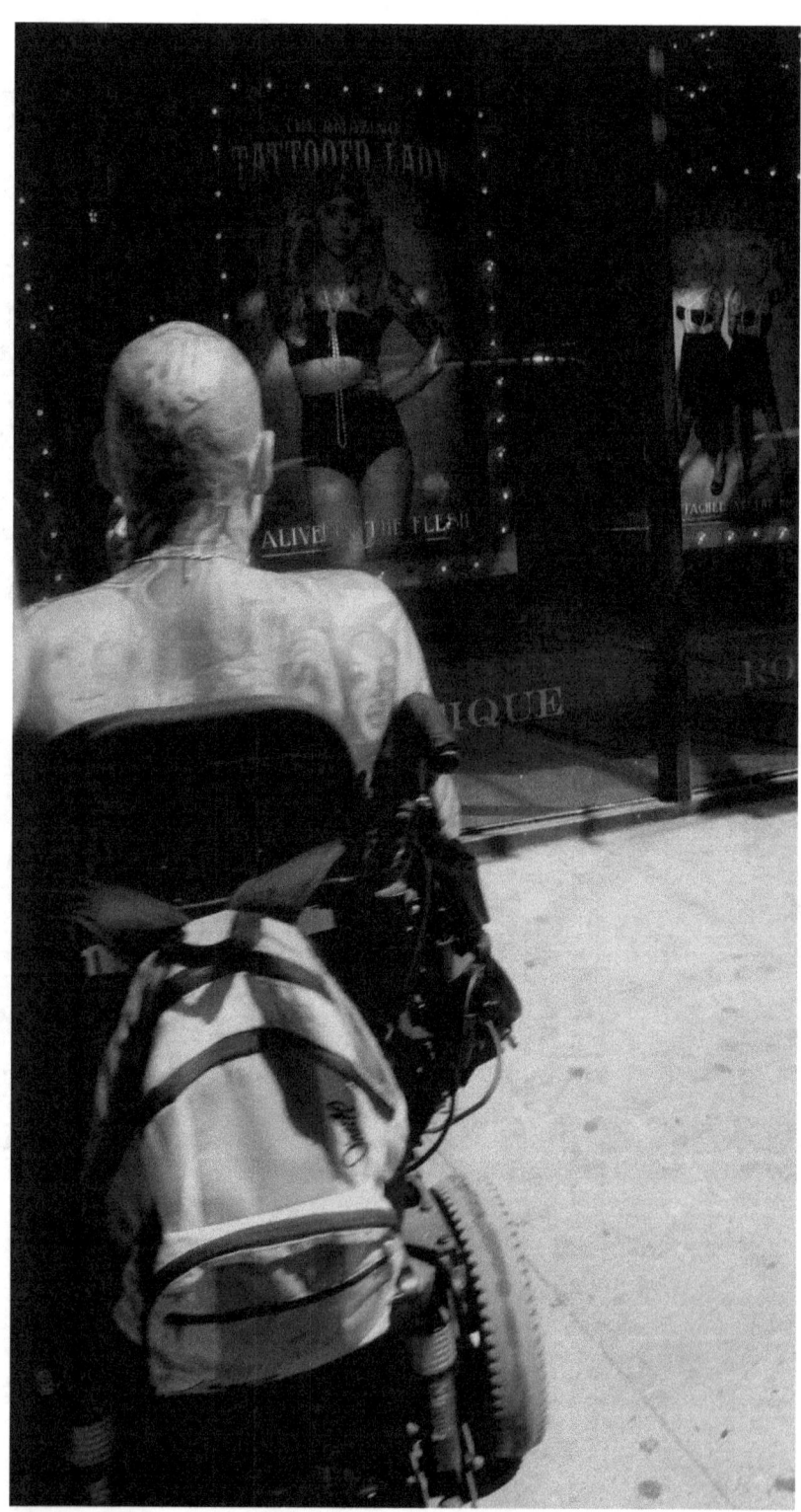

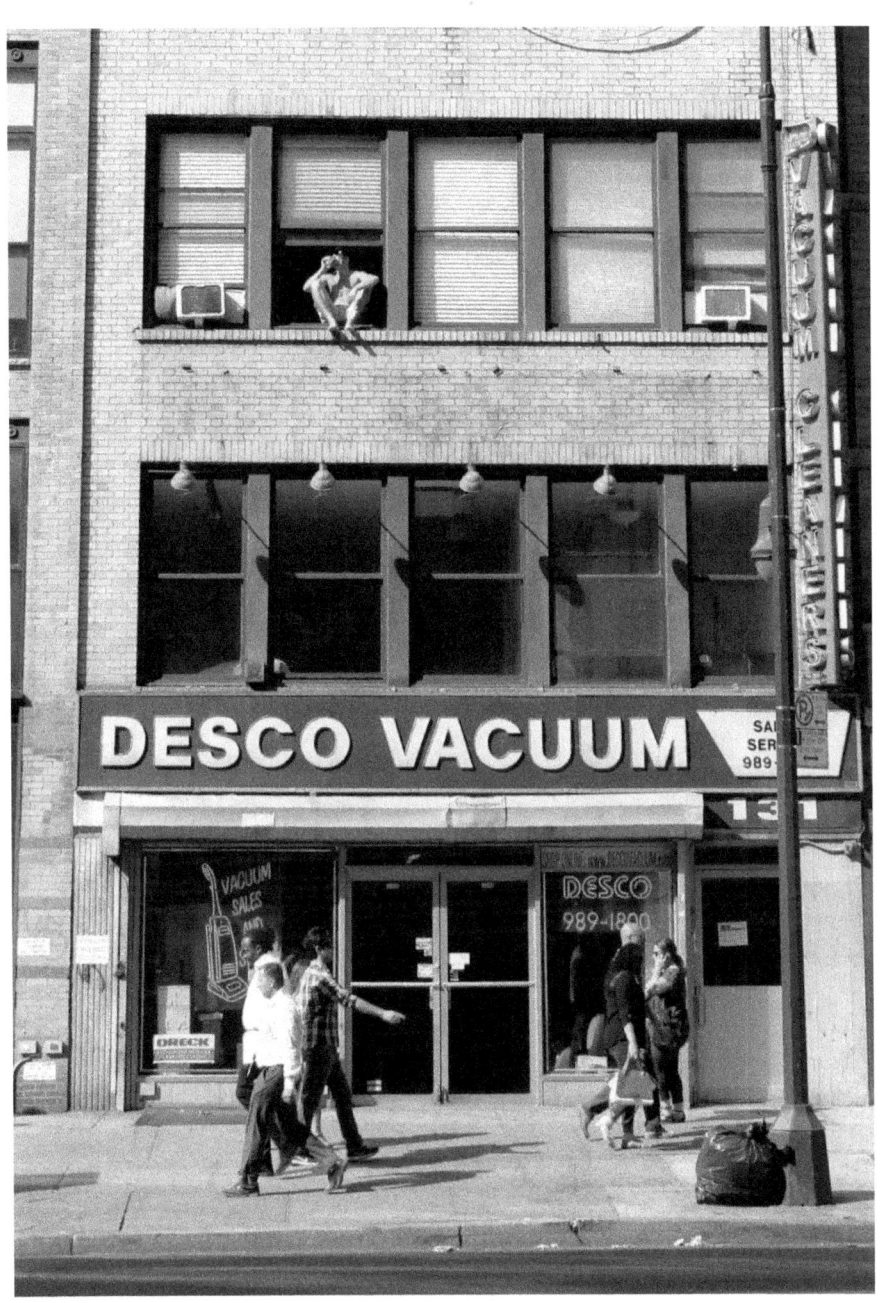

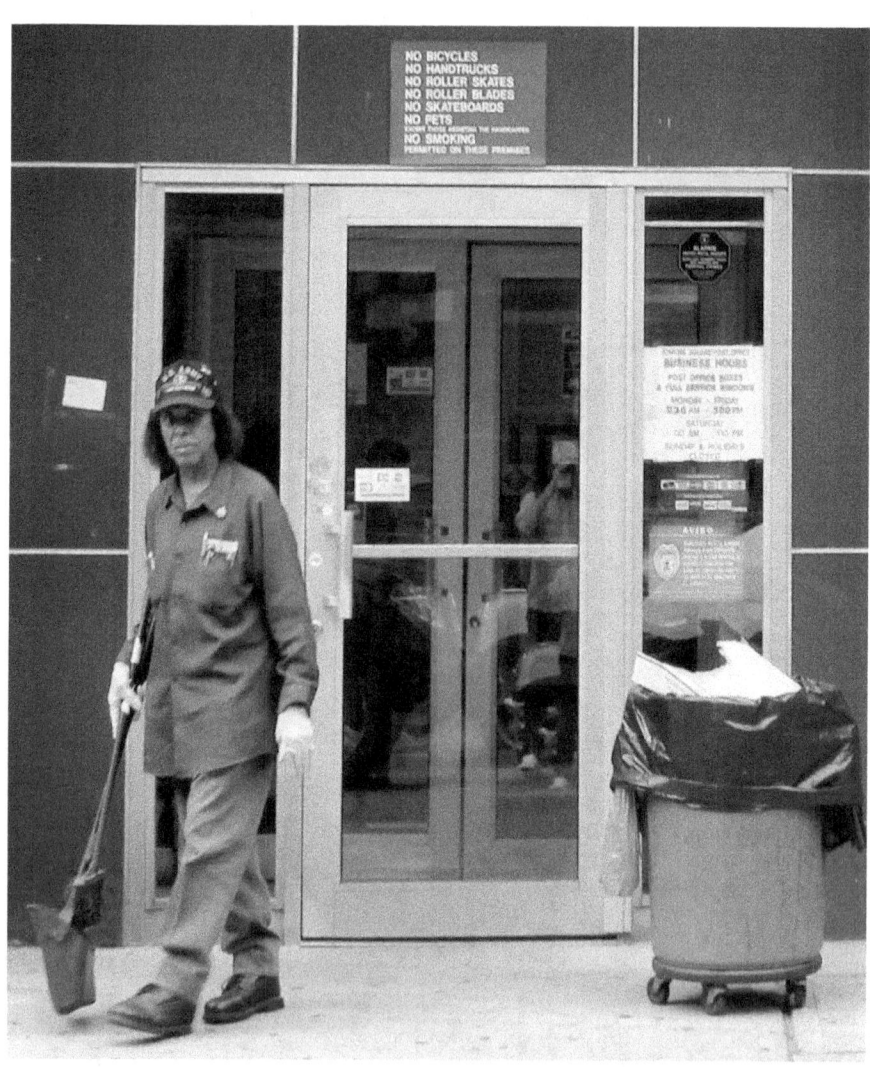

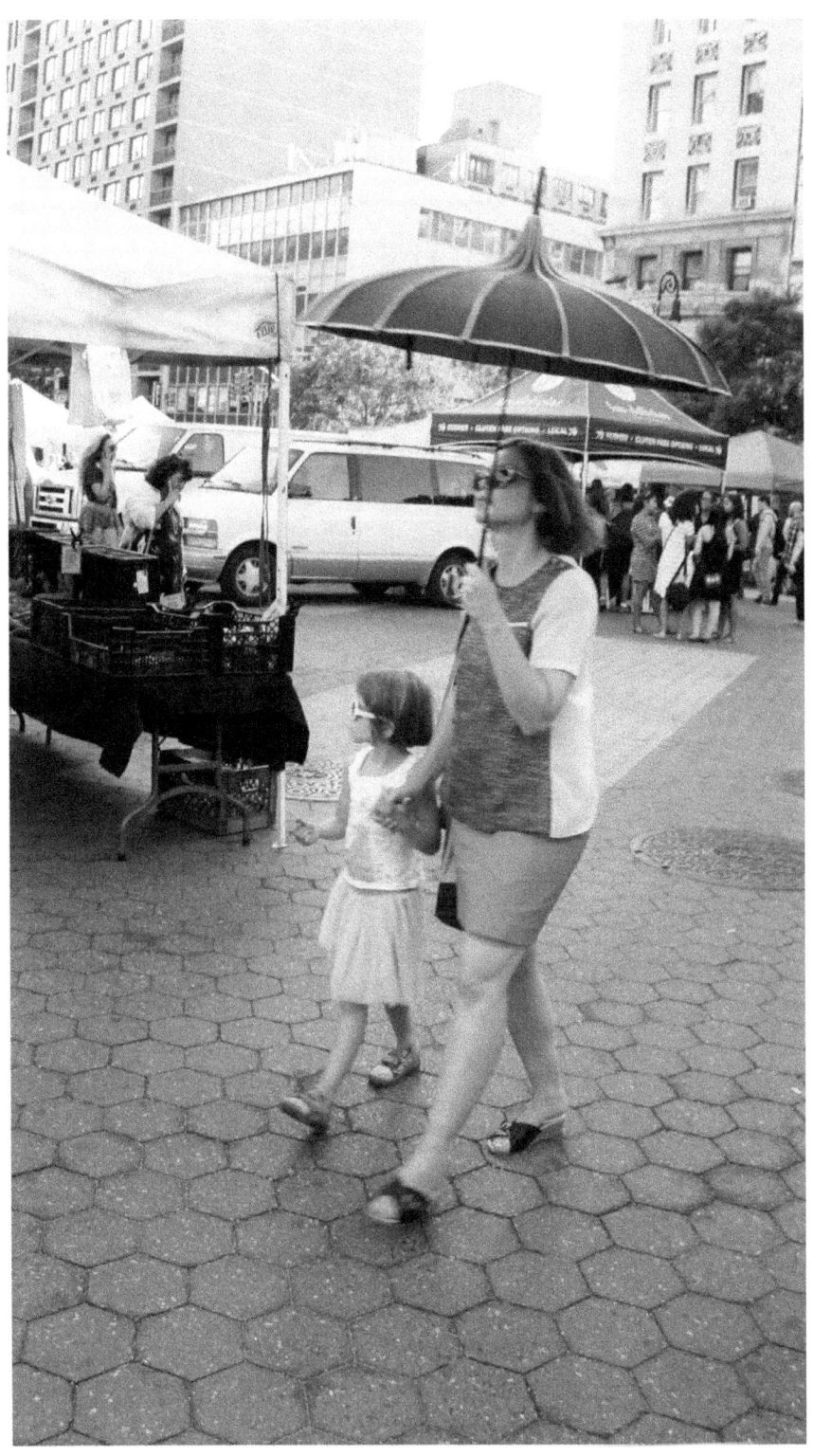

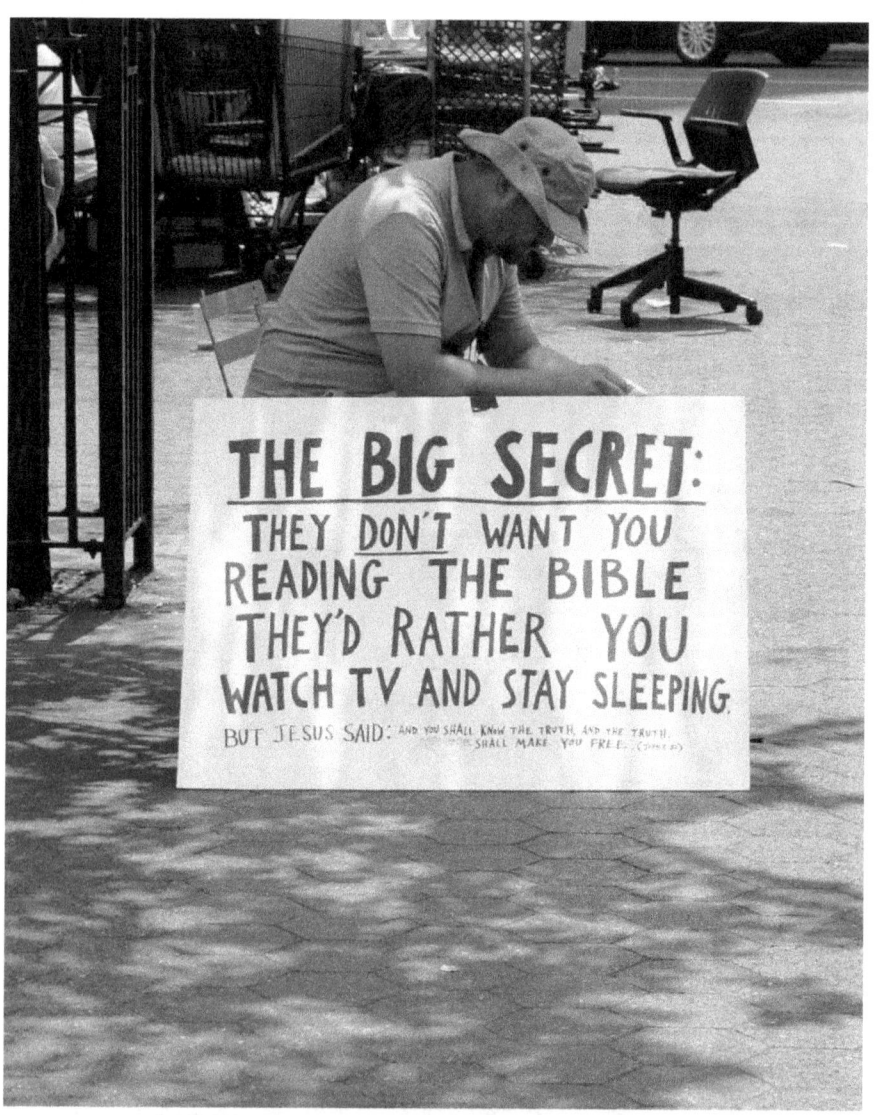

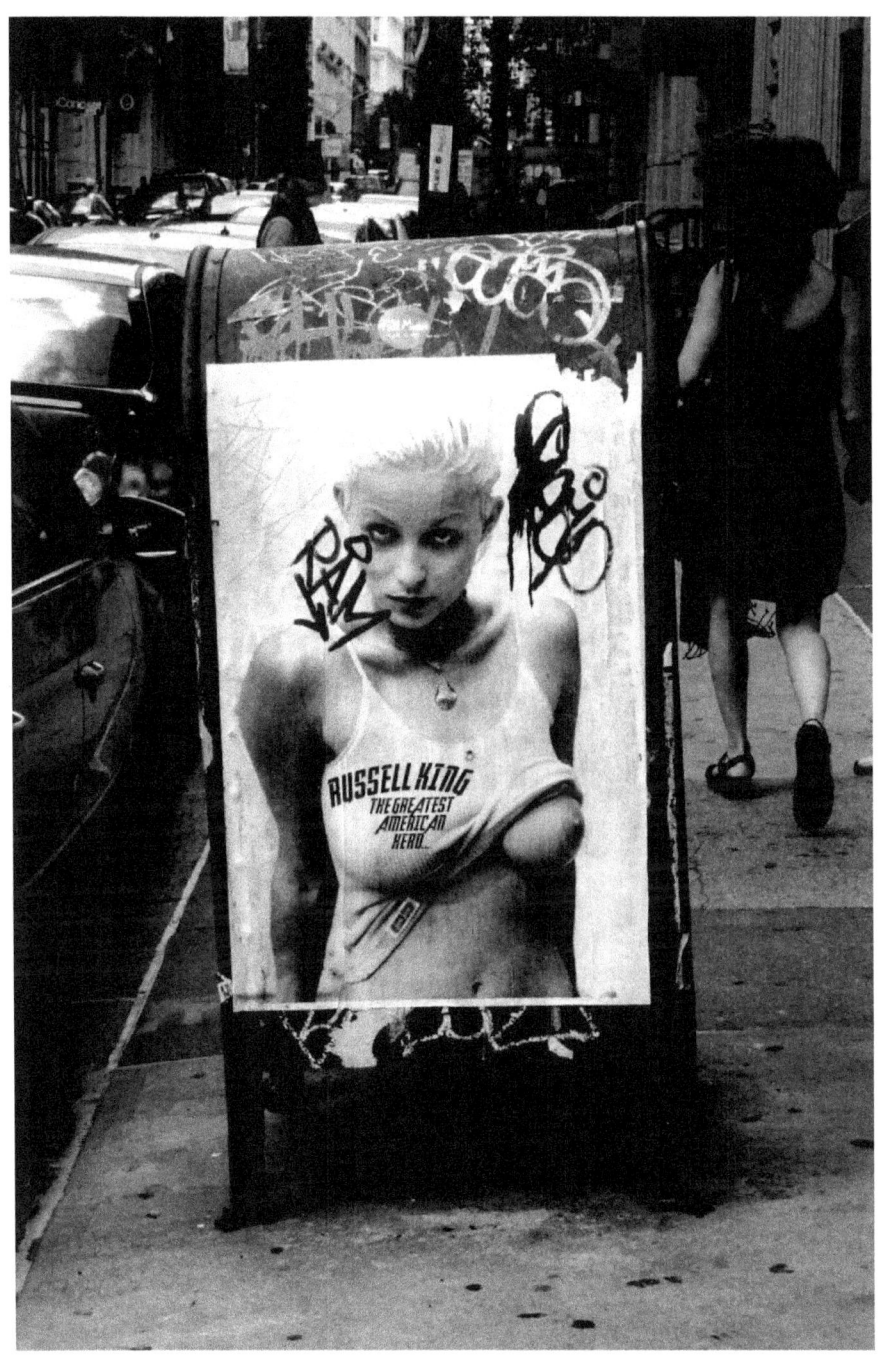

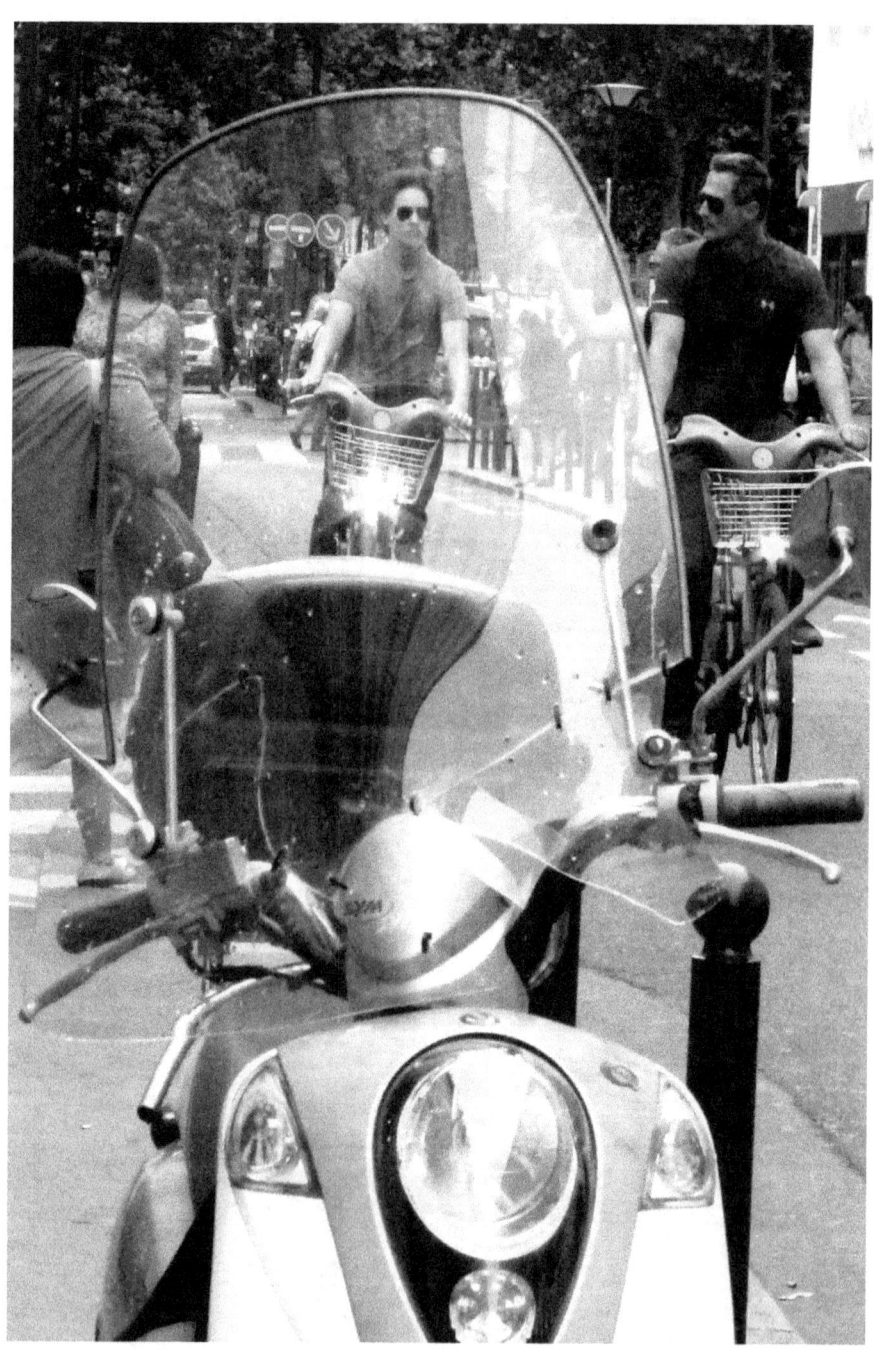

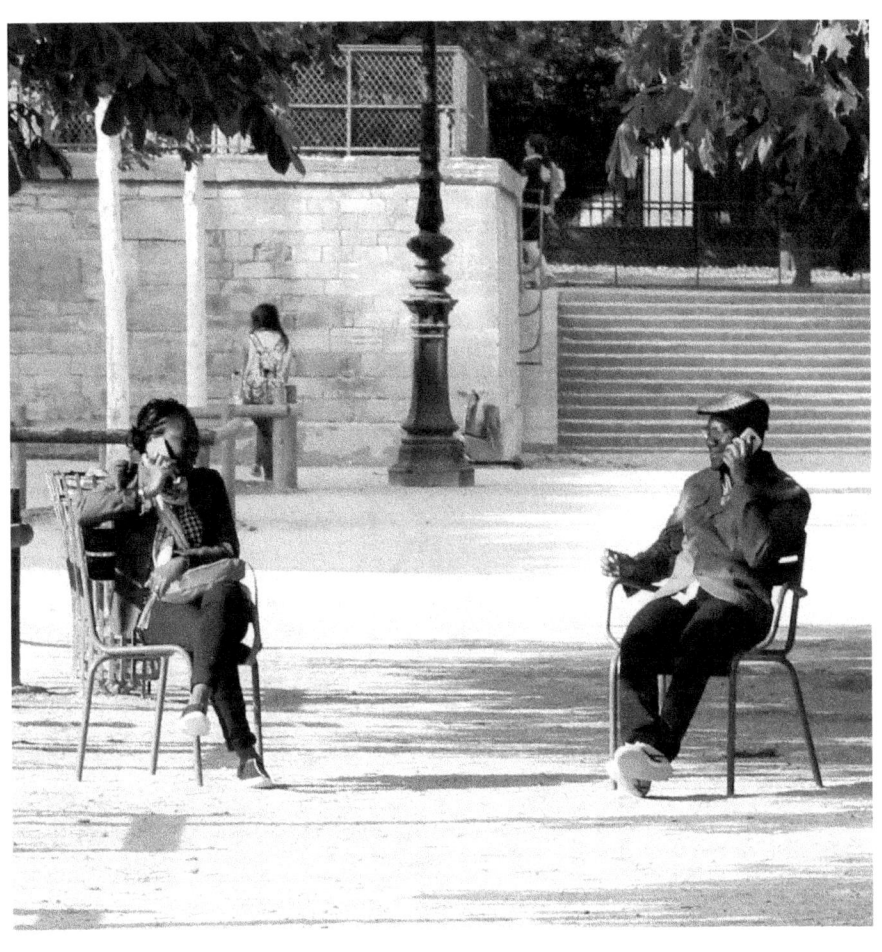

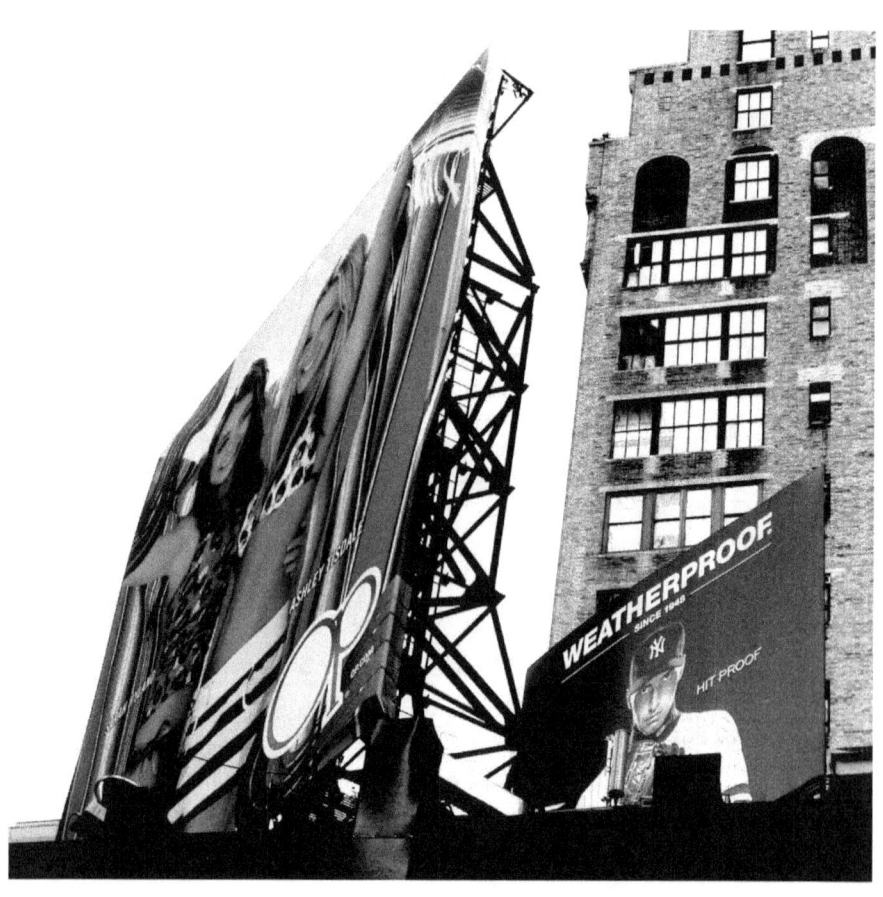

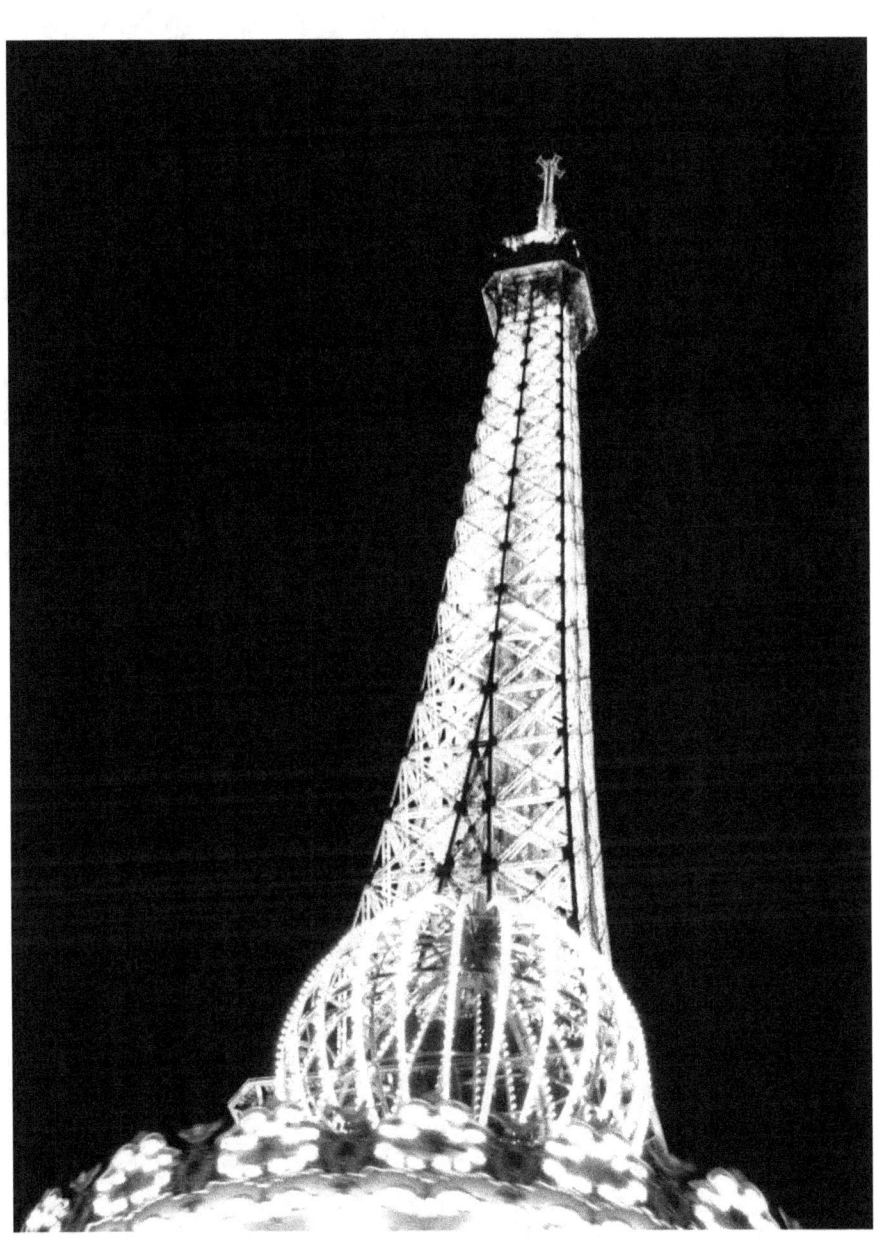

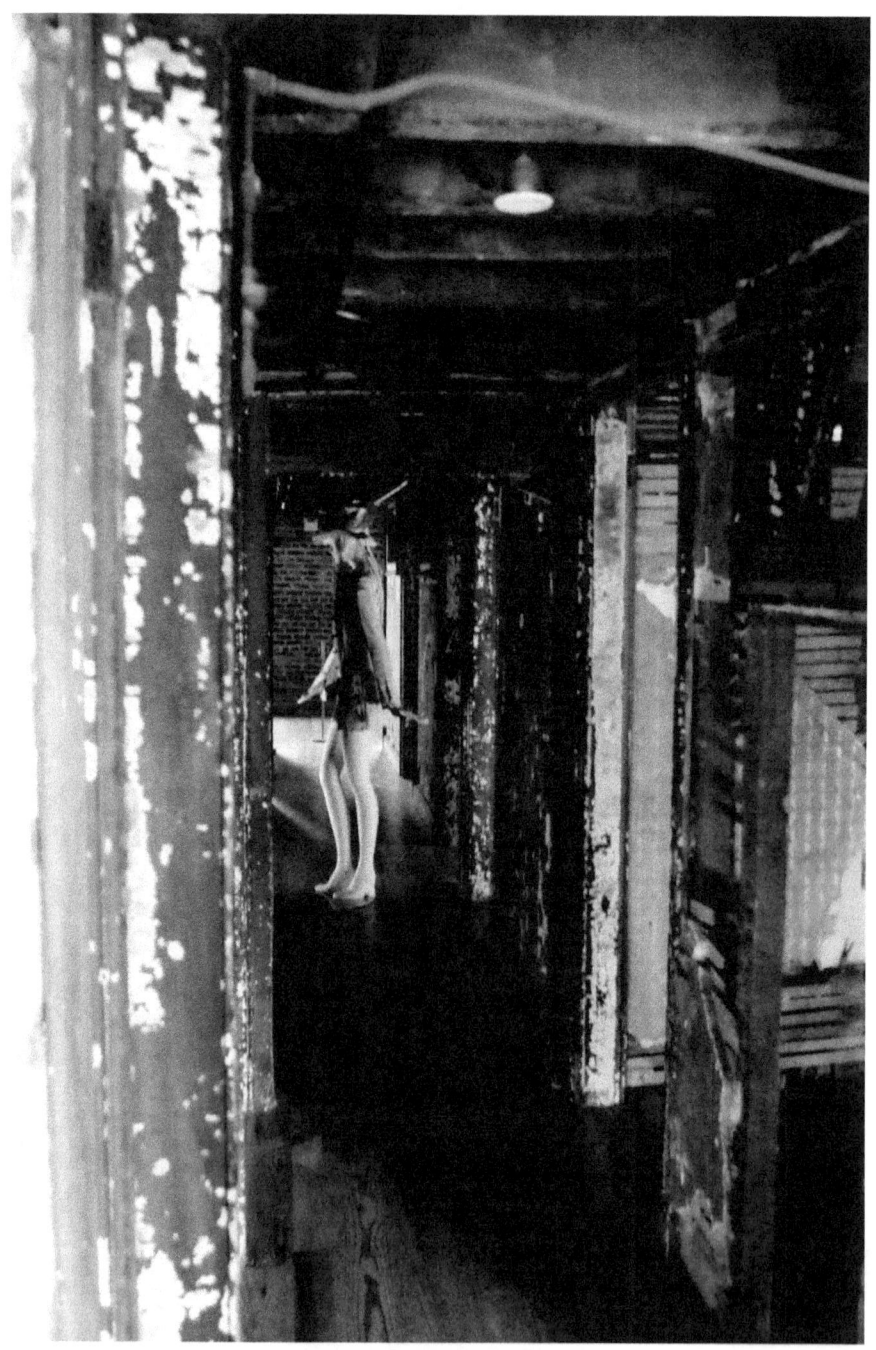

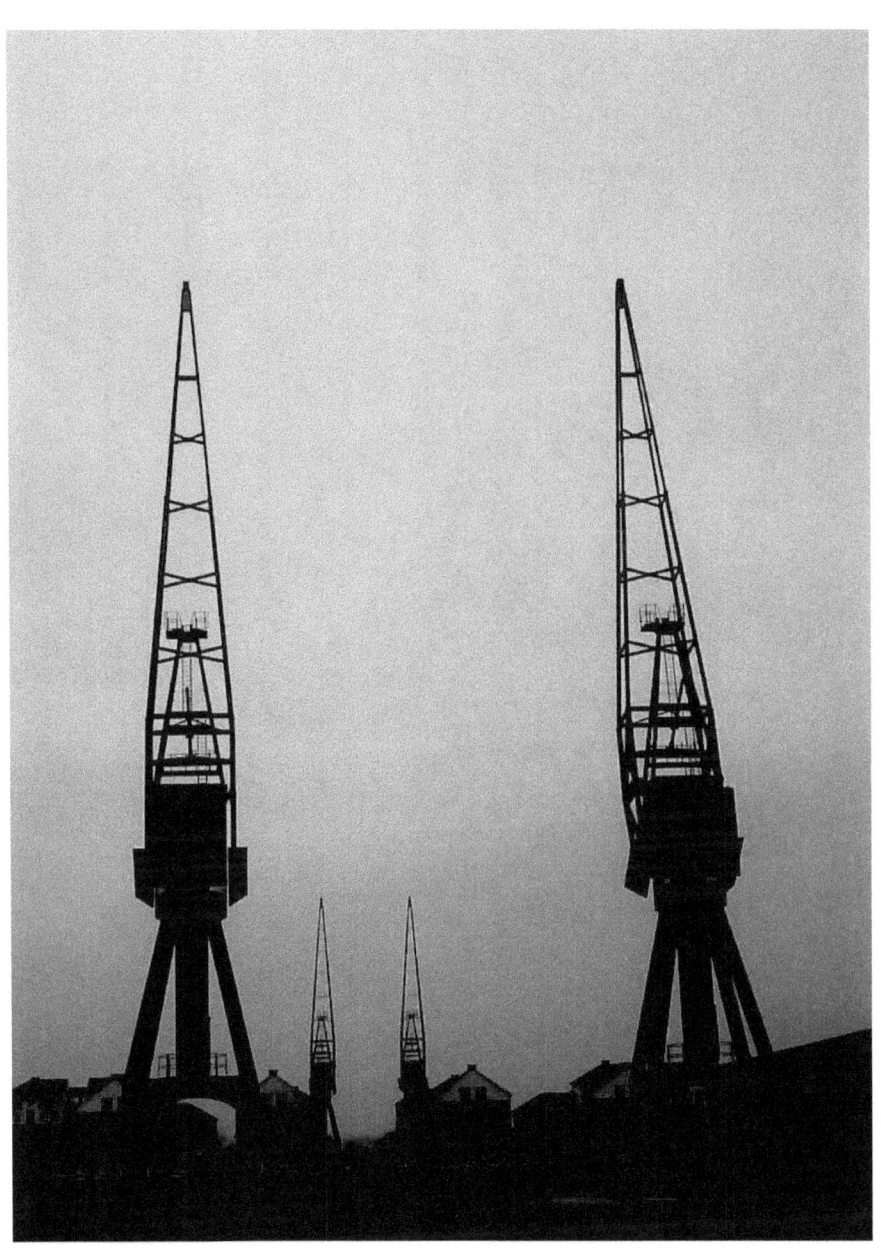

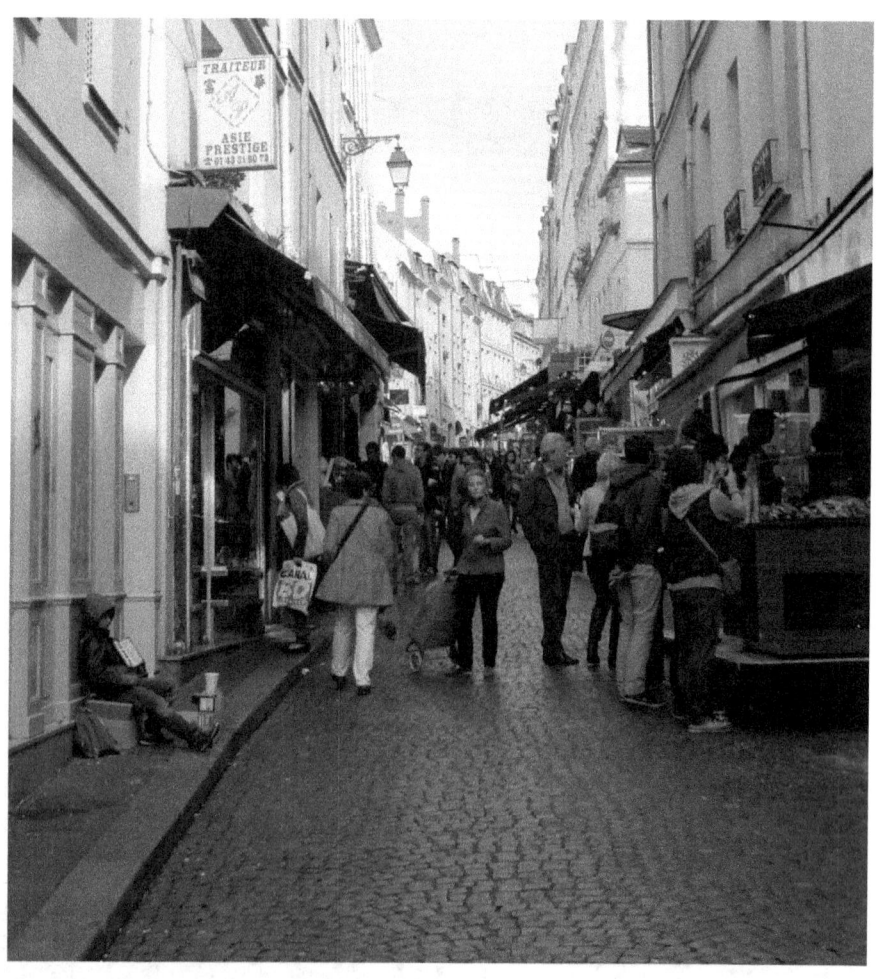

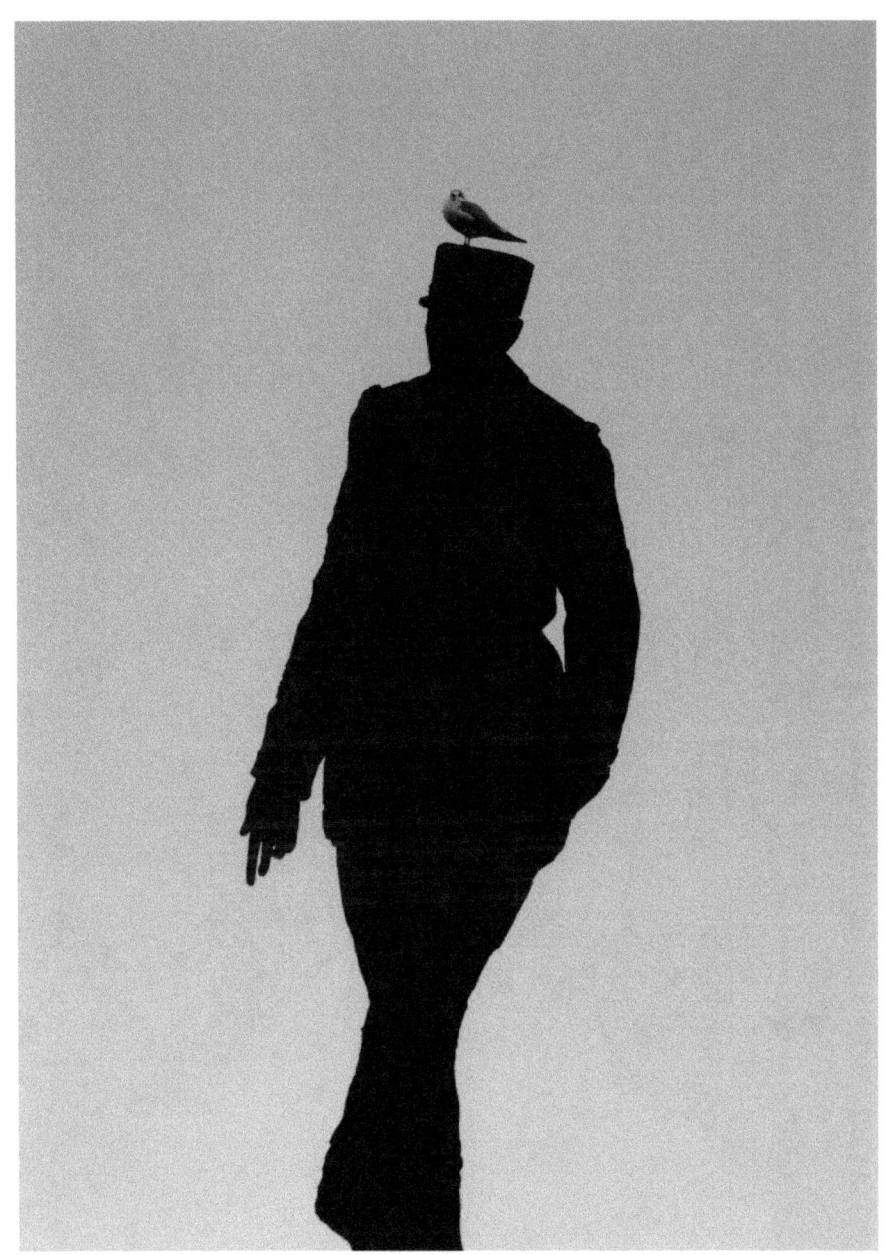

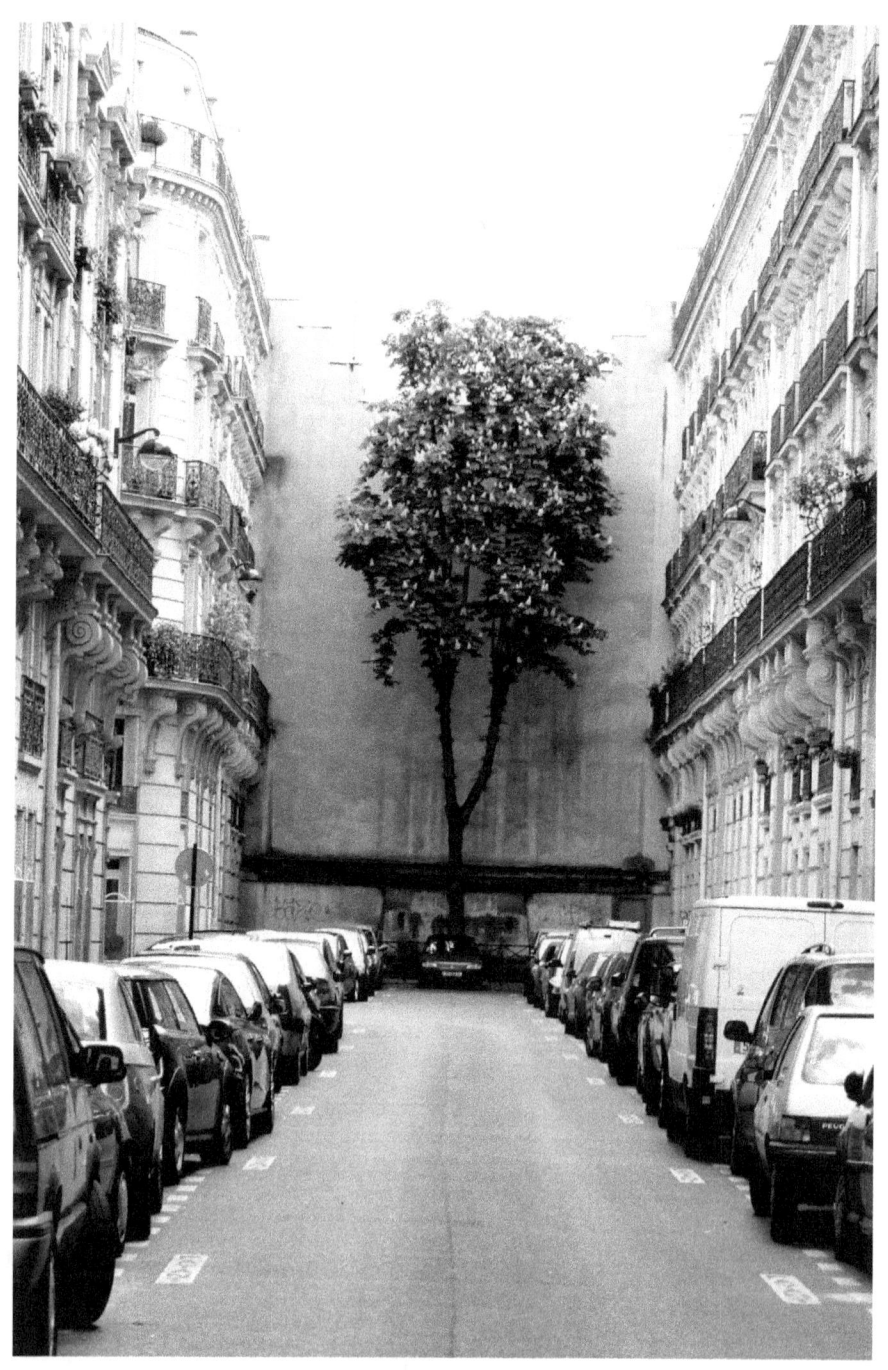

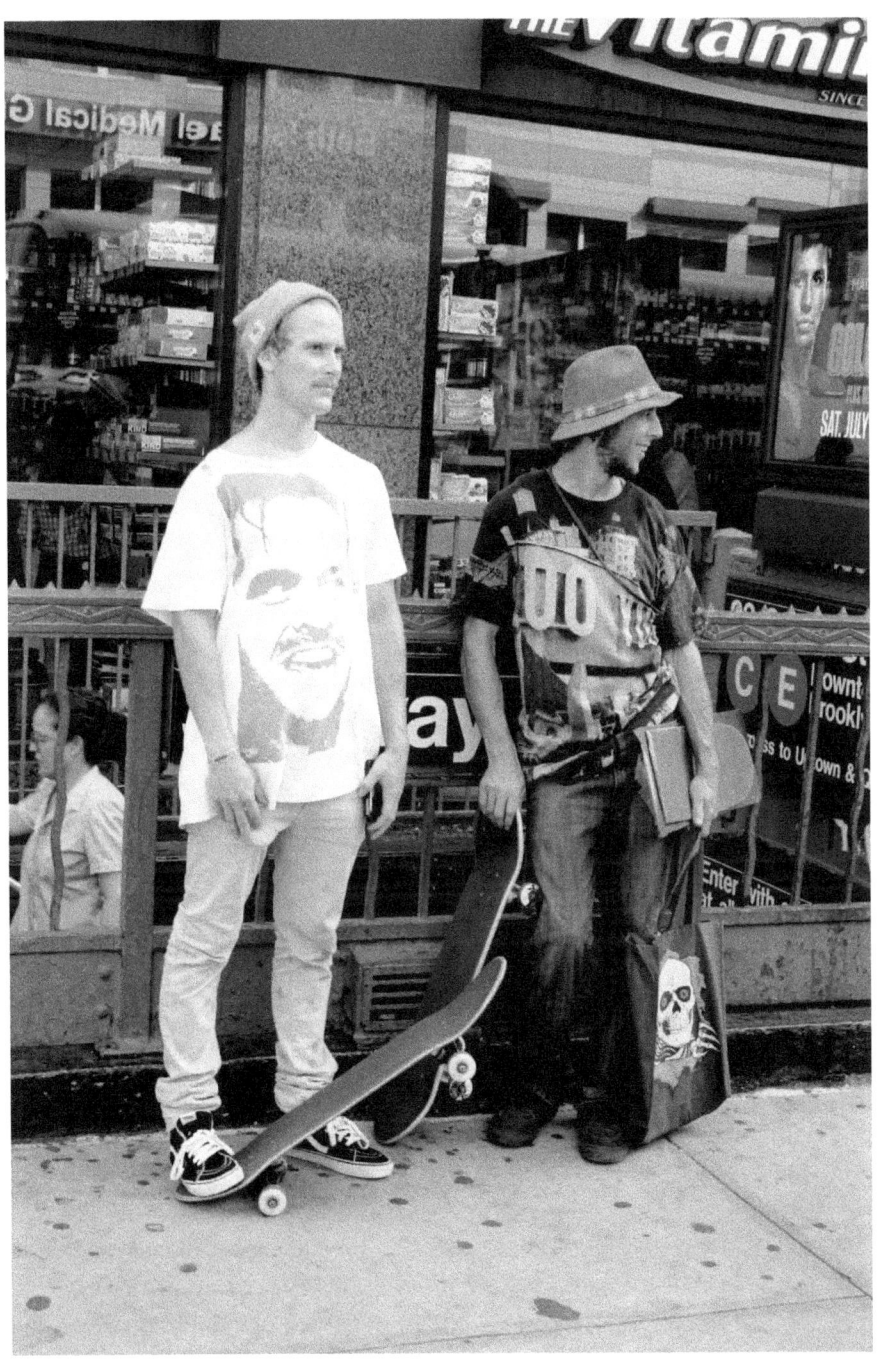

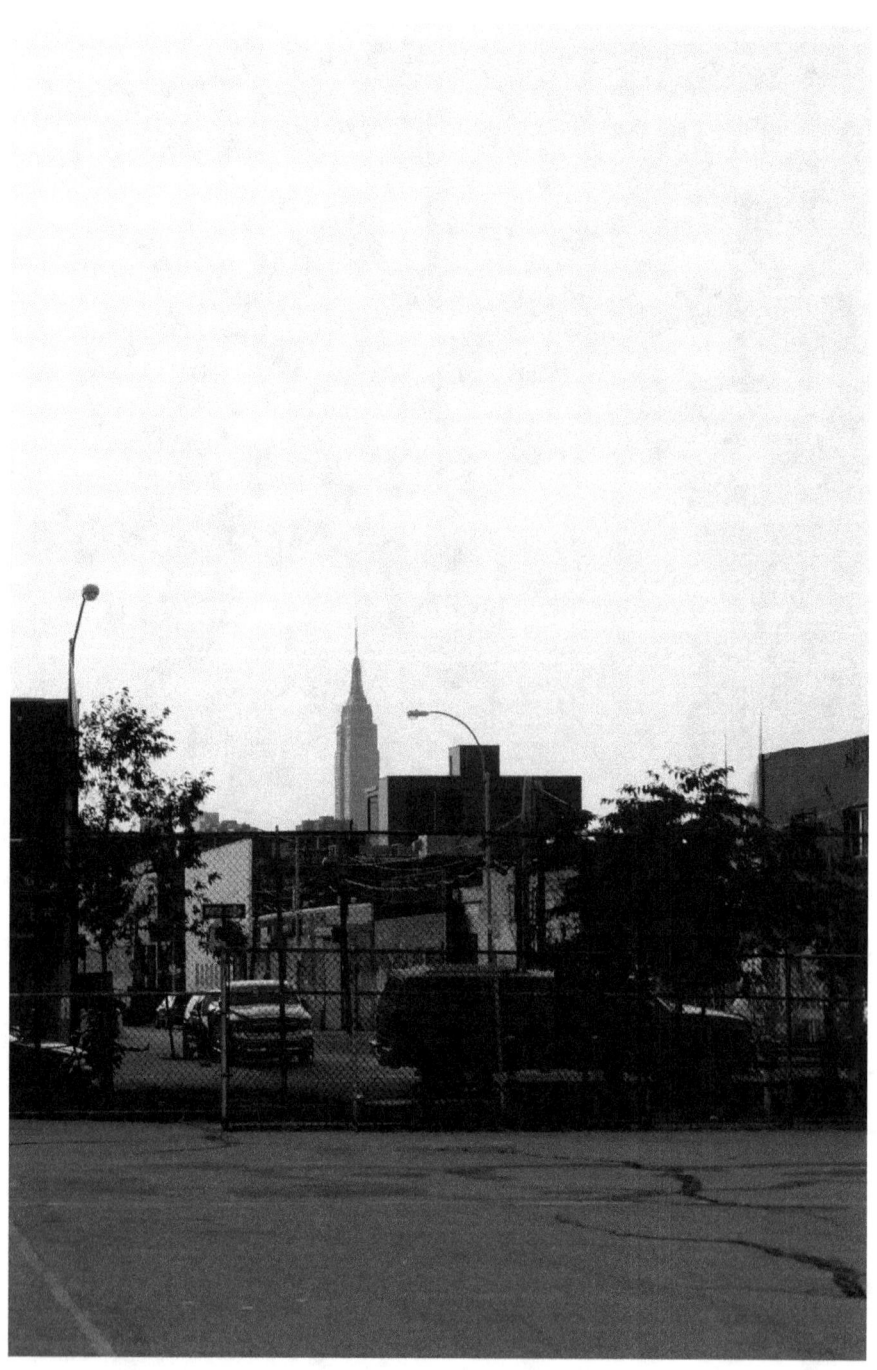

34

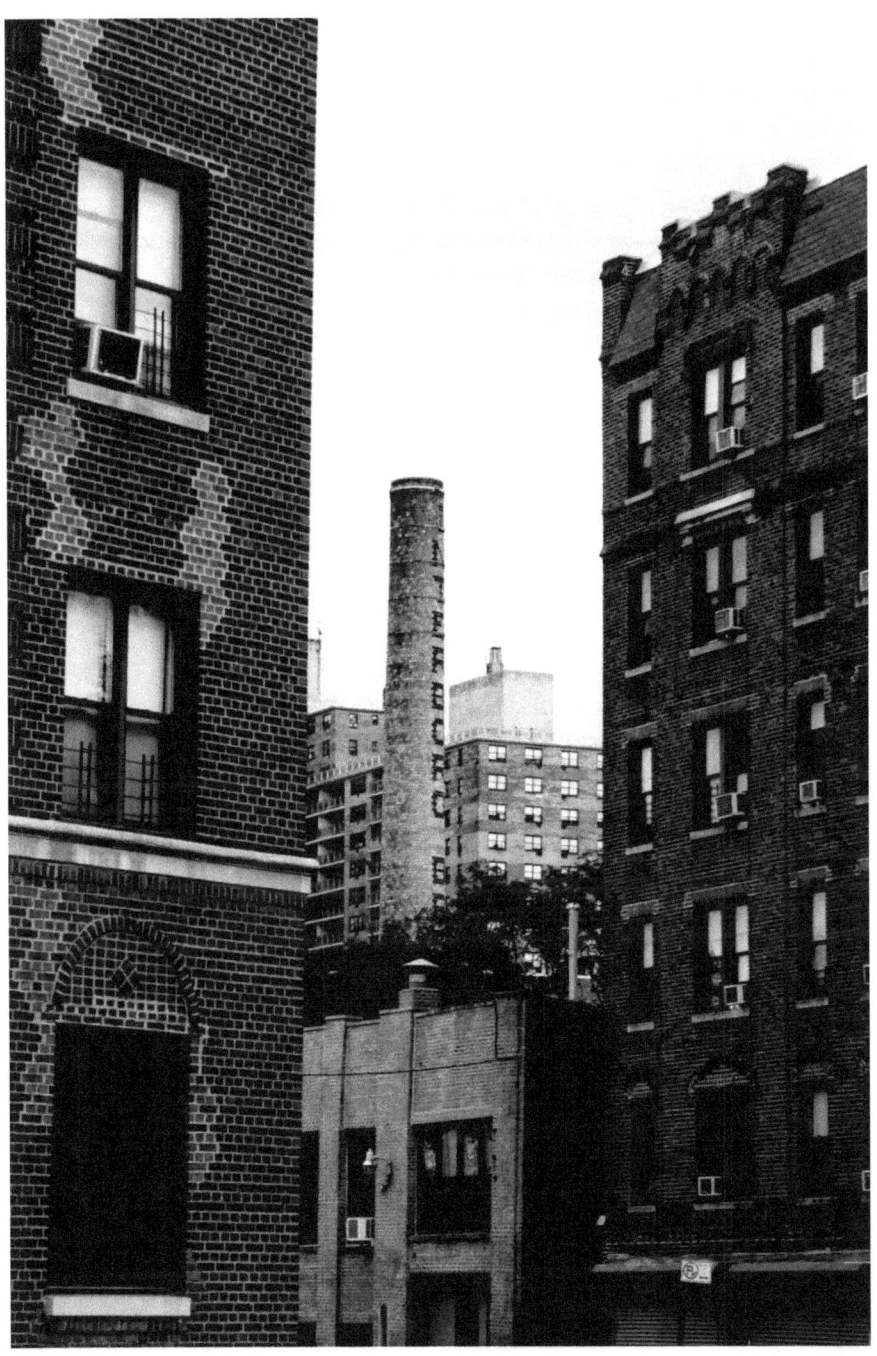

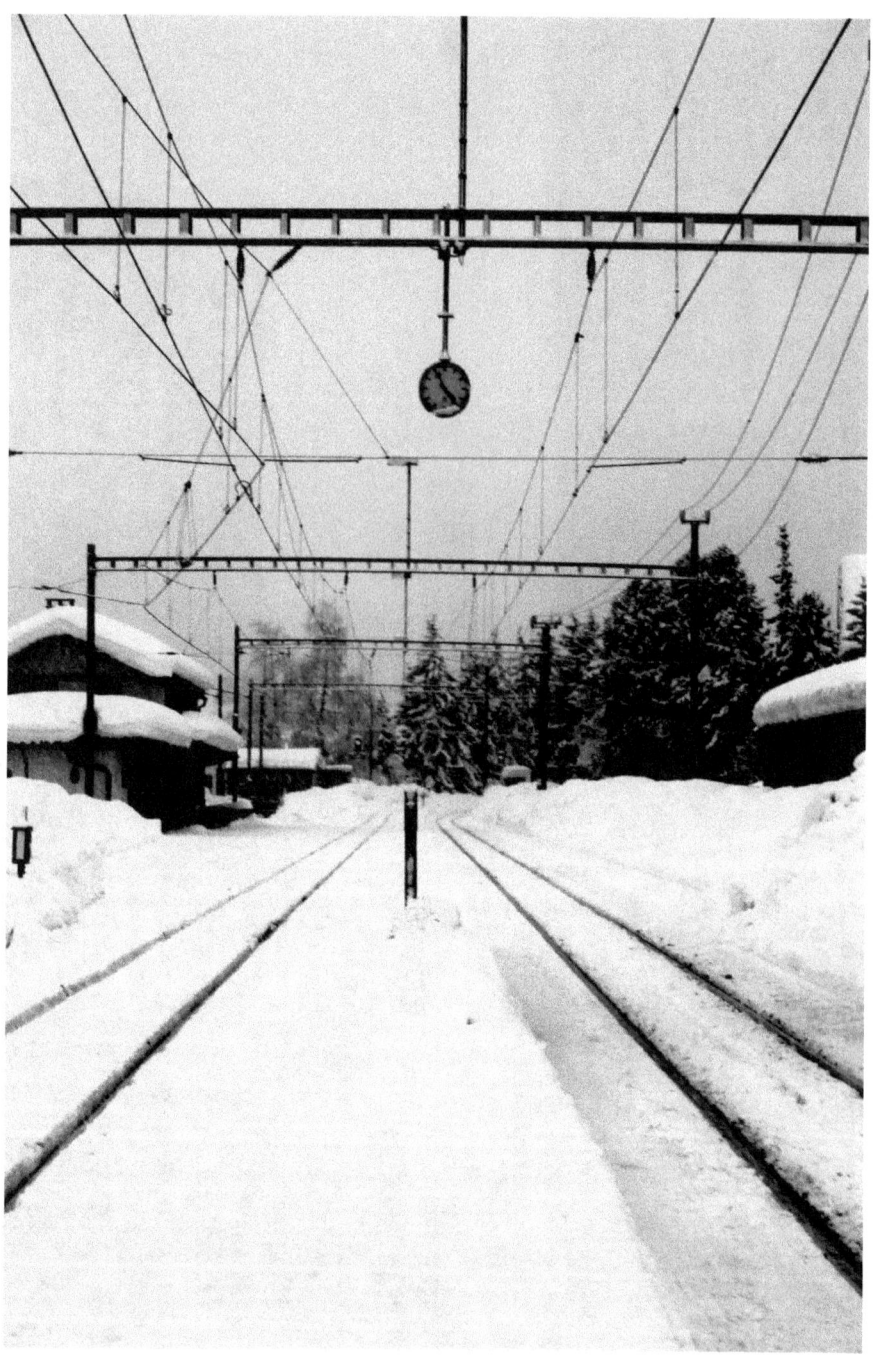

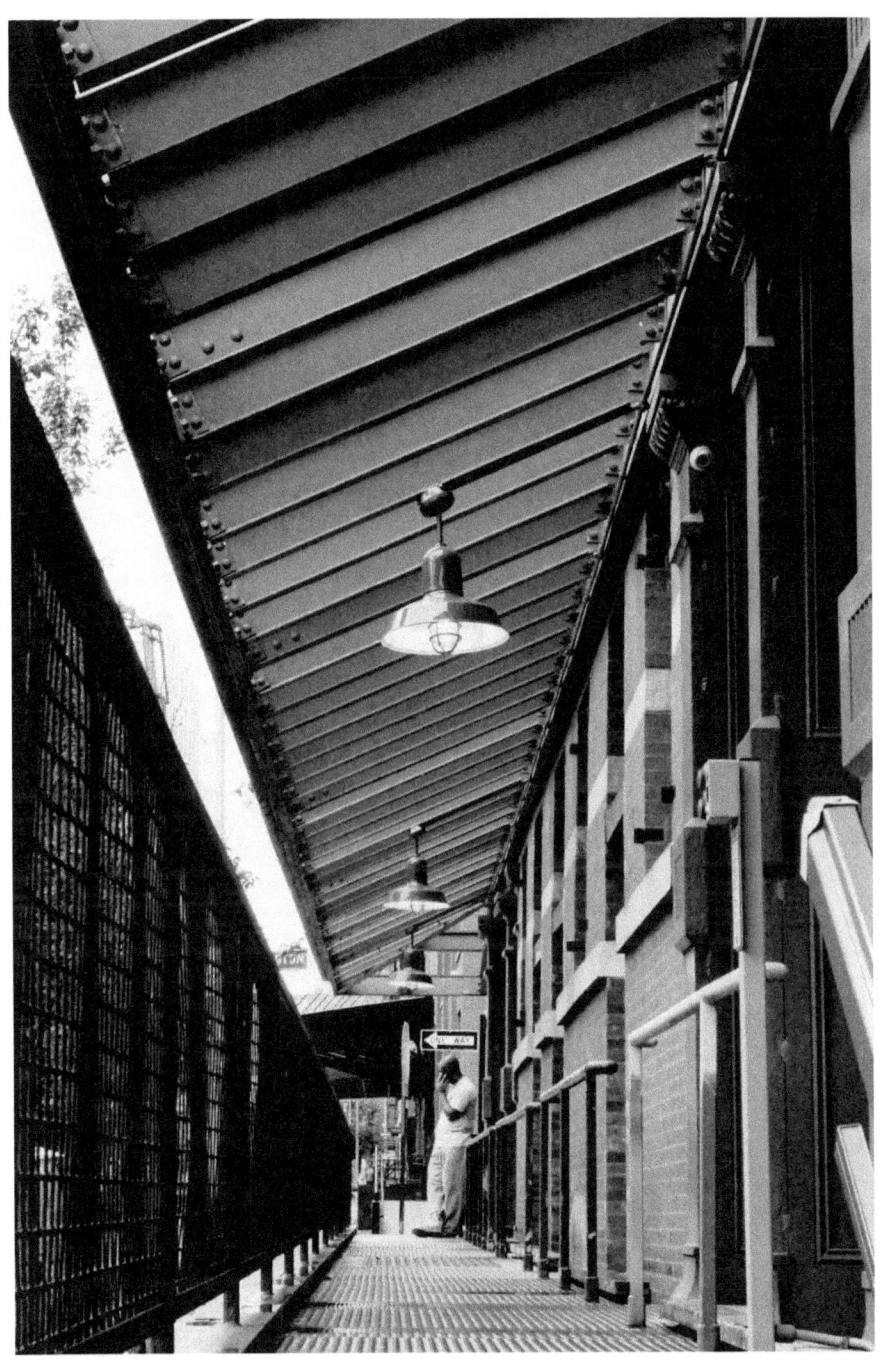

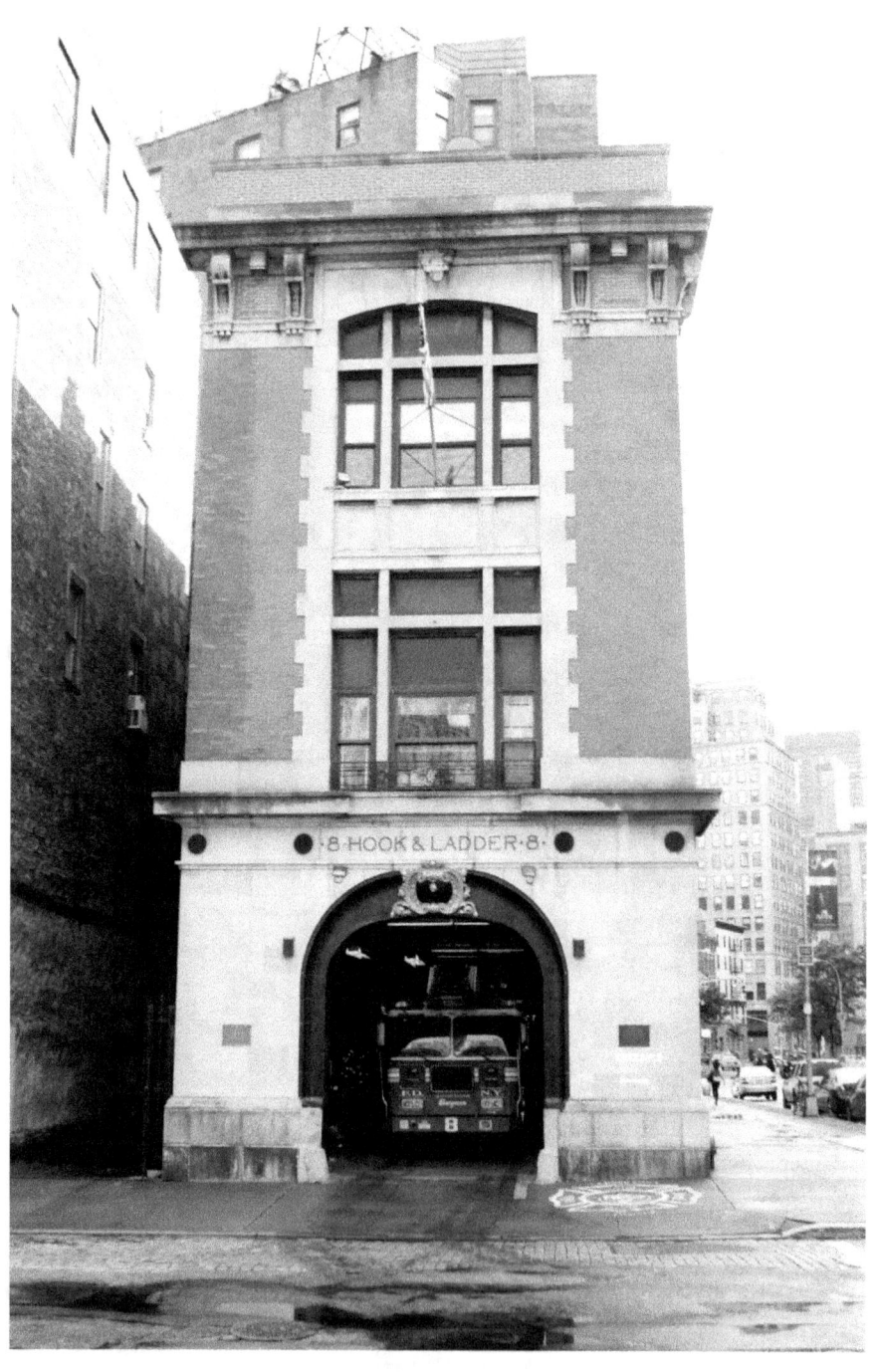

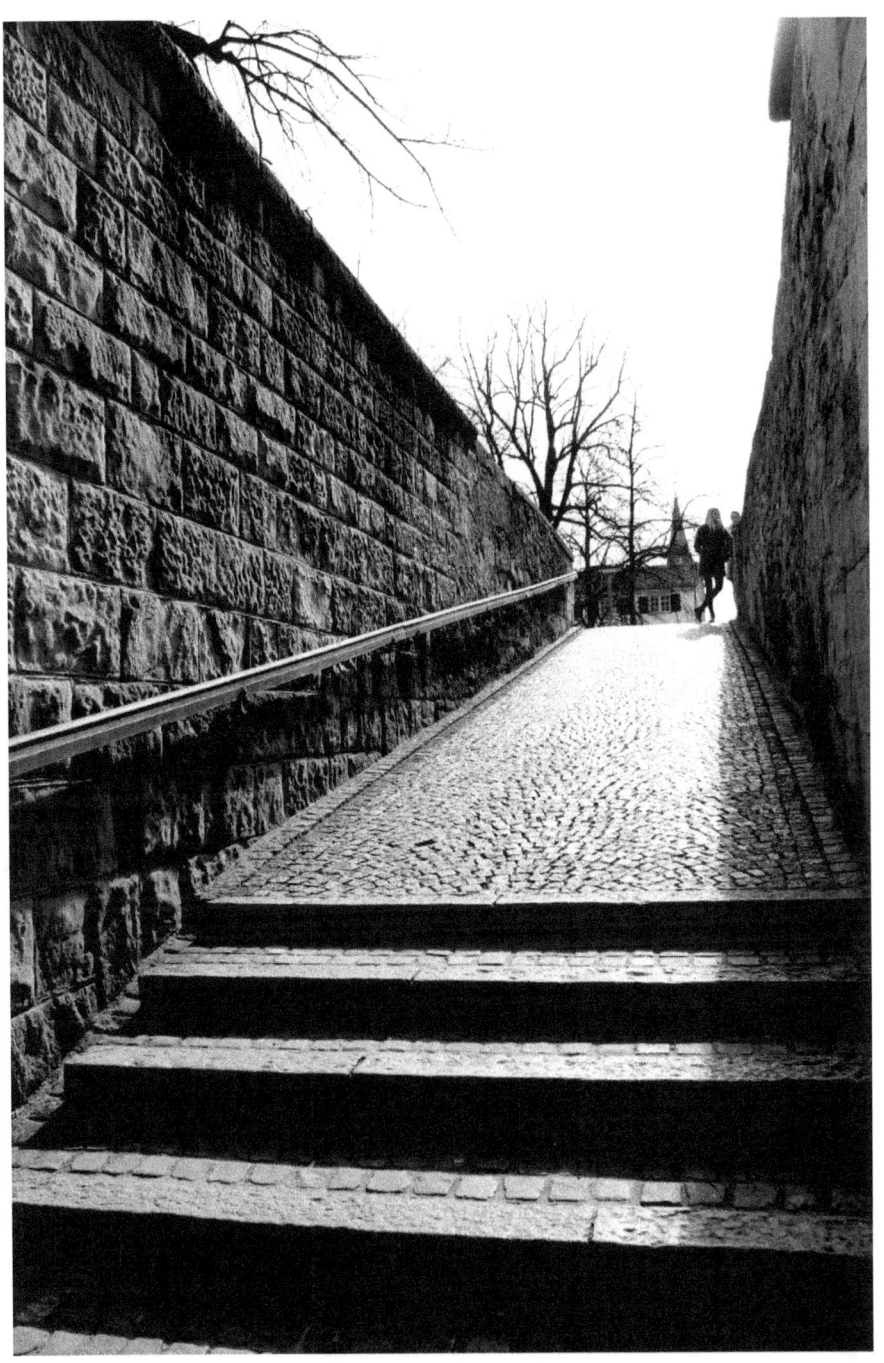

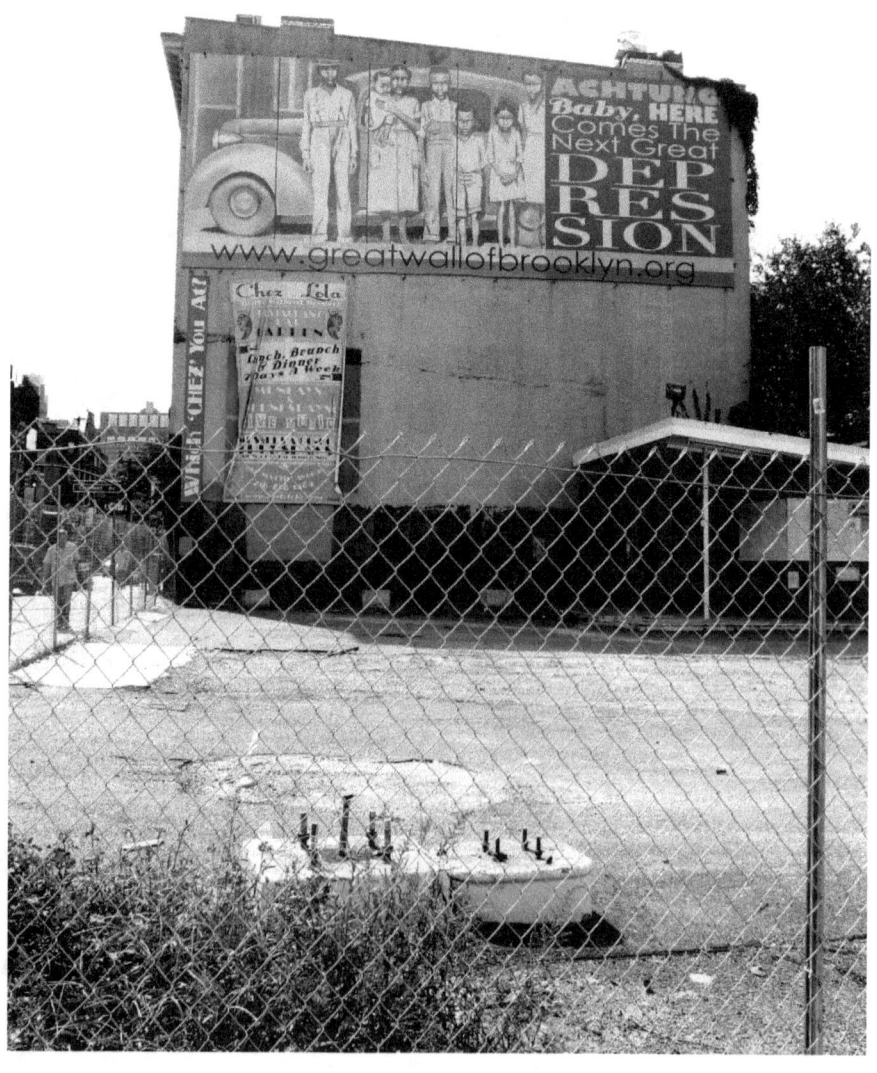

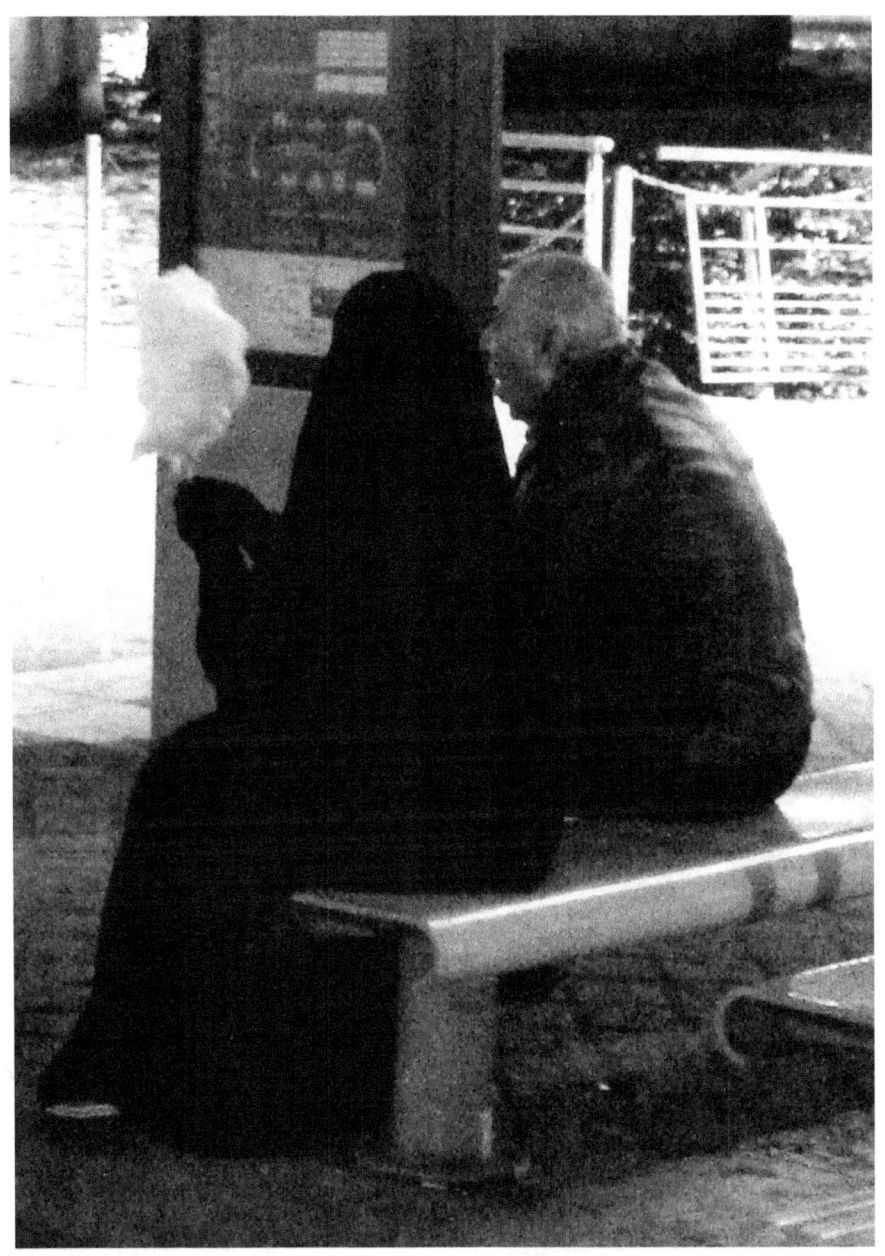

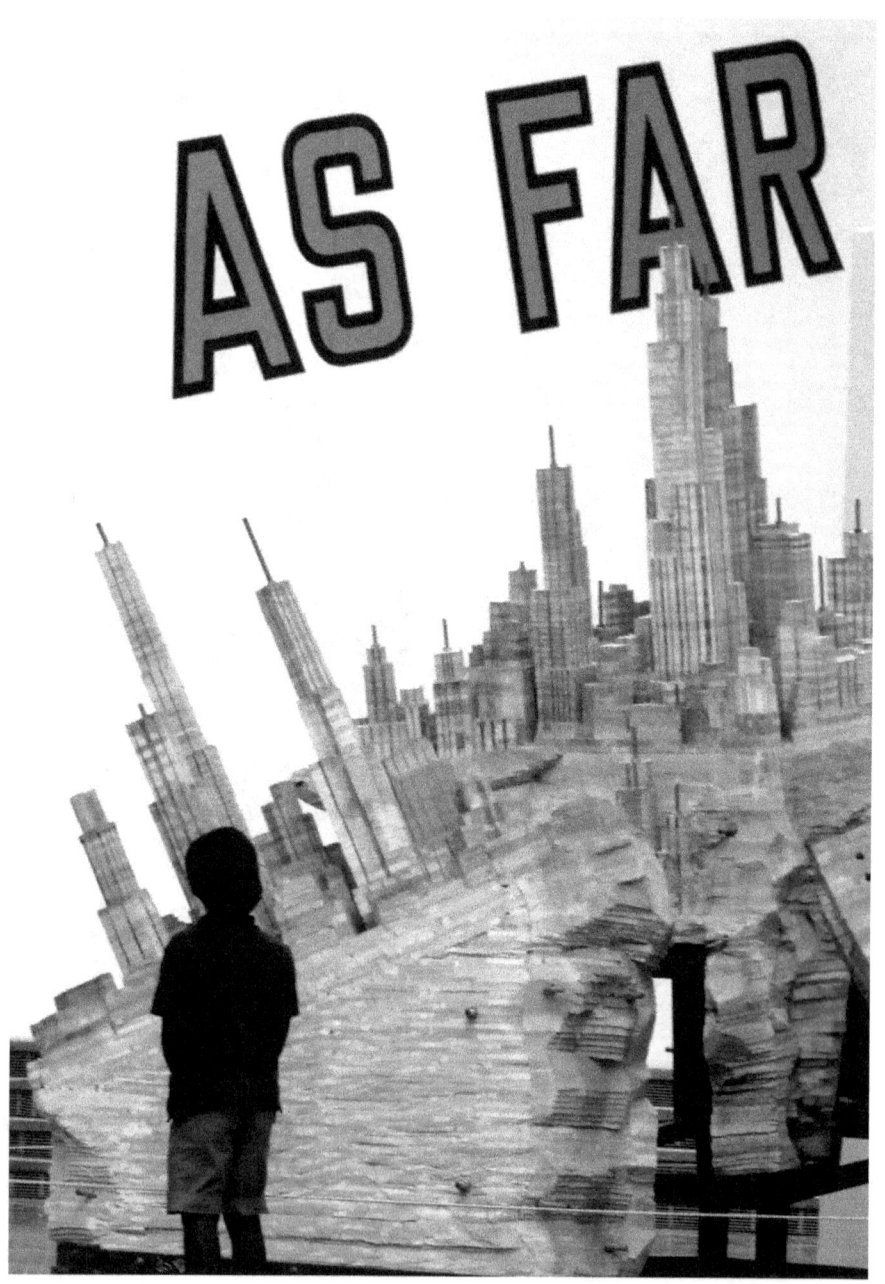

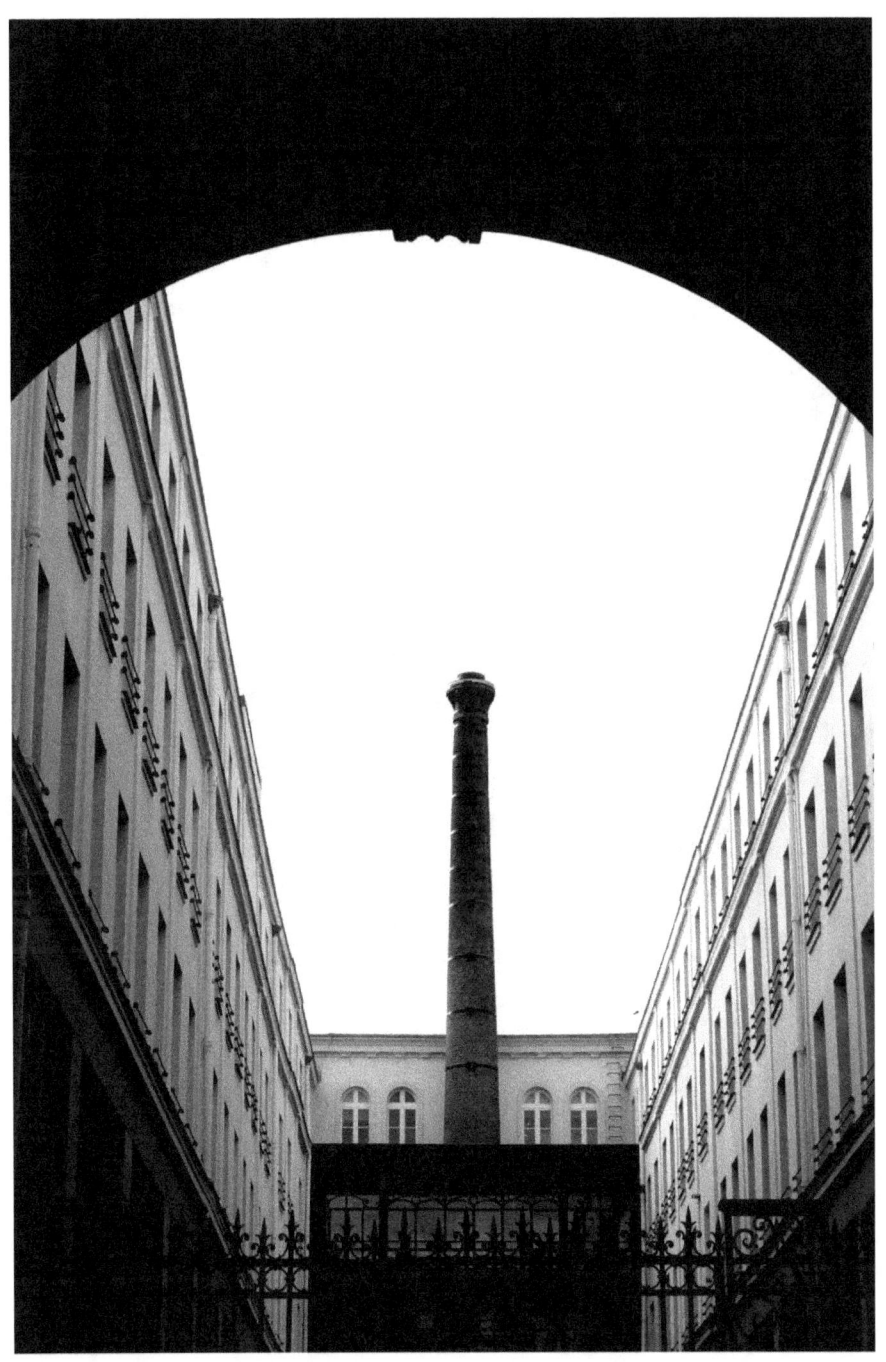

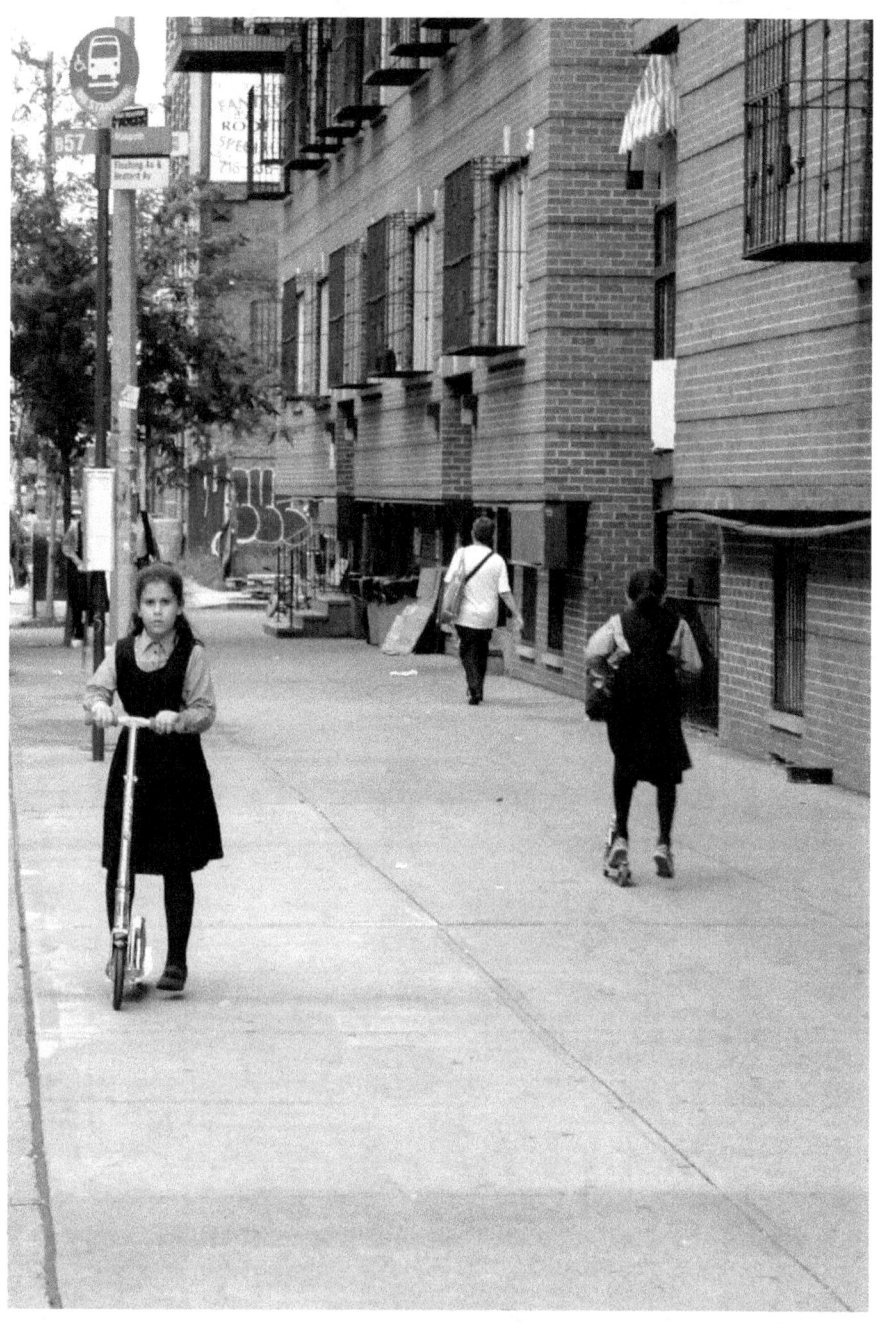

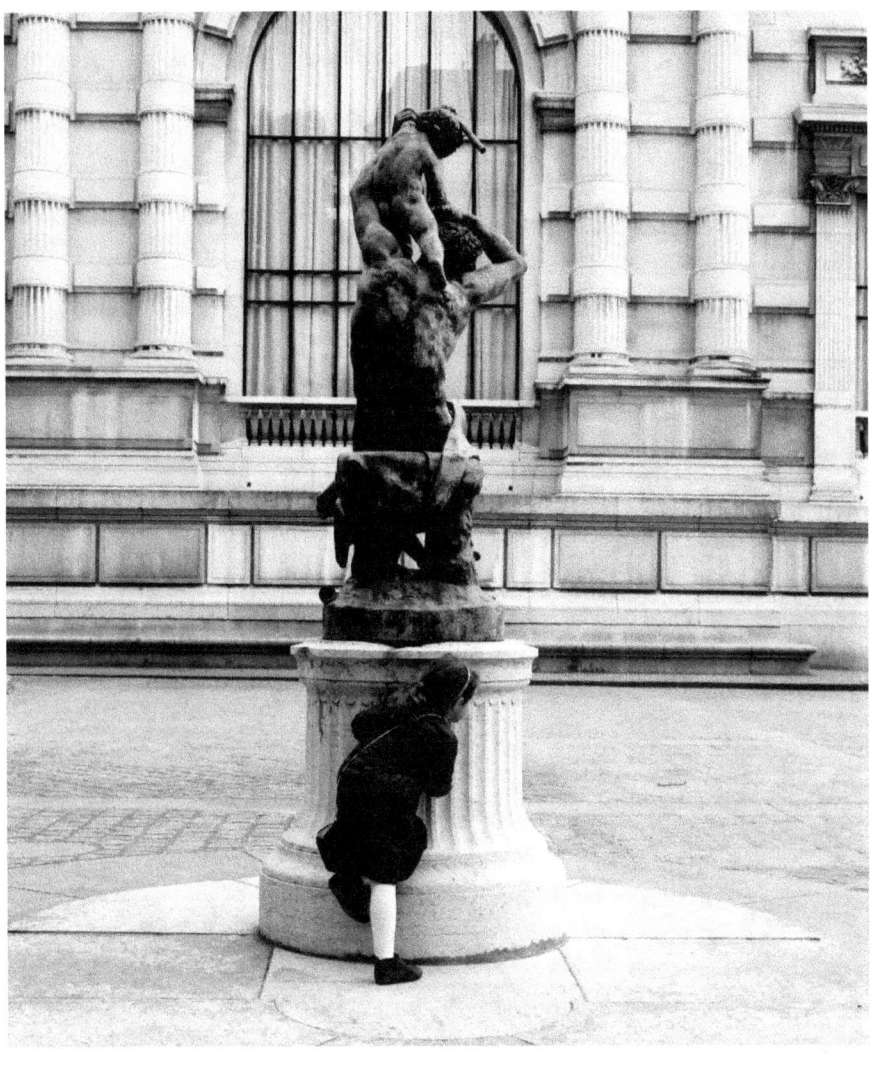

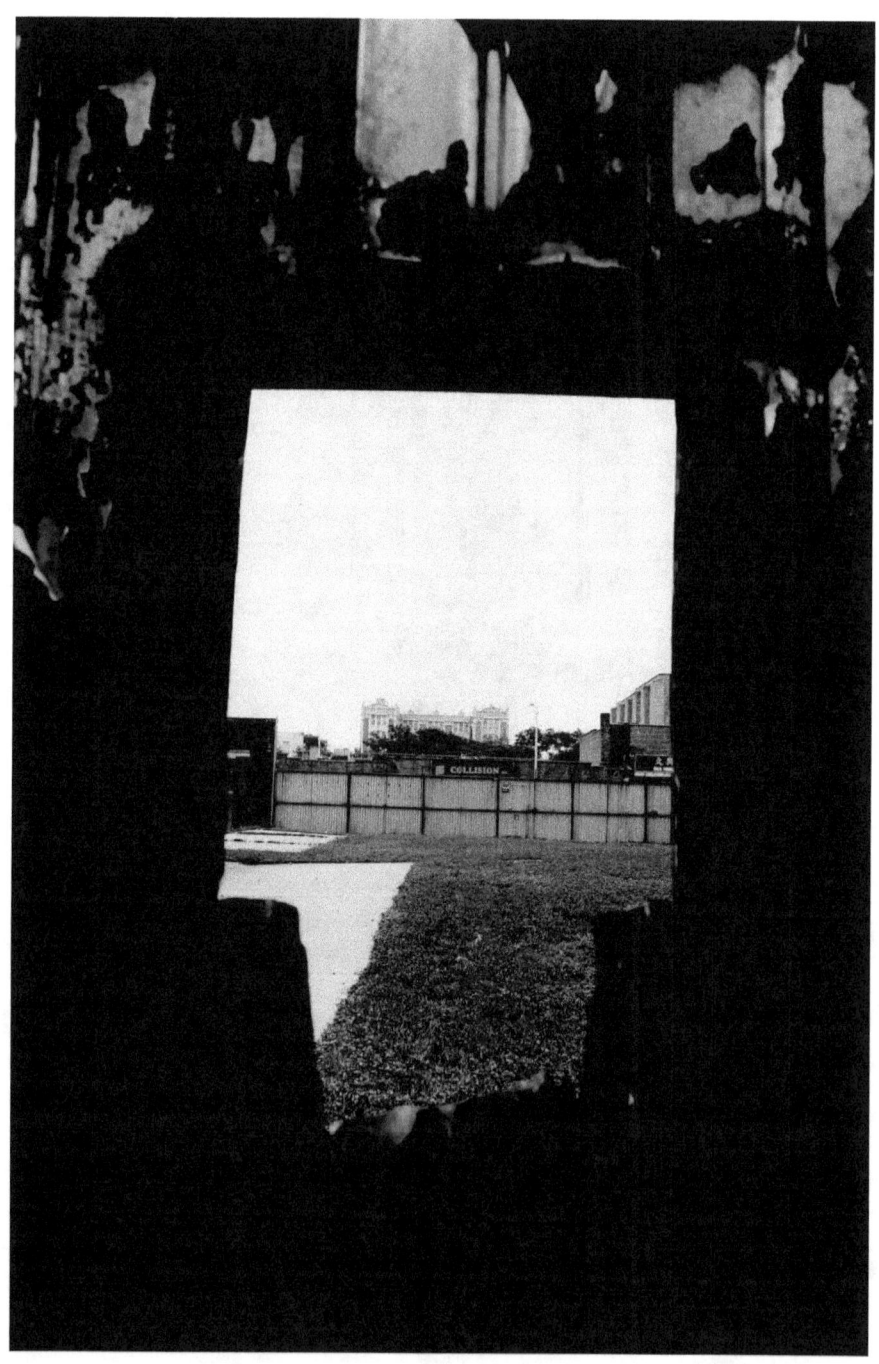

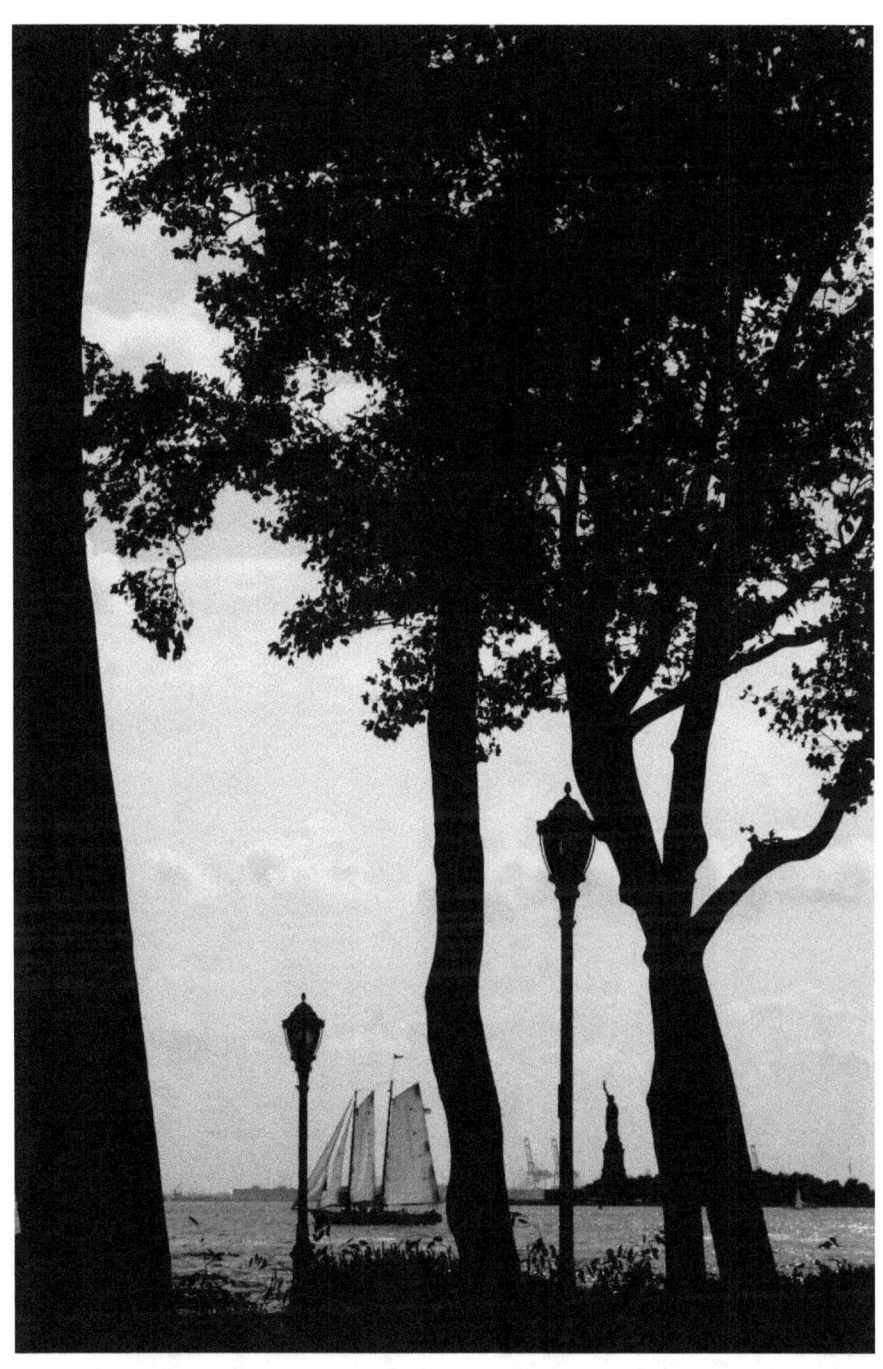

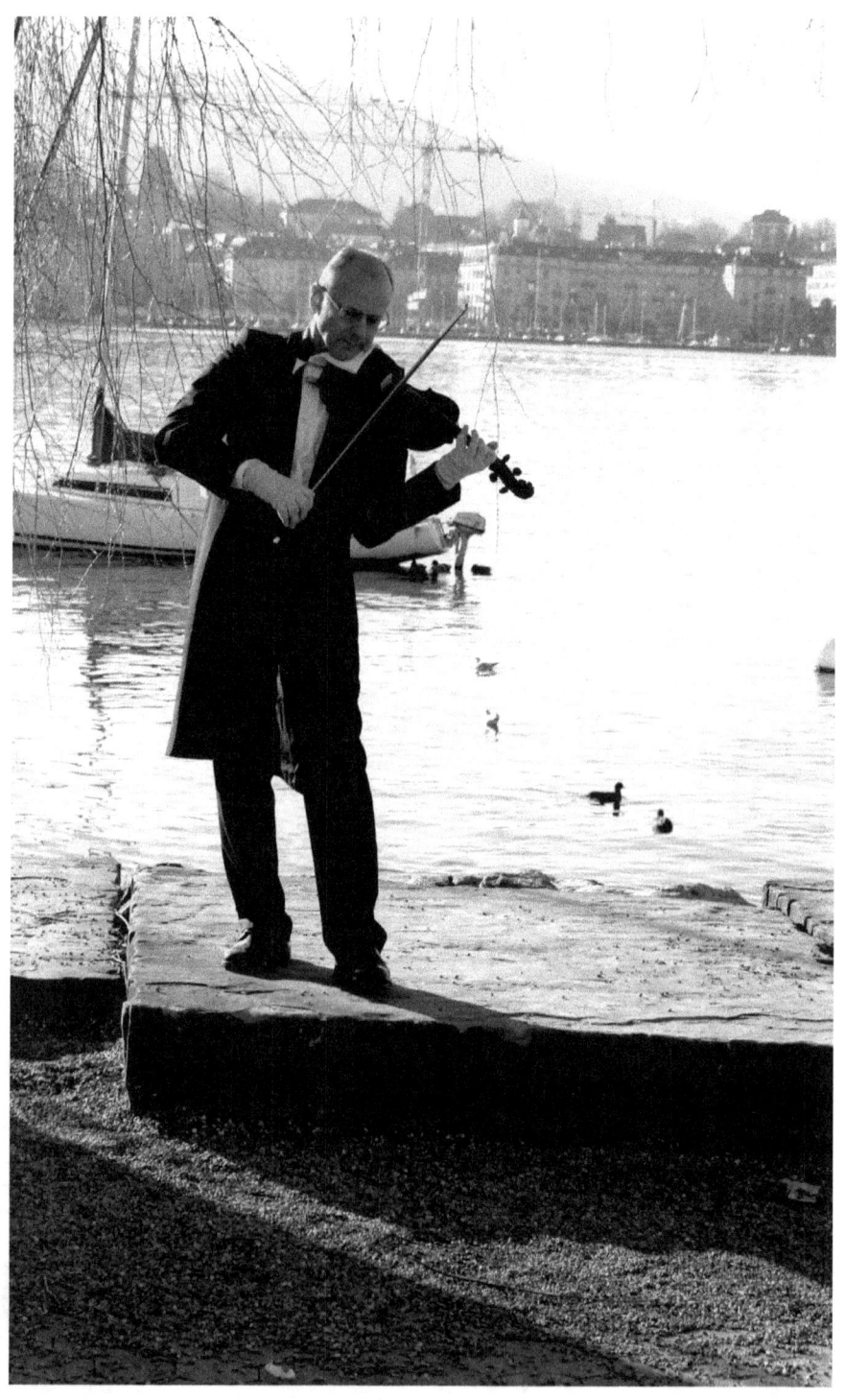

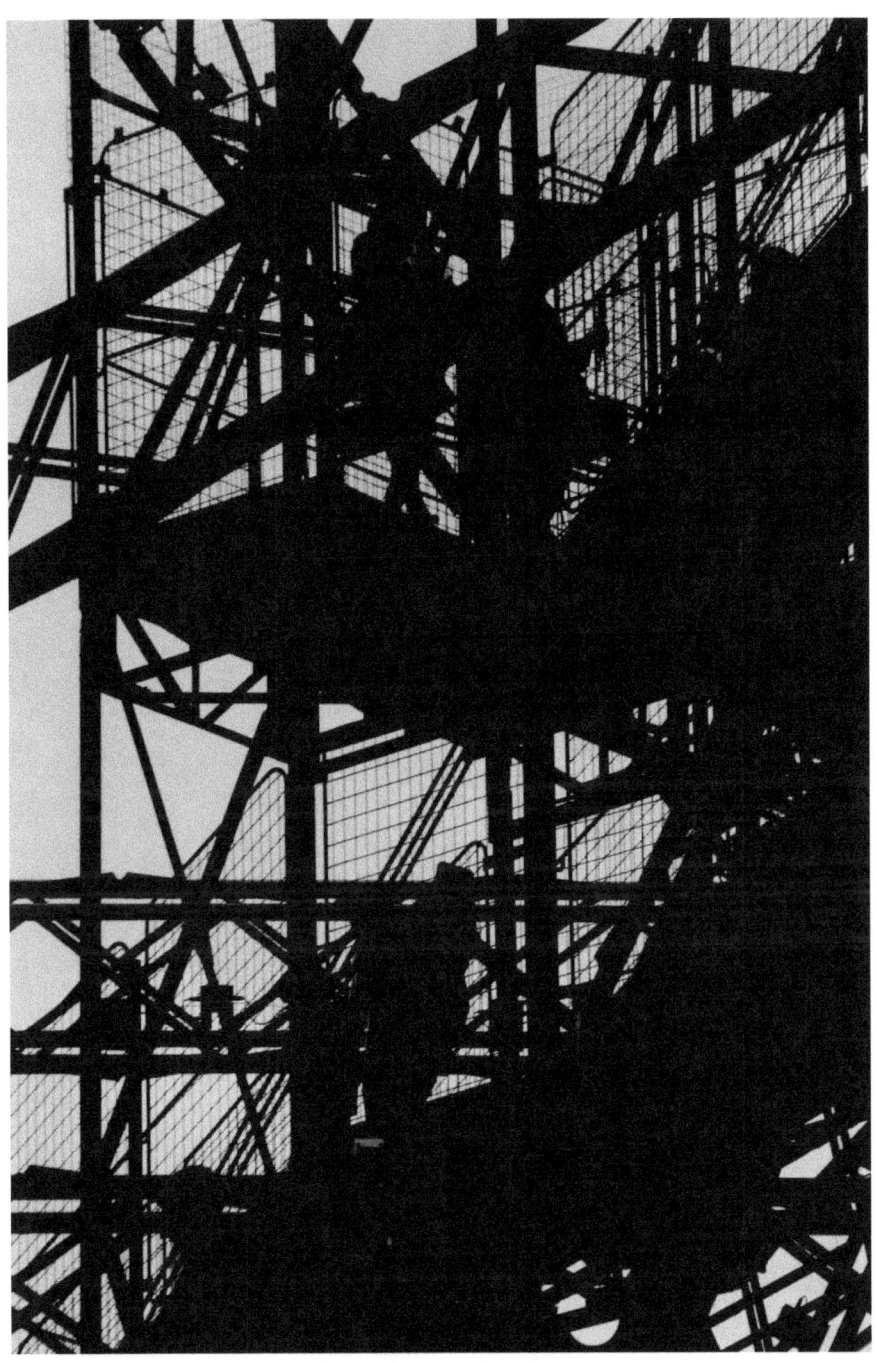

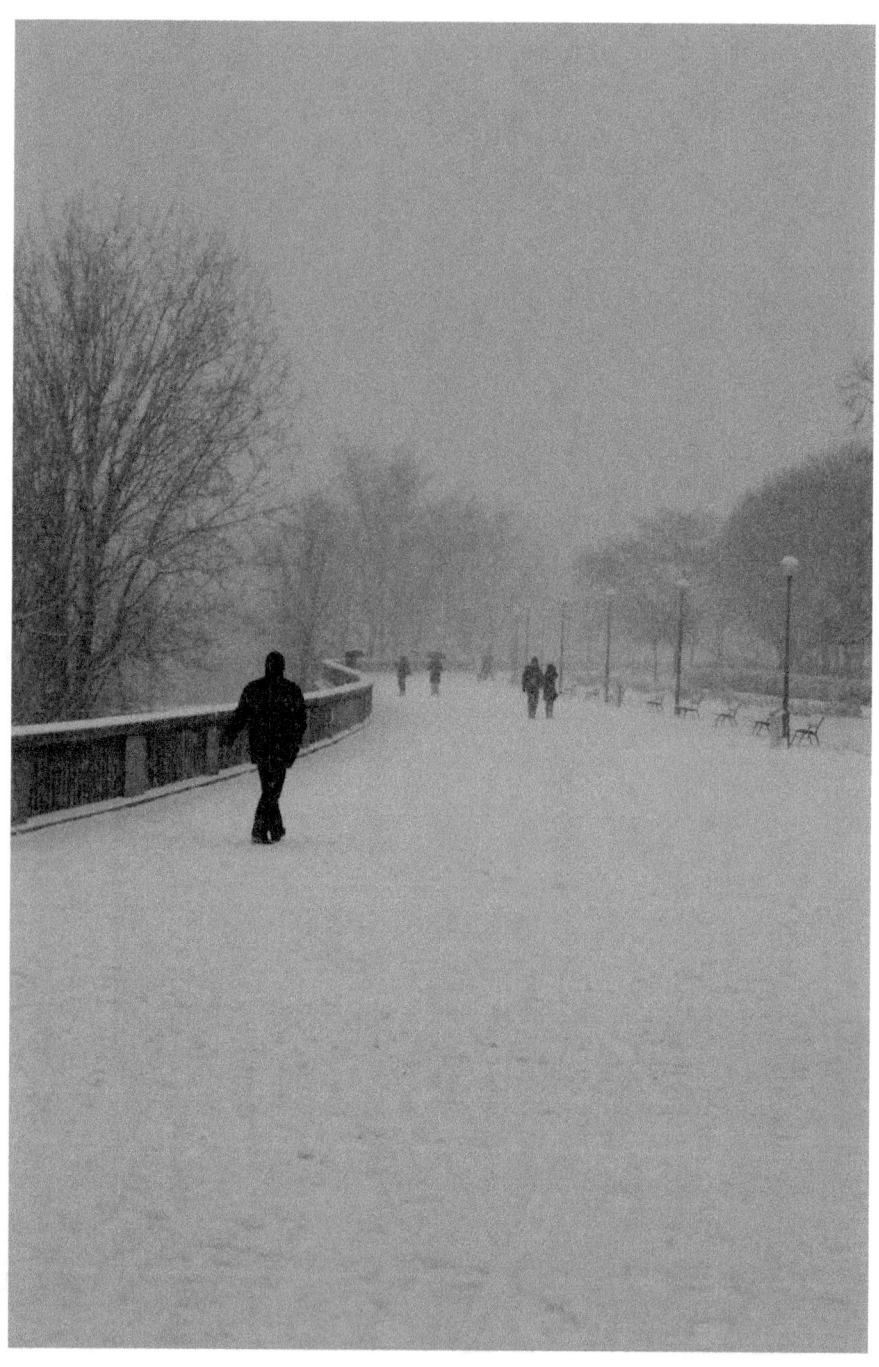

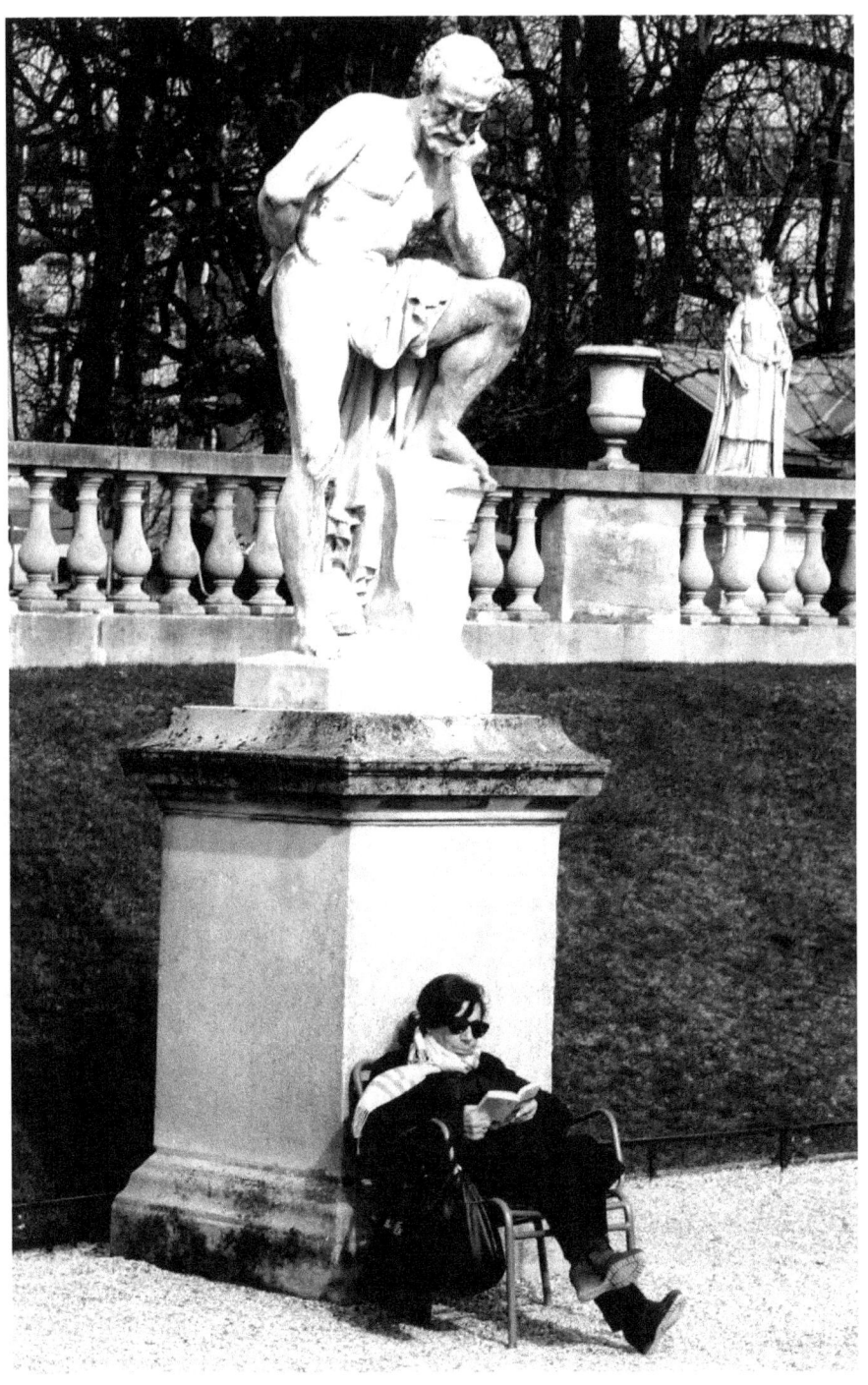

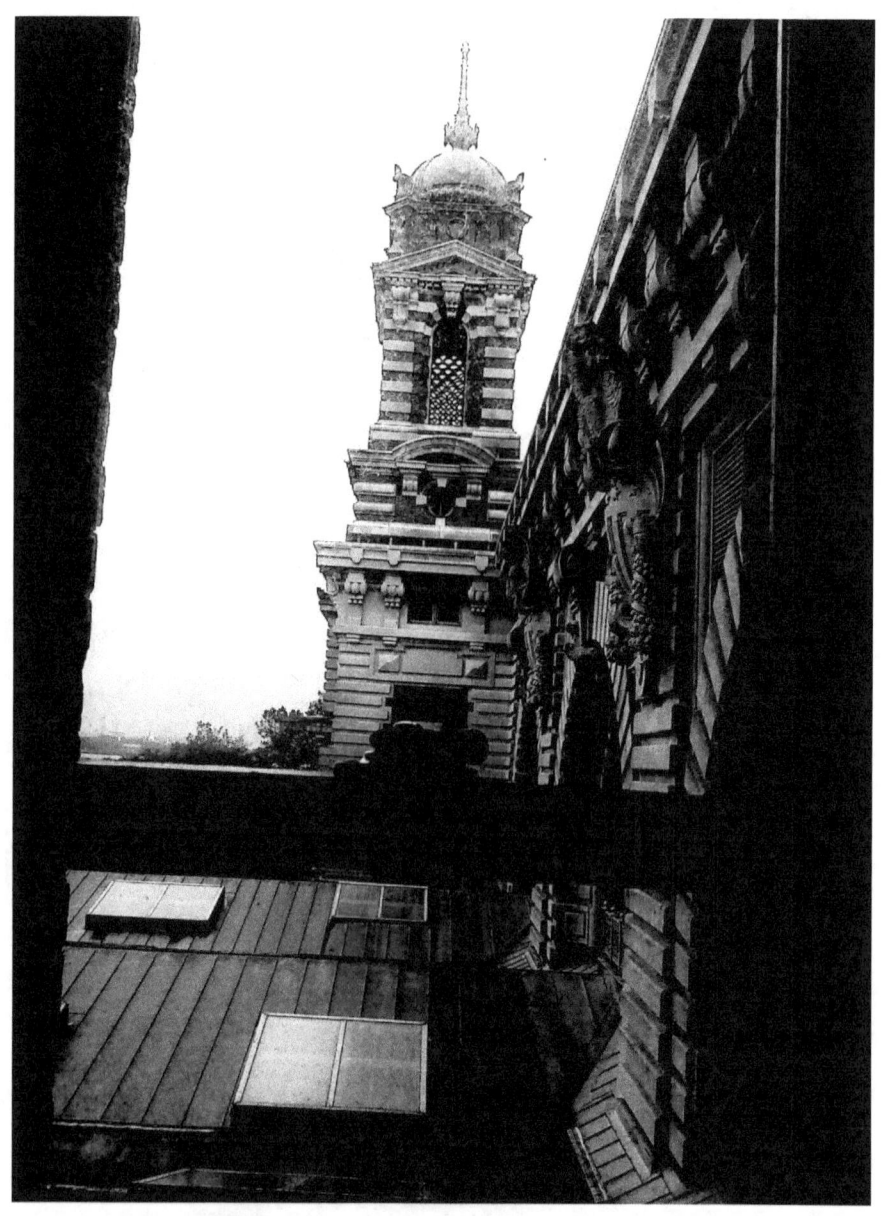

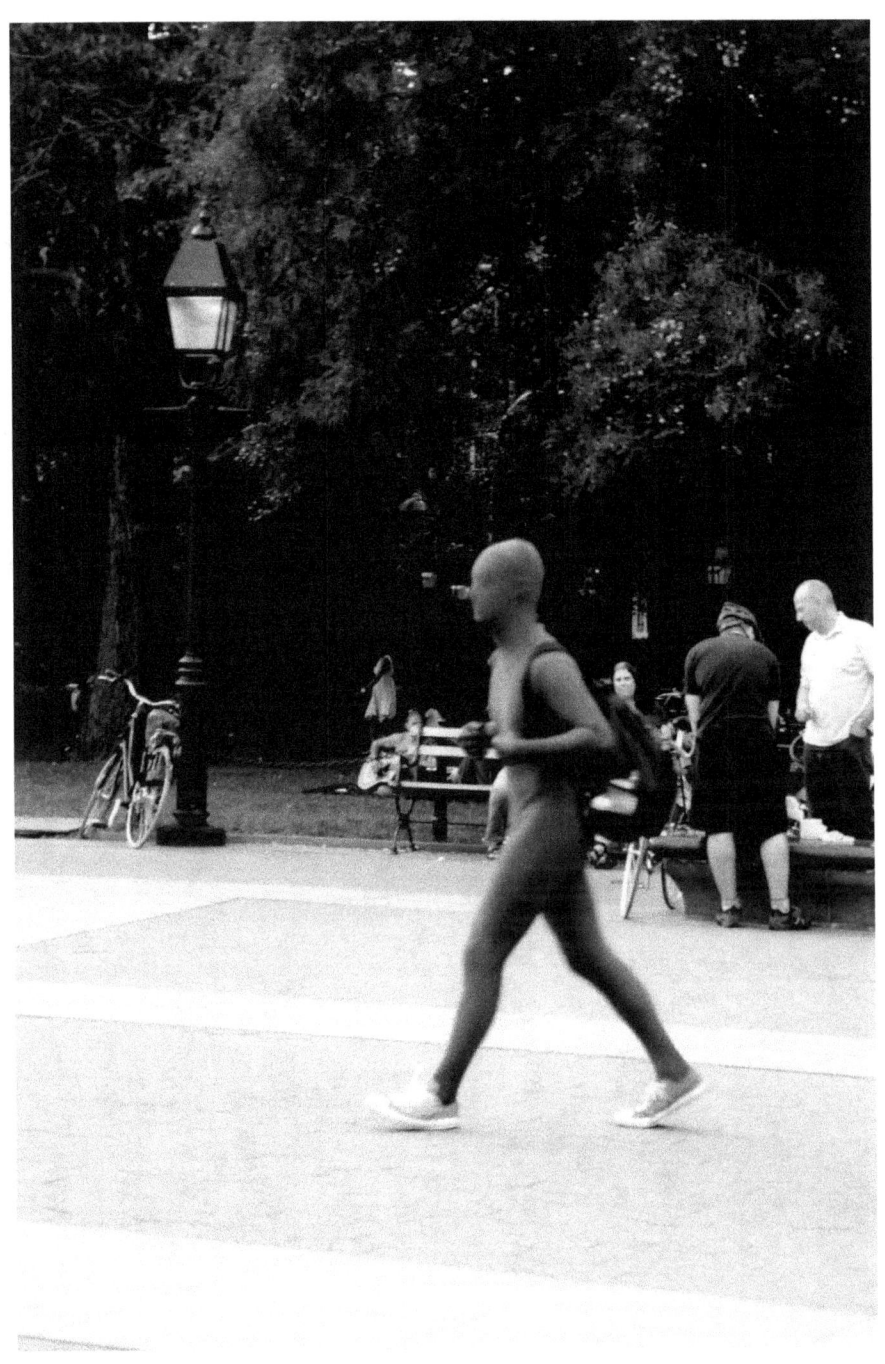

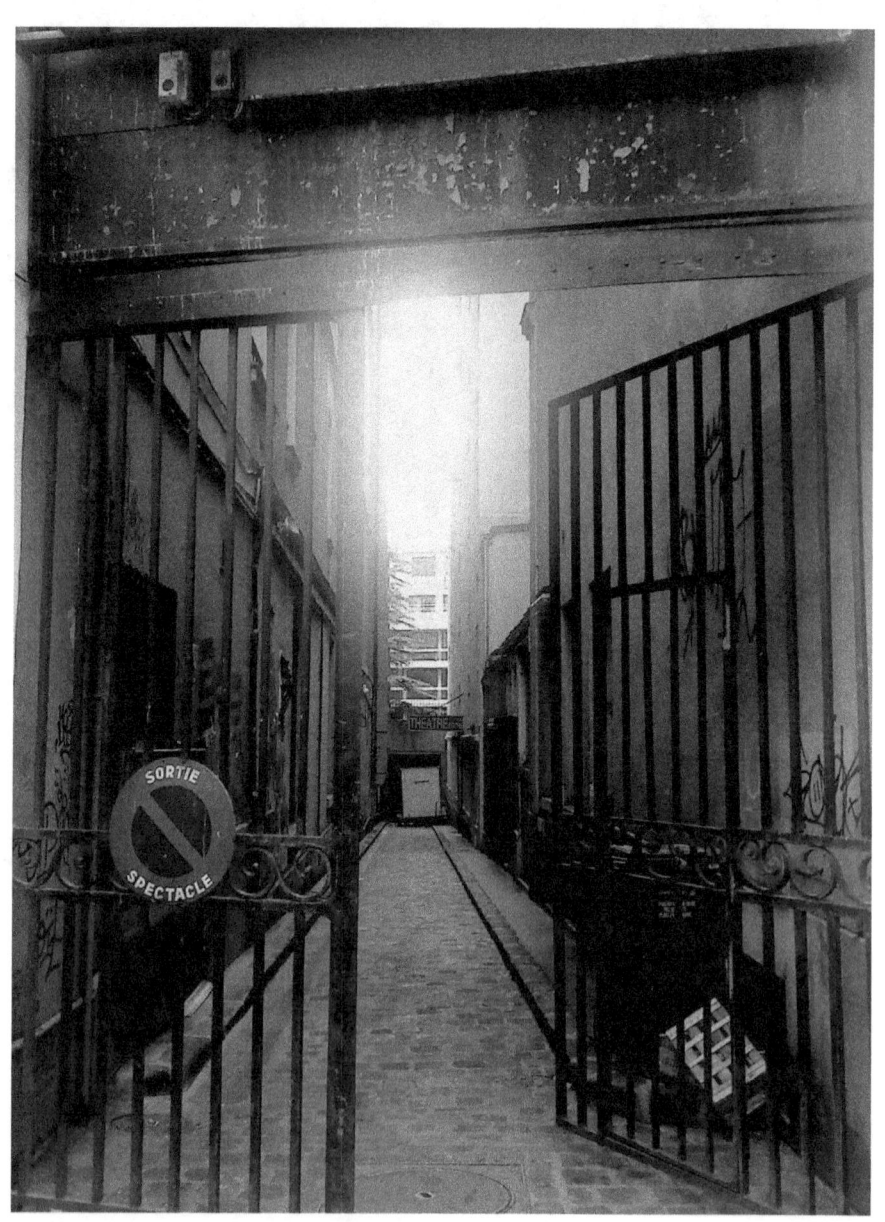

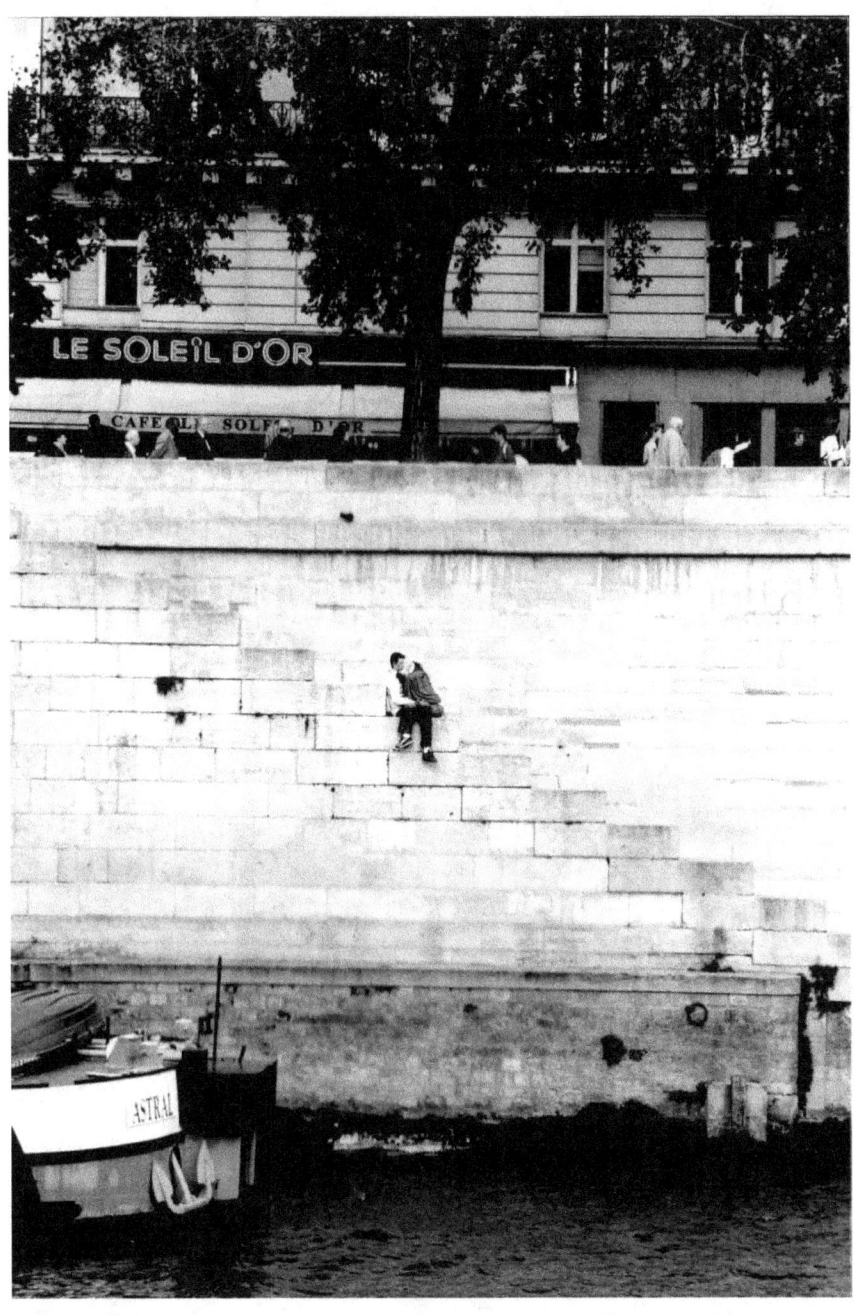

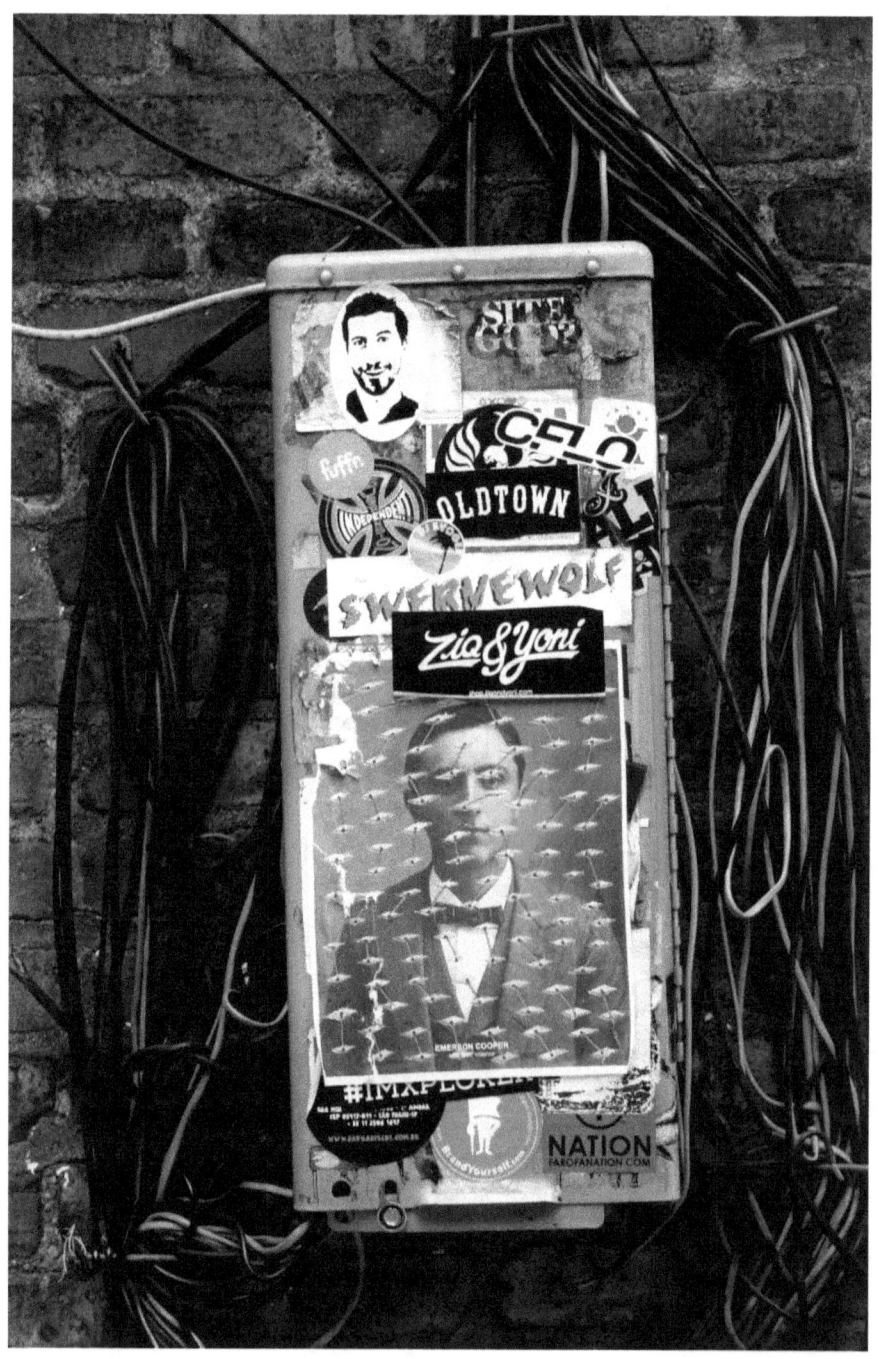

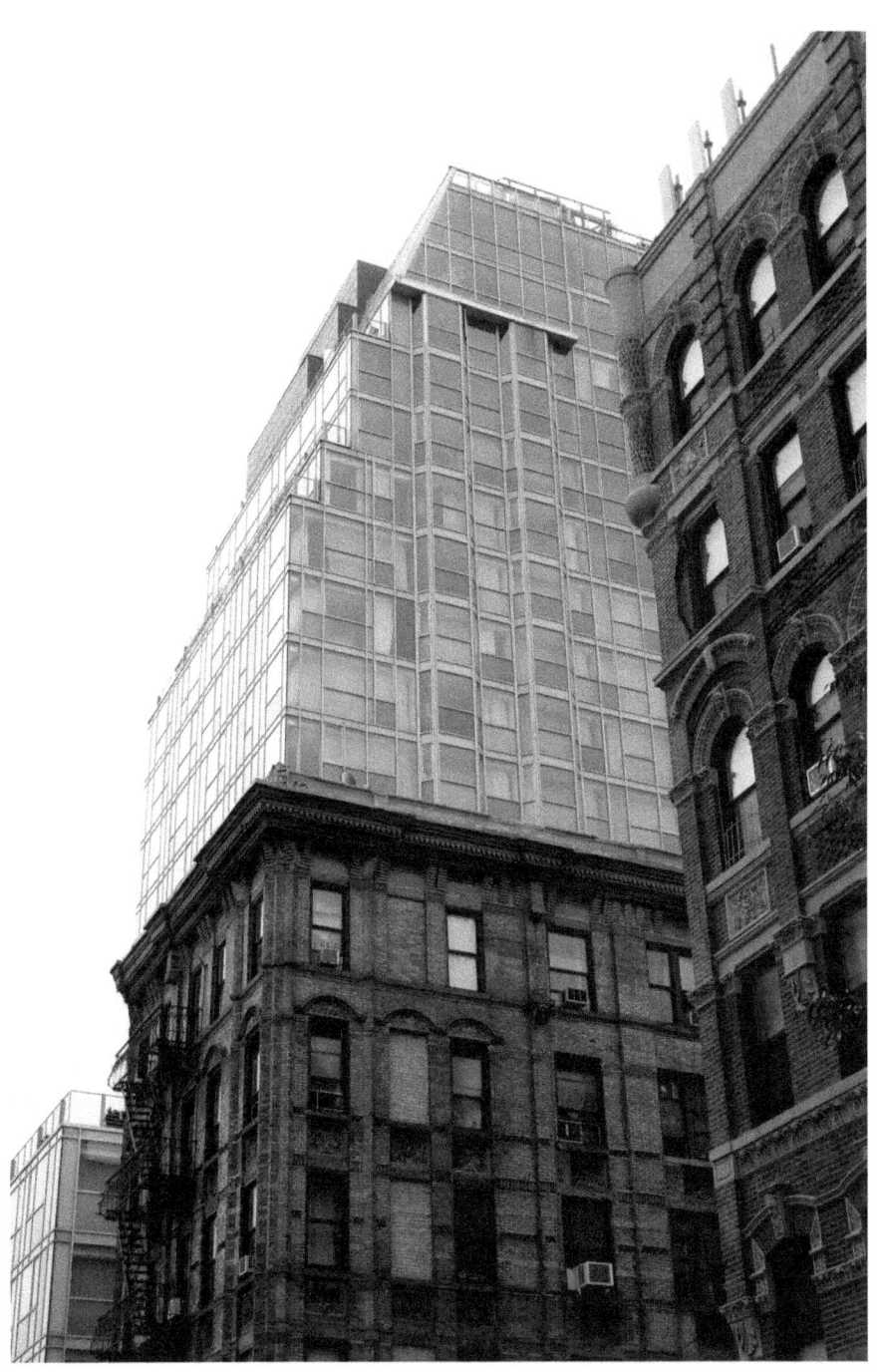

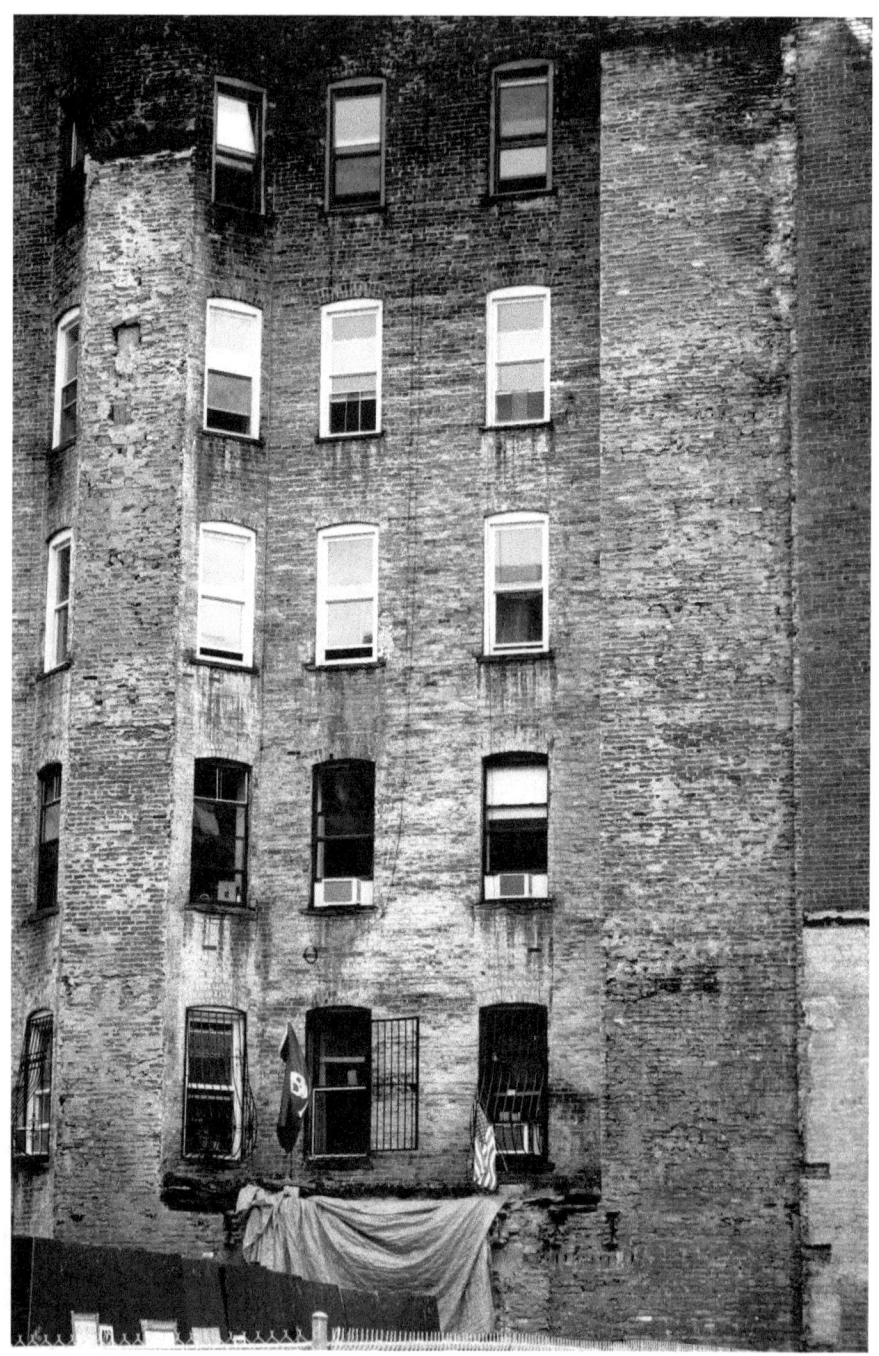

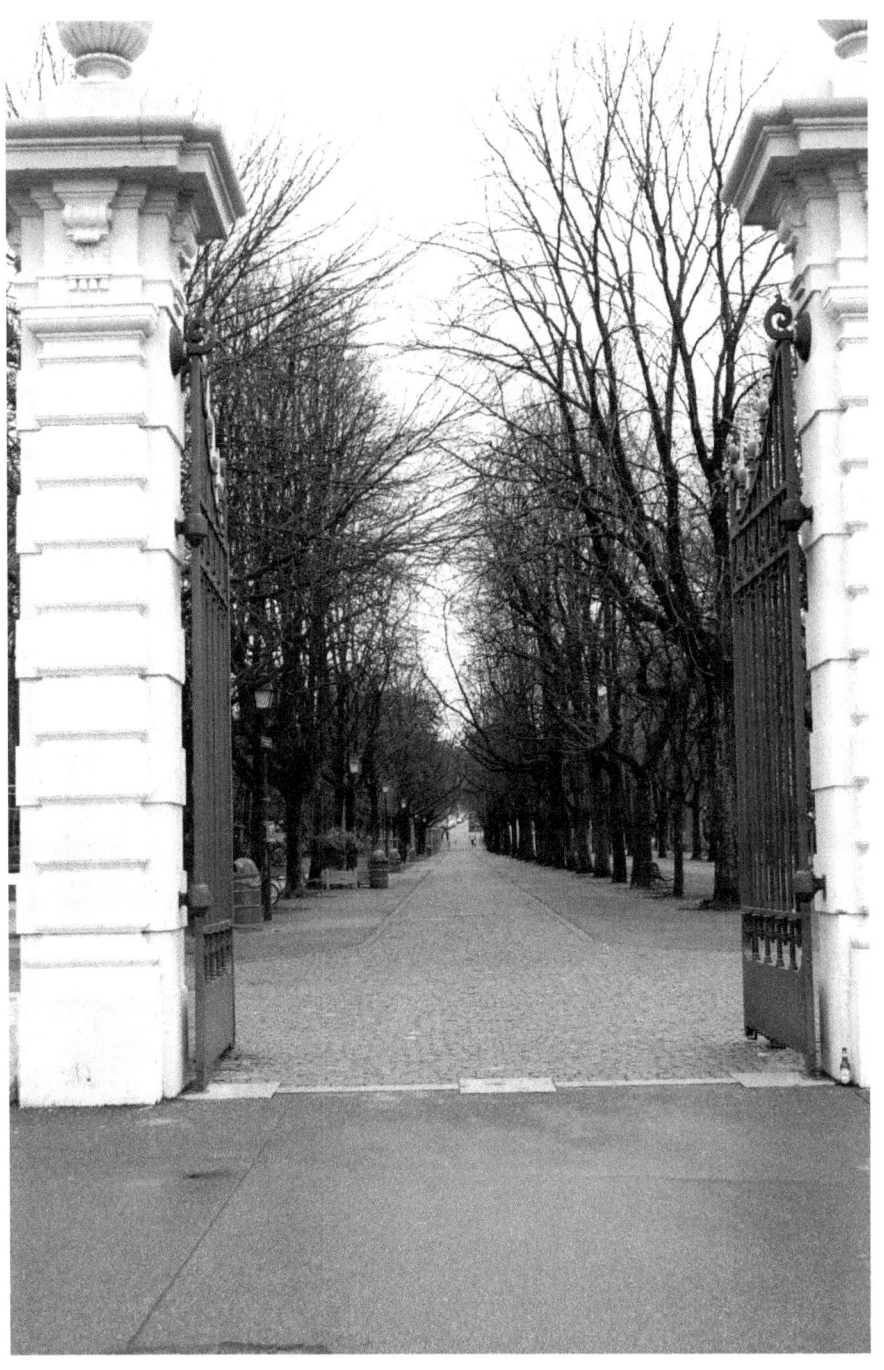

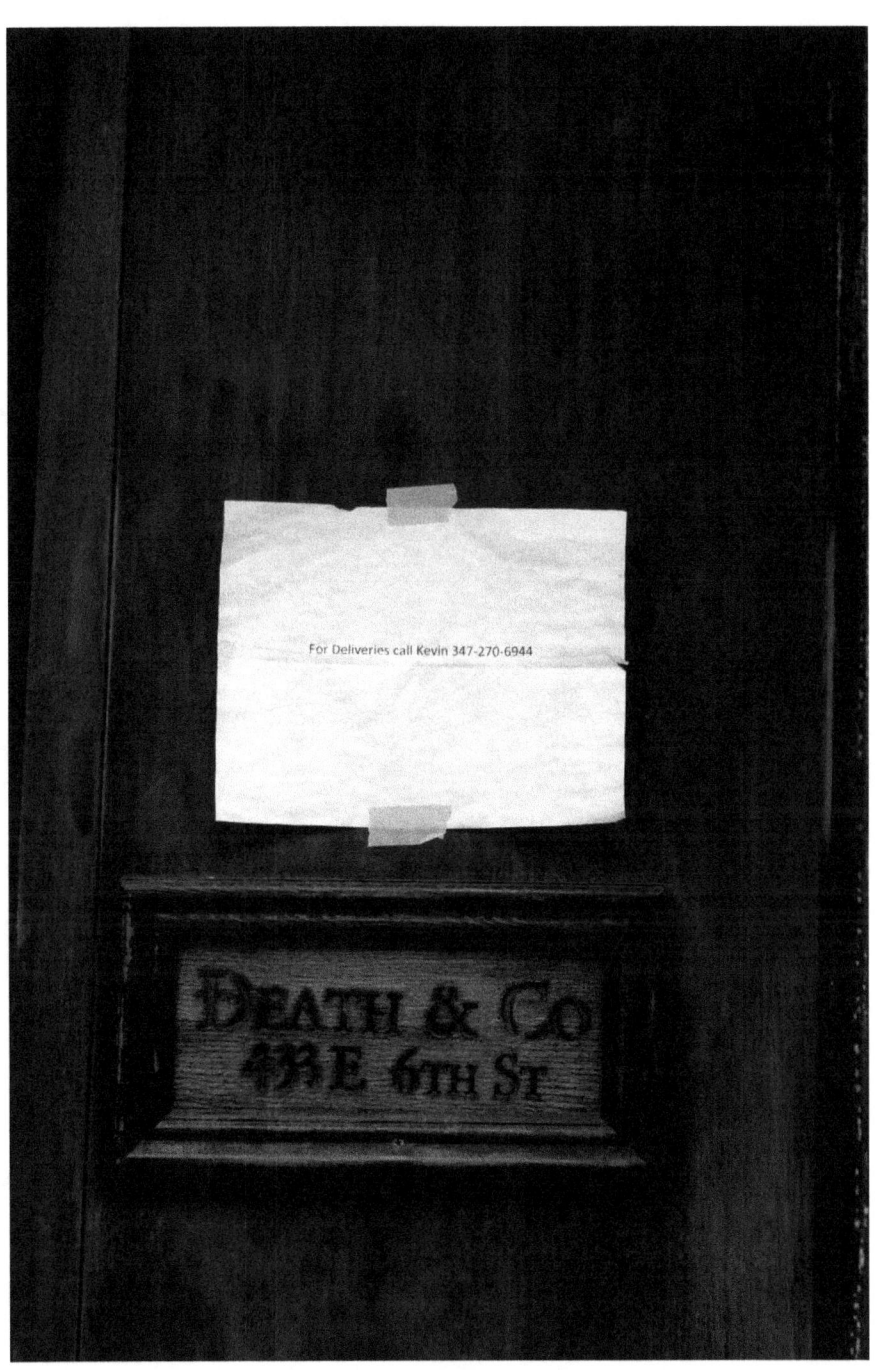

For Deliveries call Kevin 347-270-6944

DEATH & CO
433 E 6TH ST

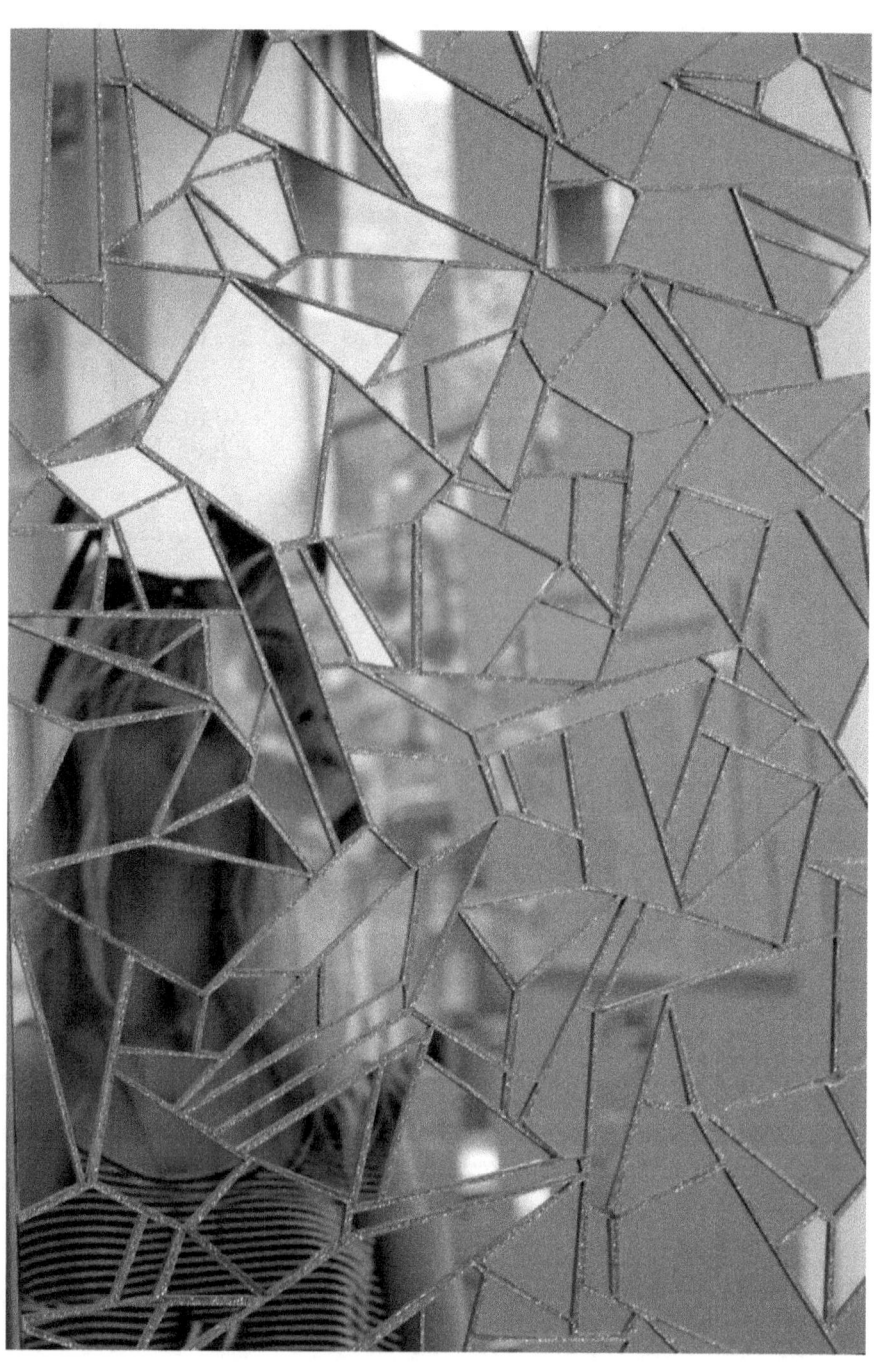

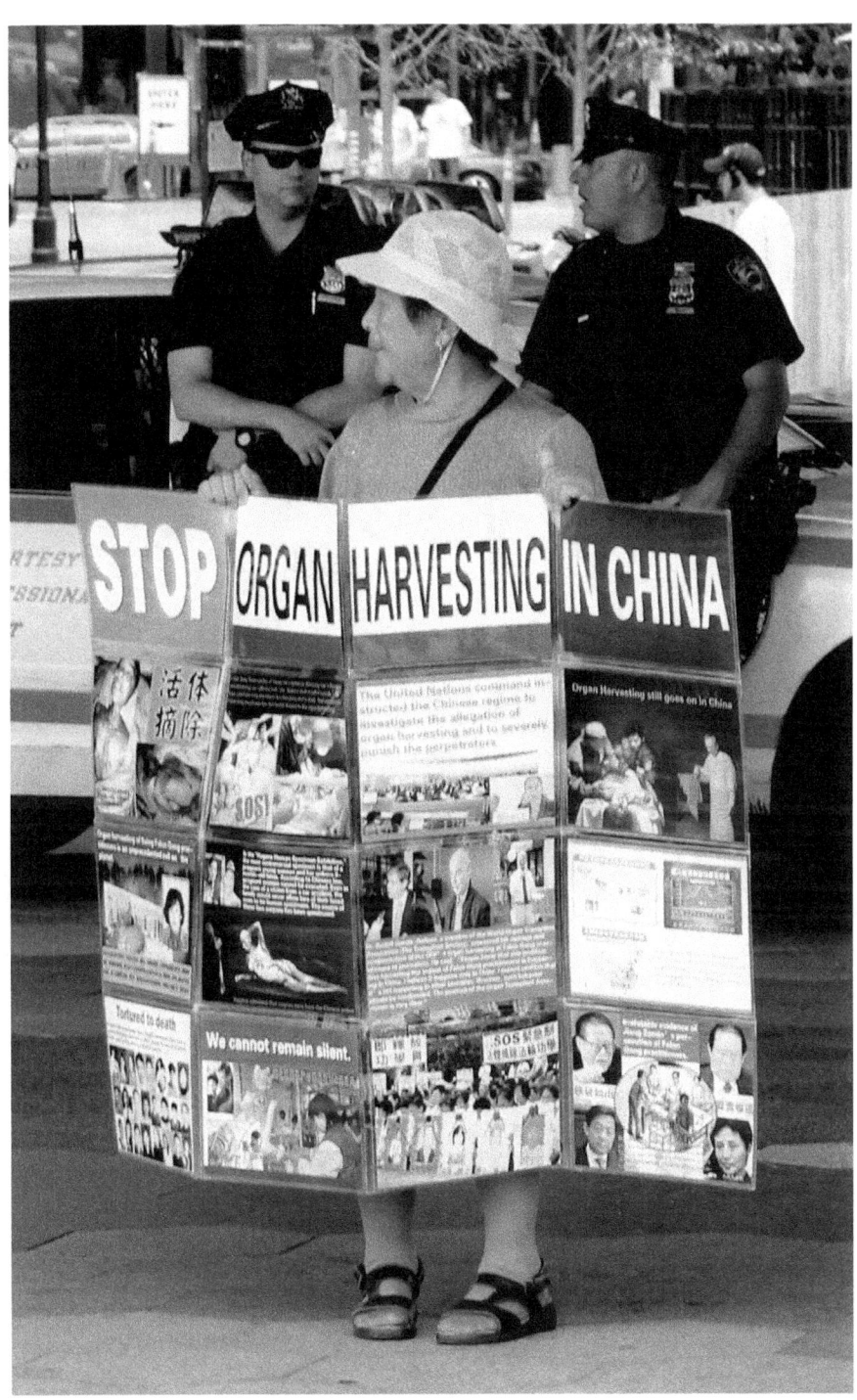

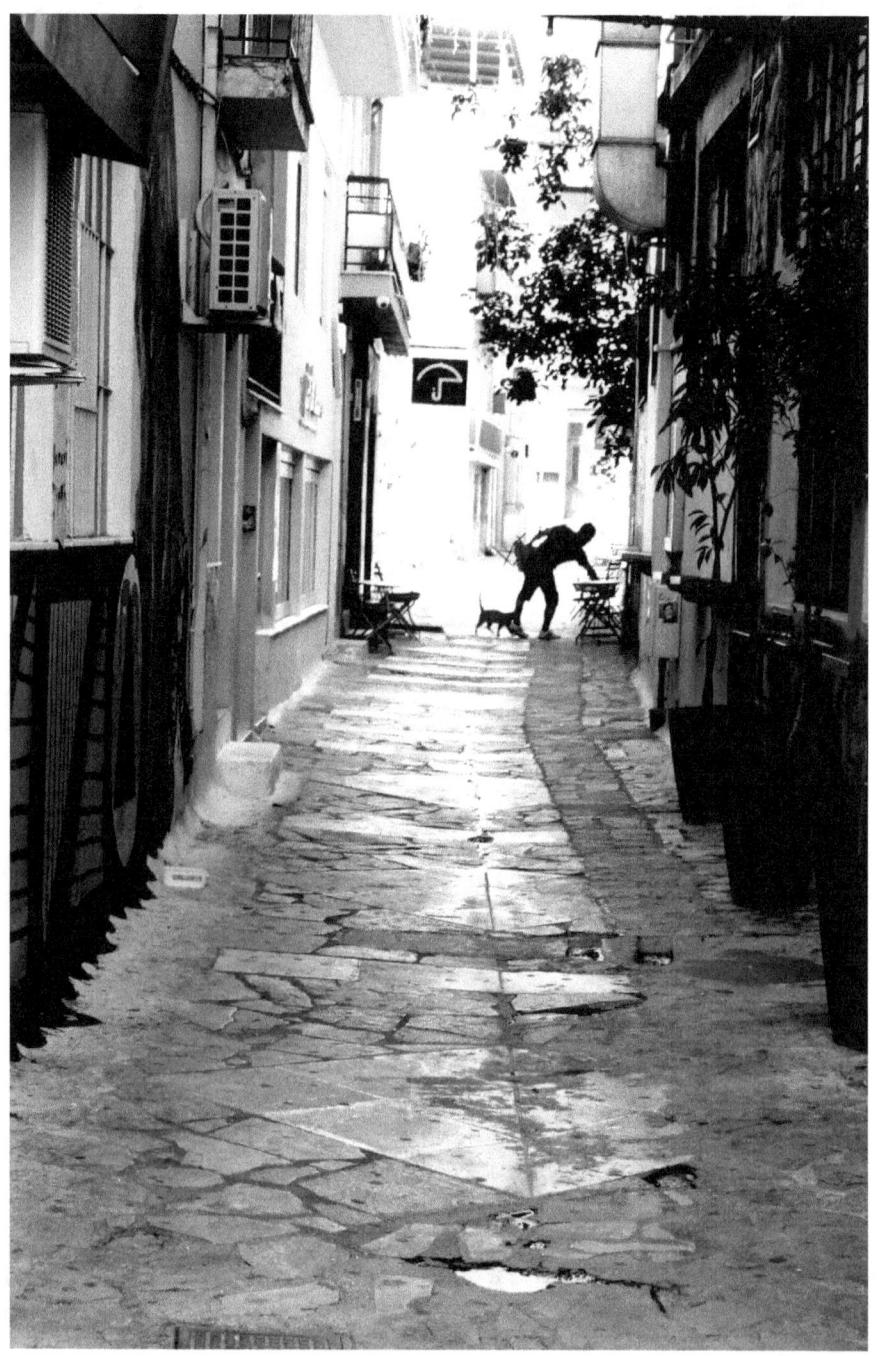

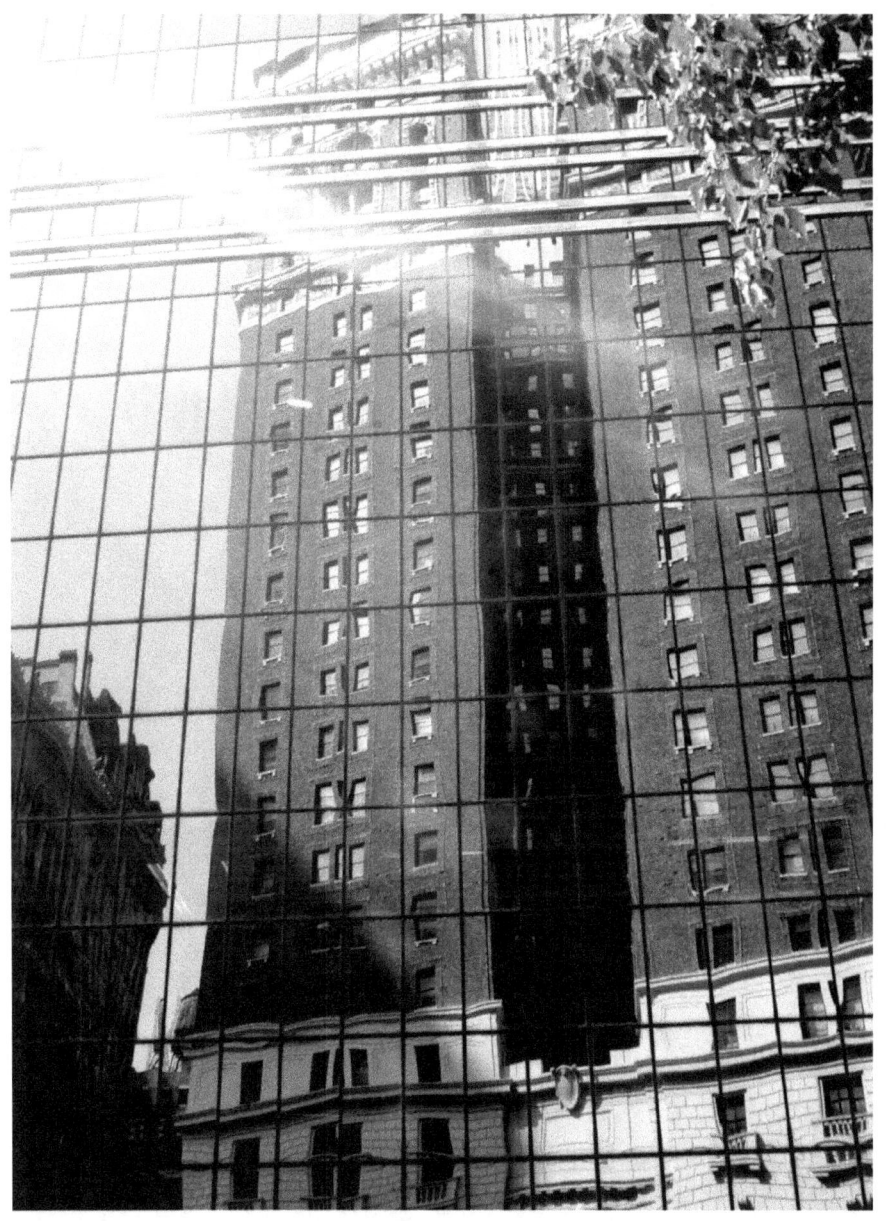

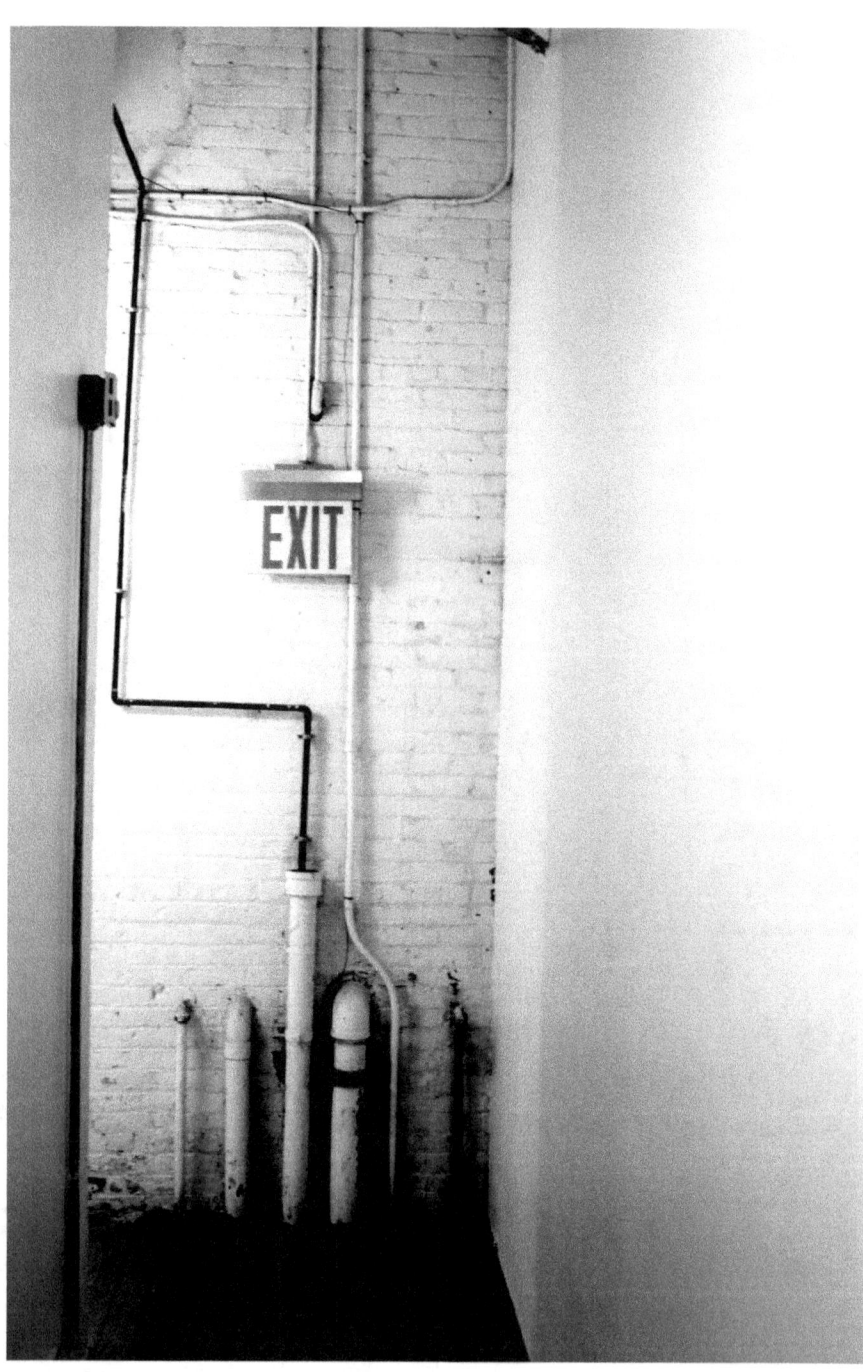

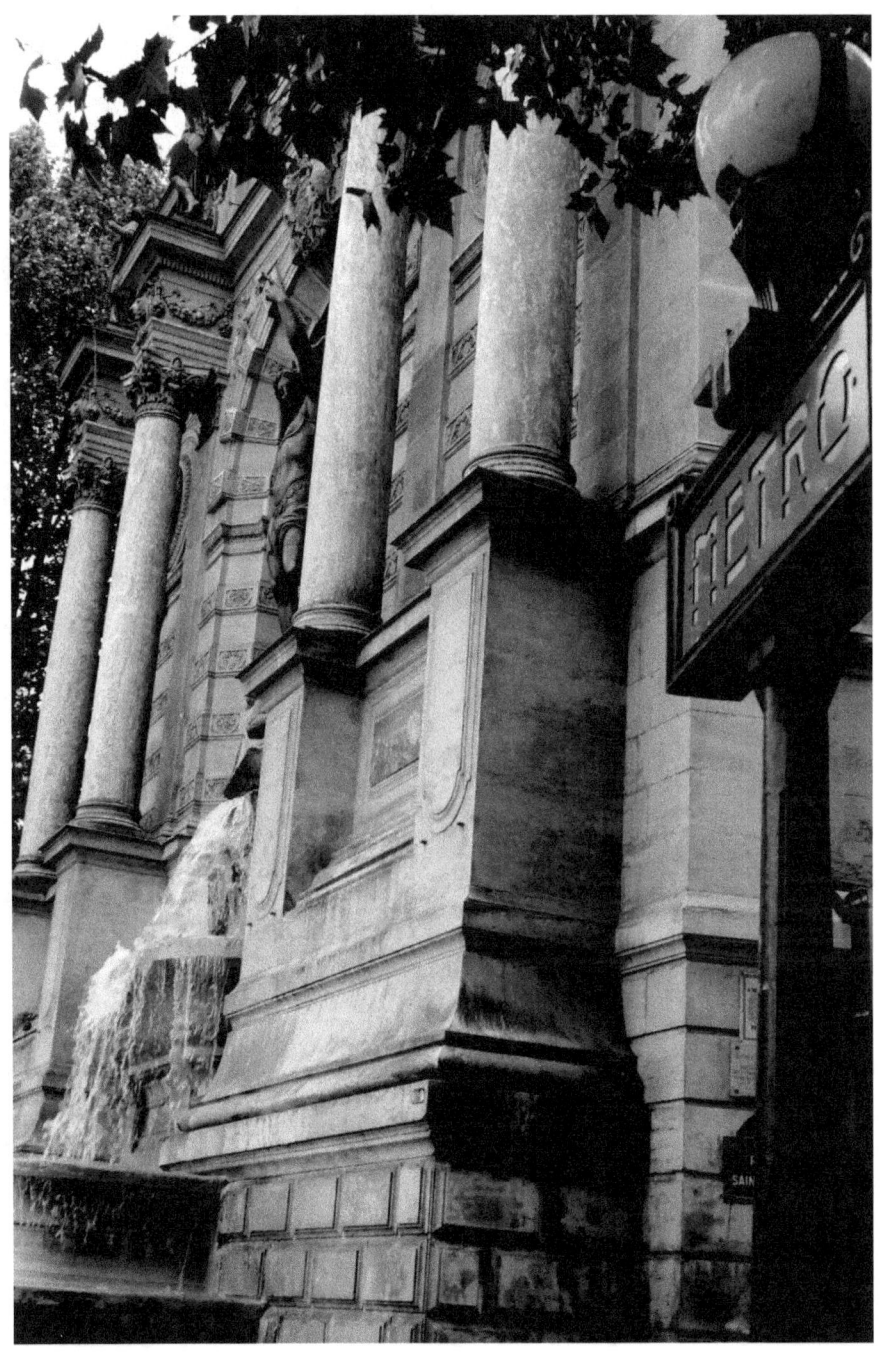

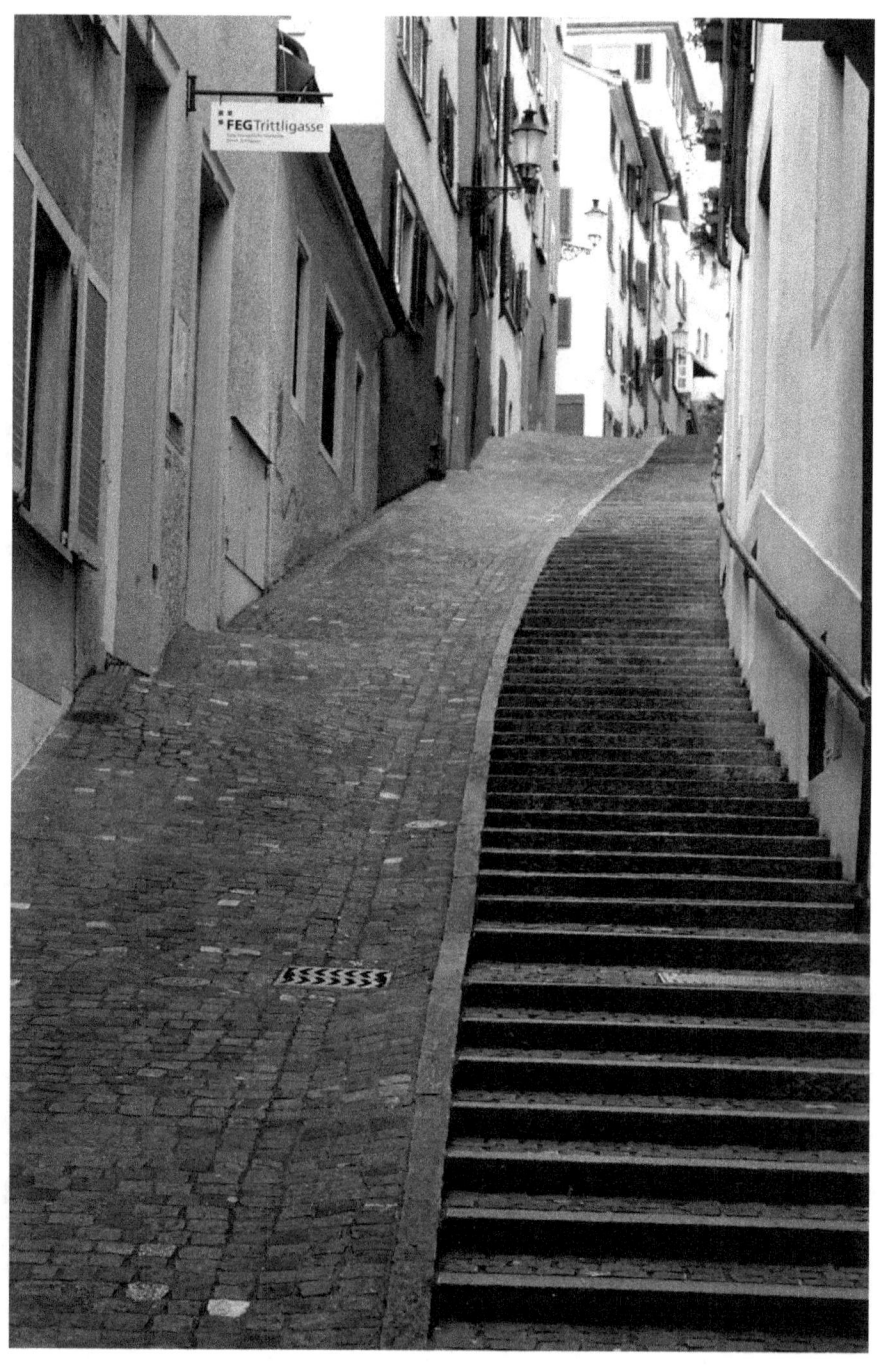

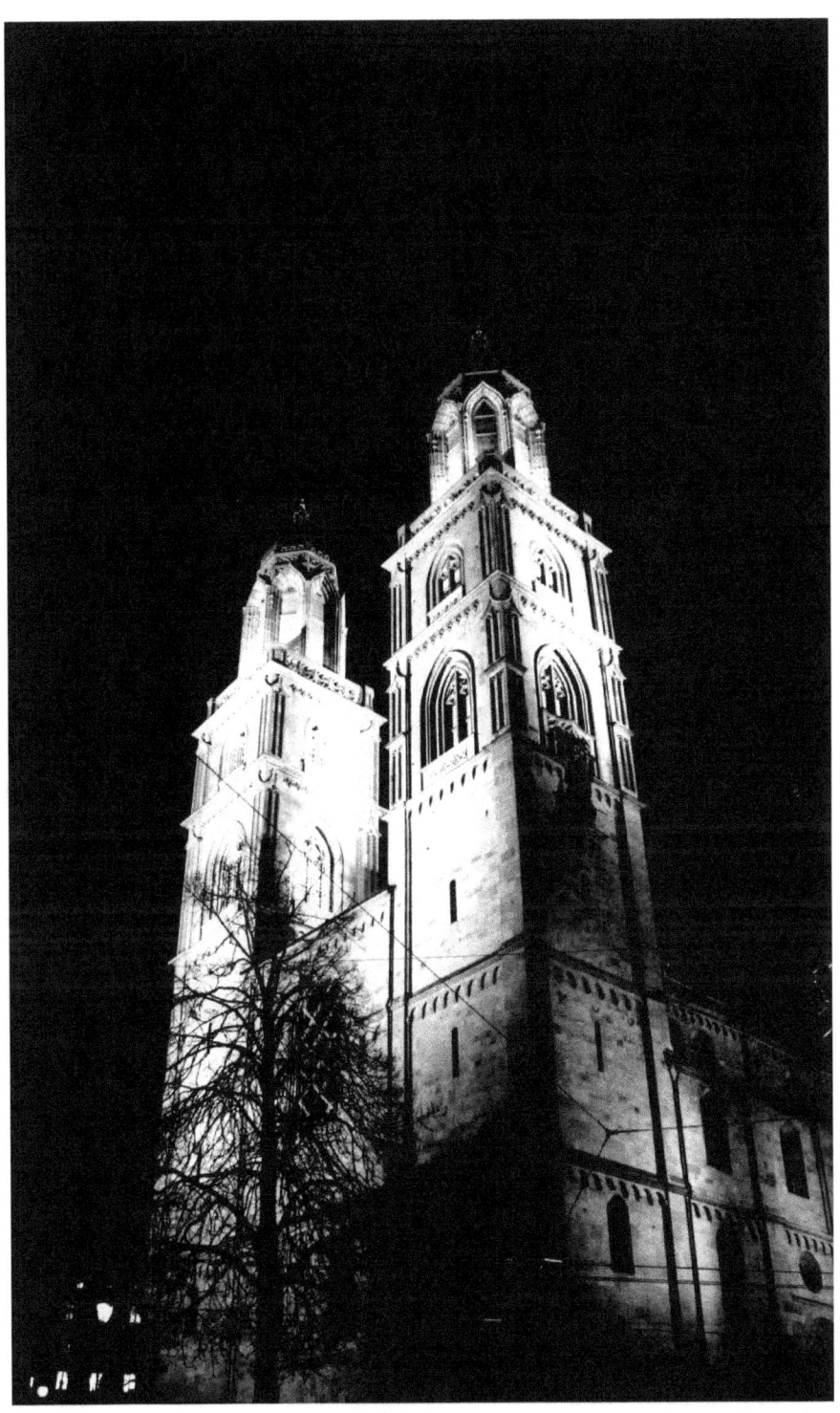

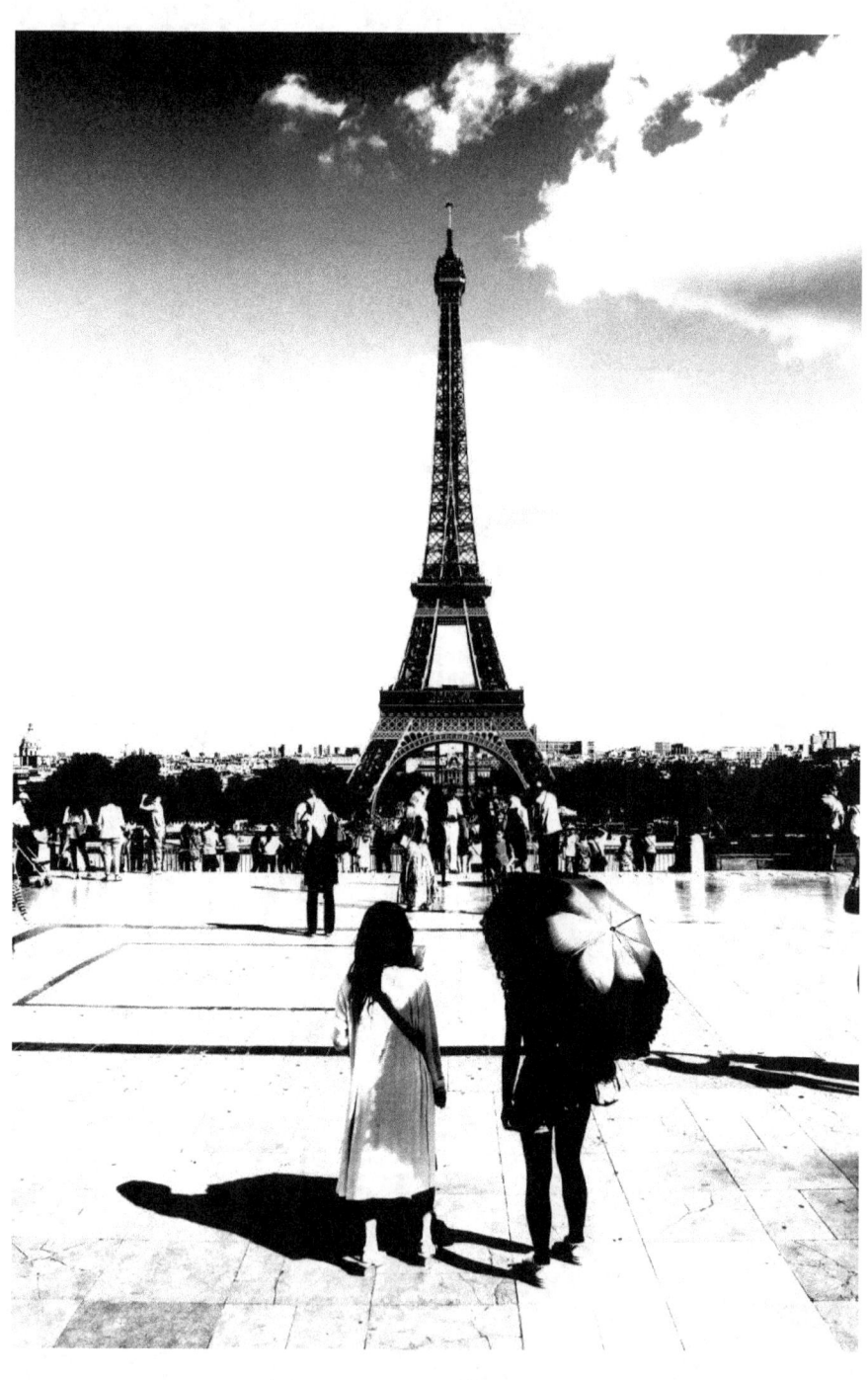

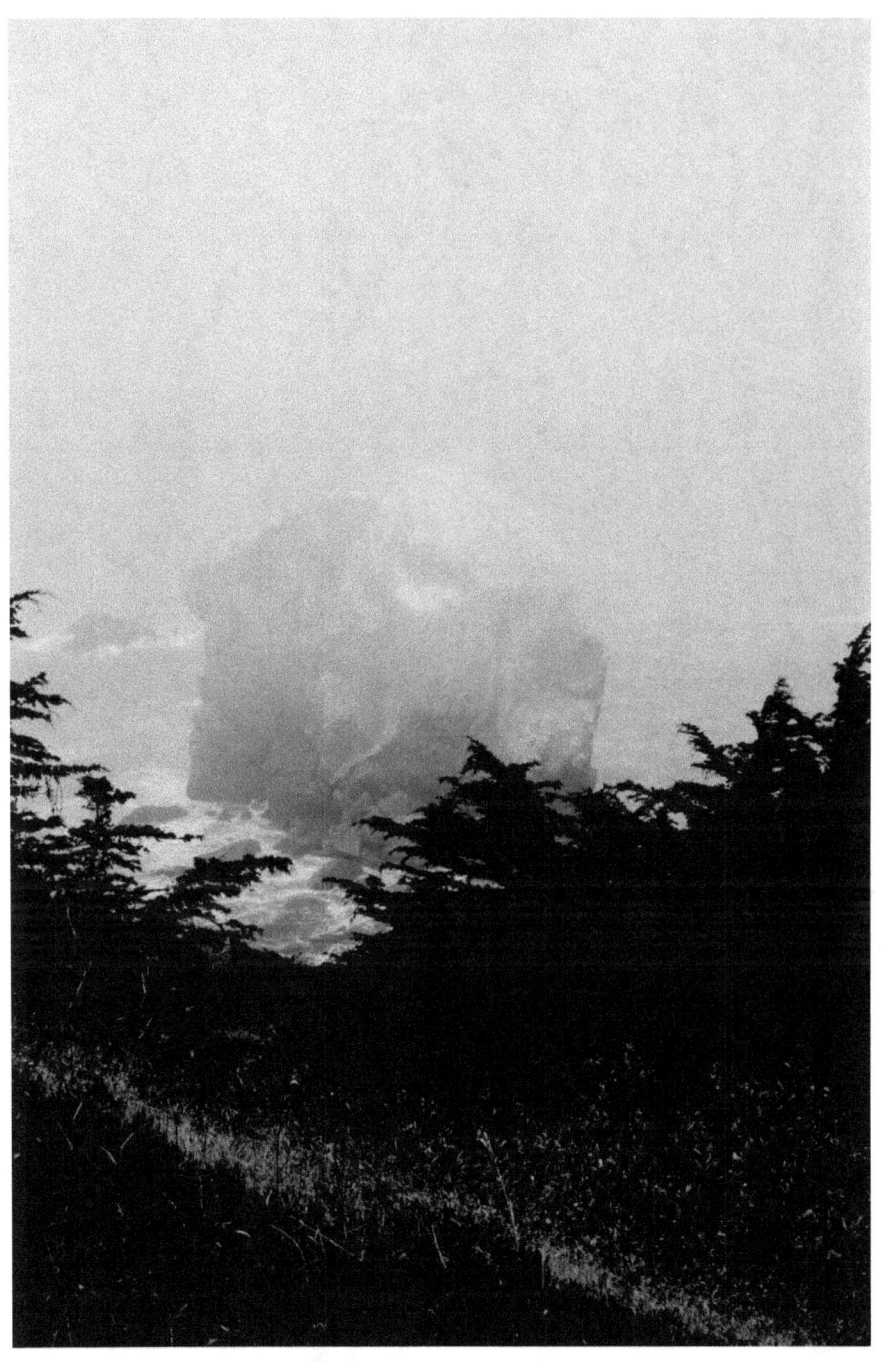

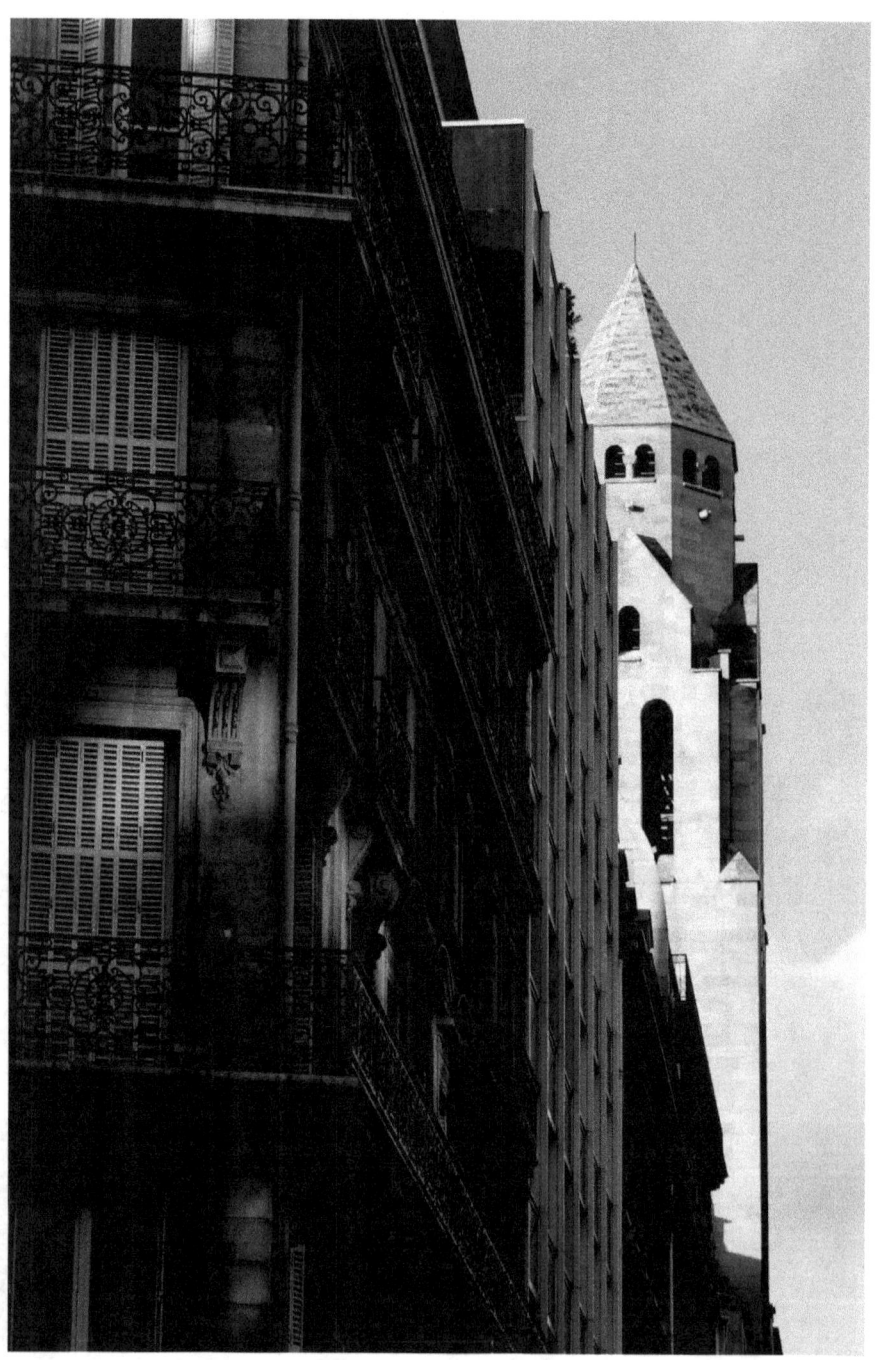

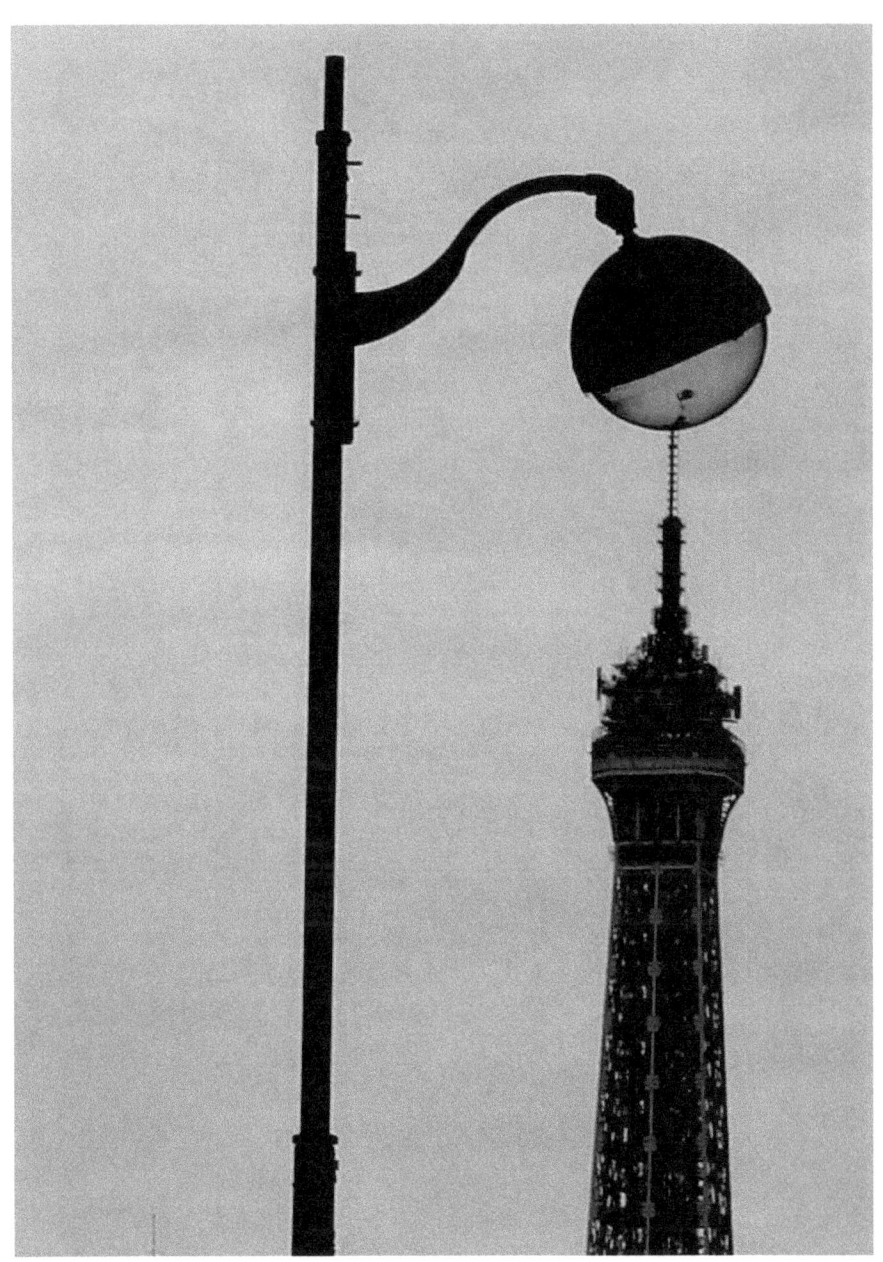

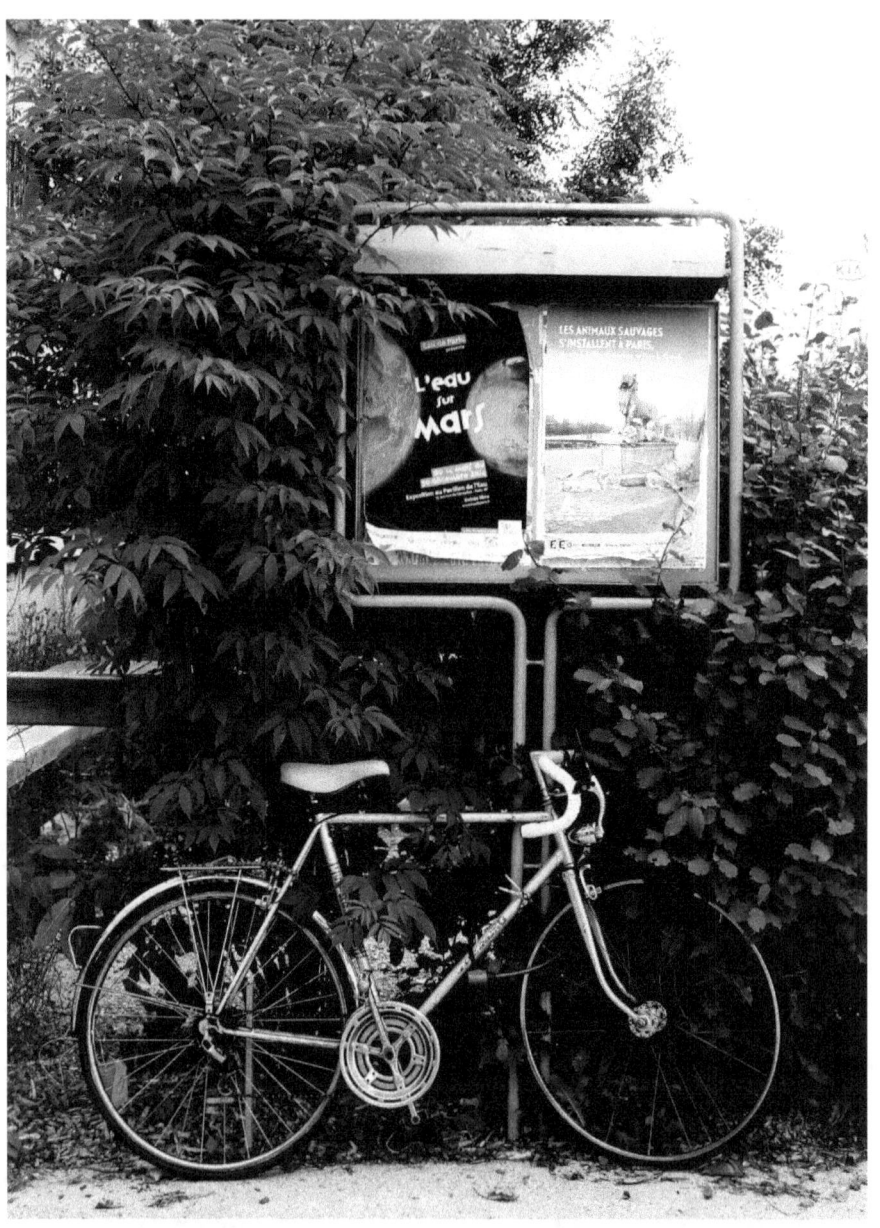

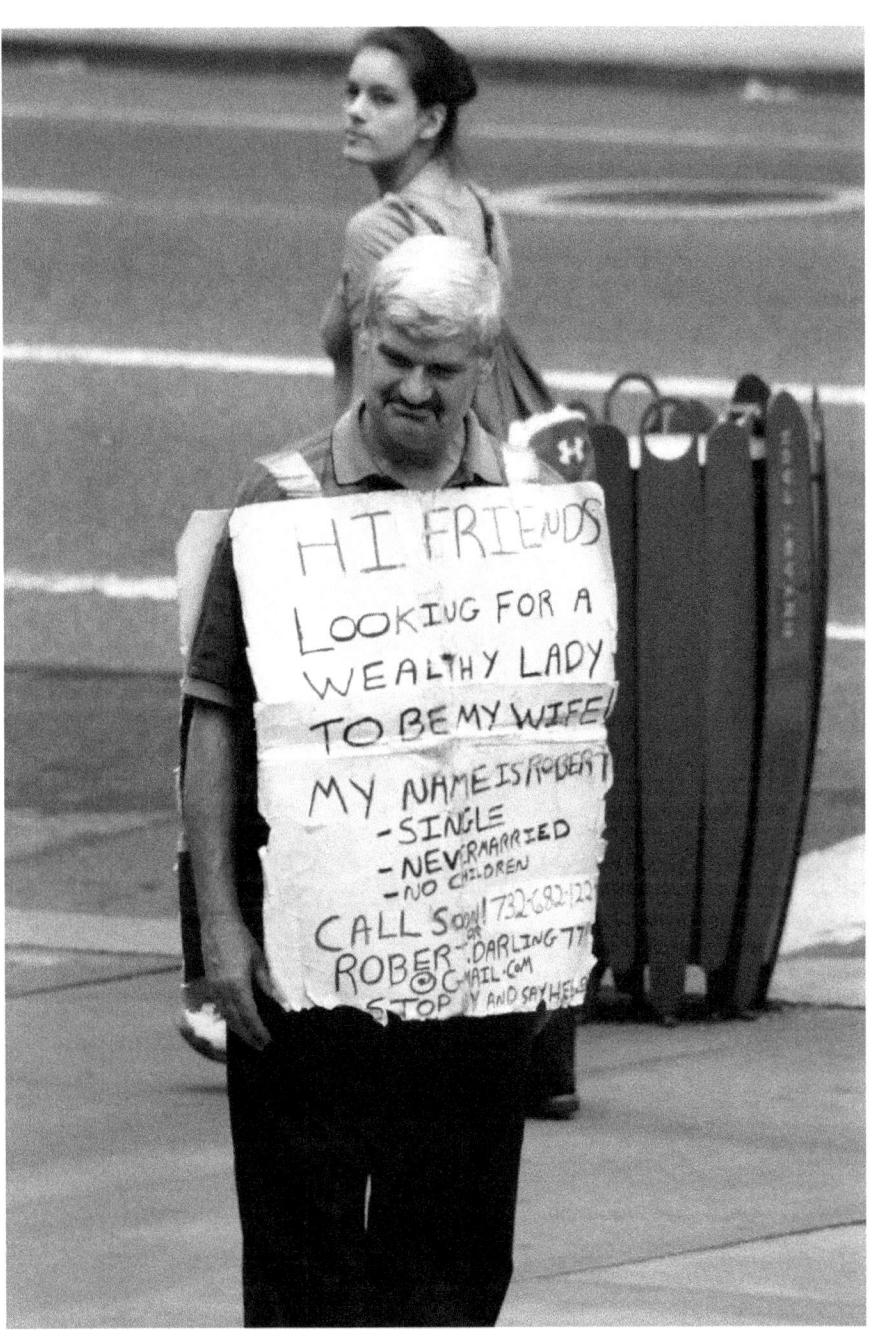

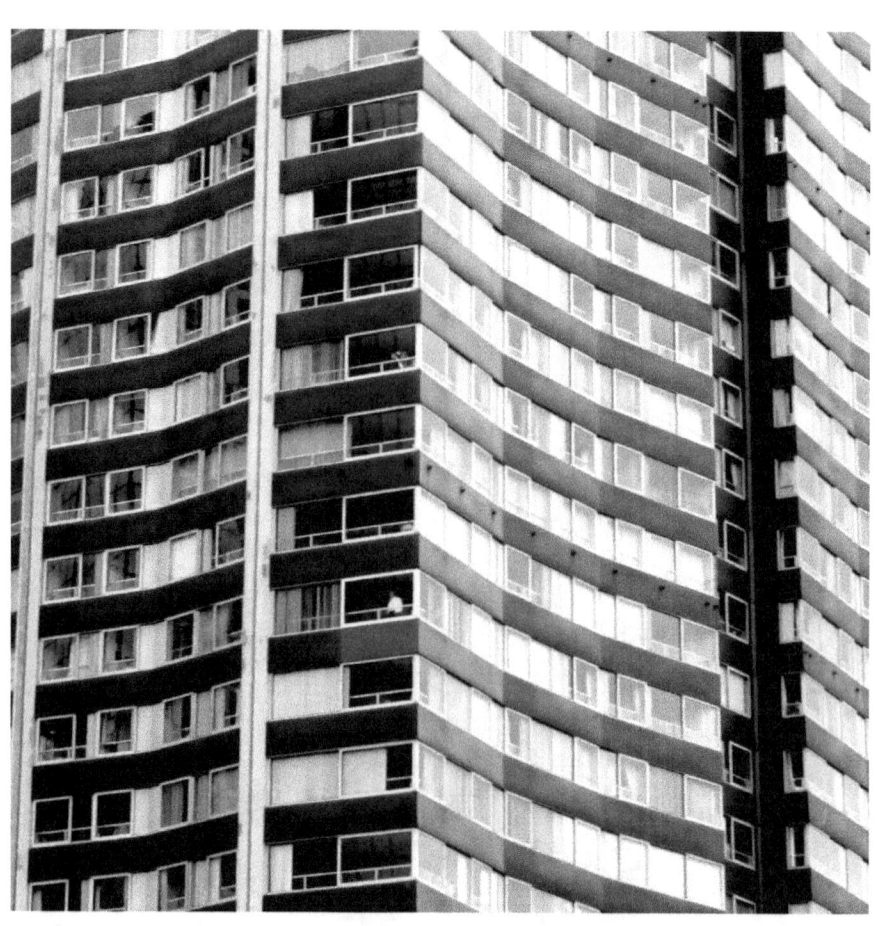

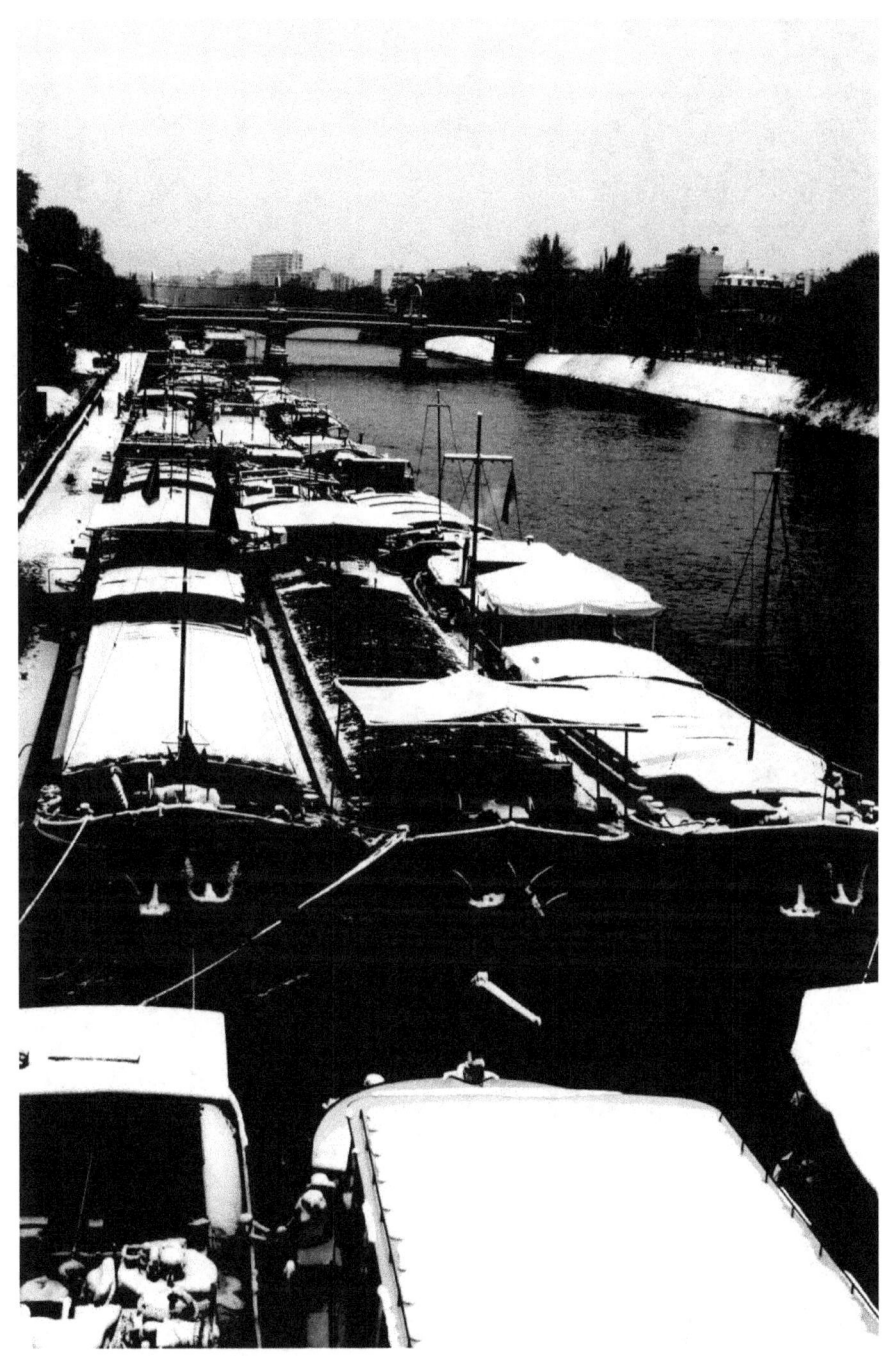

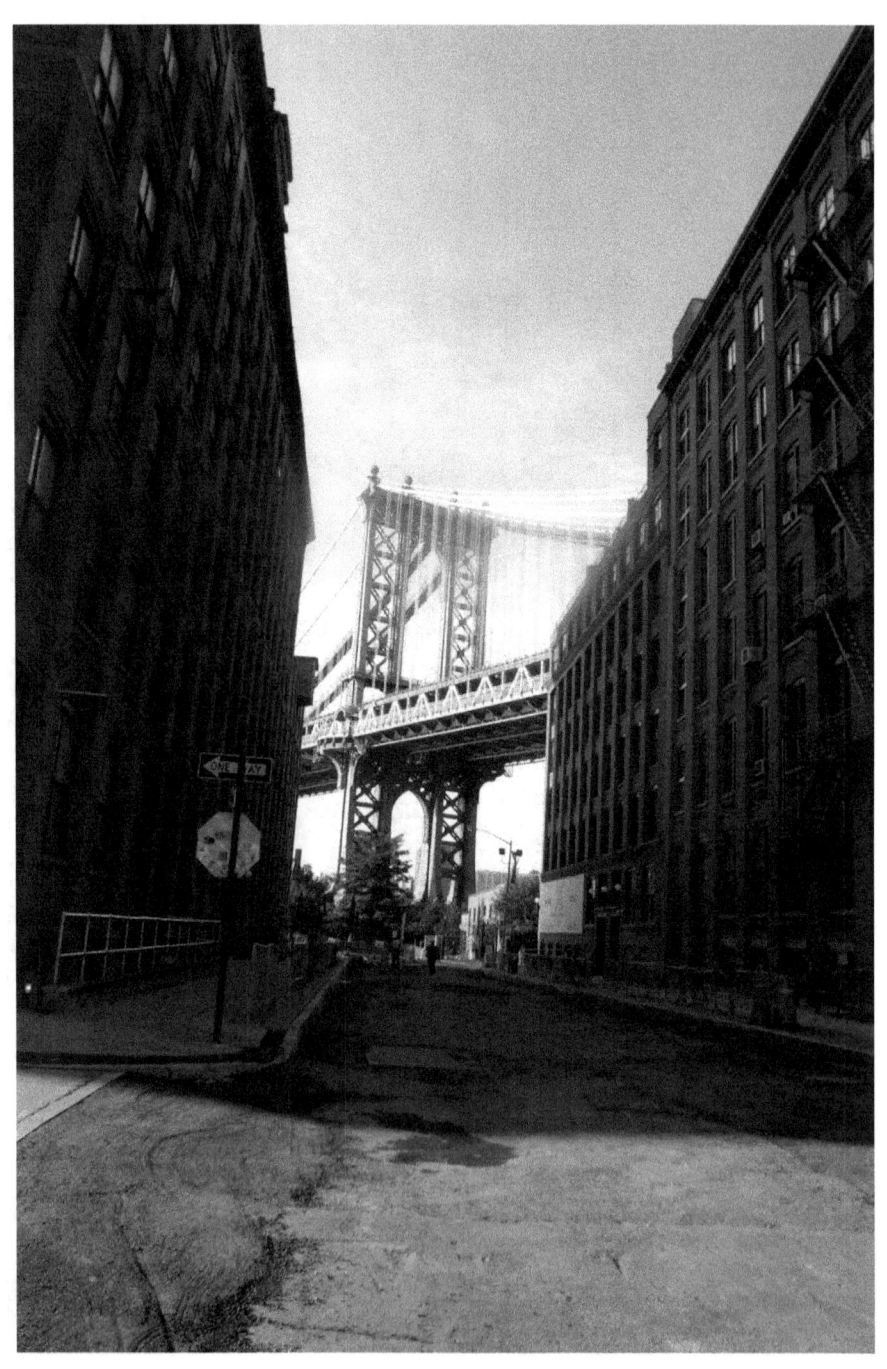

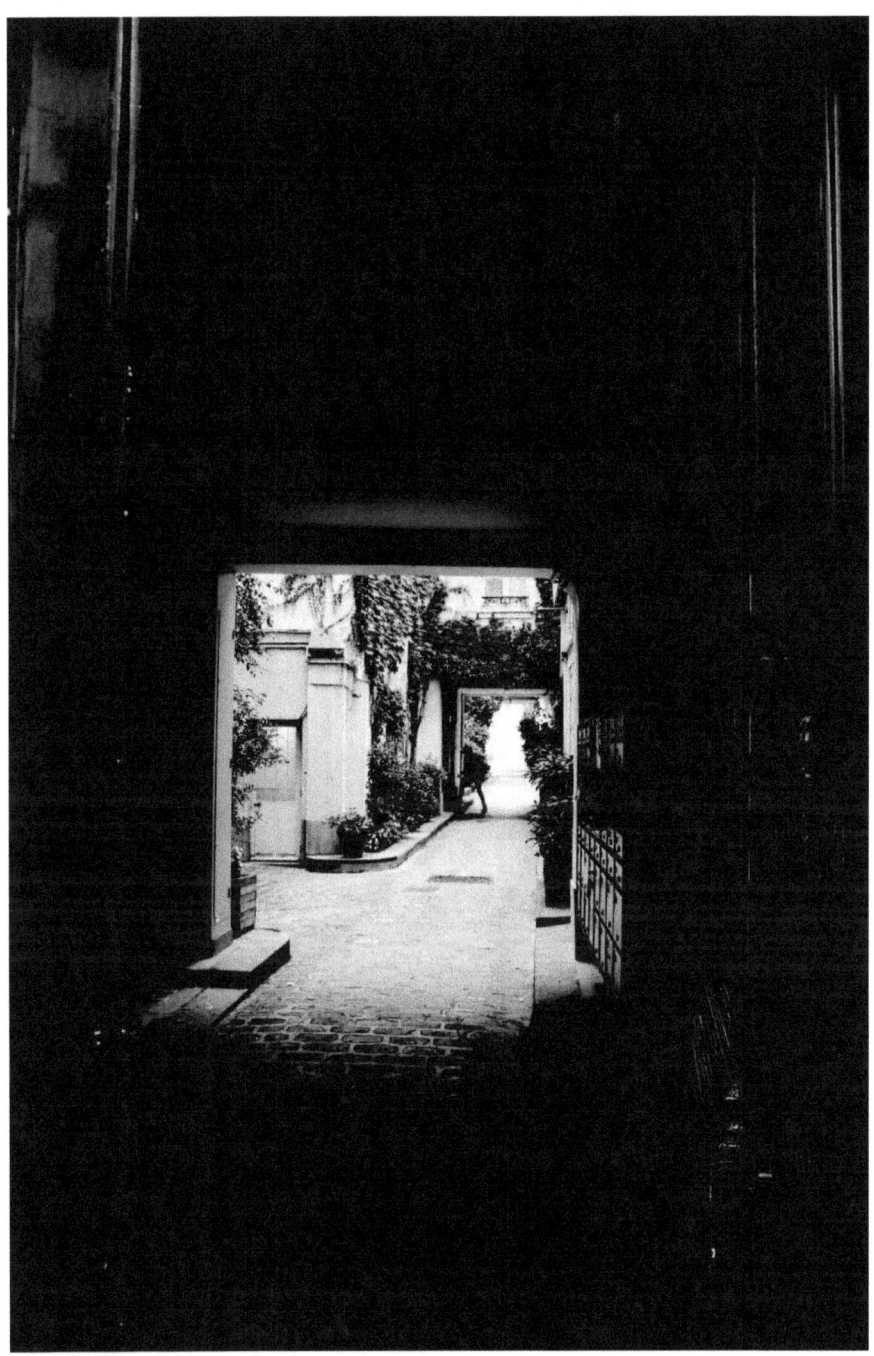

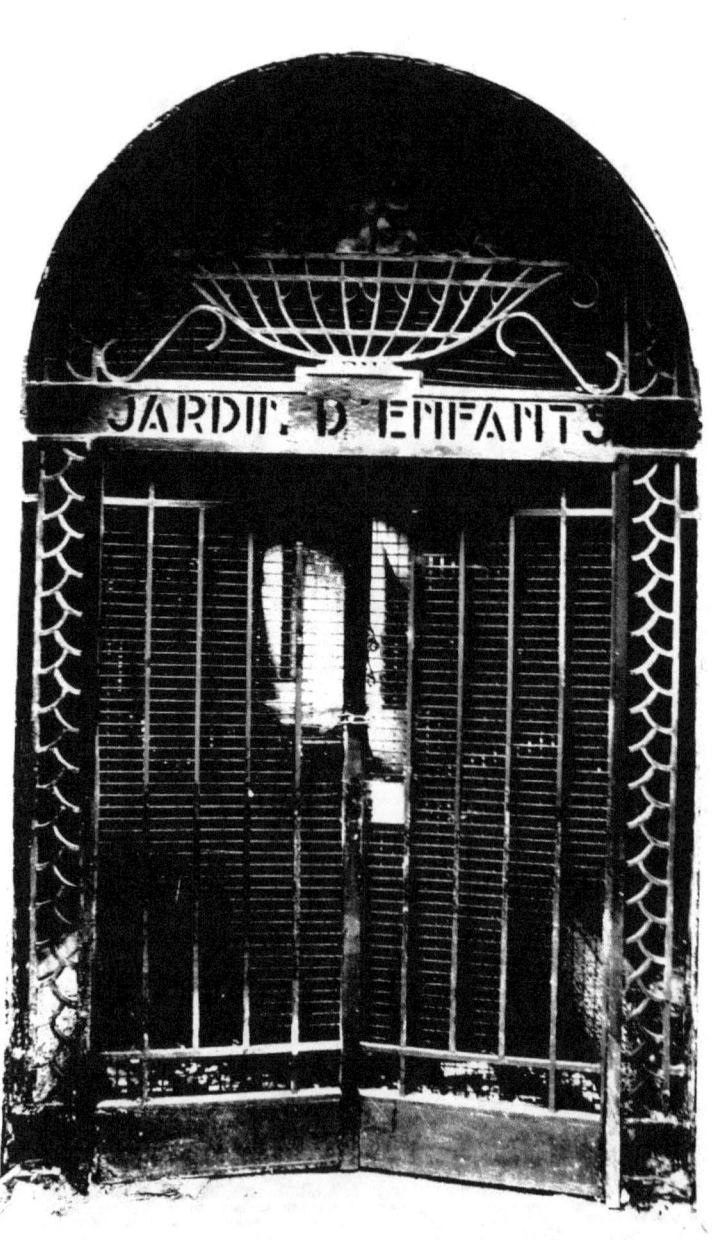

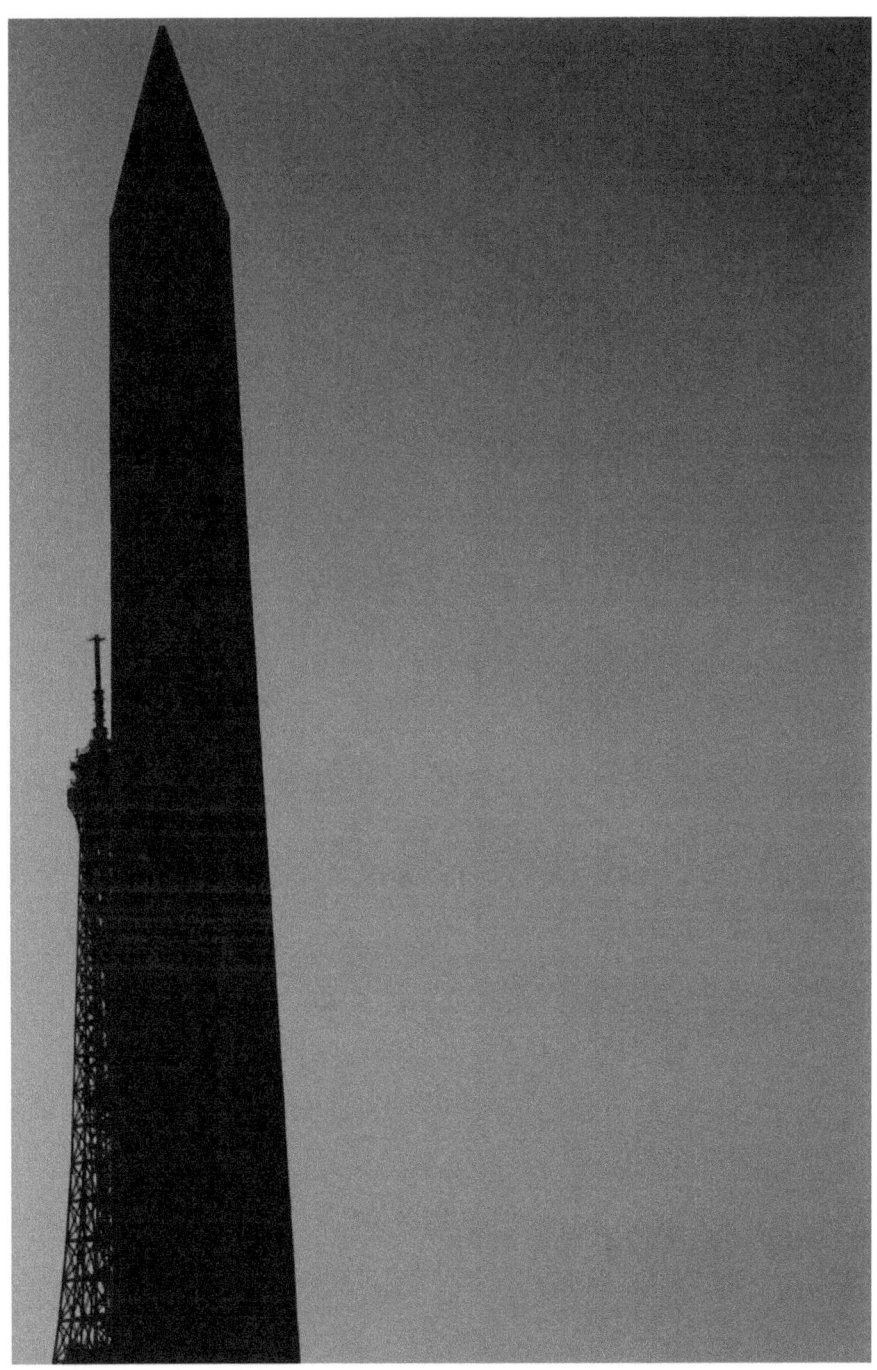

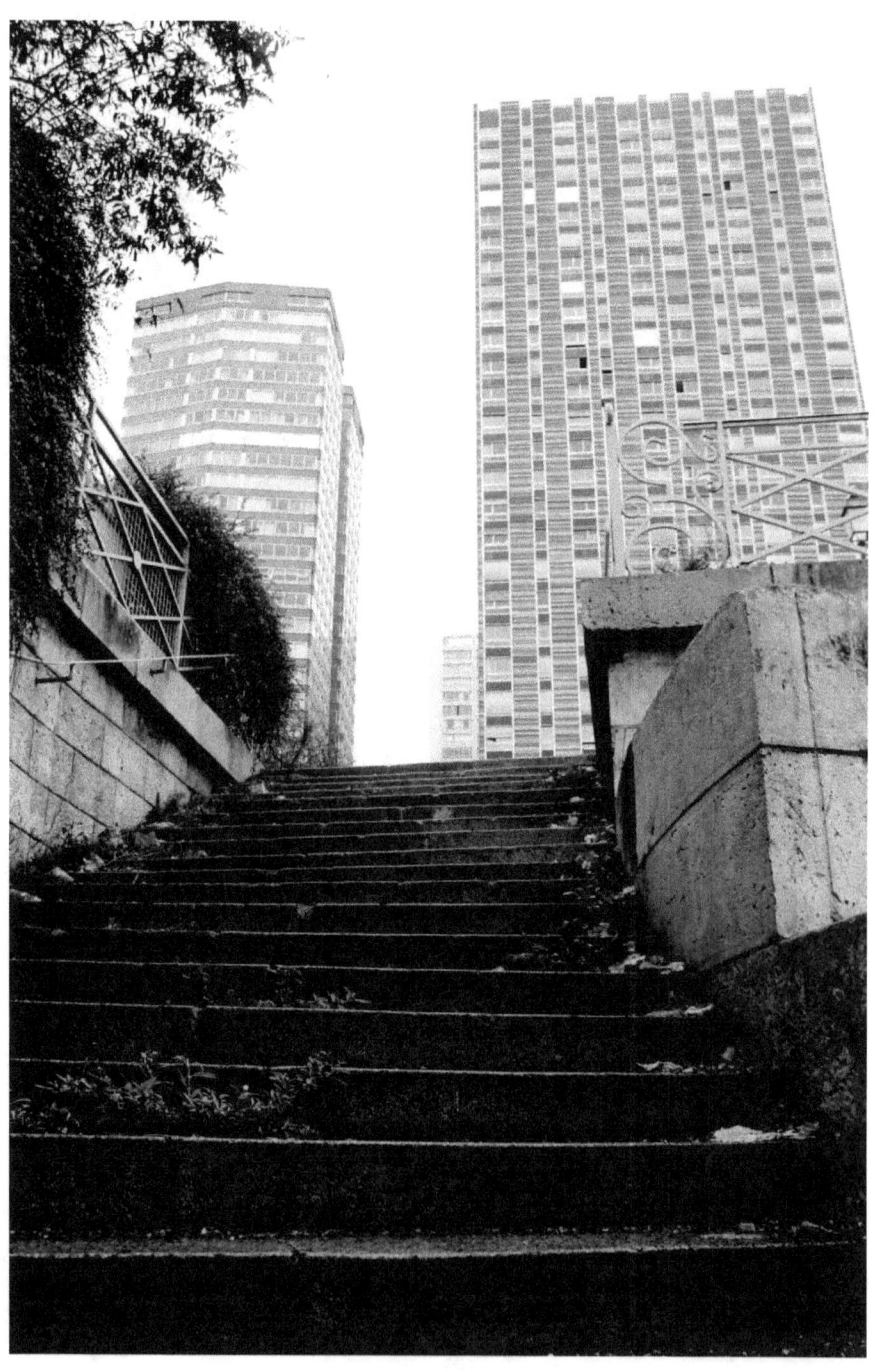

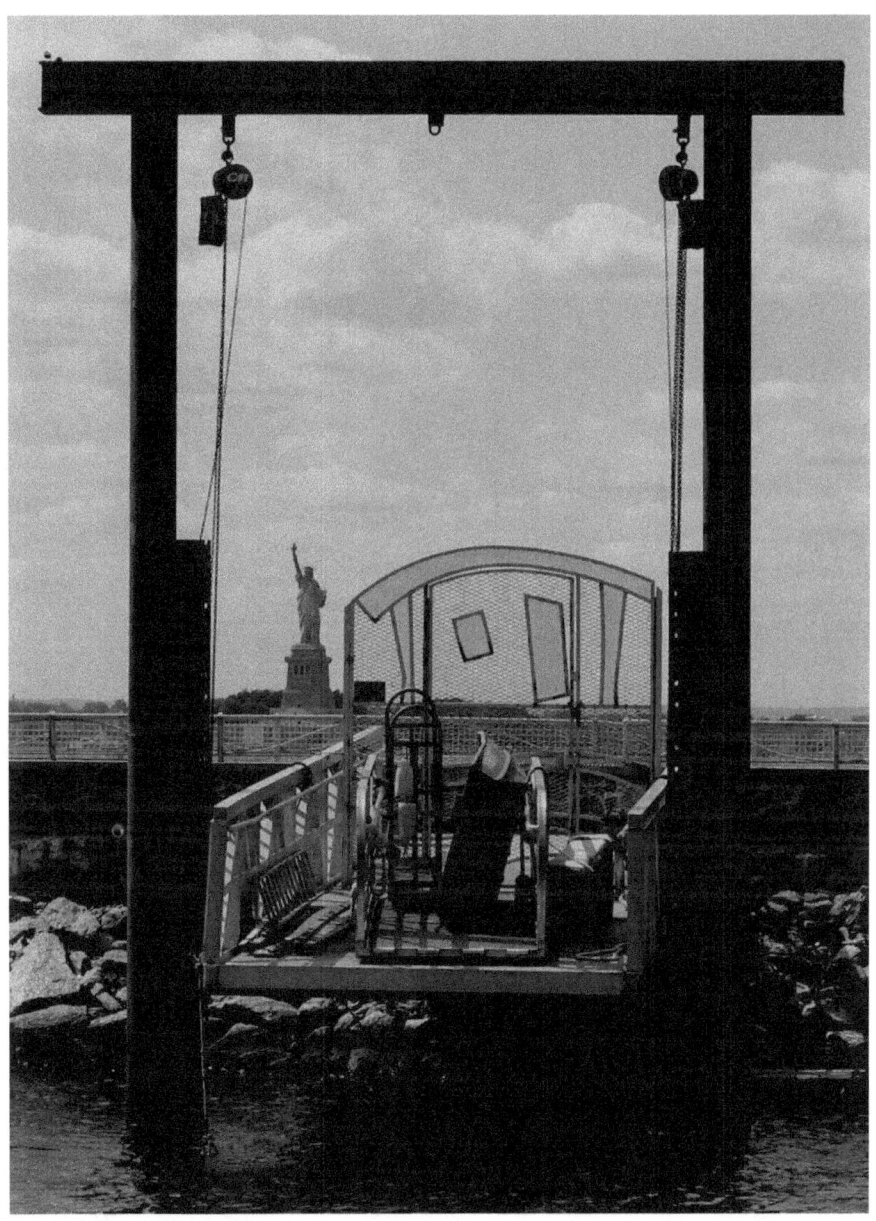

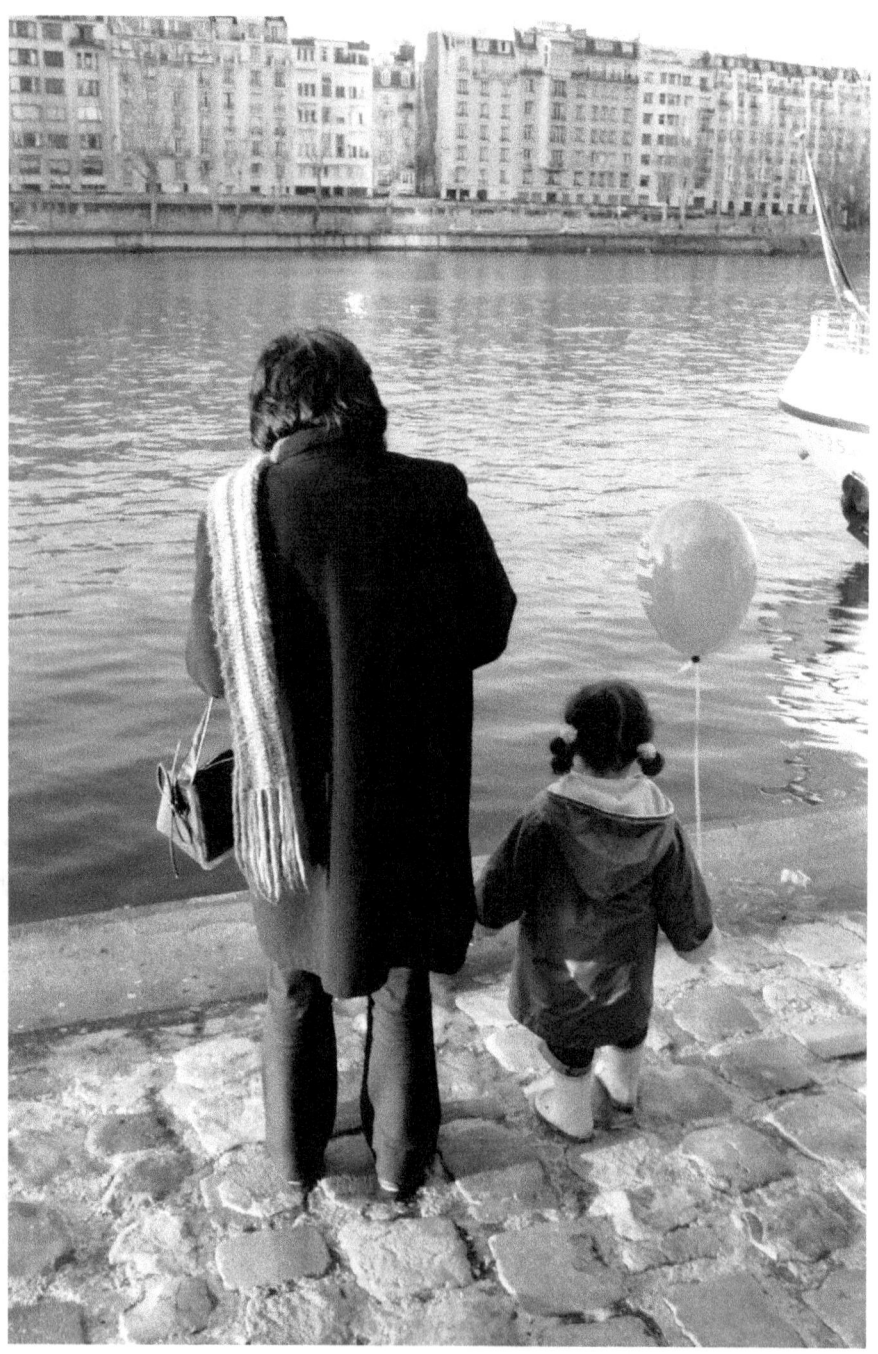

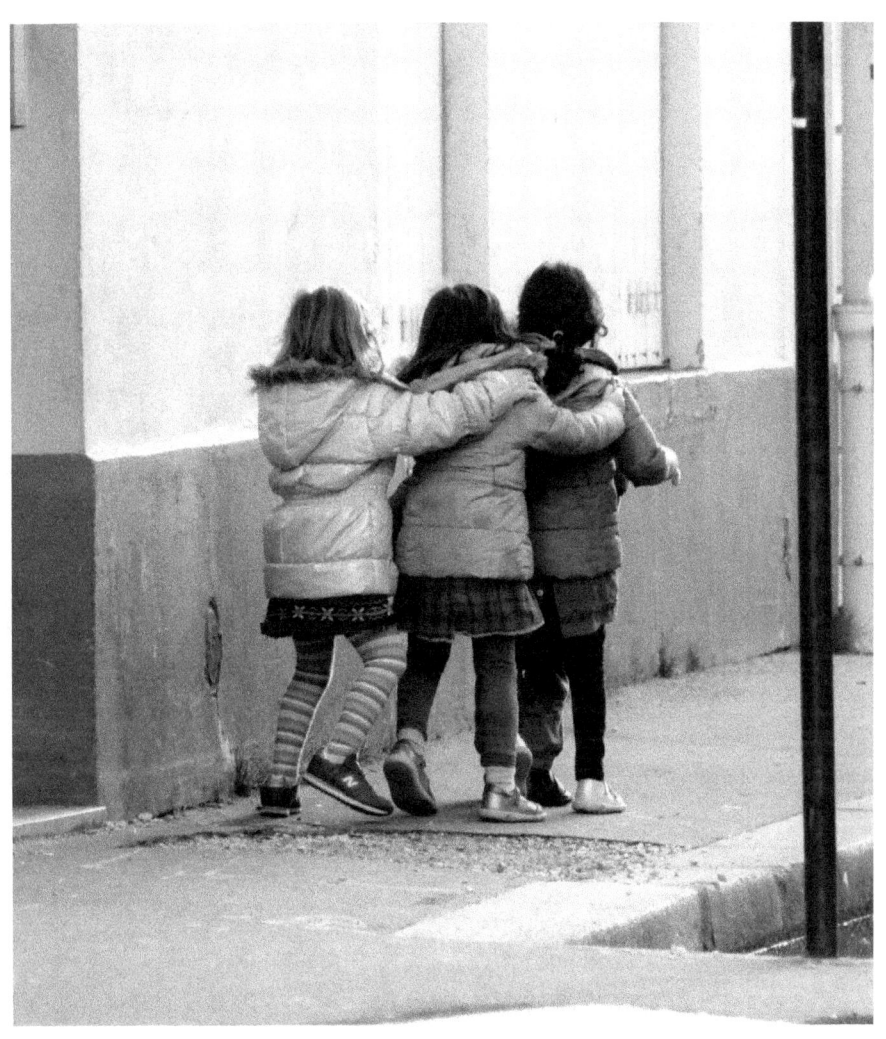

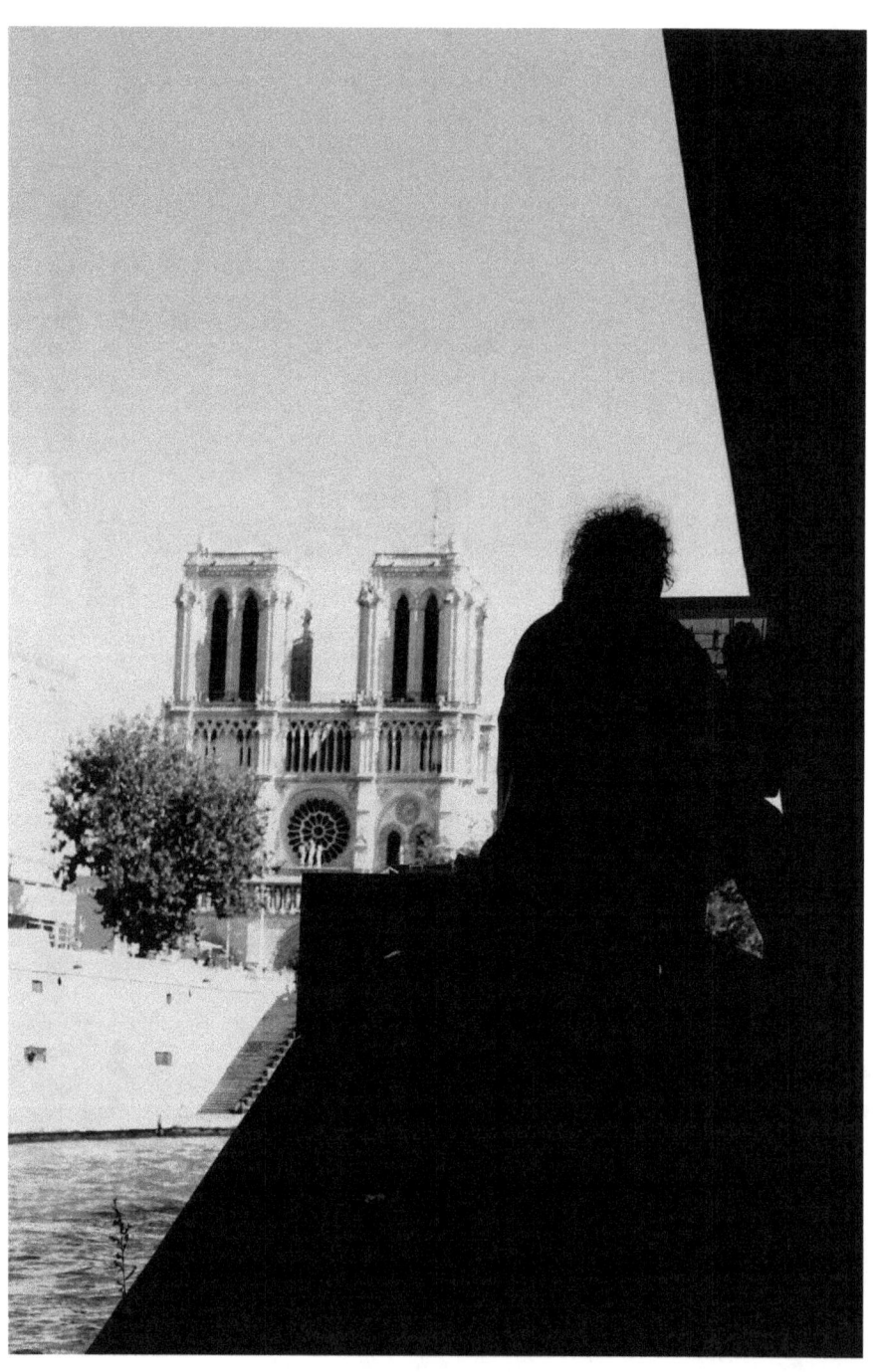

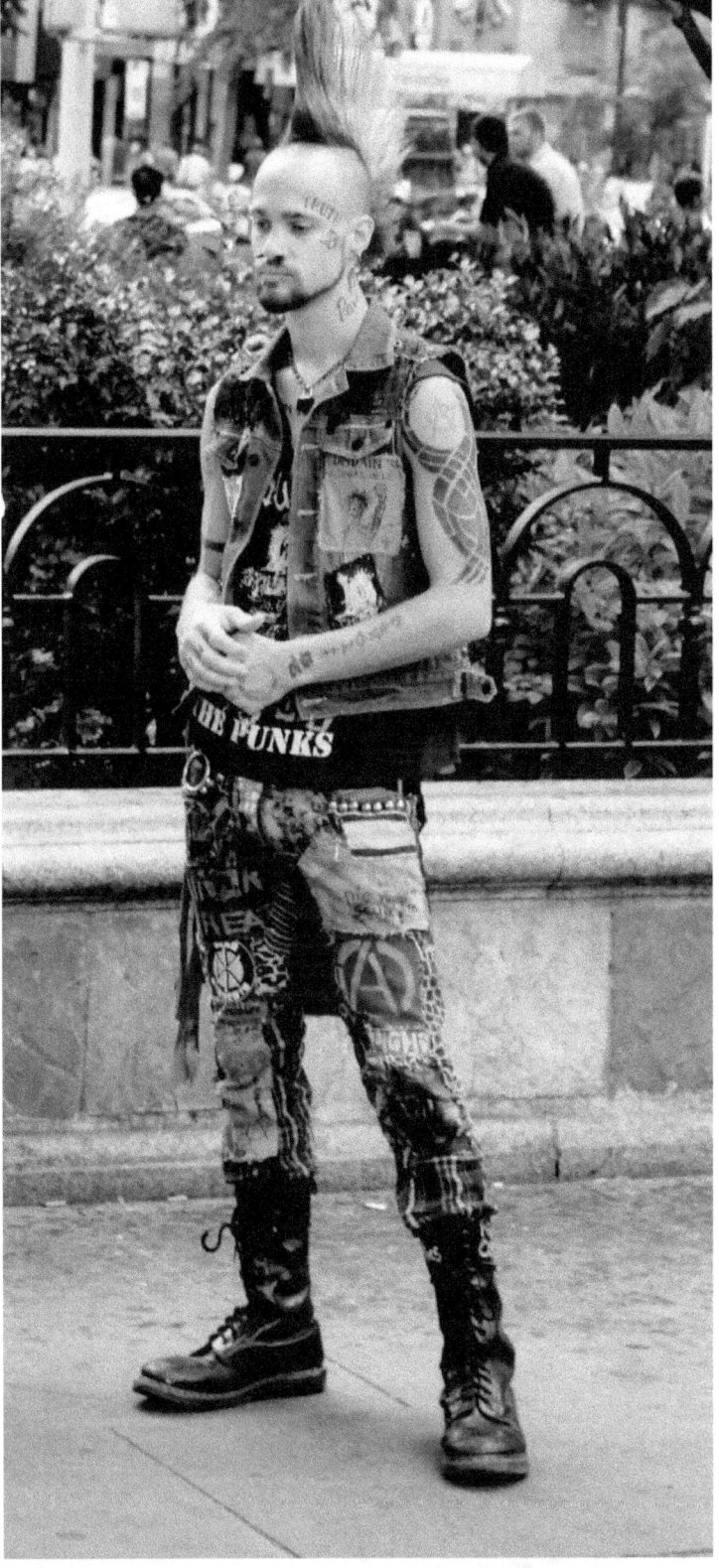

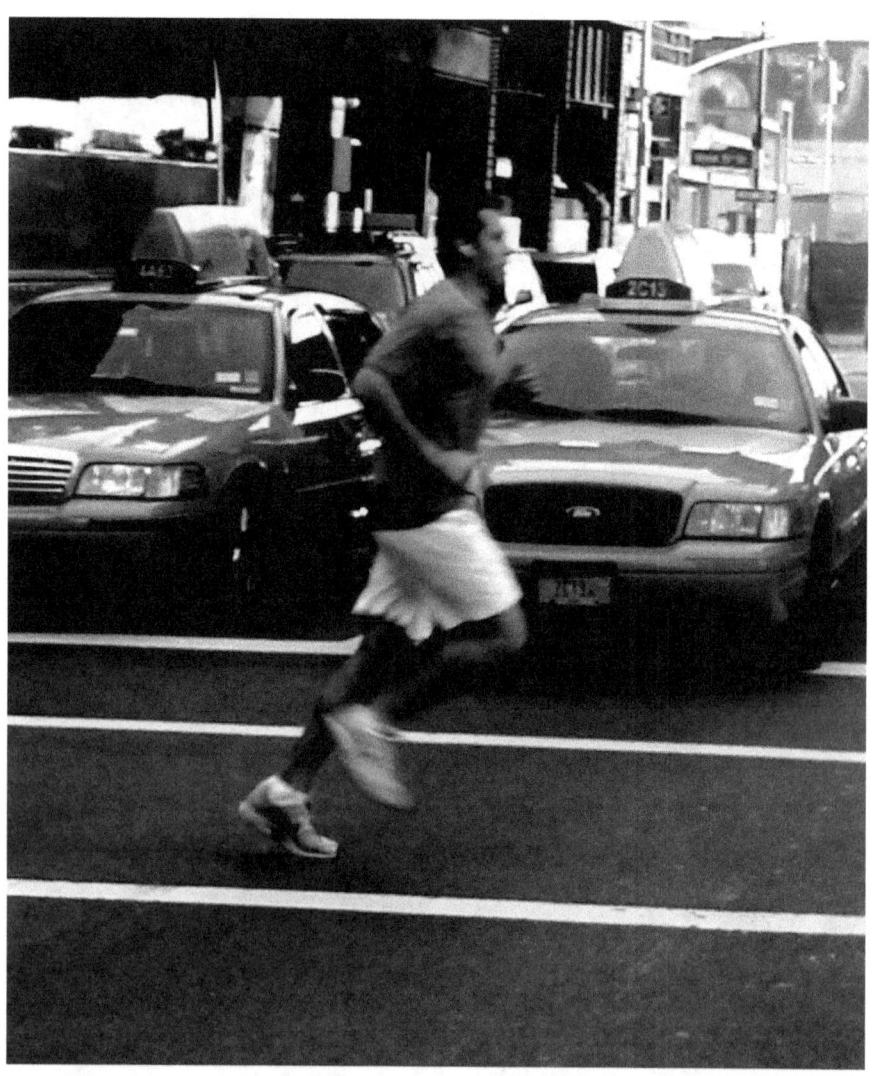

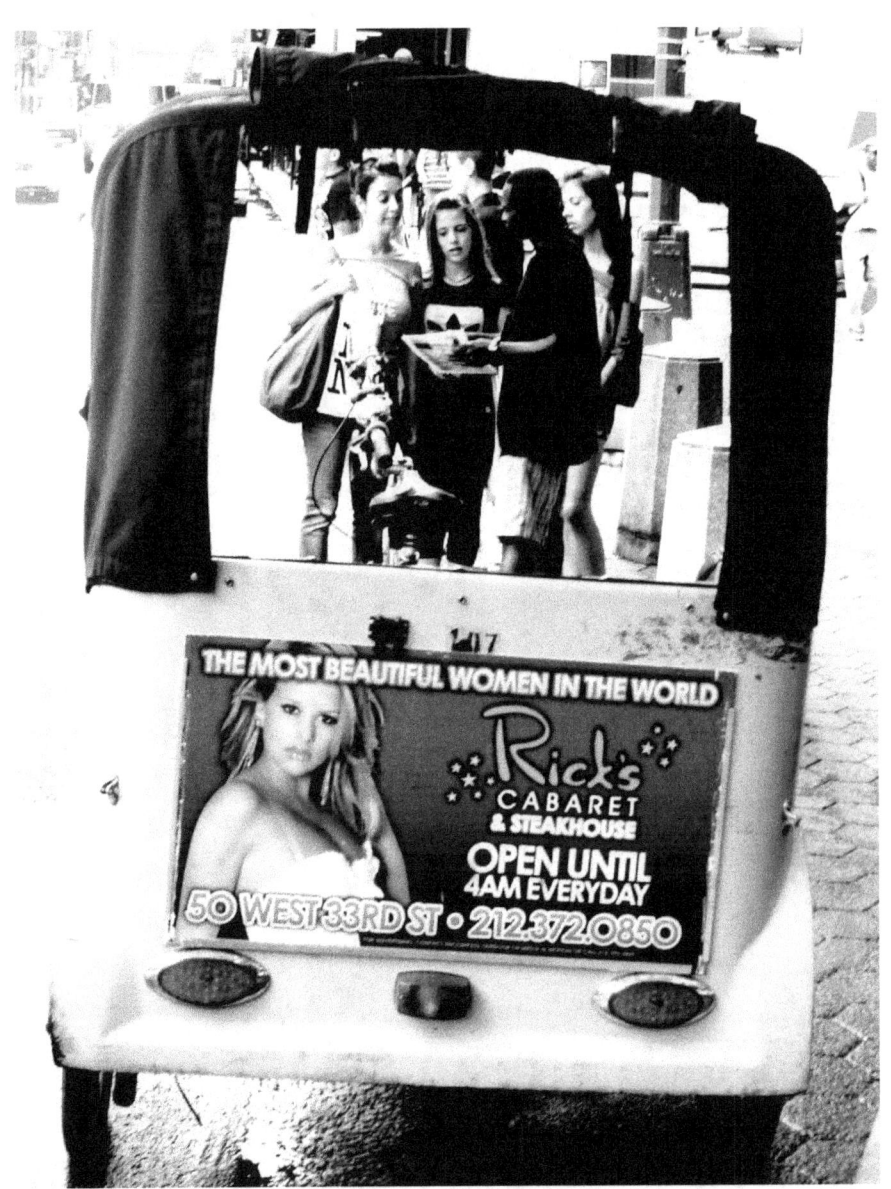

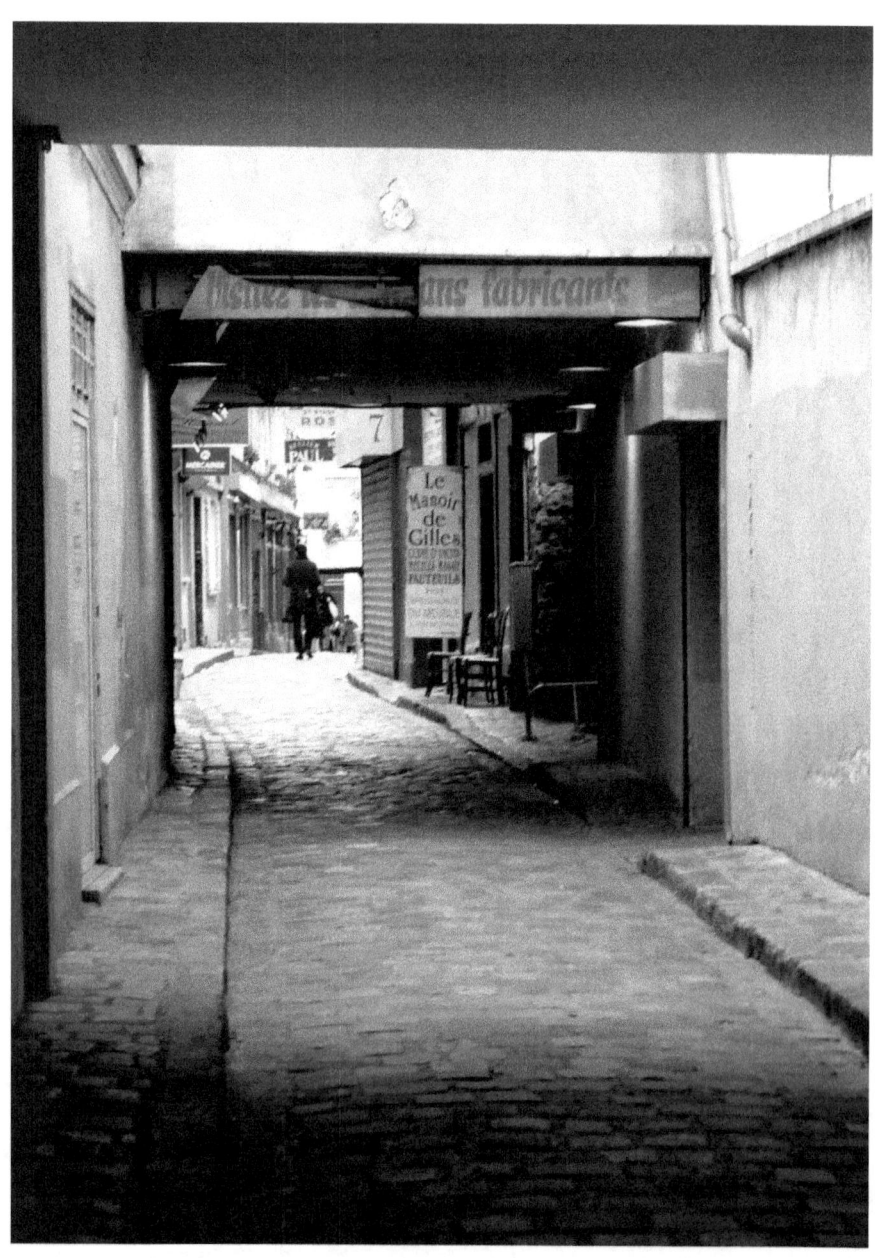

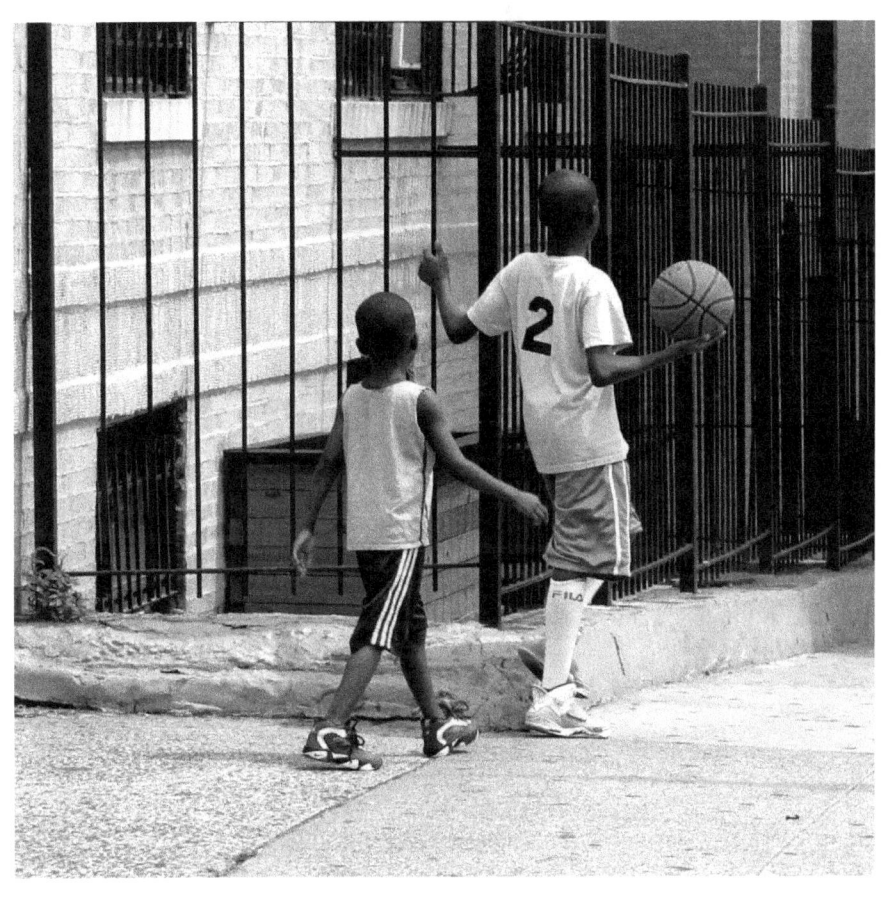

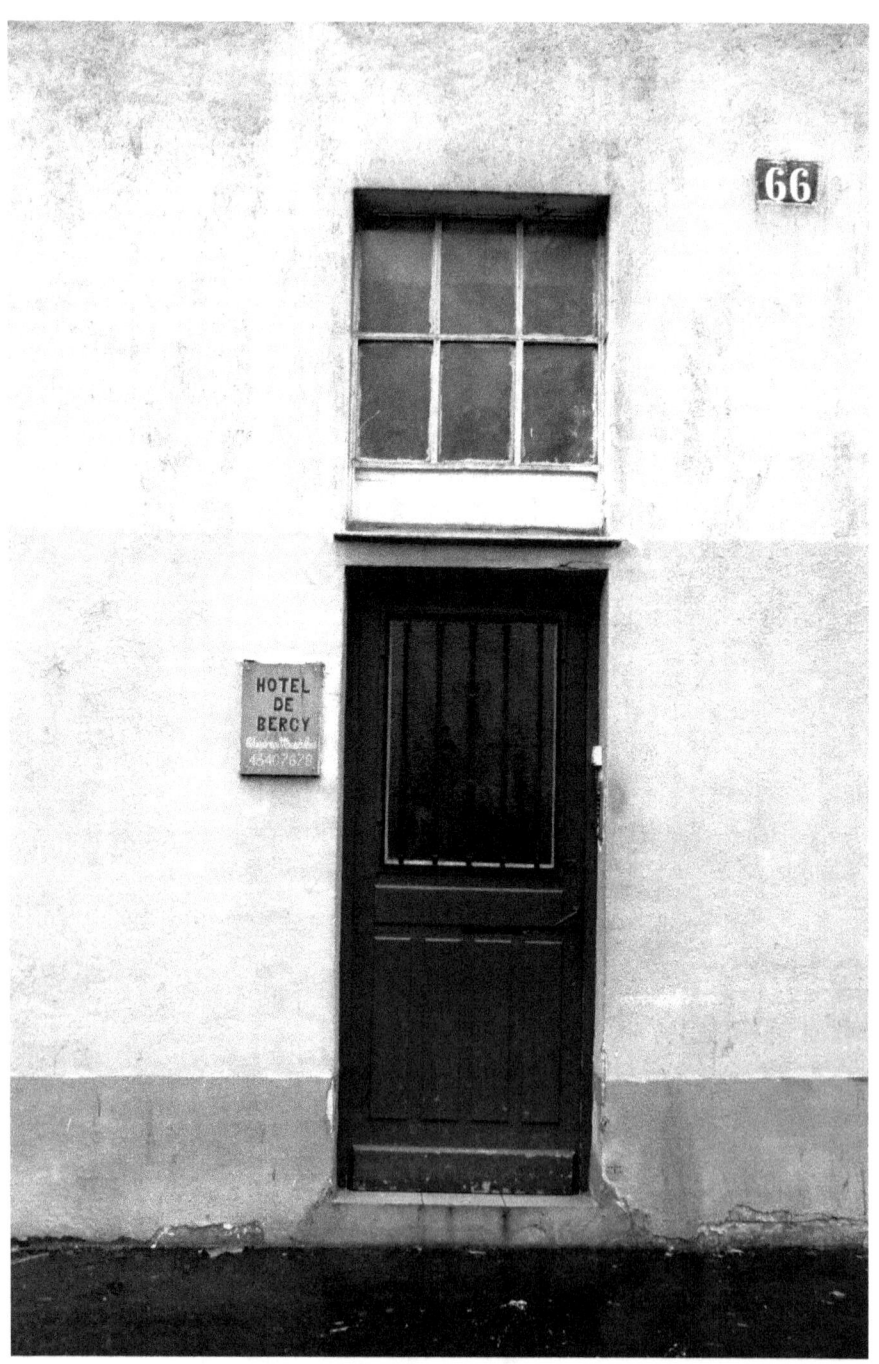

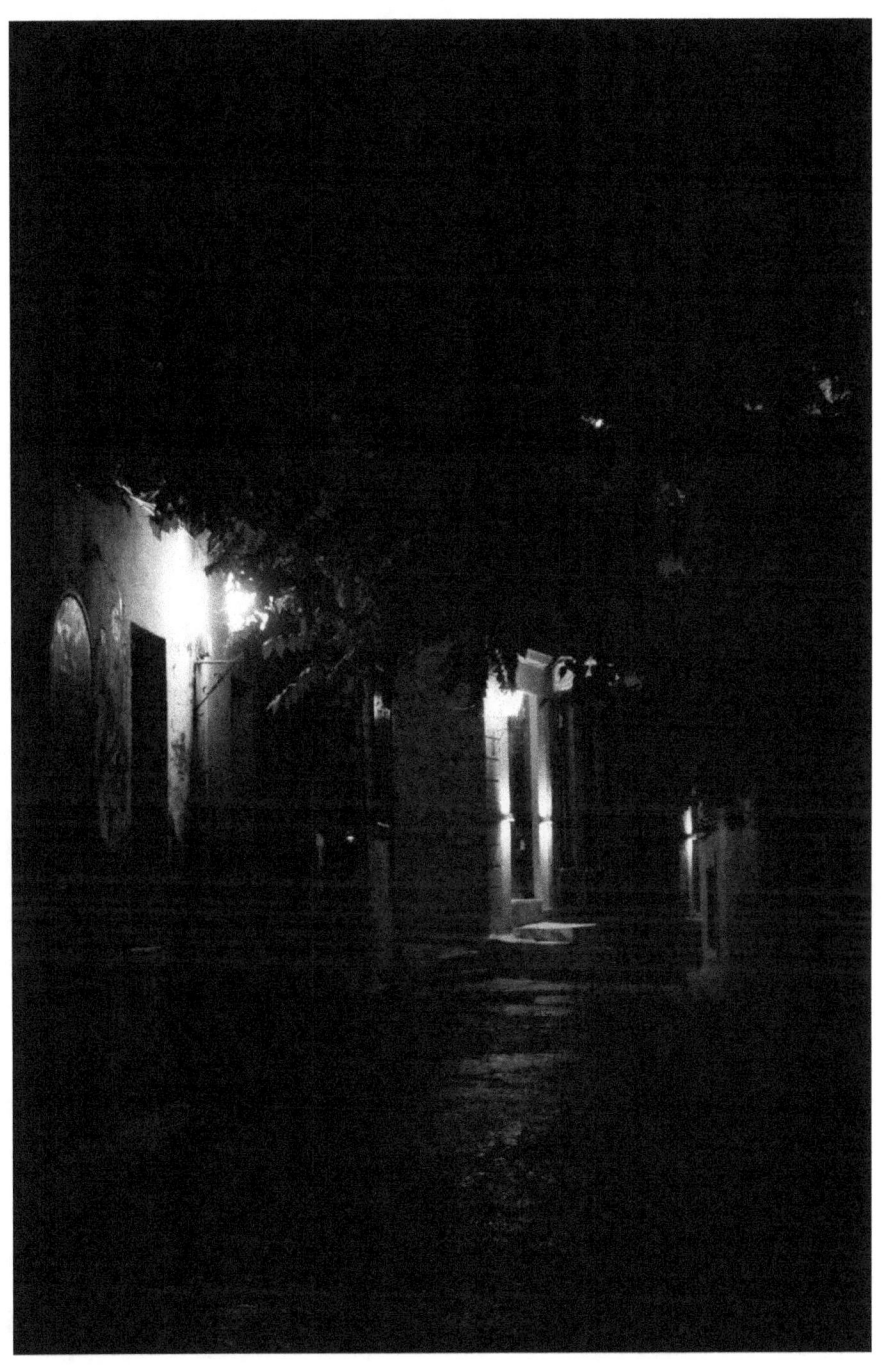

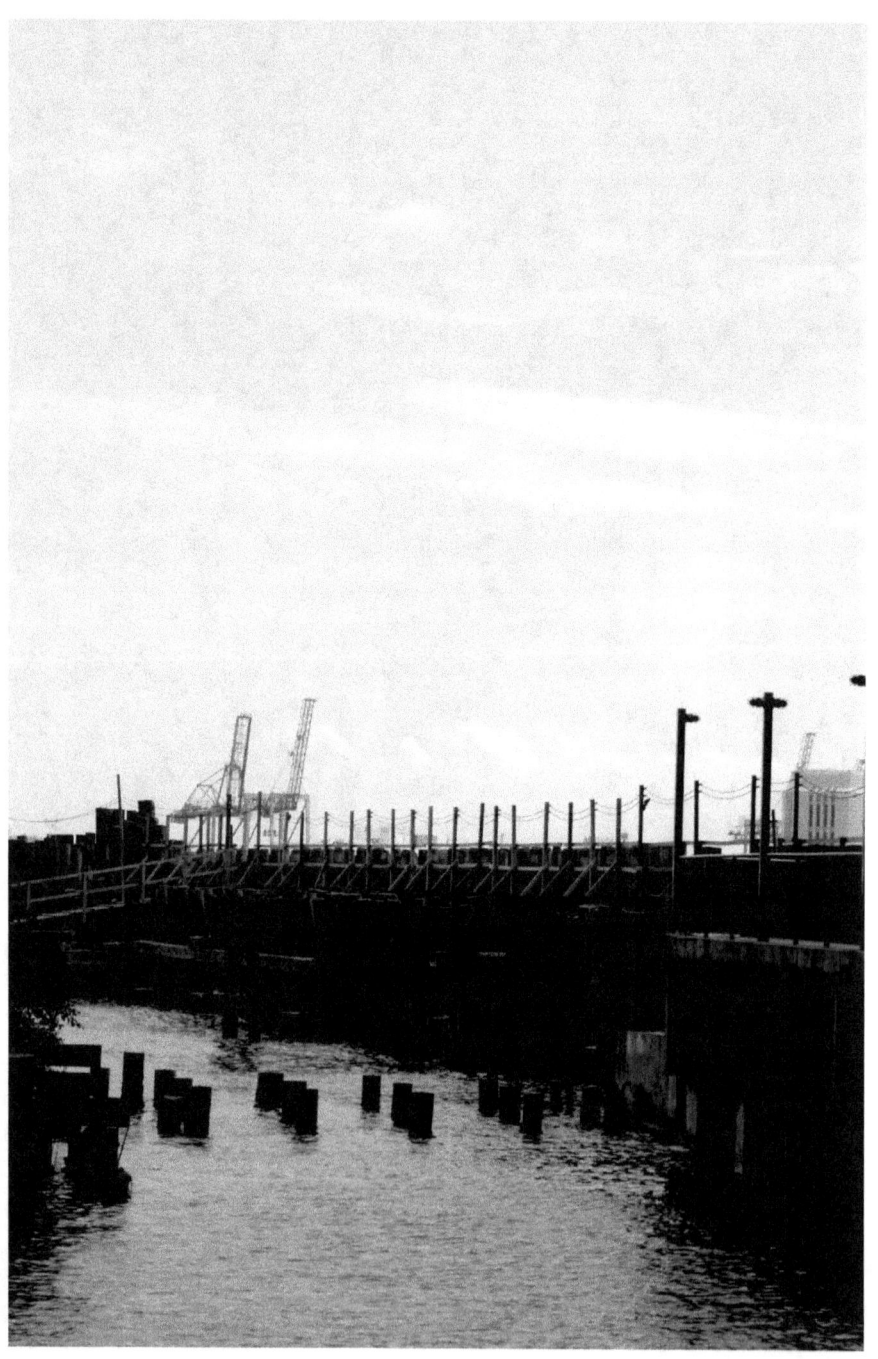

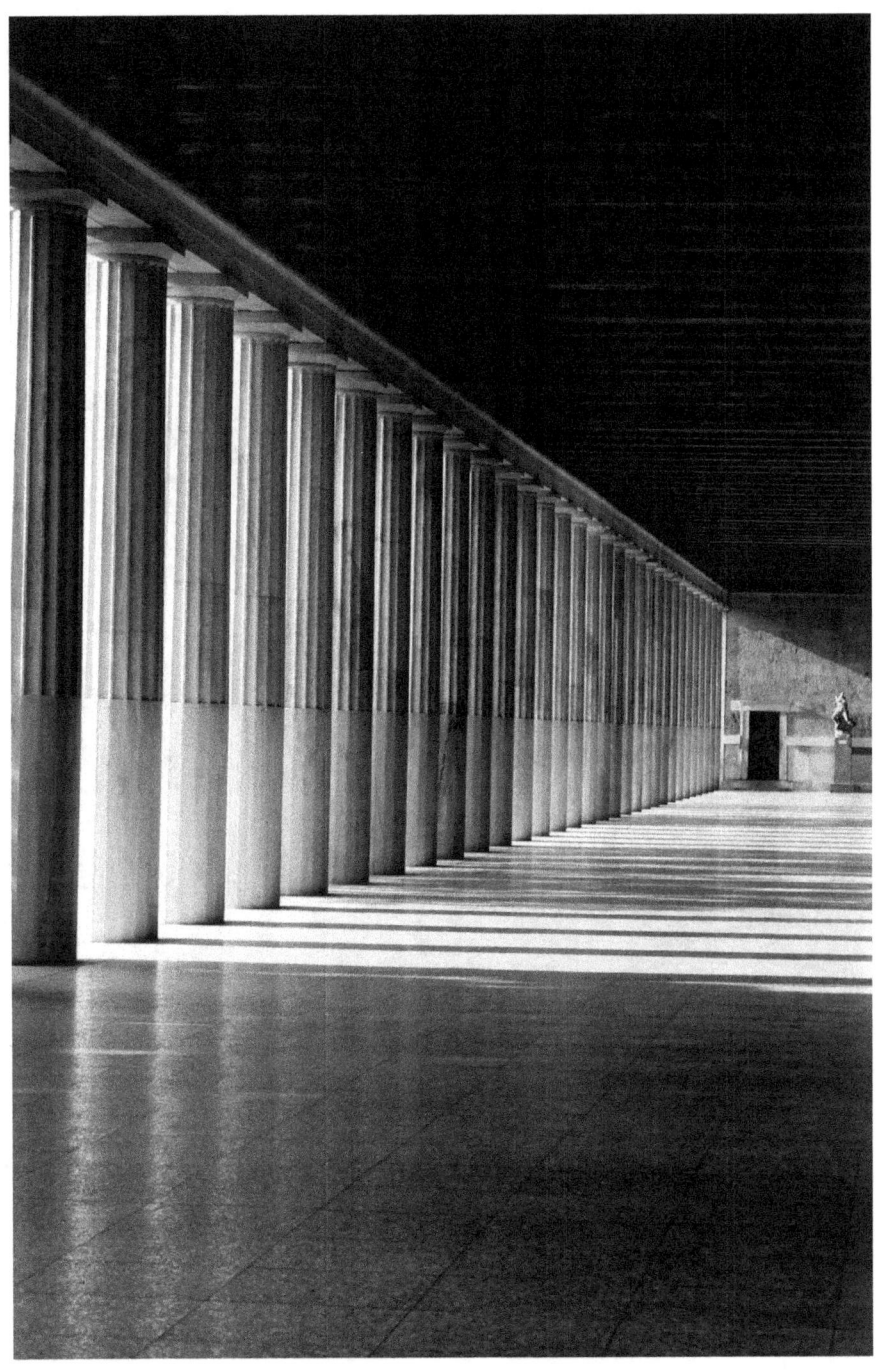

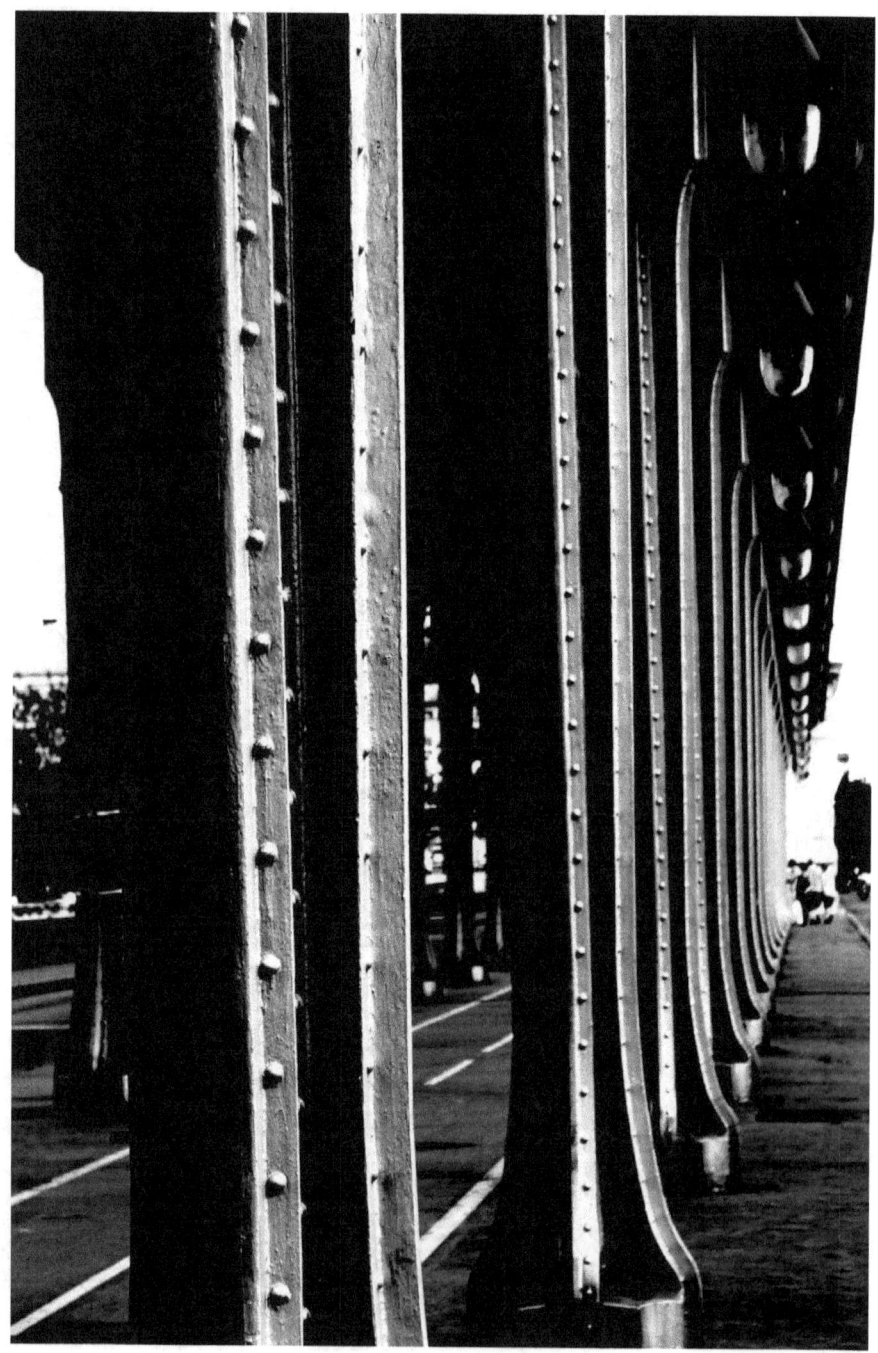

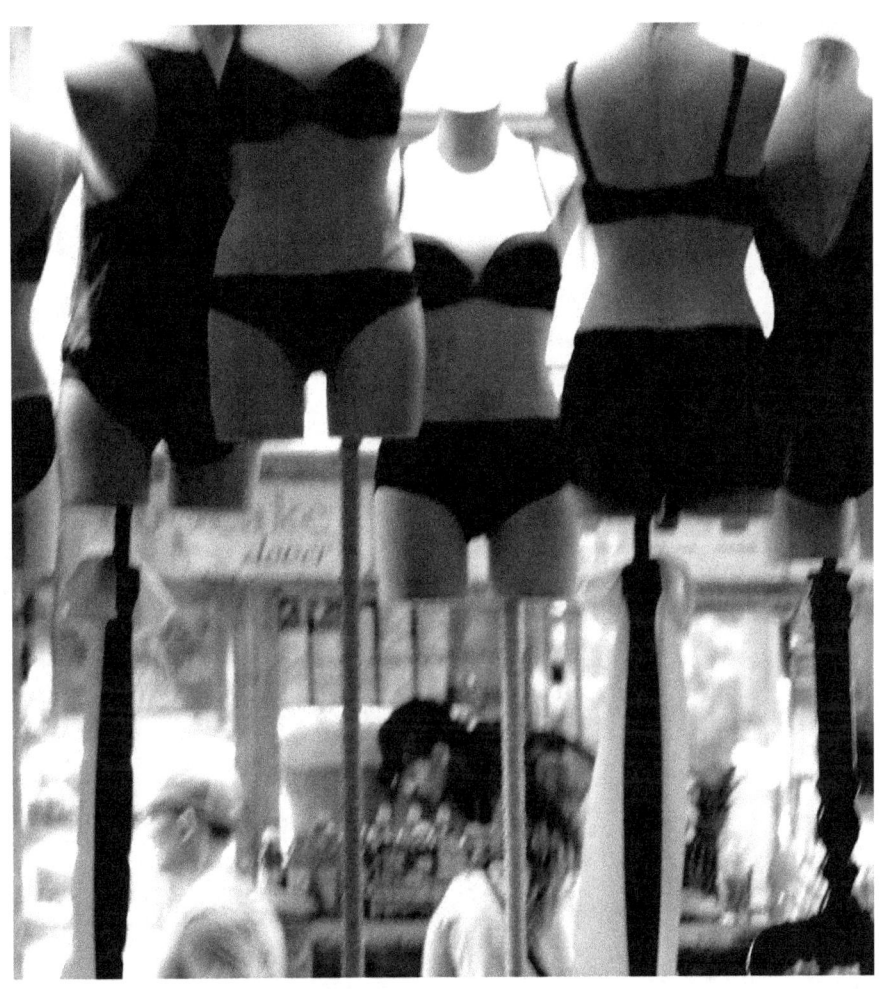

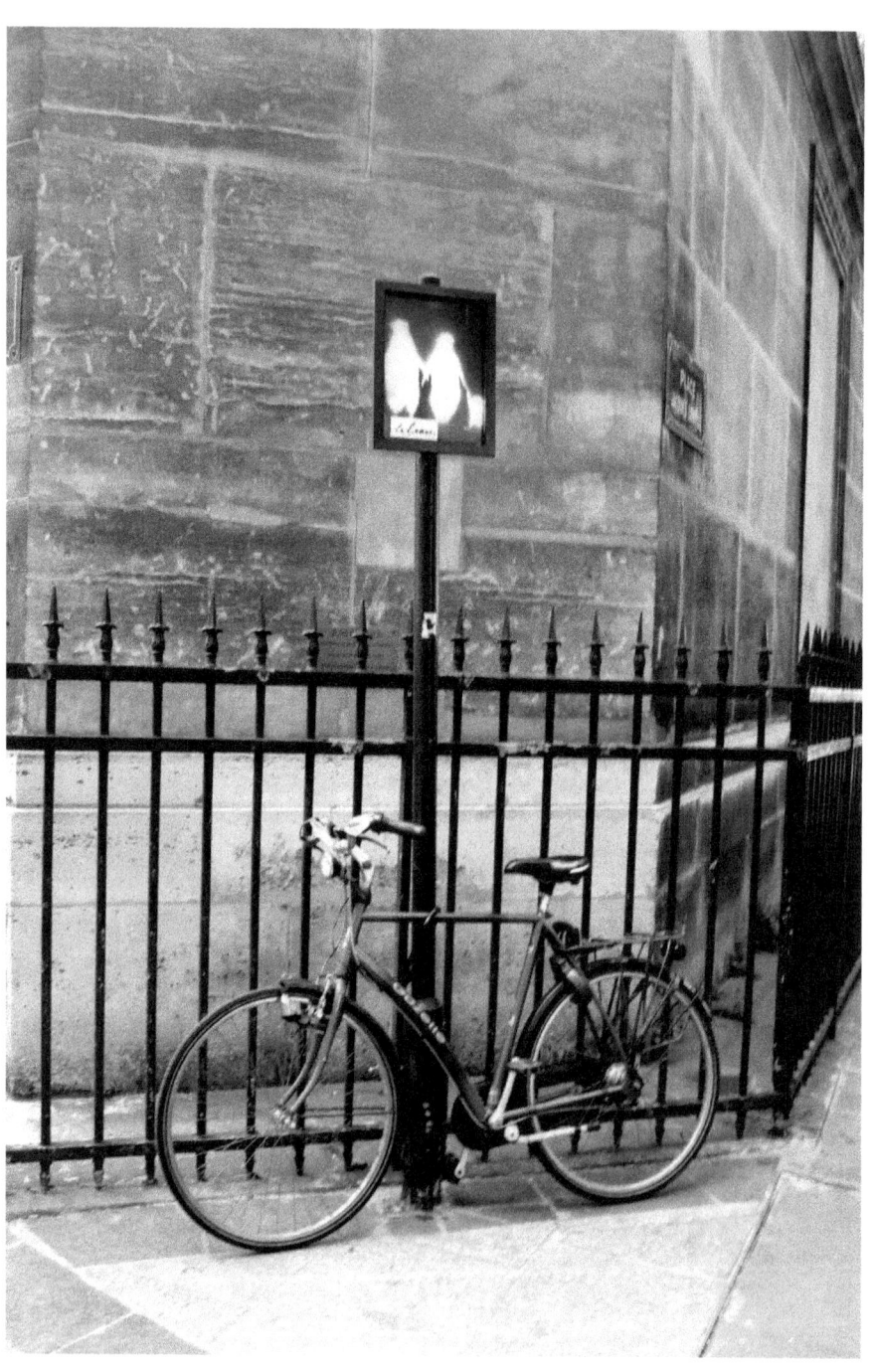

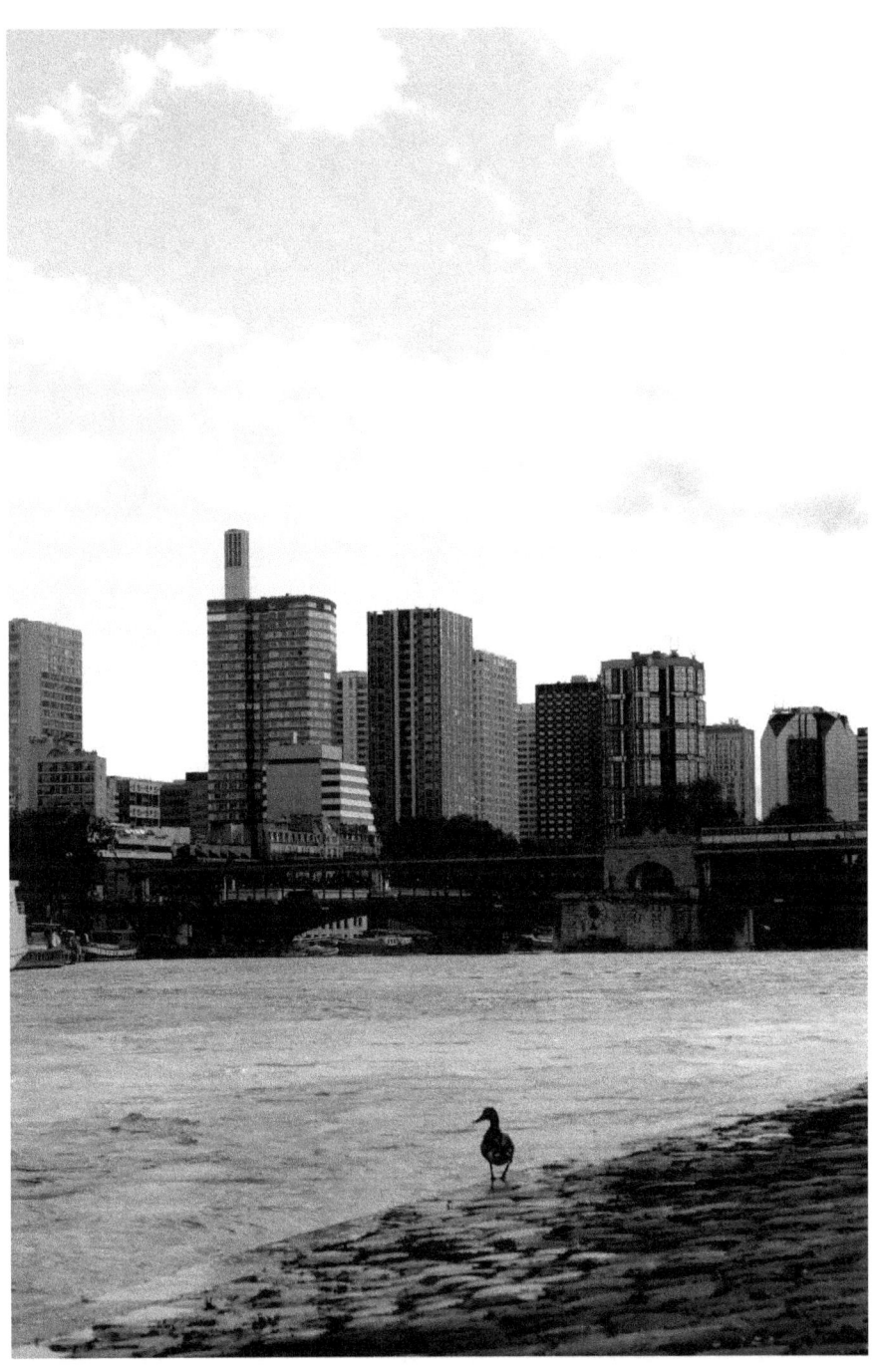

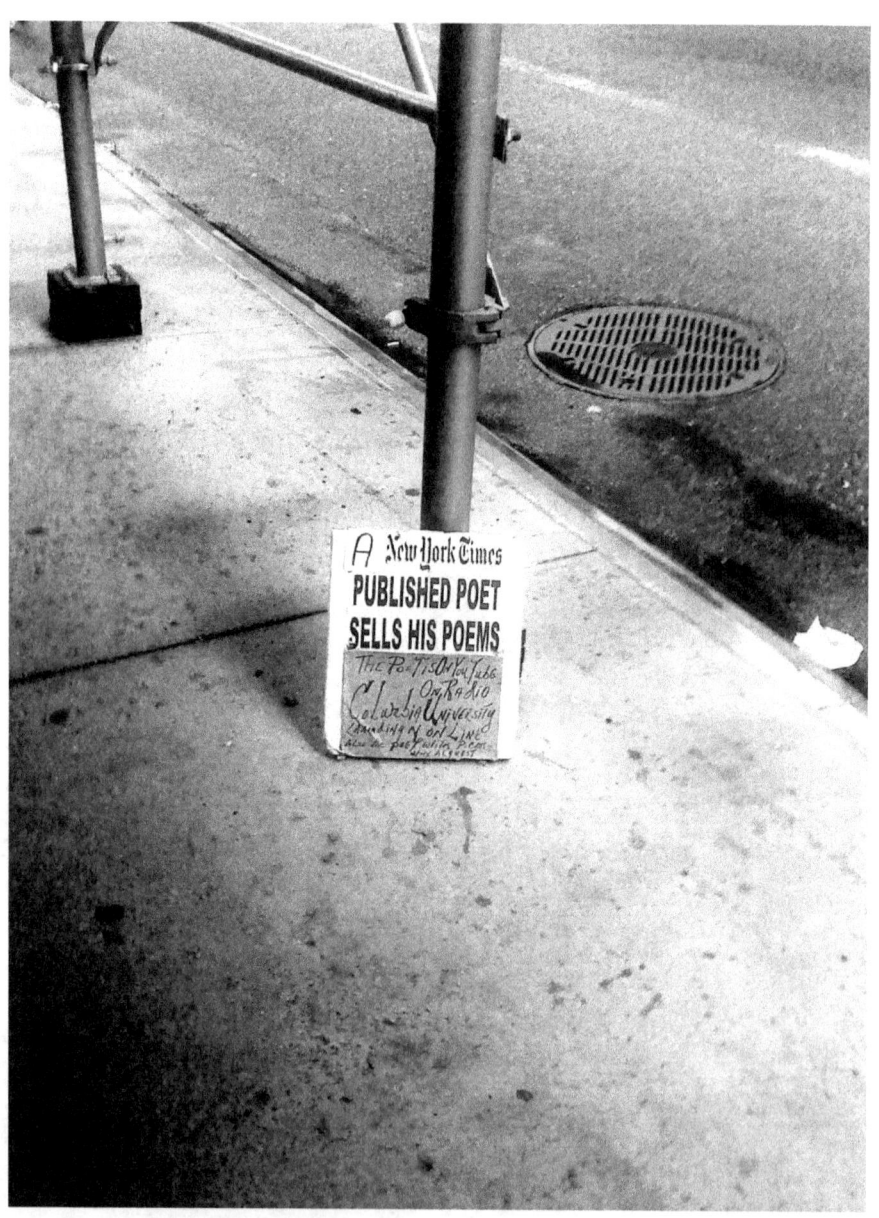

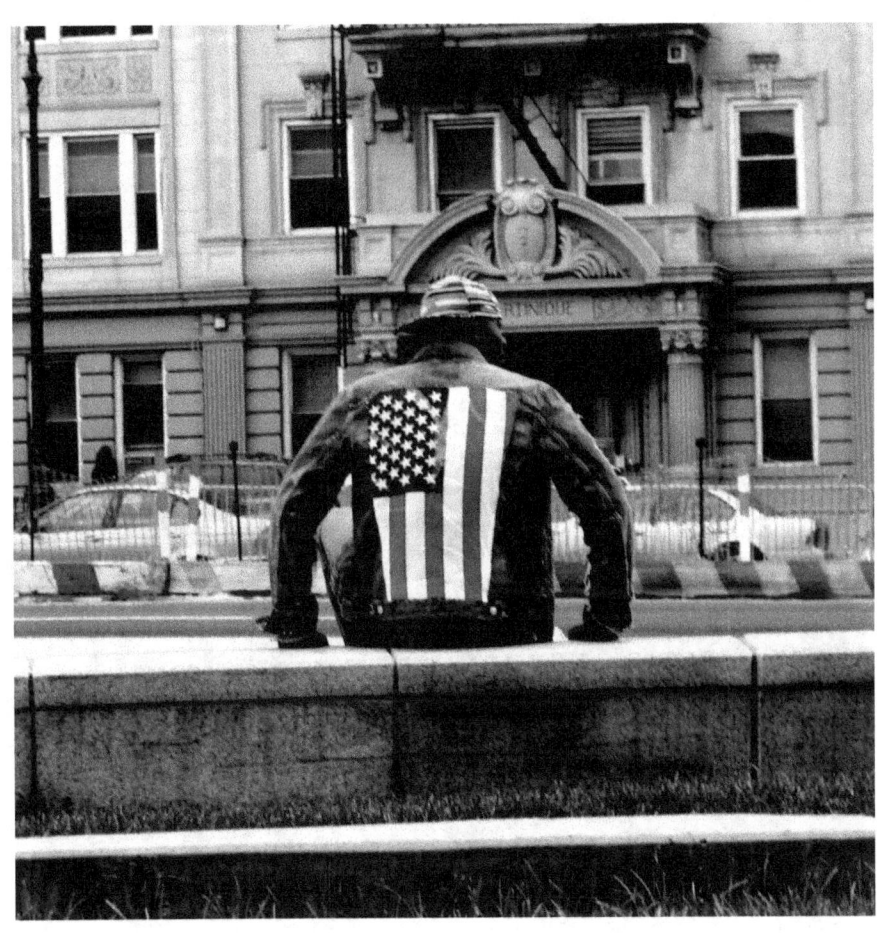

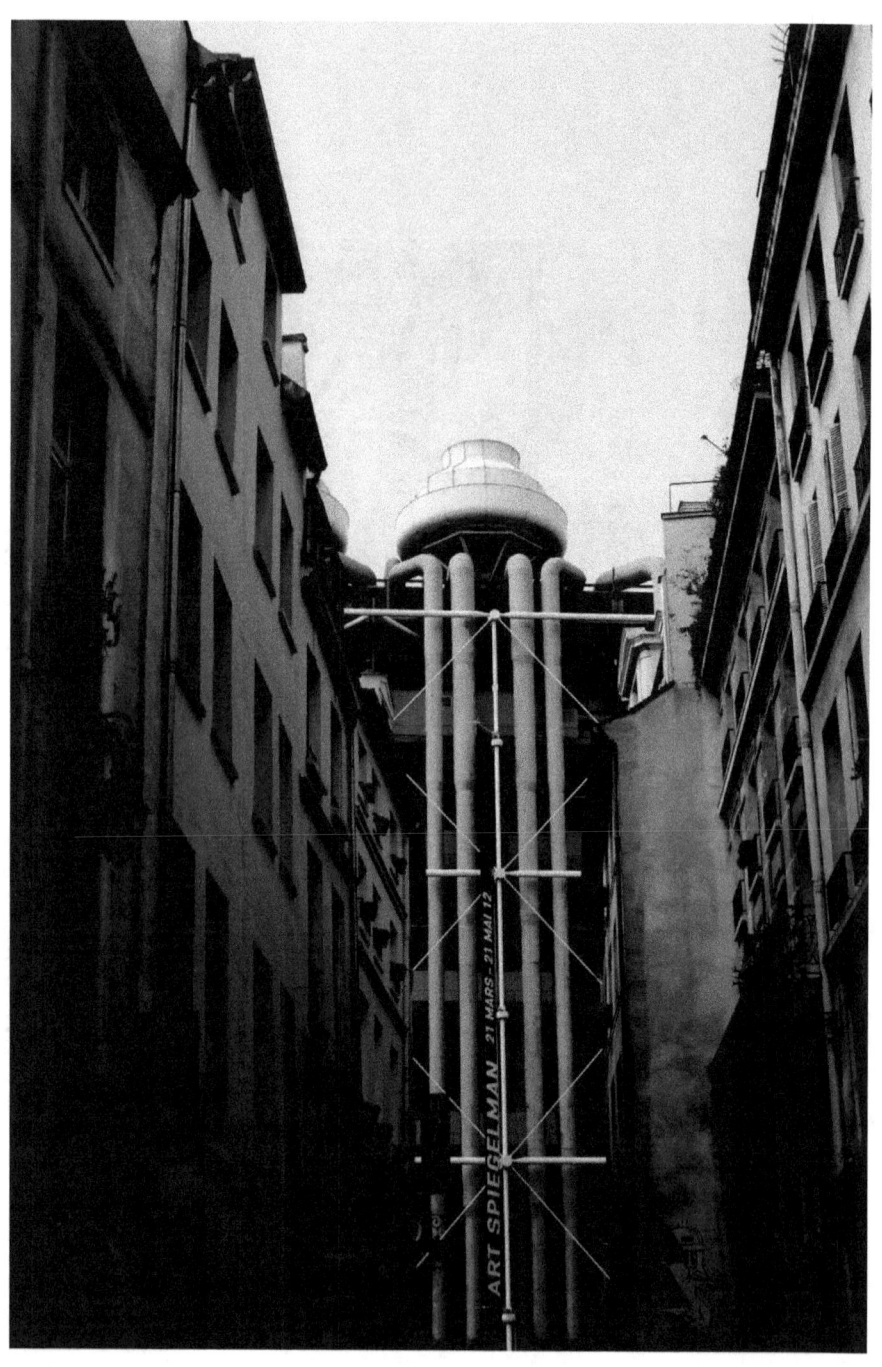

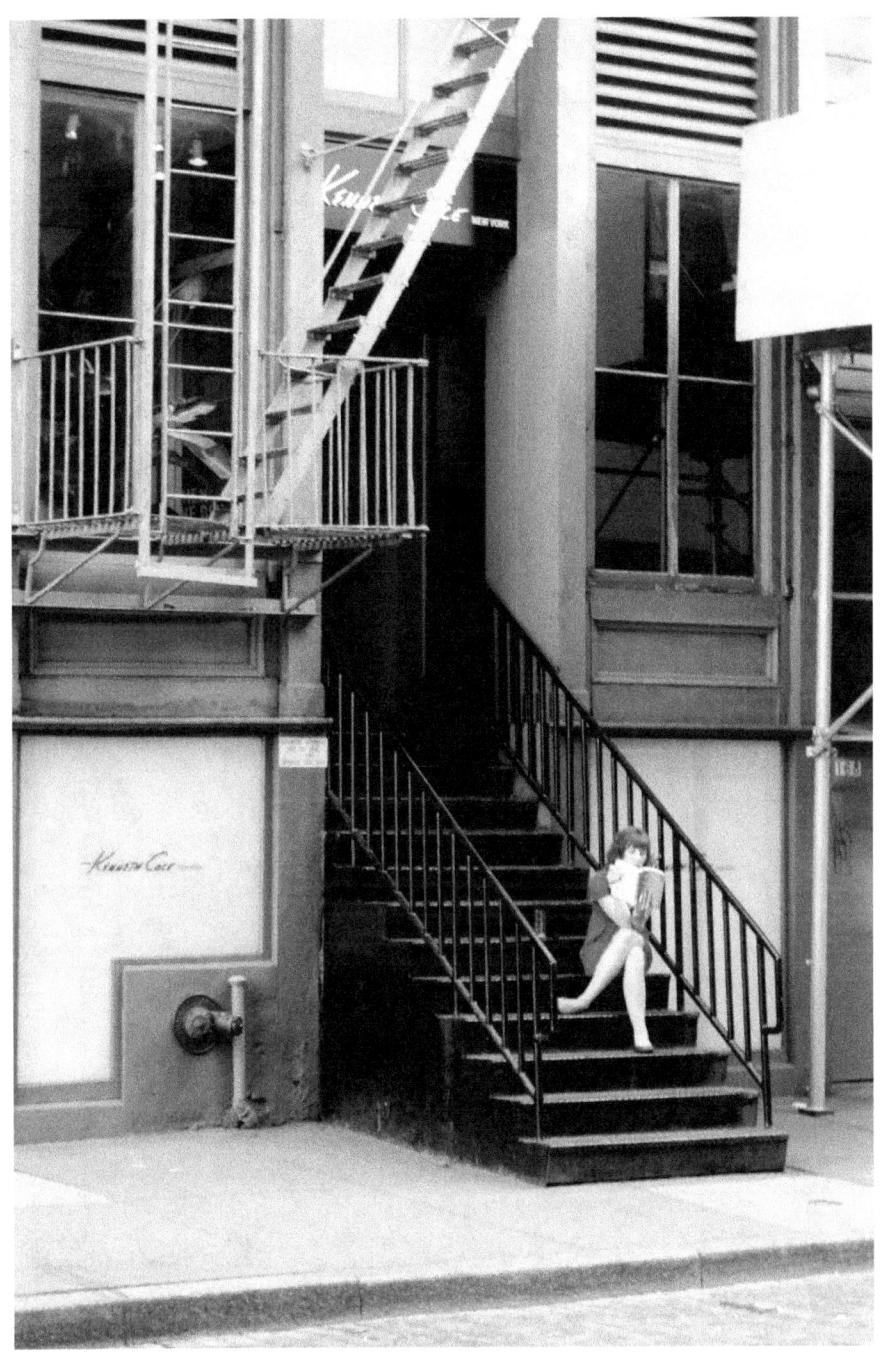

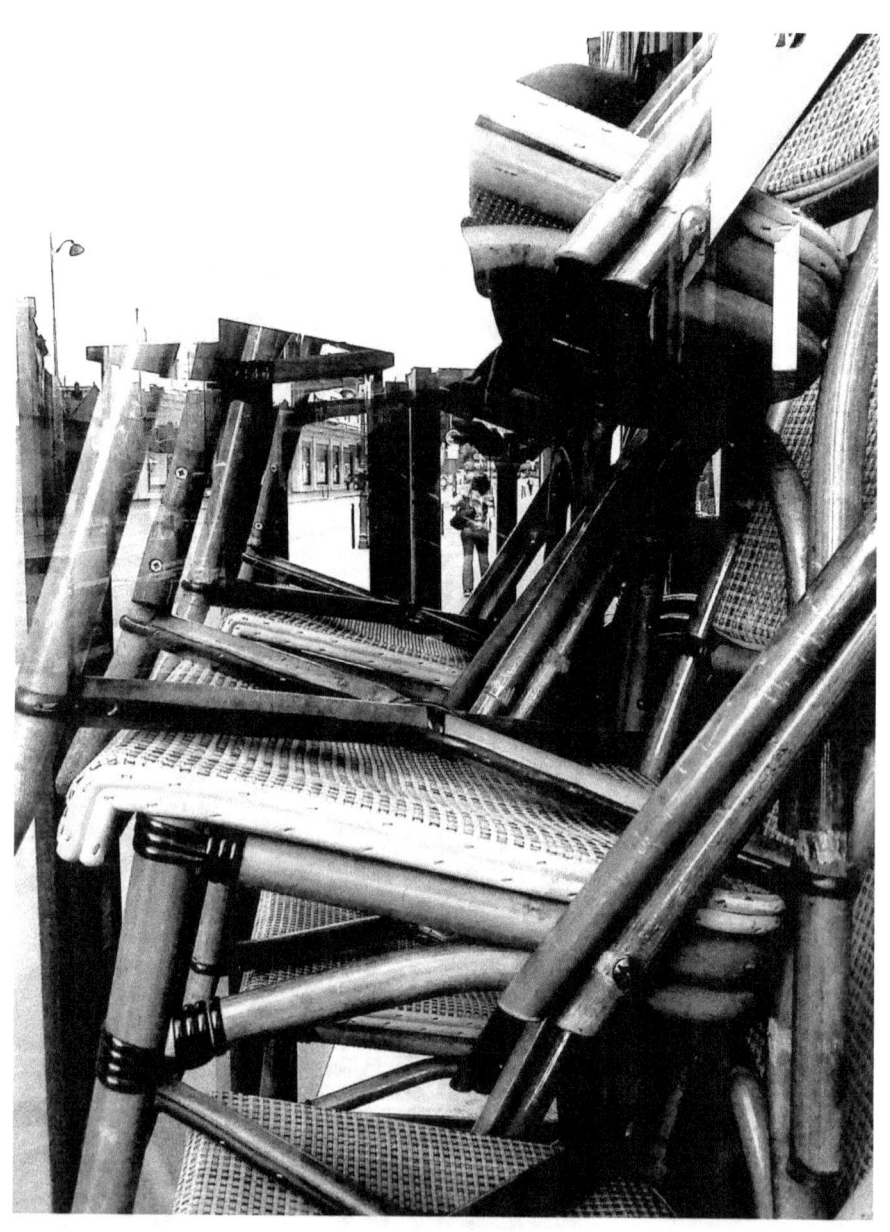

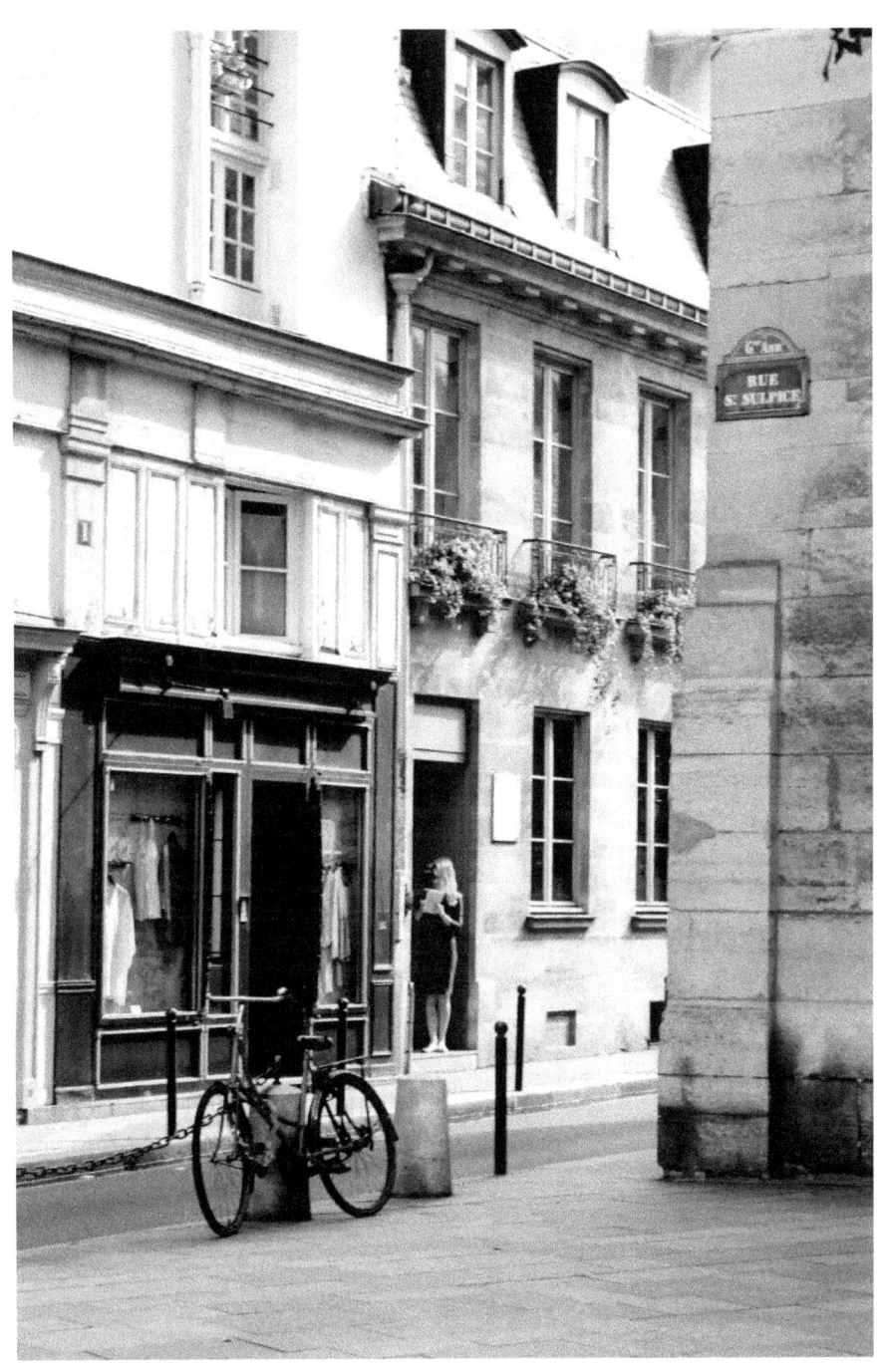

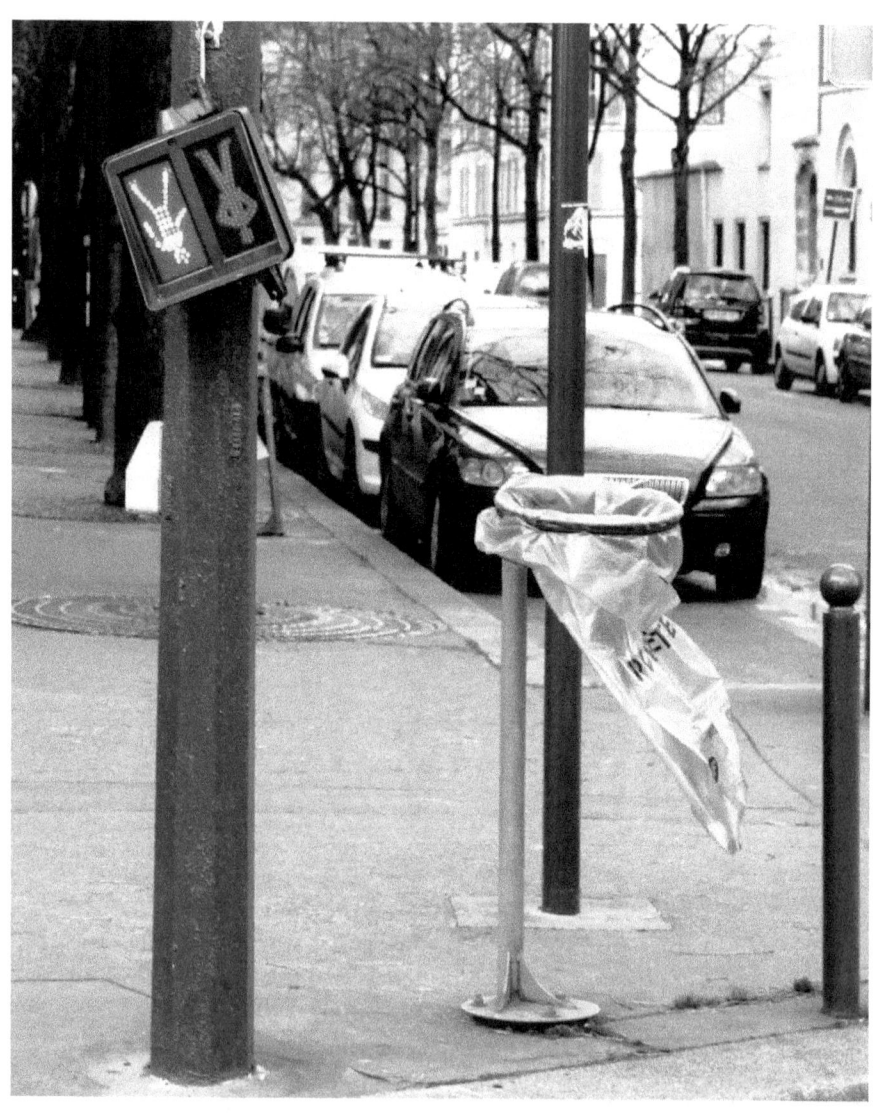

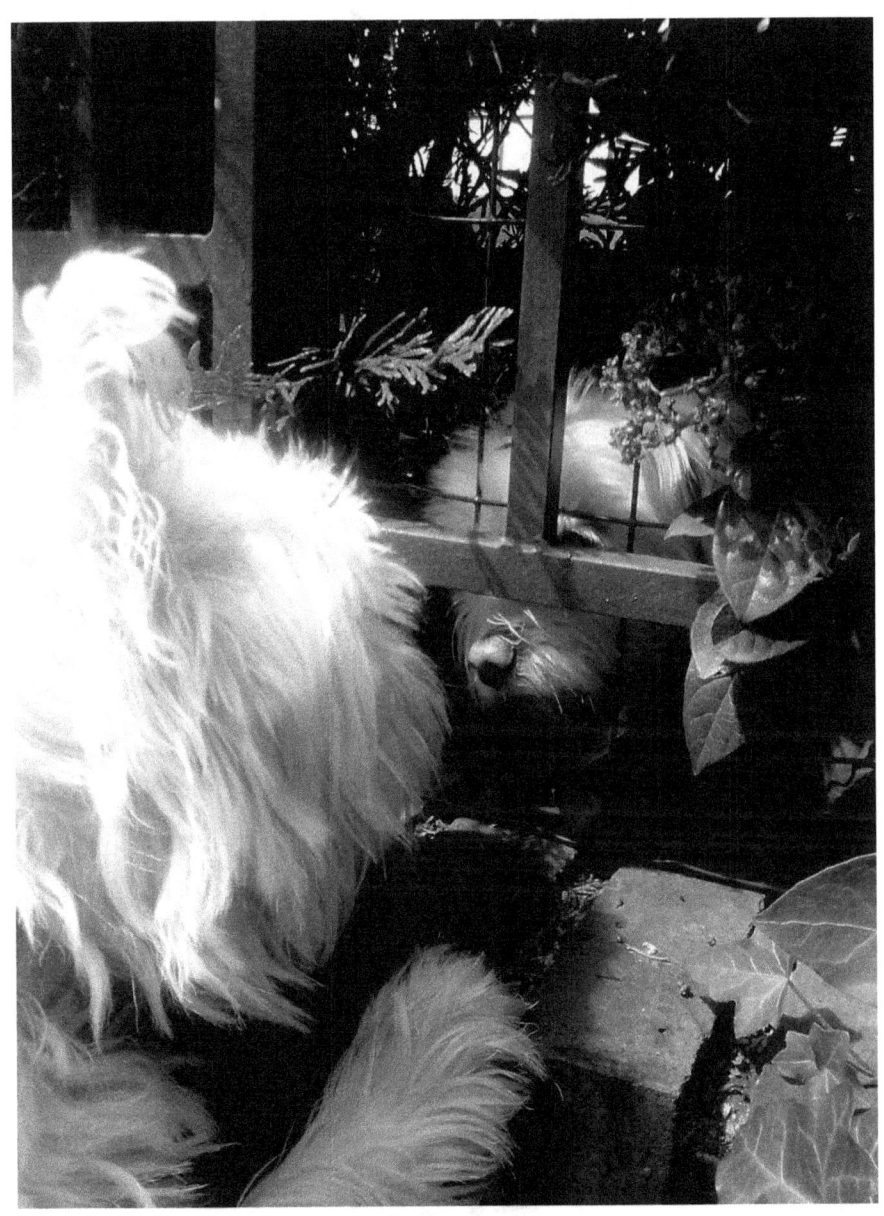

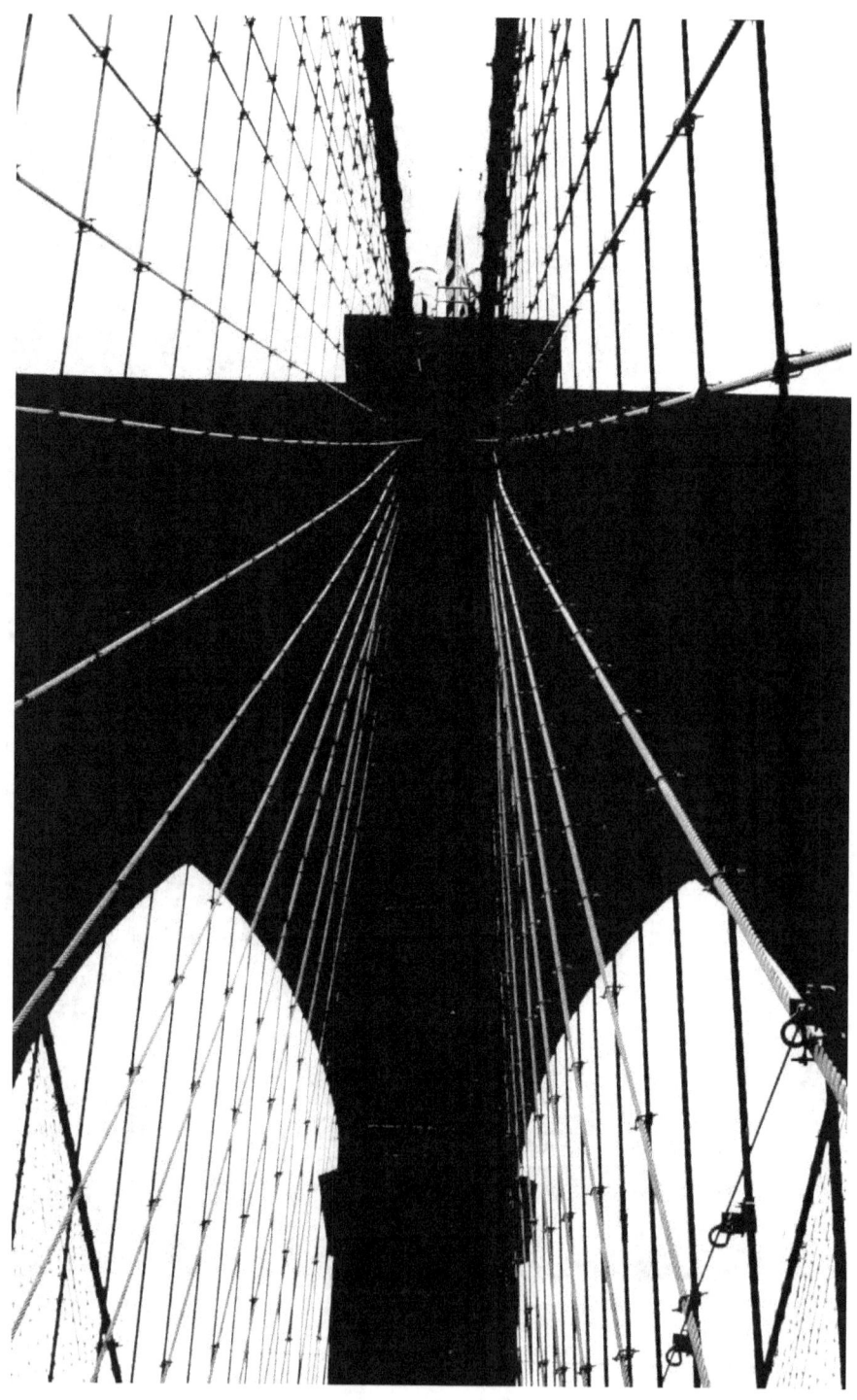

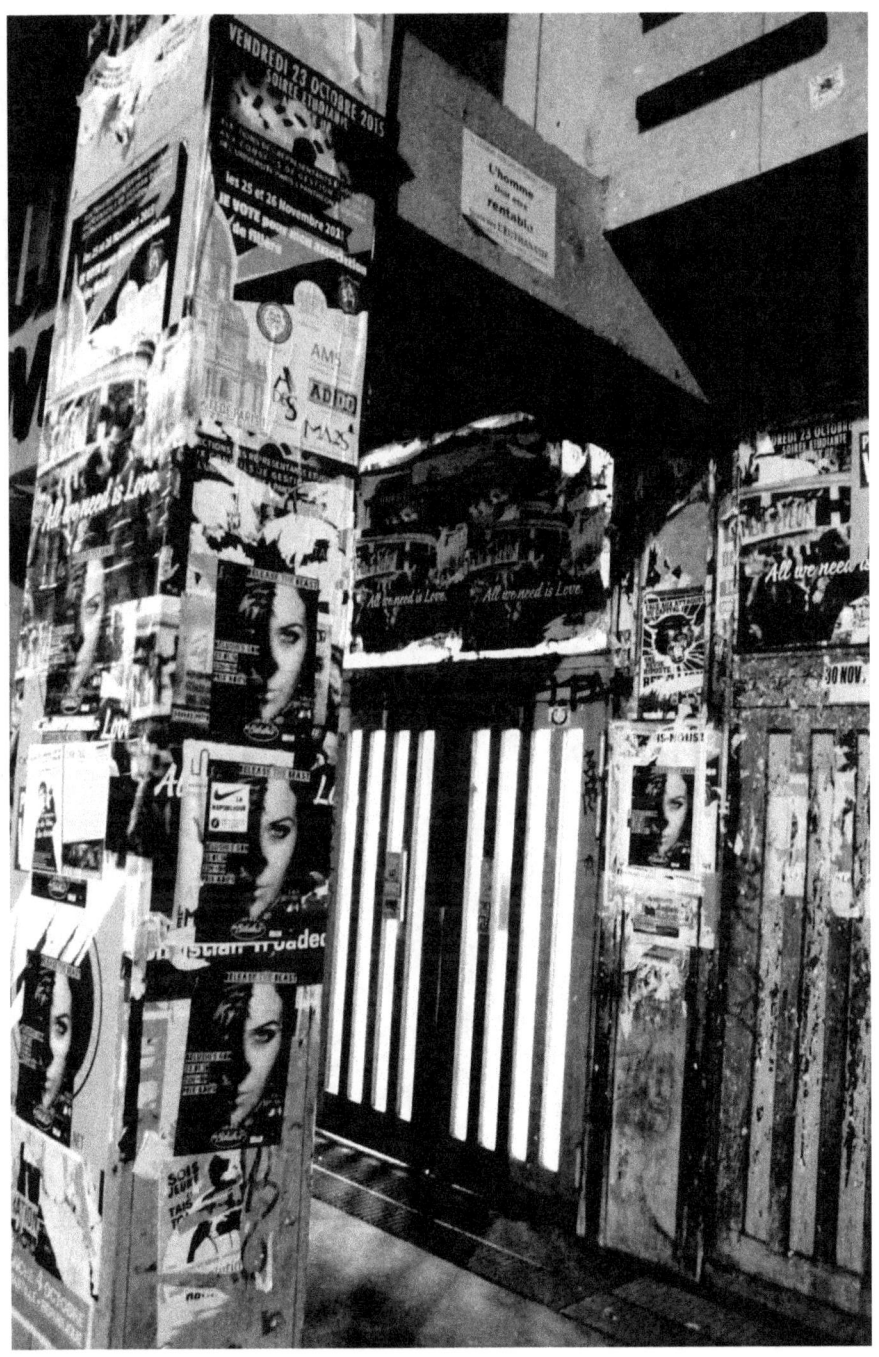

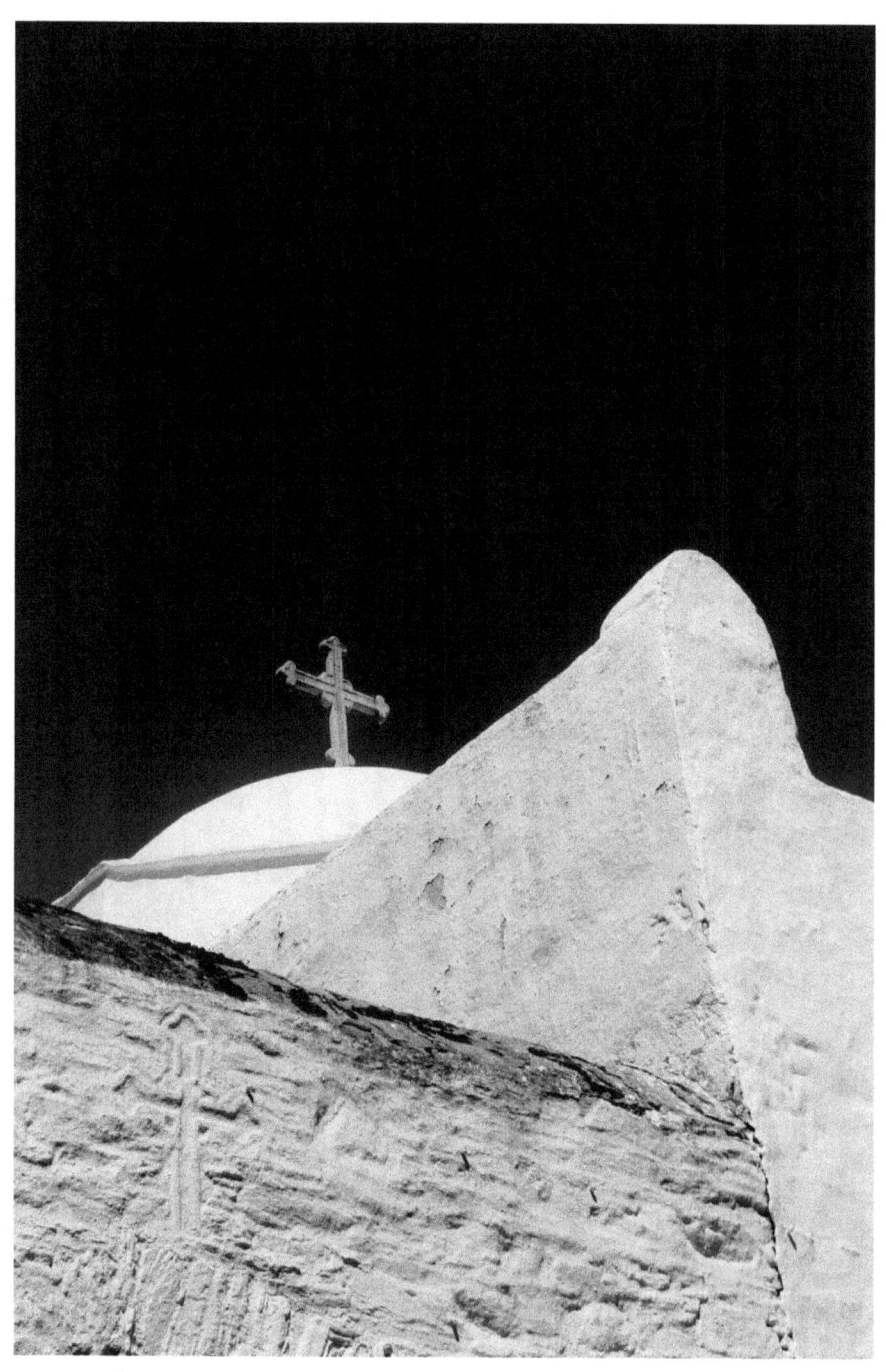

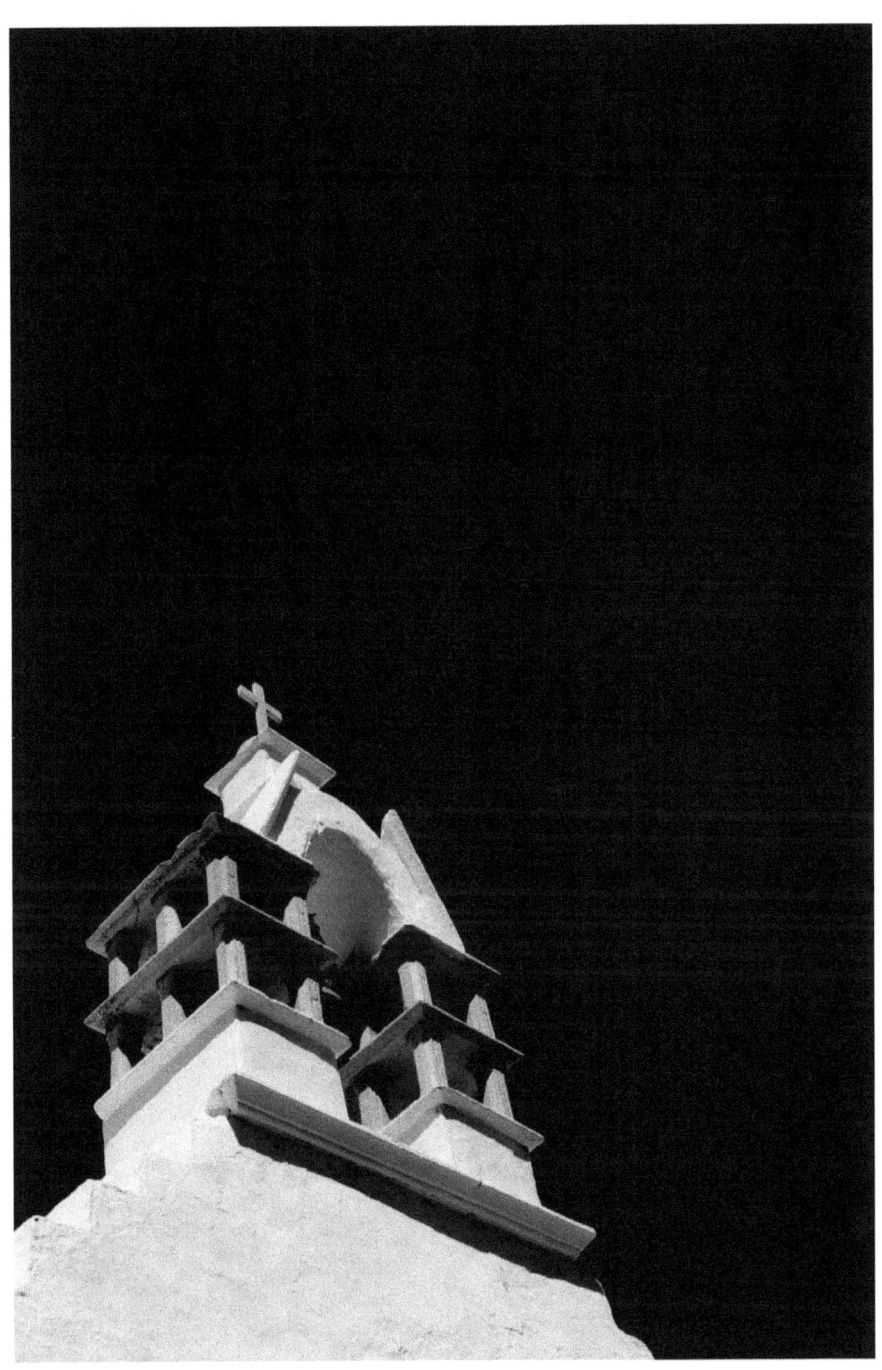

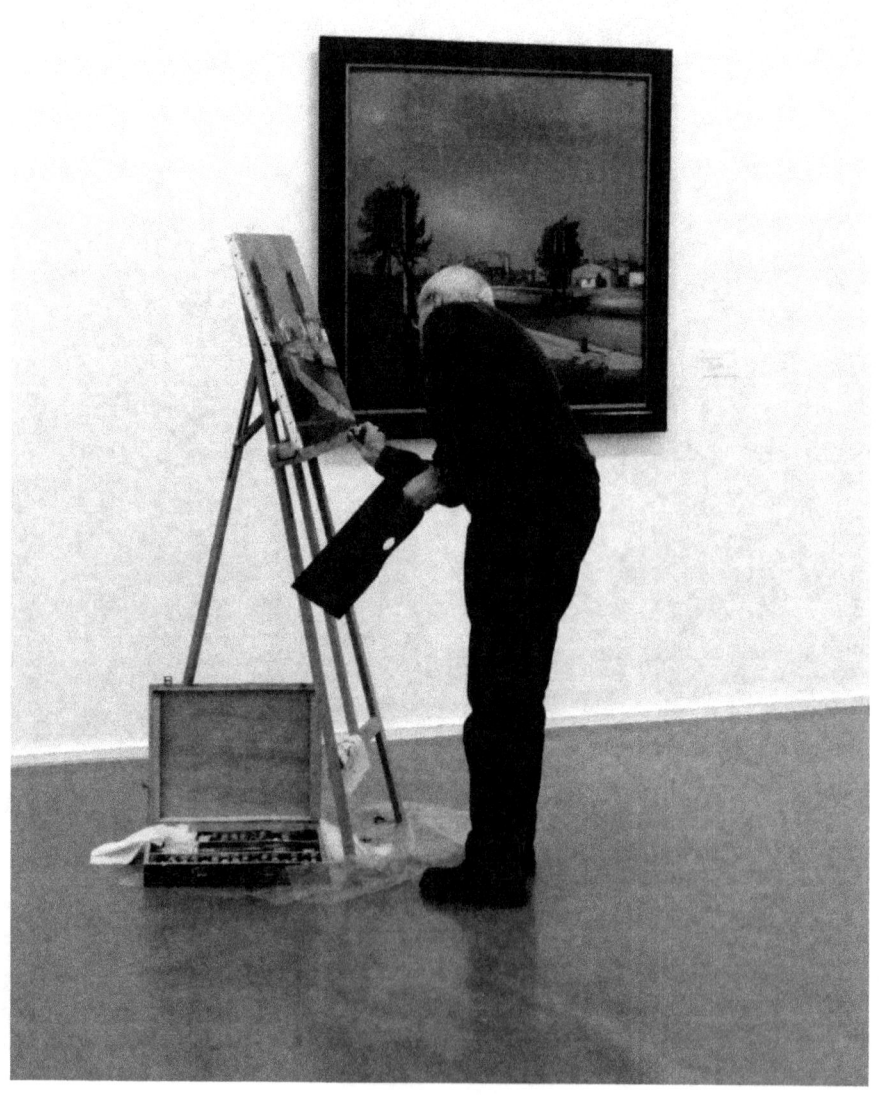

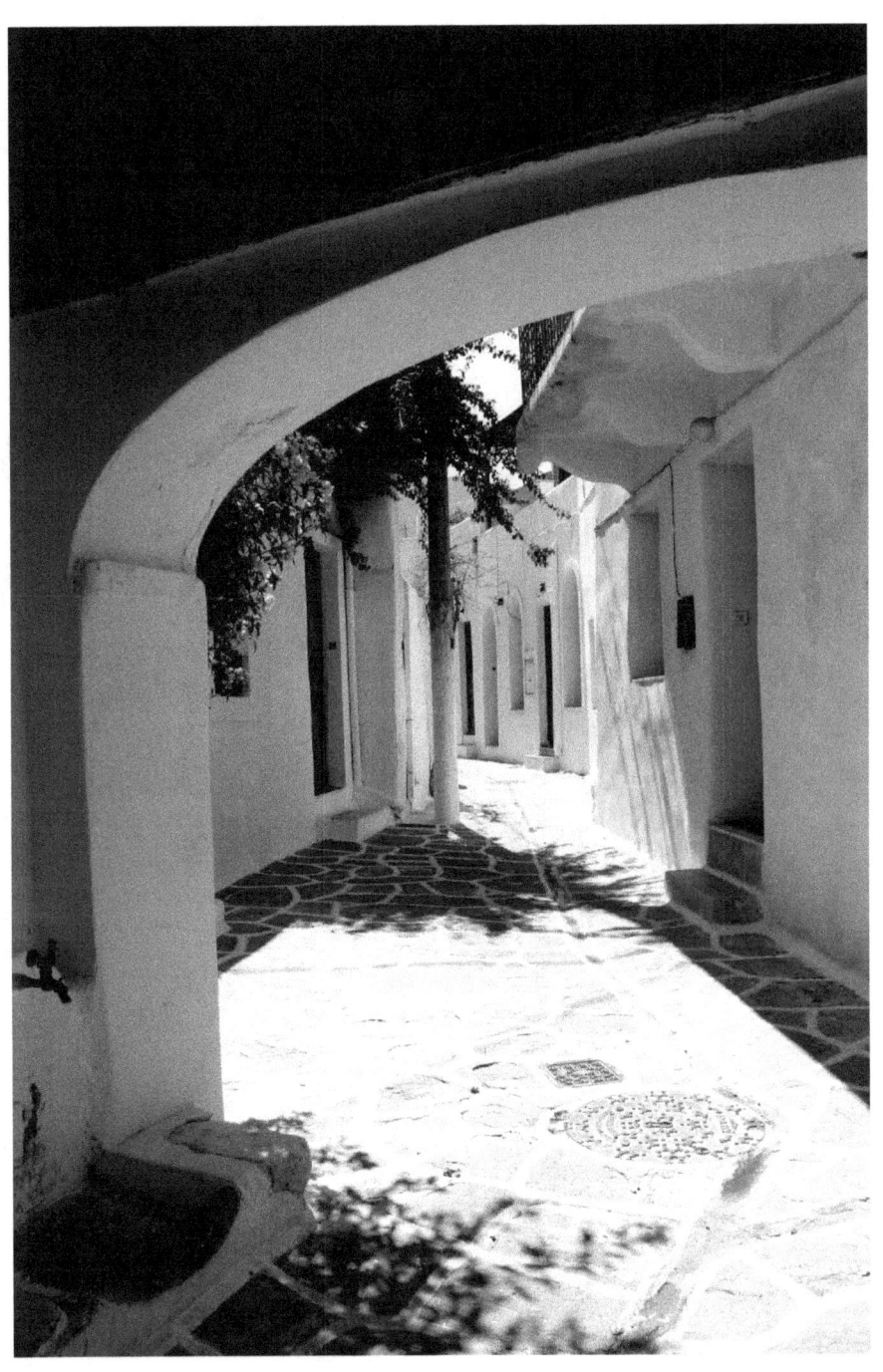

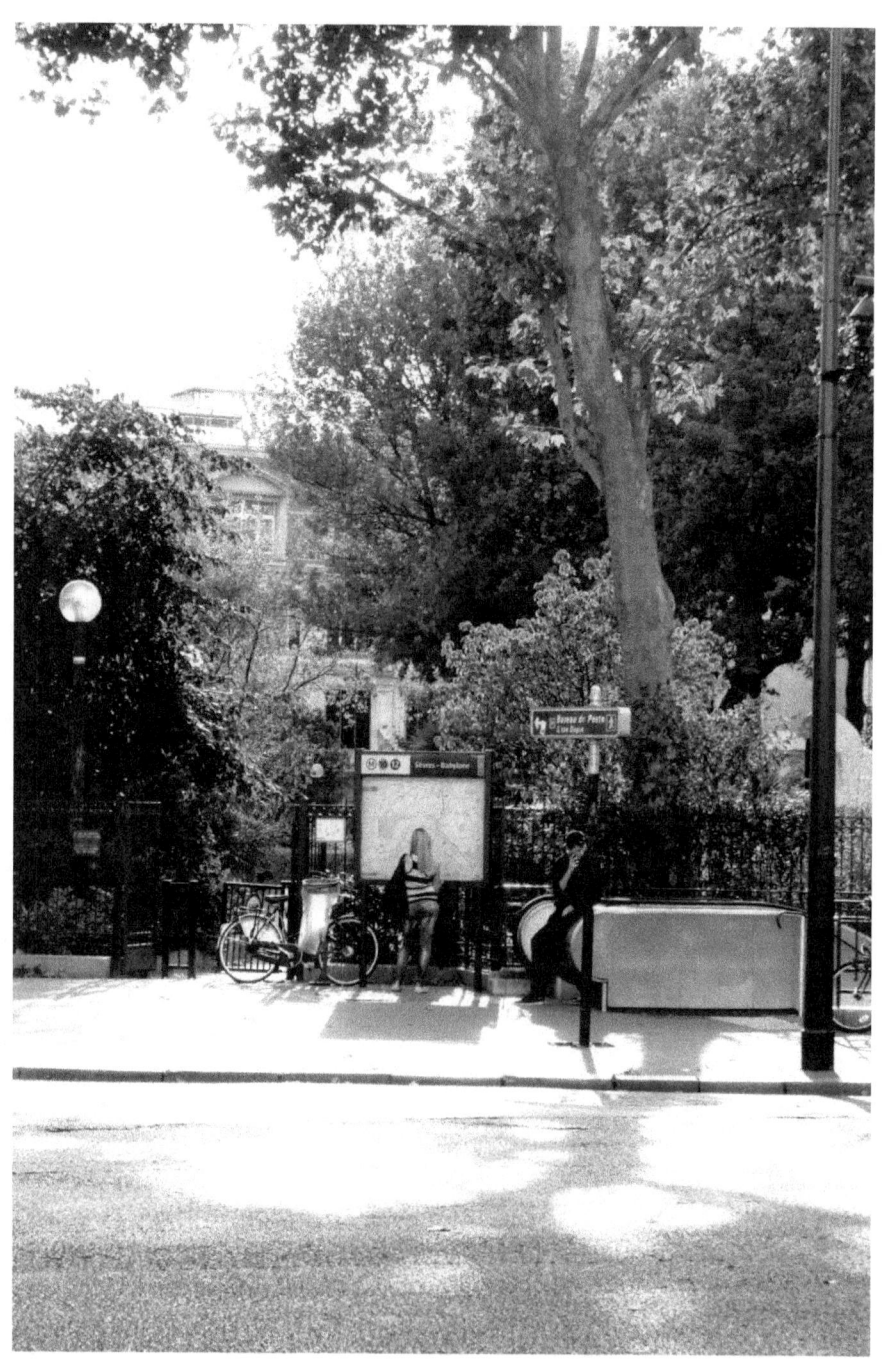

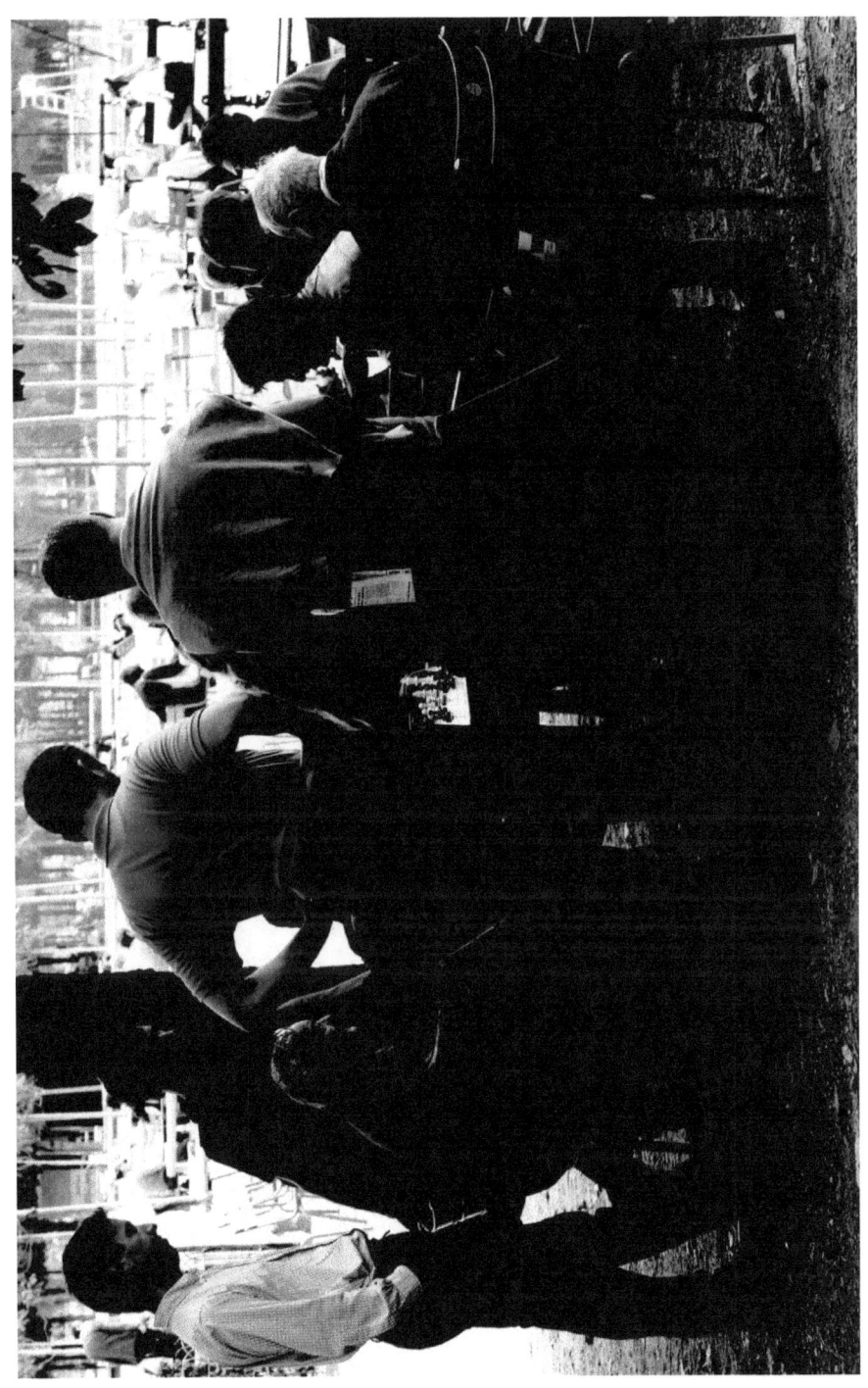

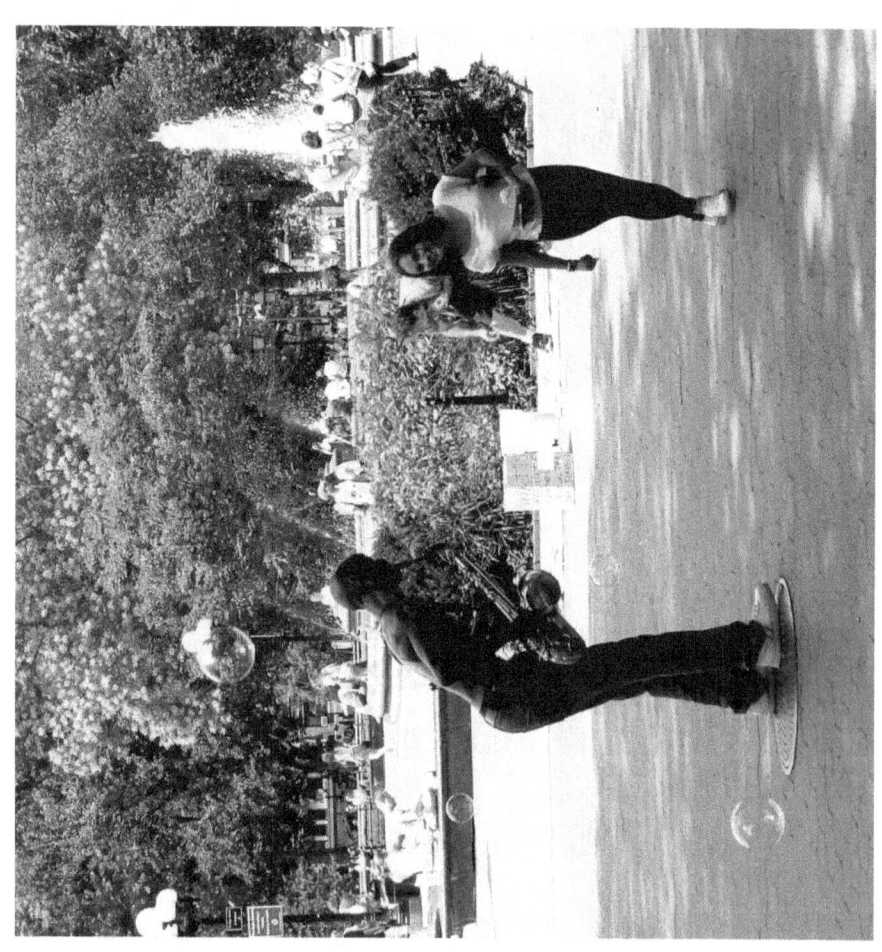

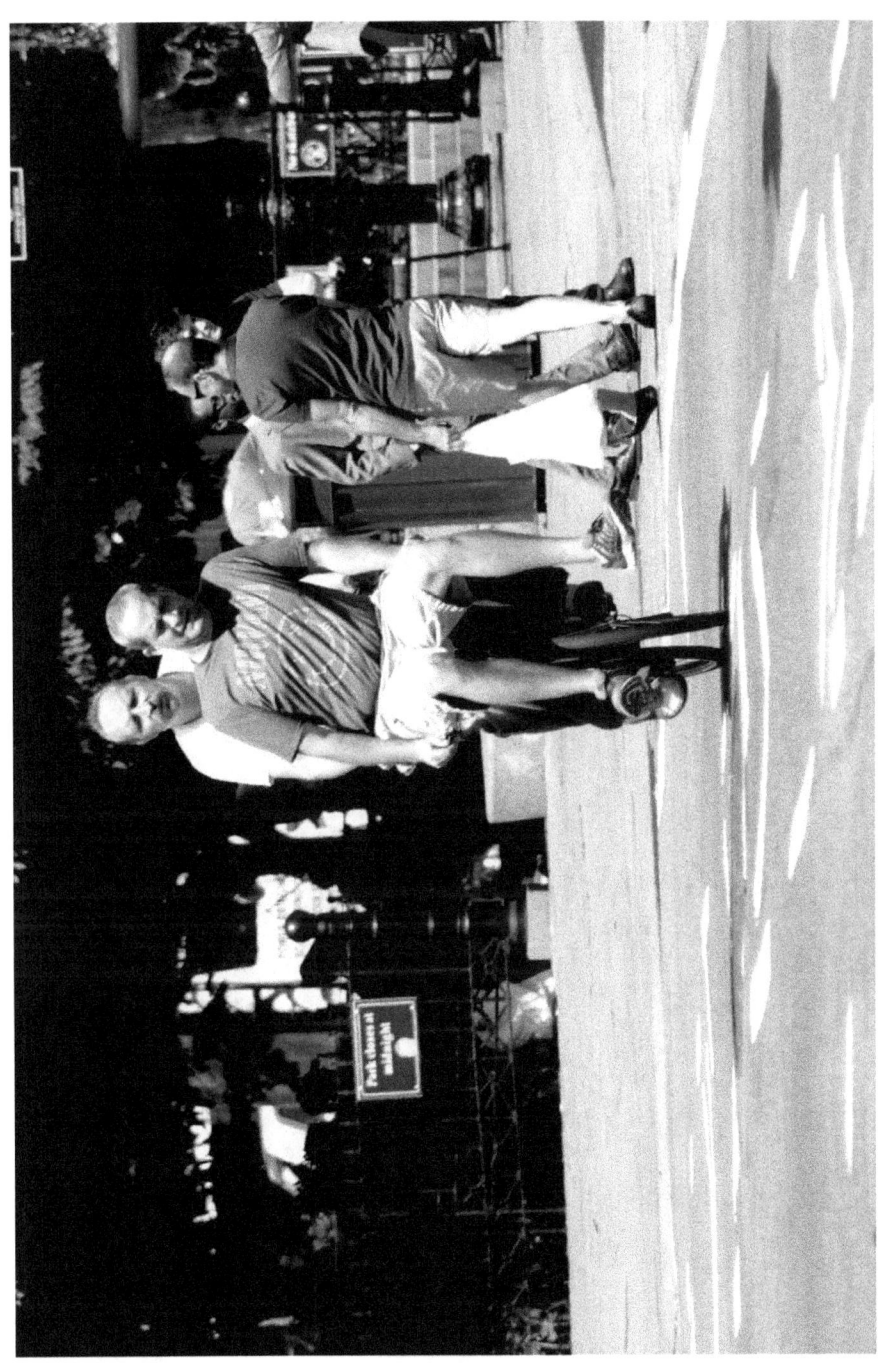

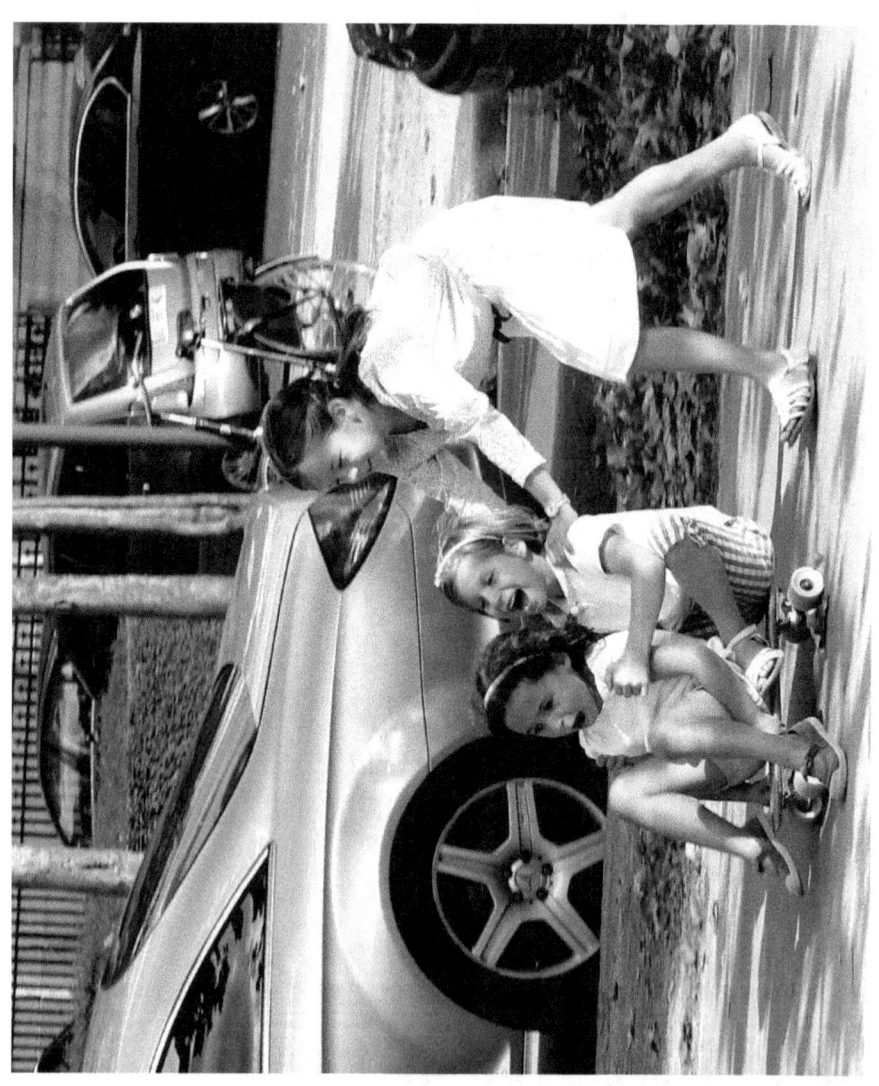

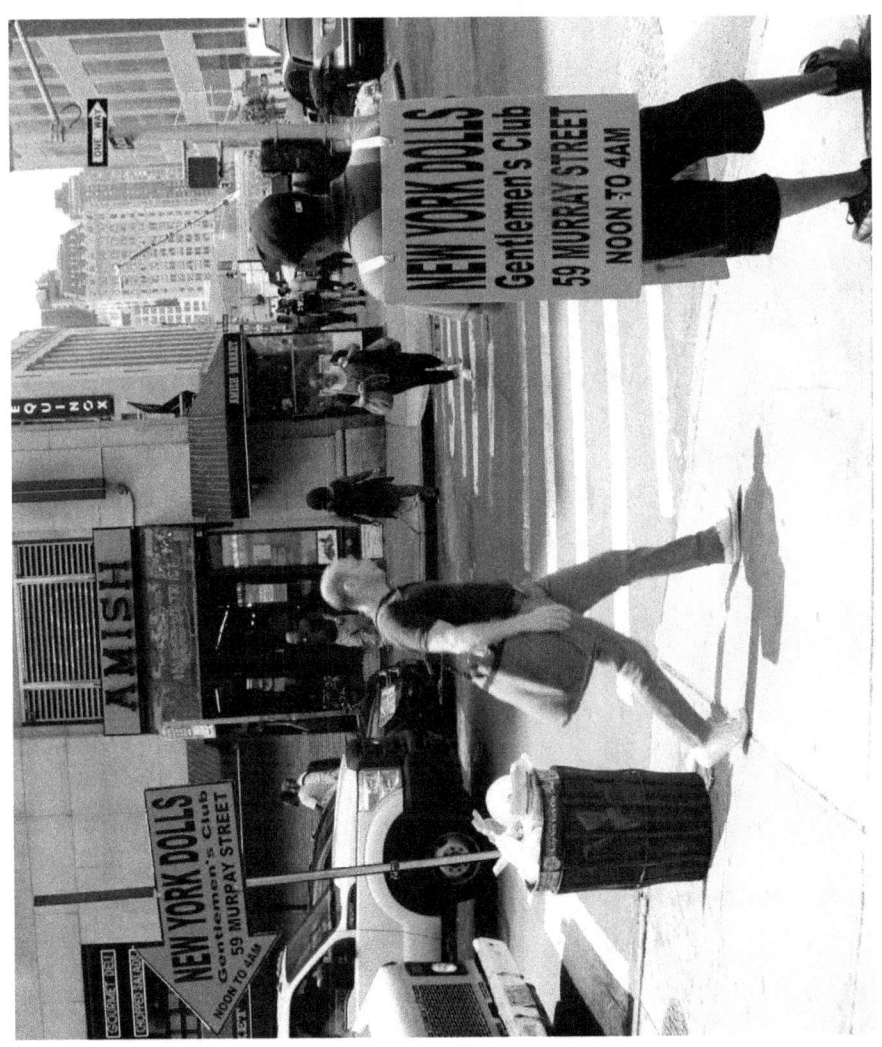

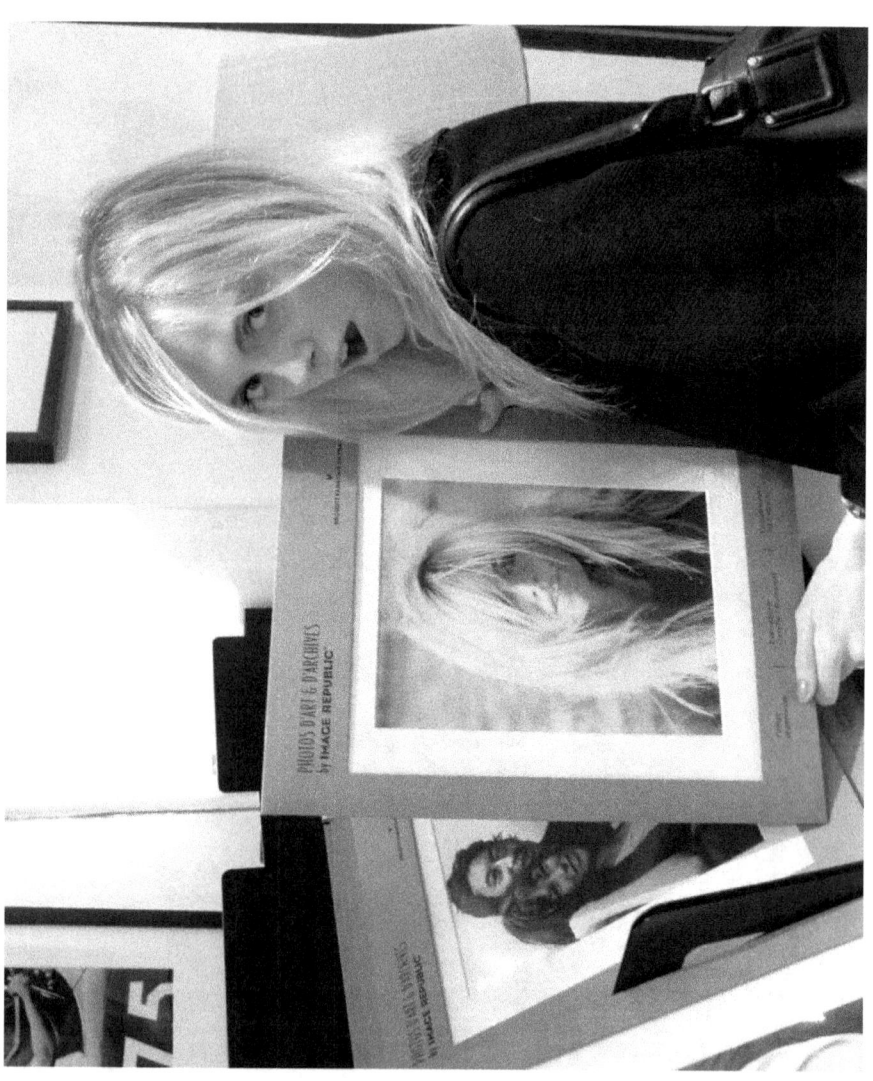

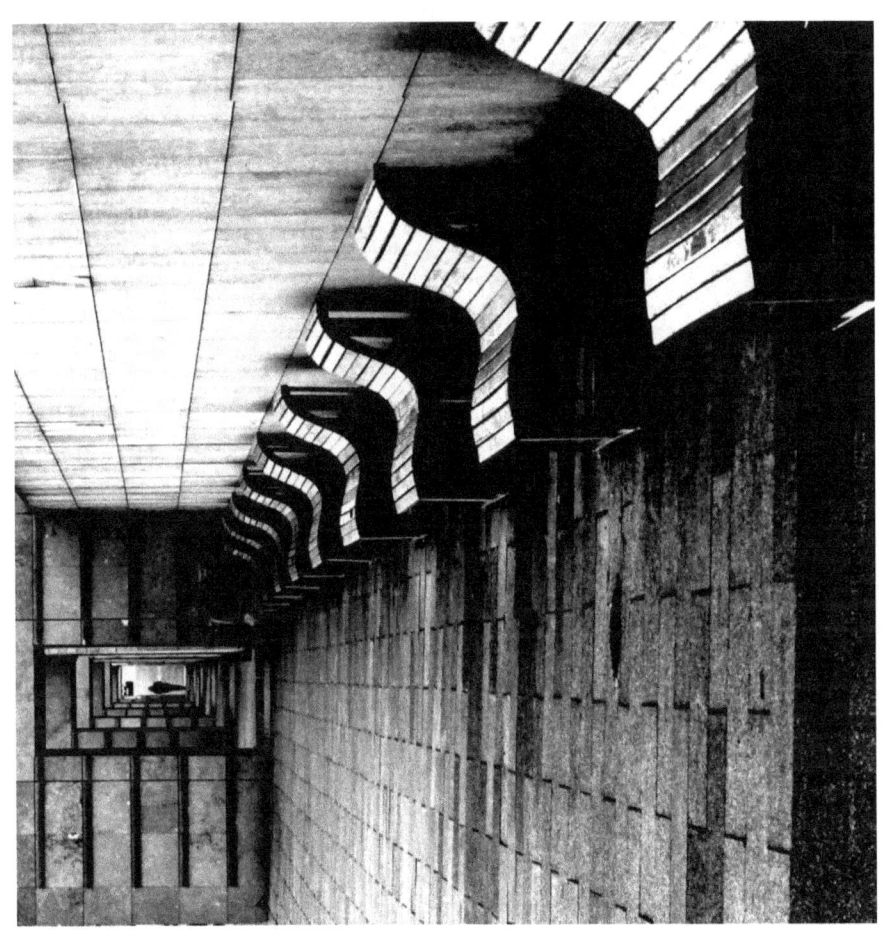

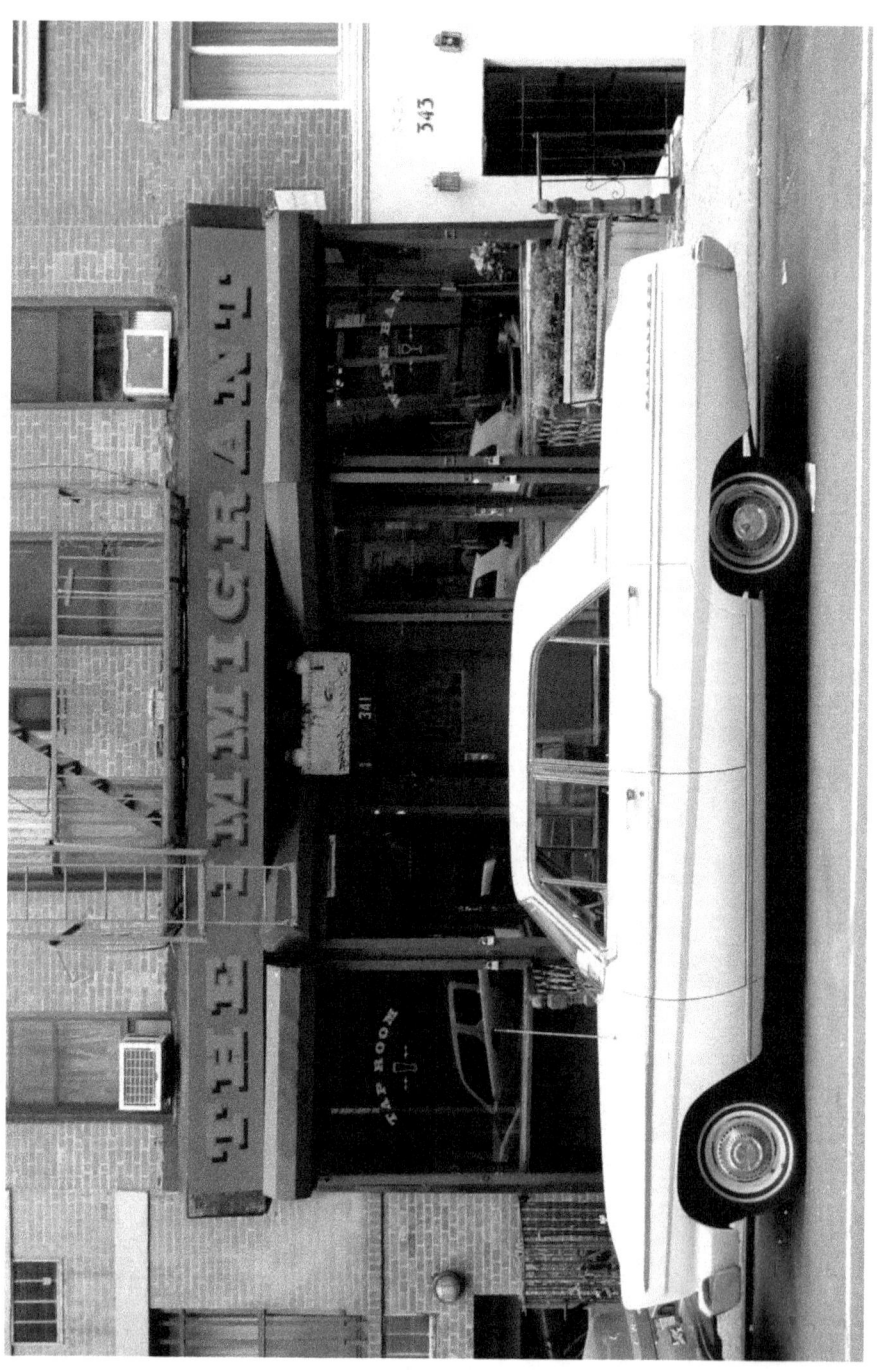

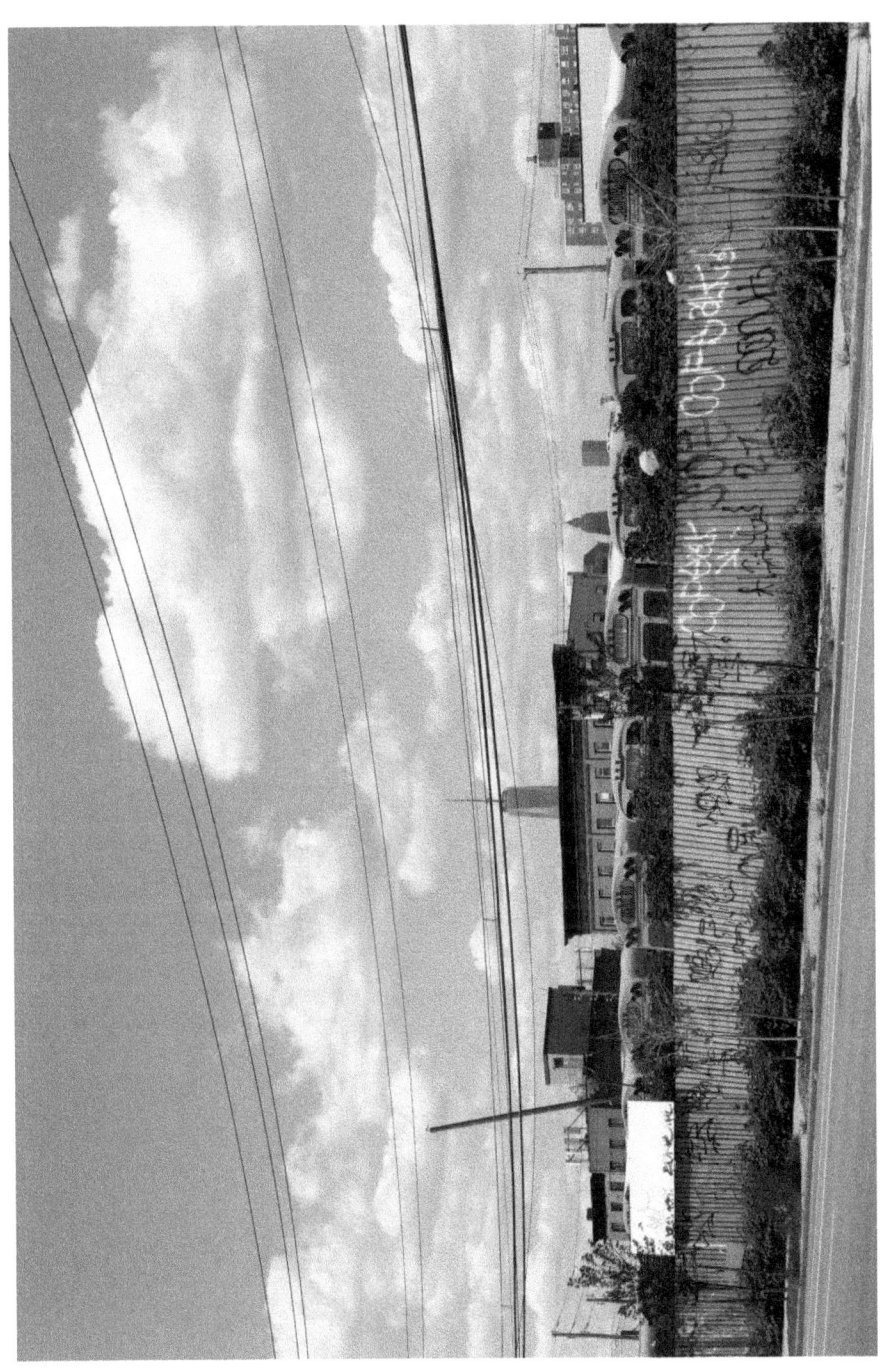

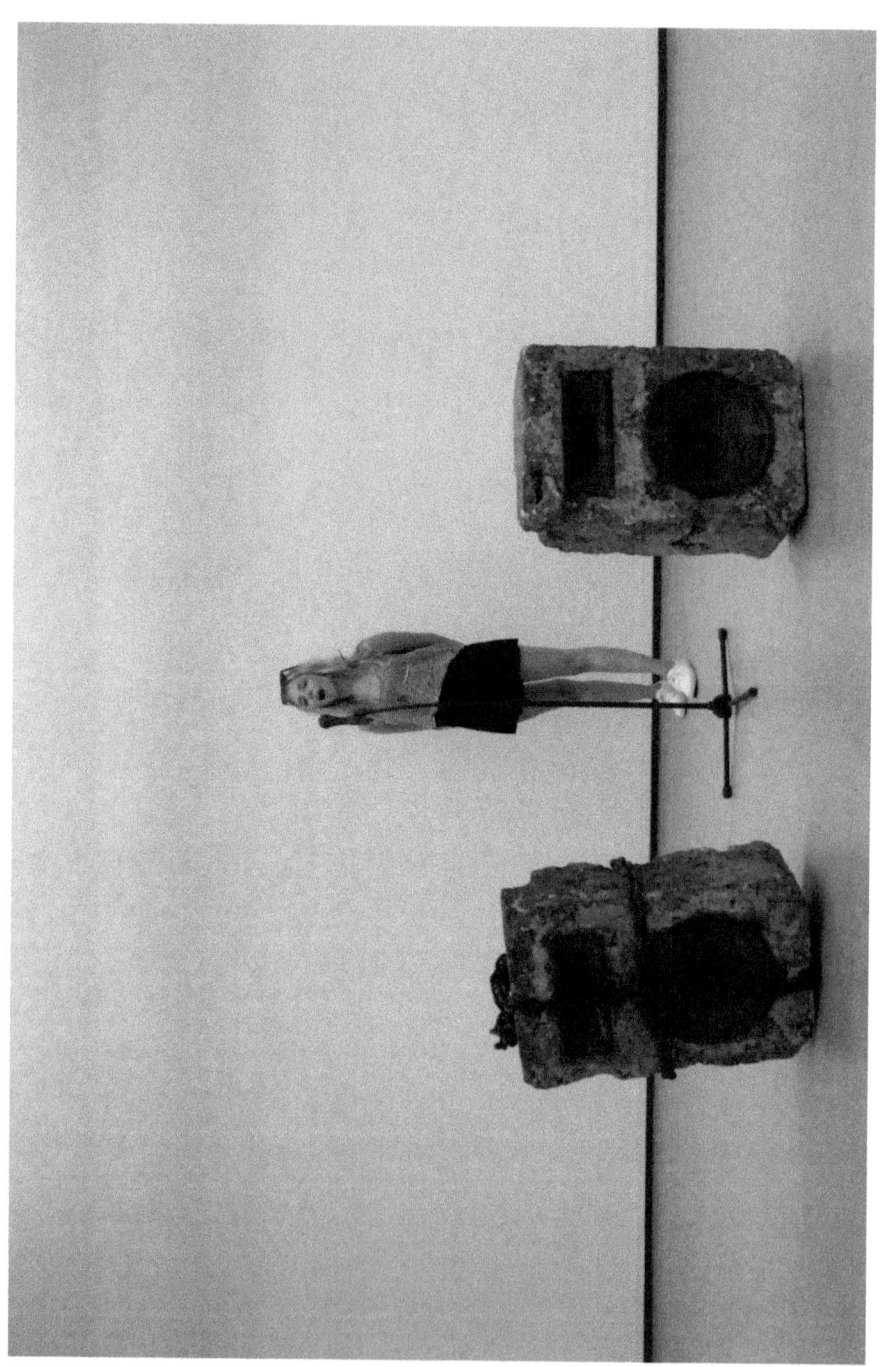

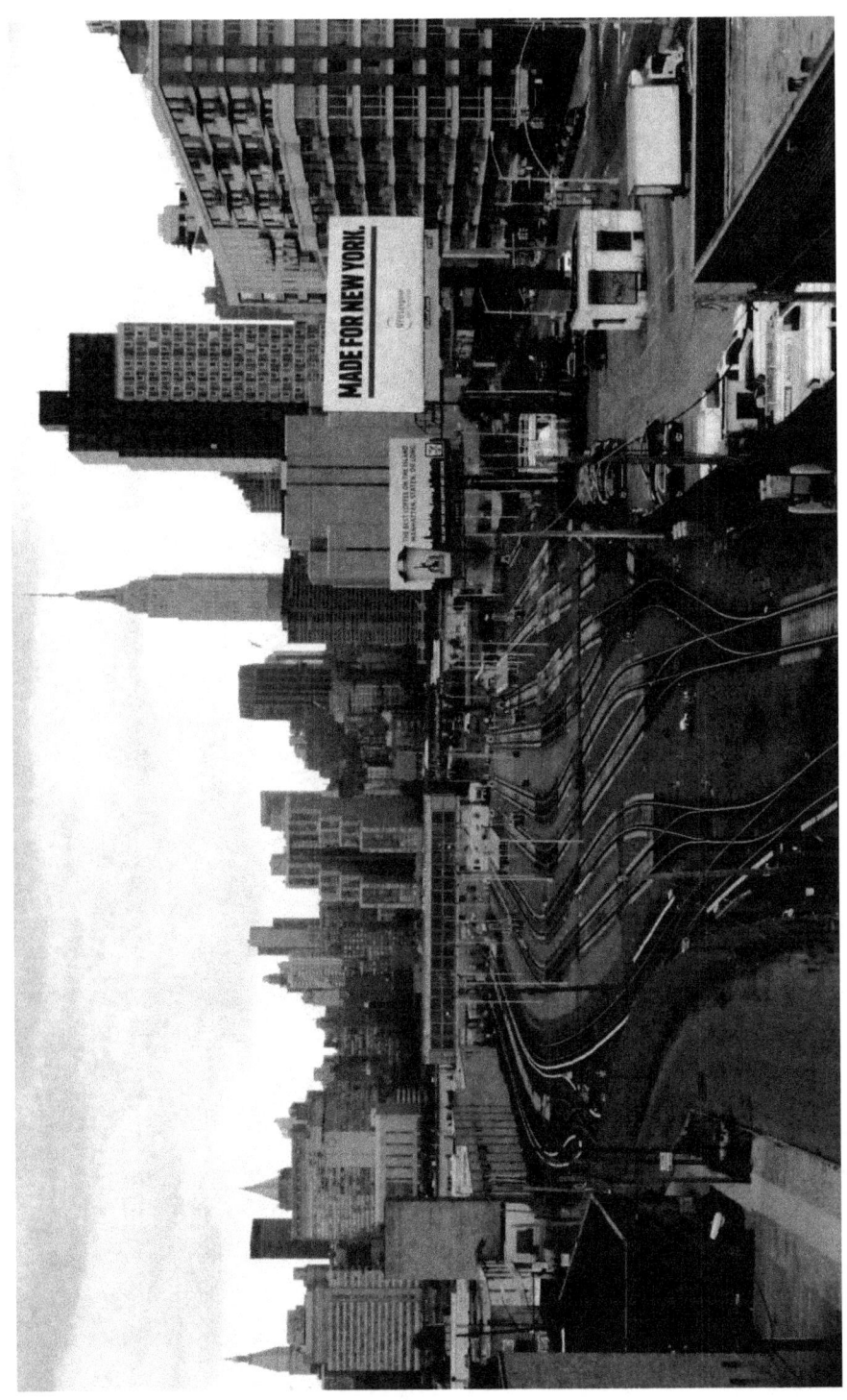

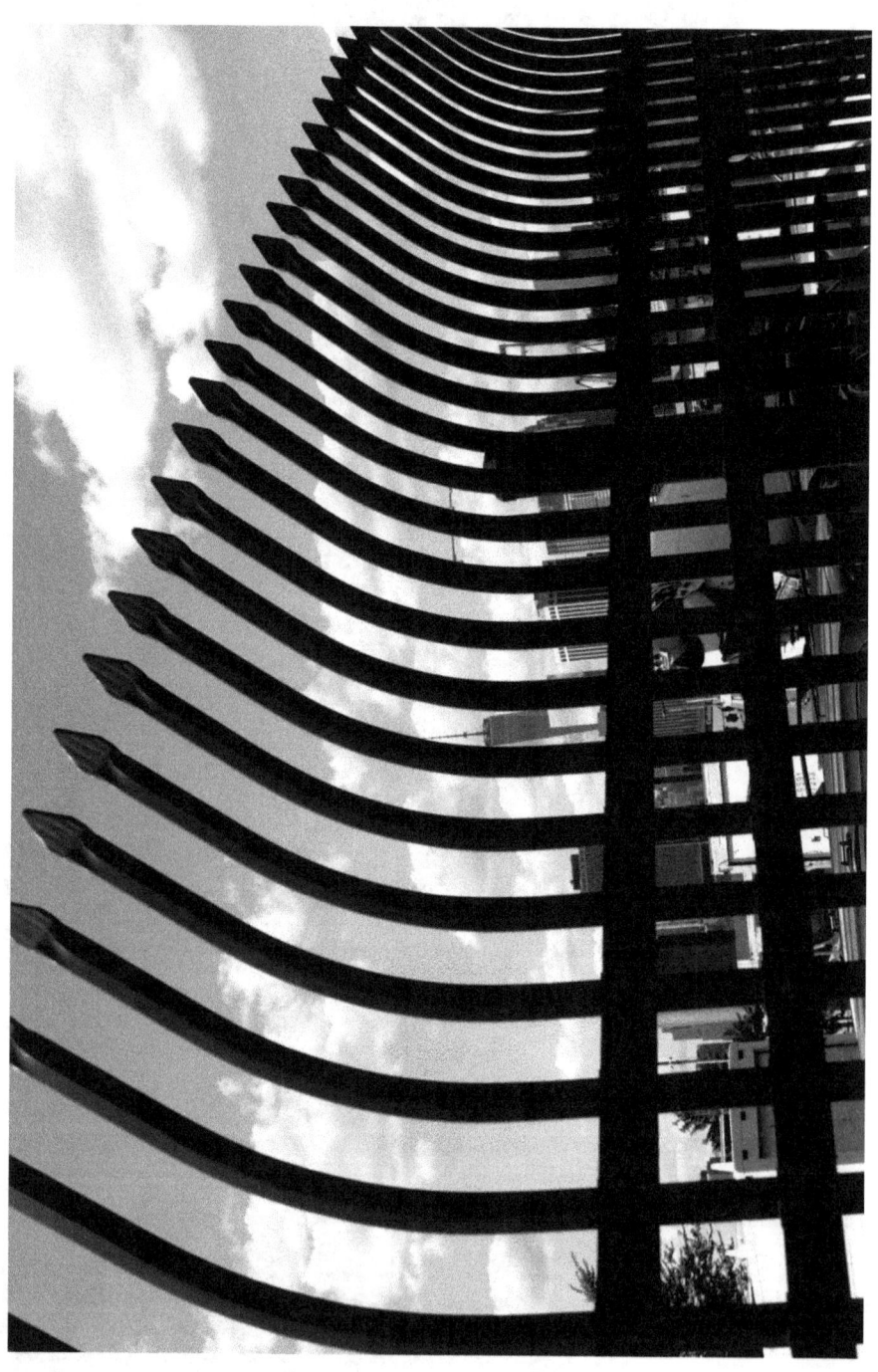

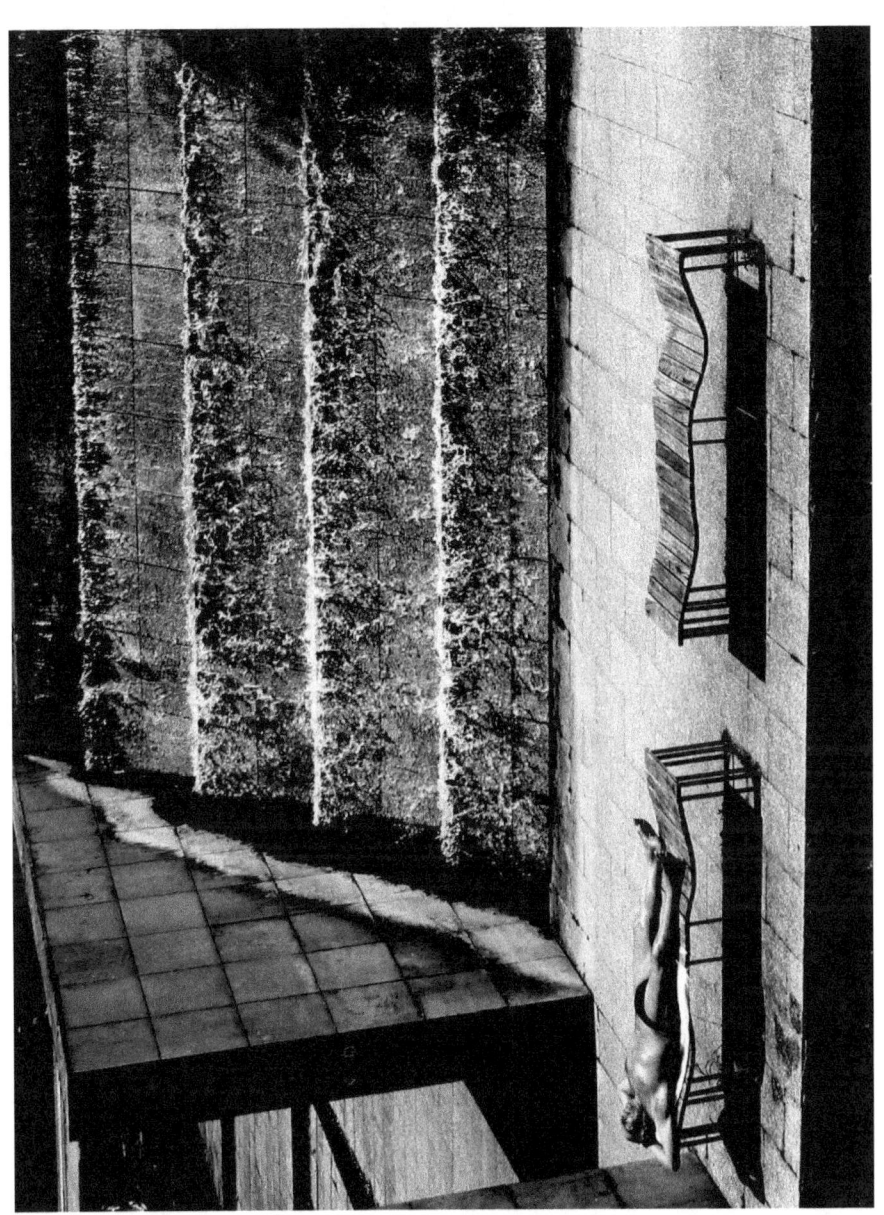

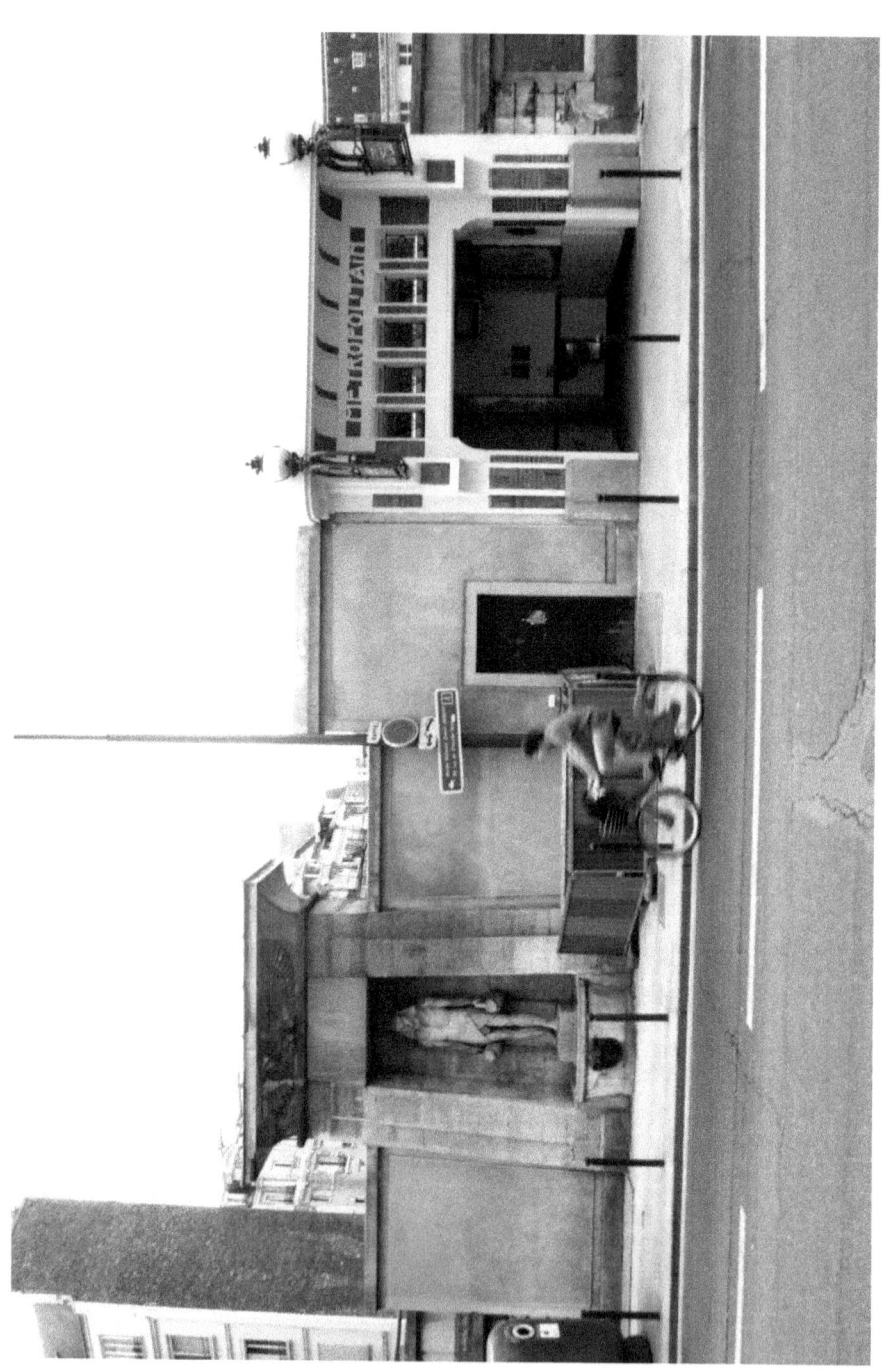

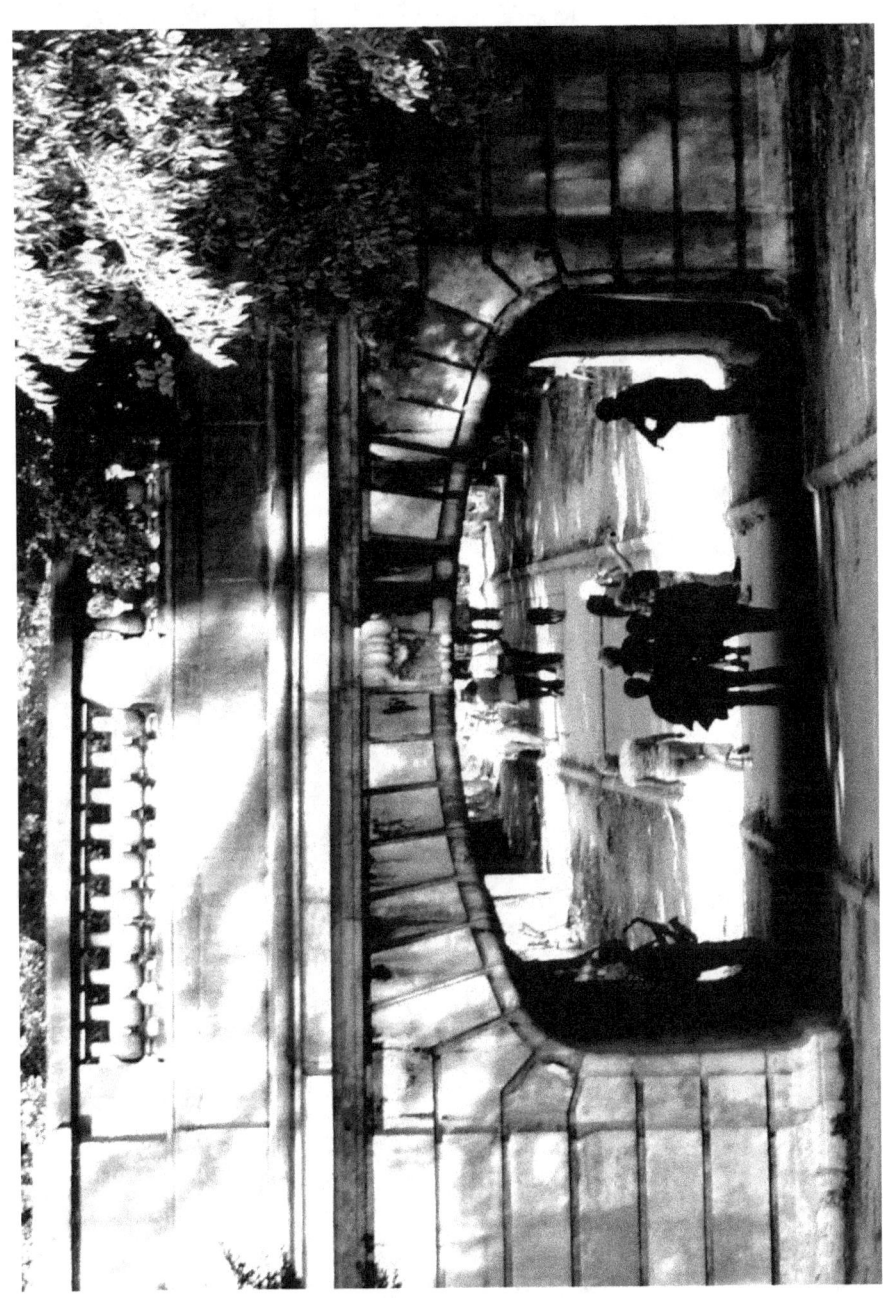

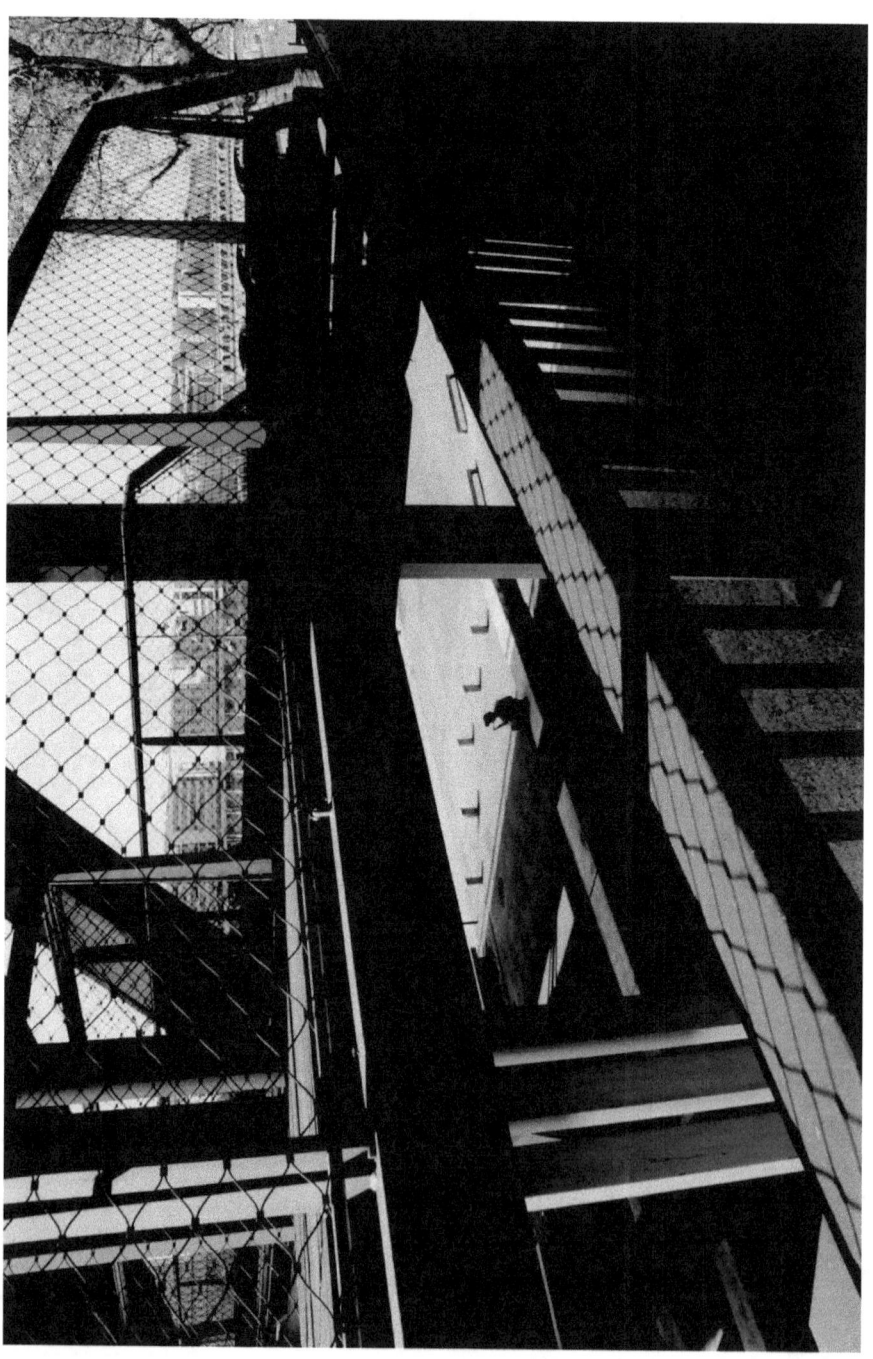

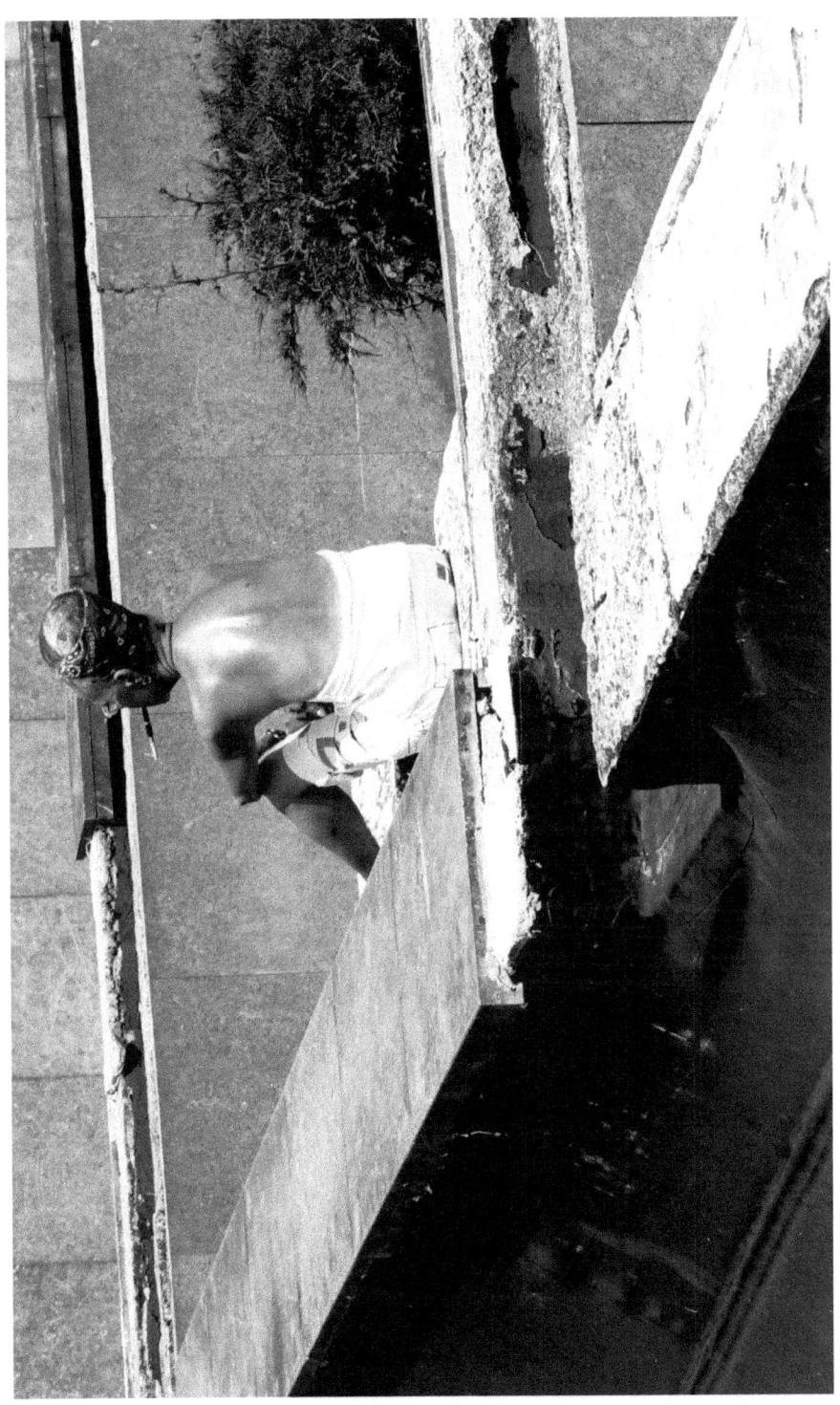

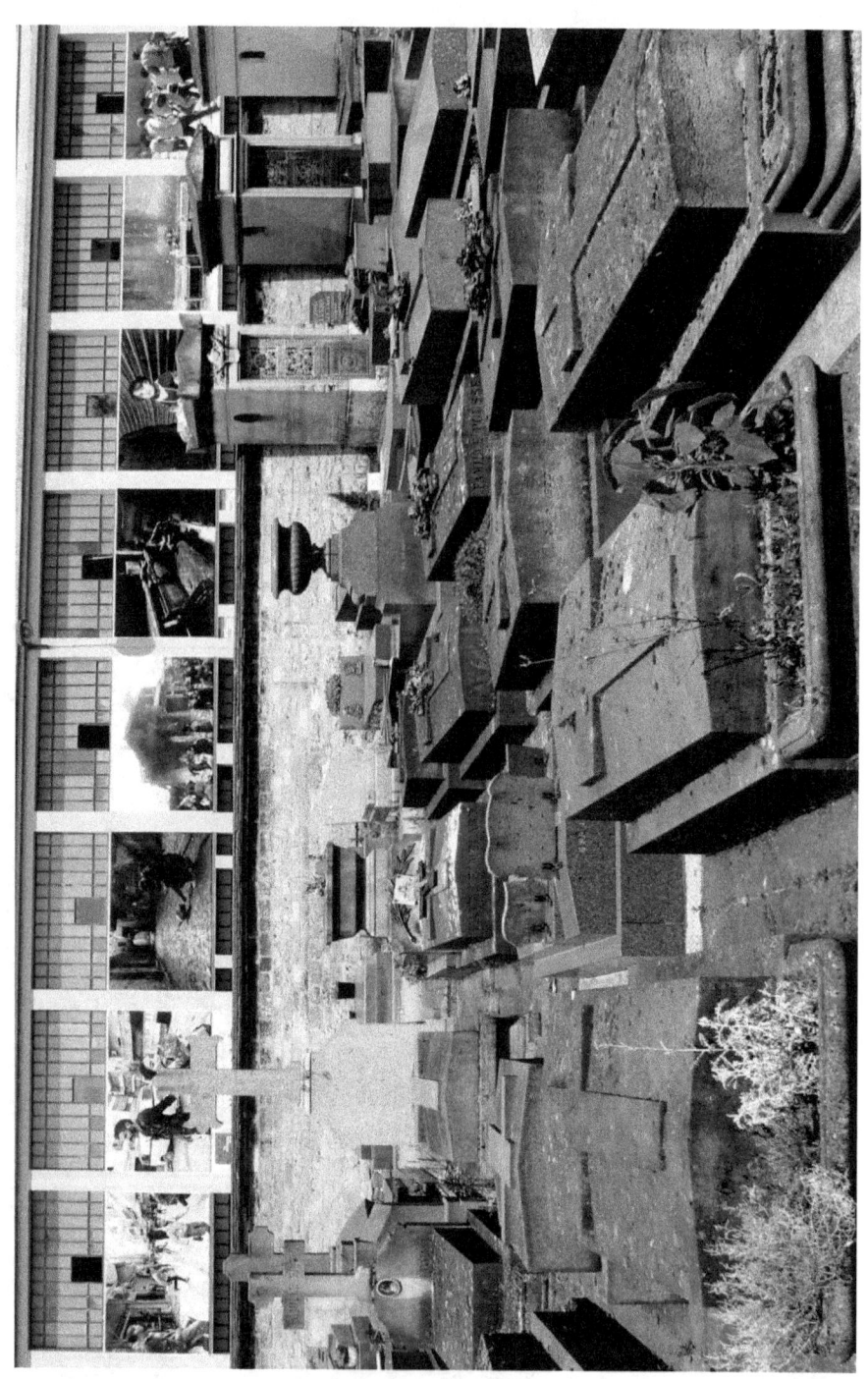

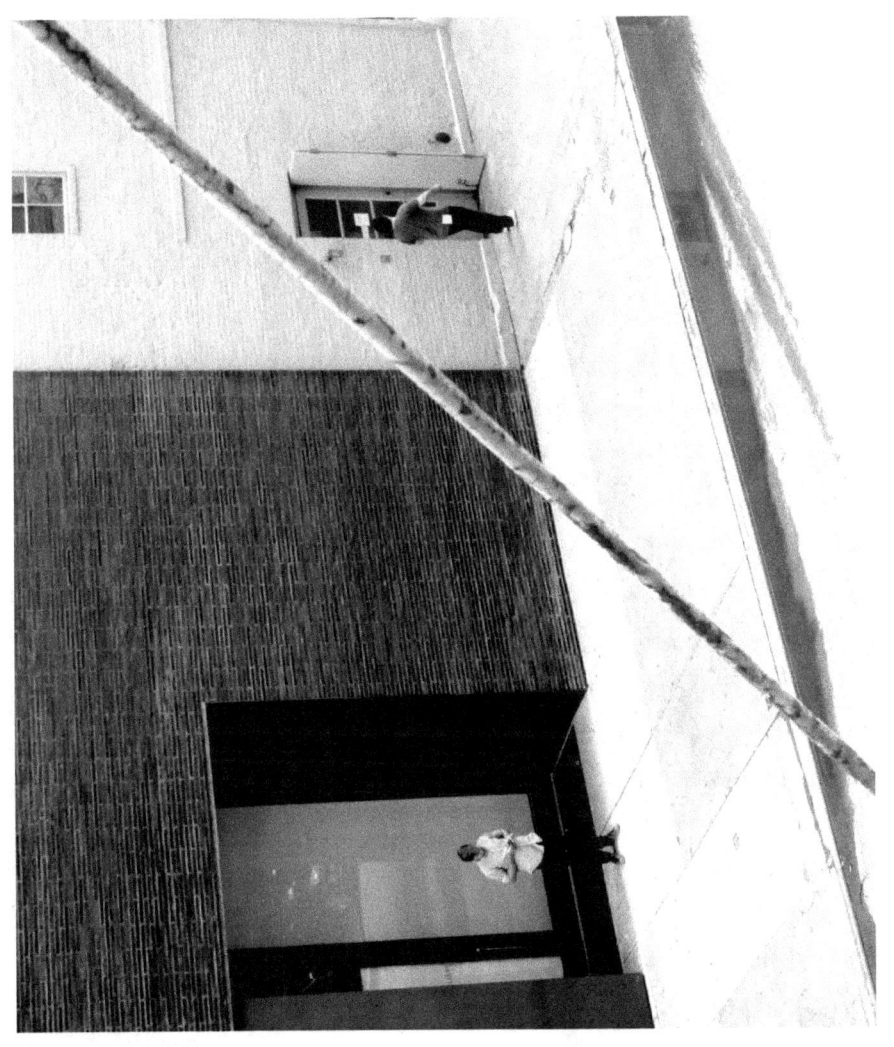

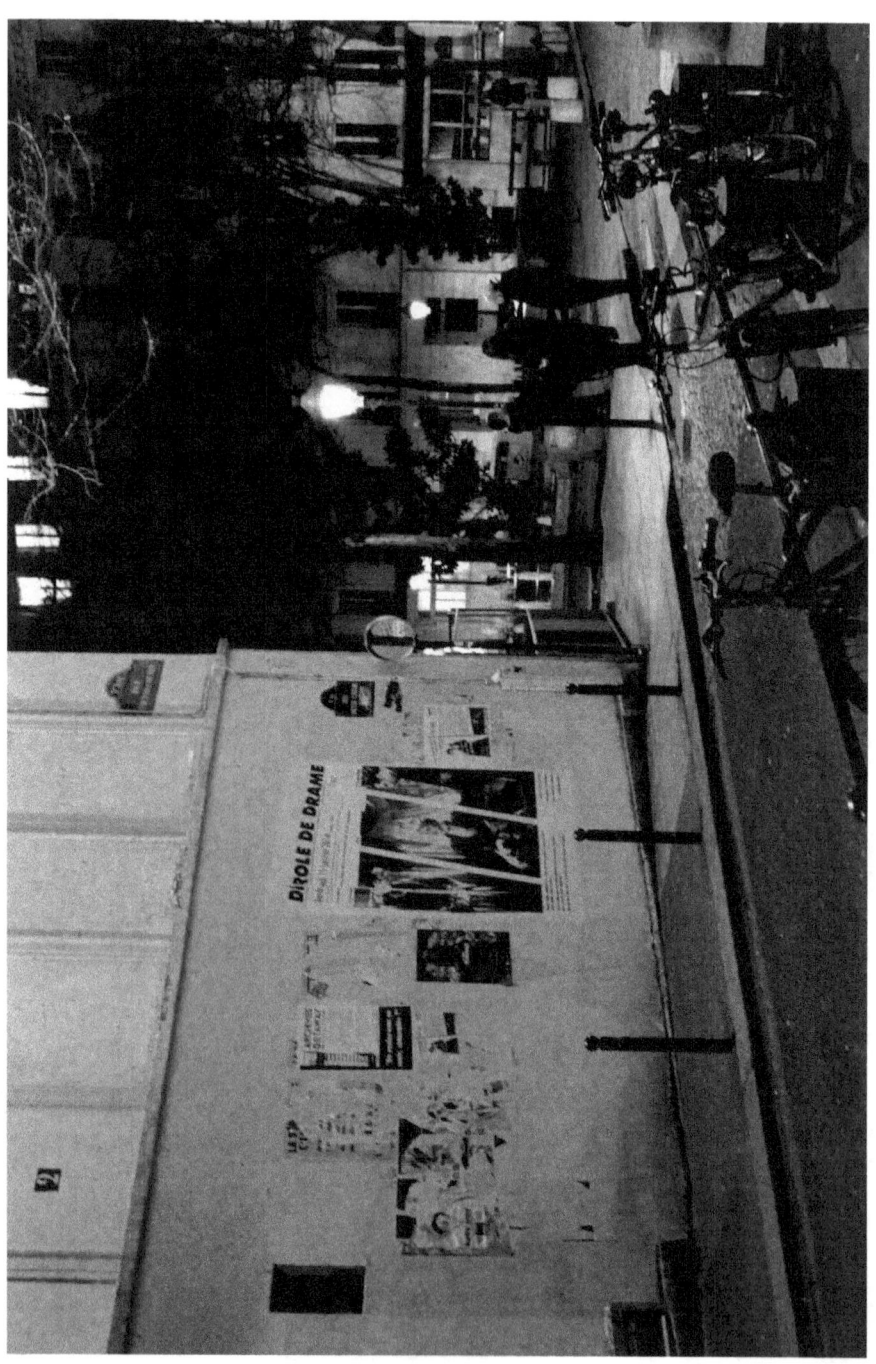

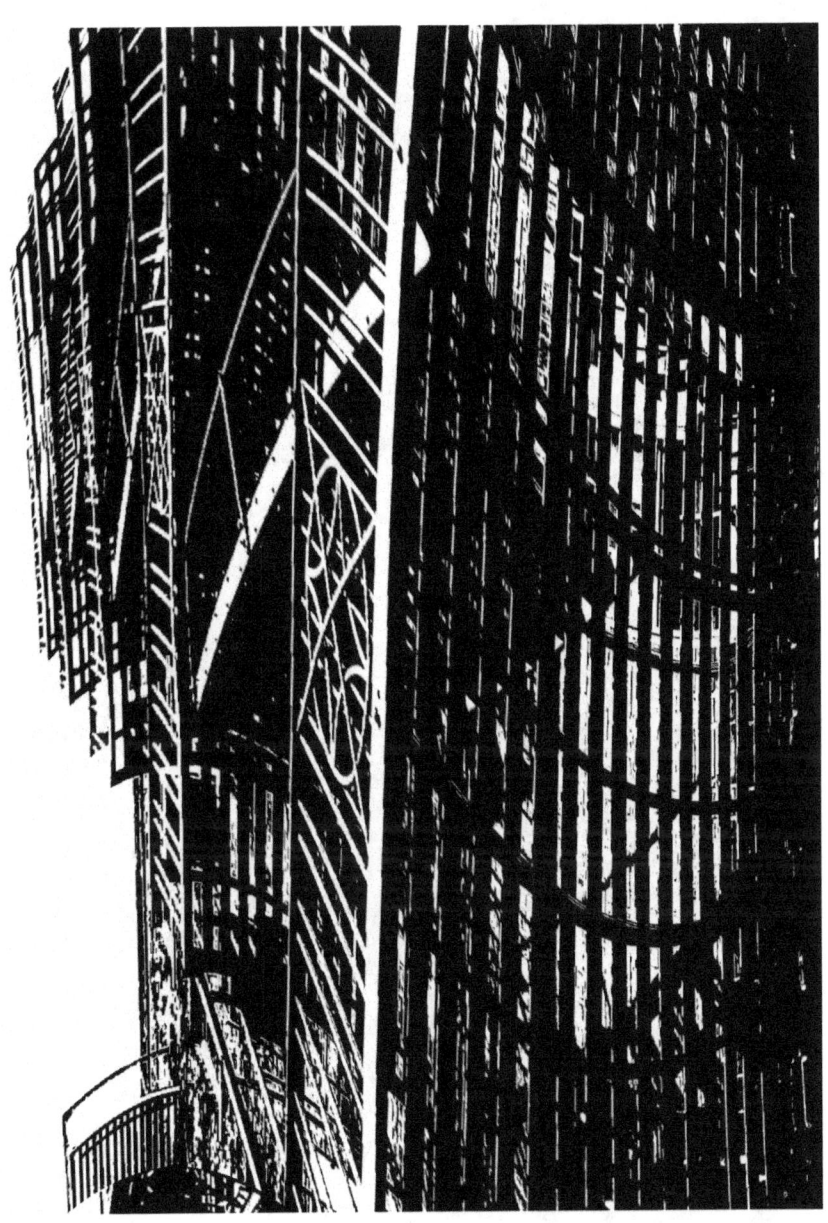

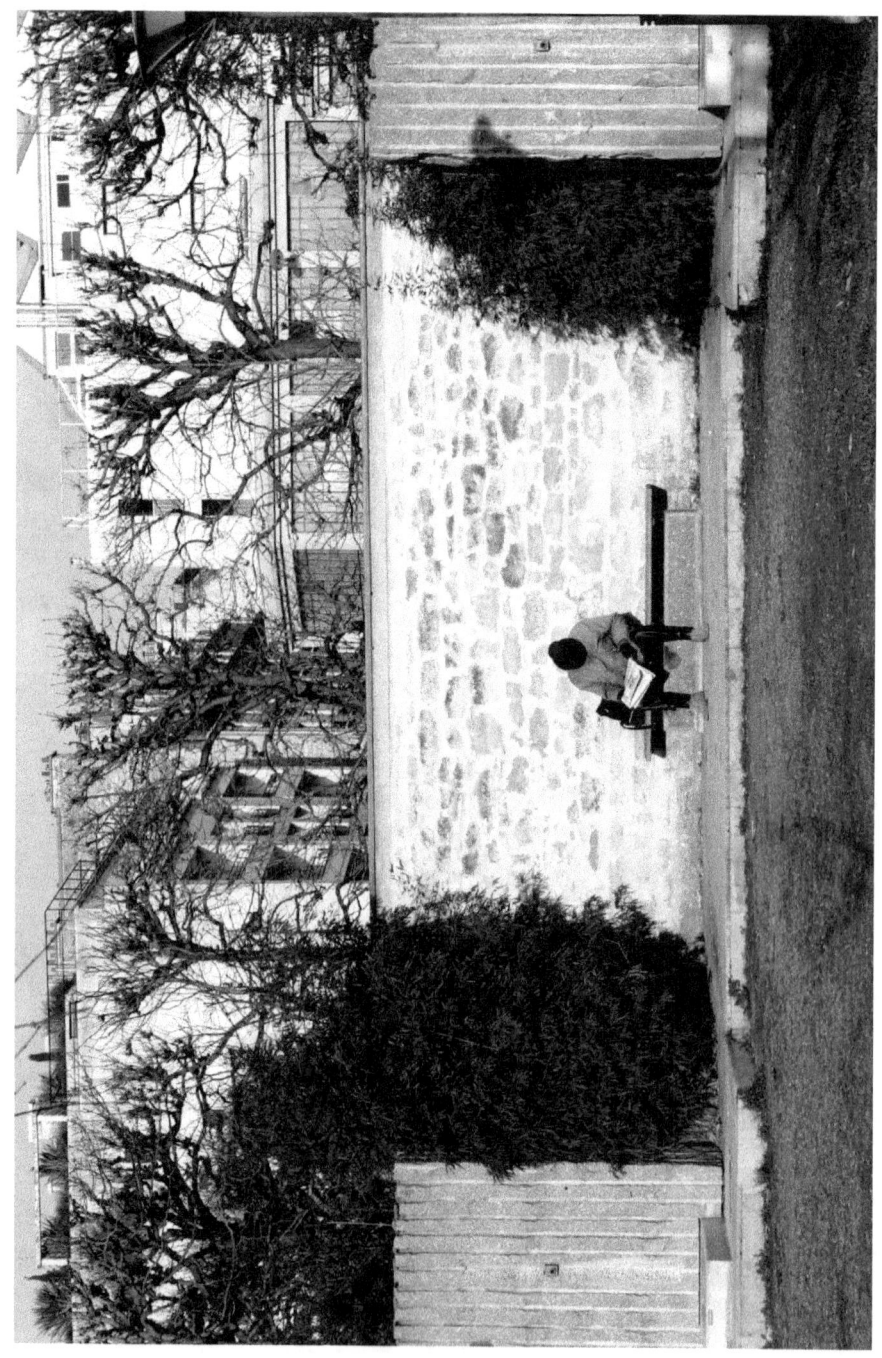

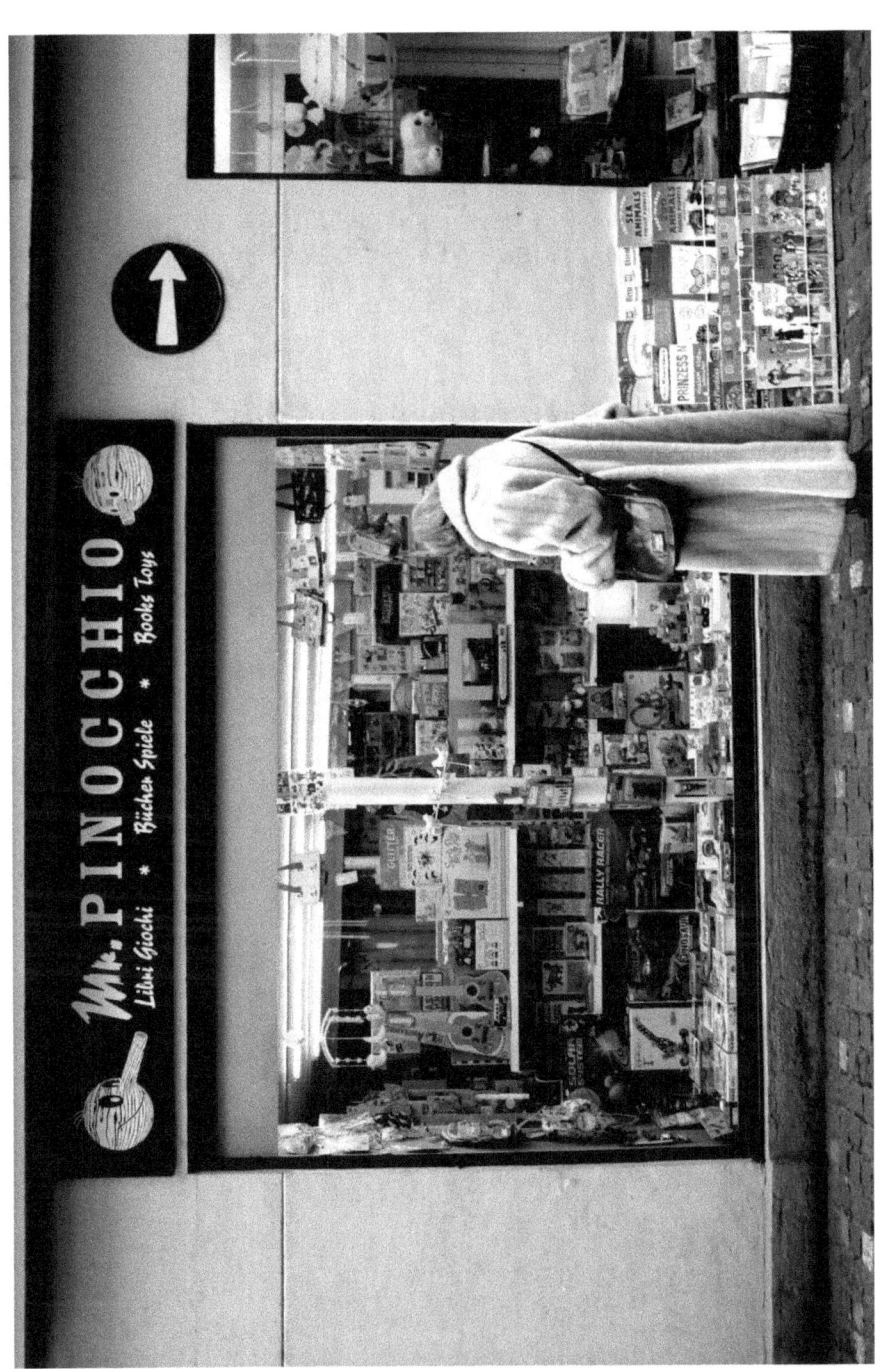

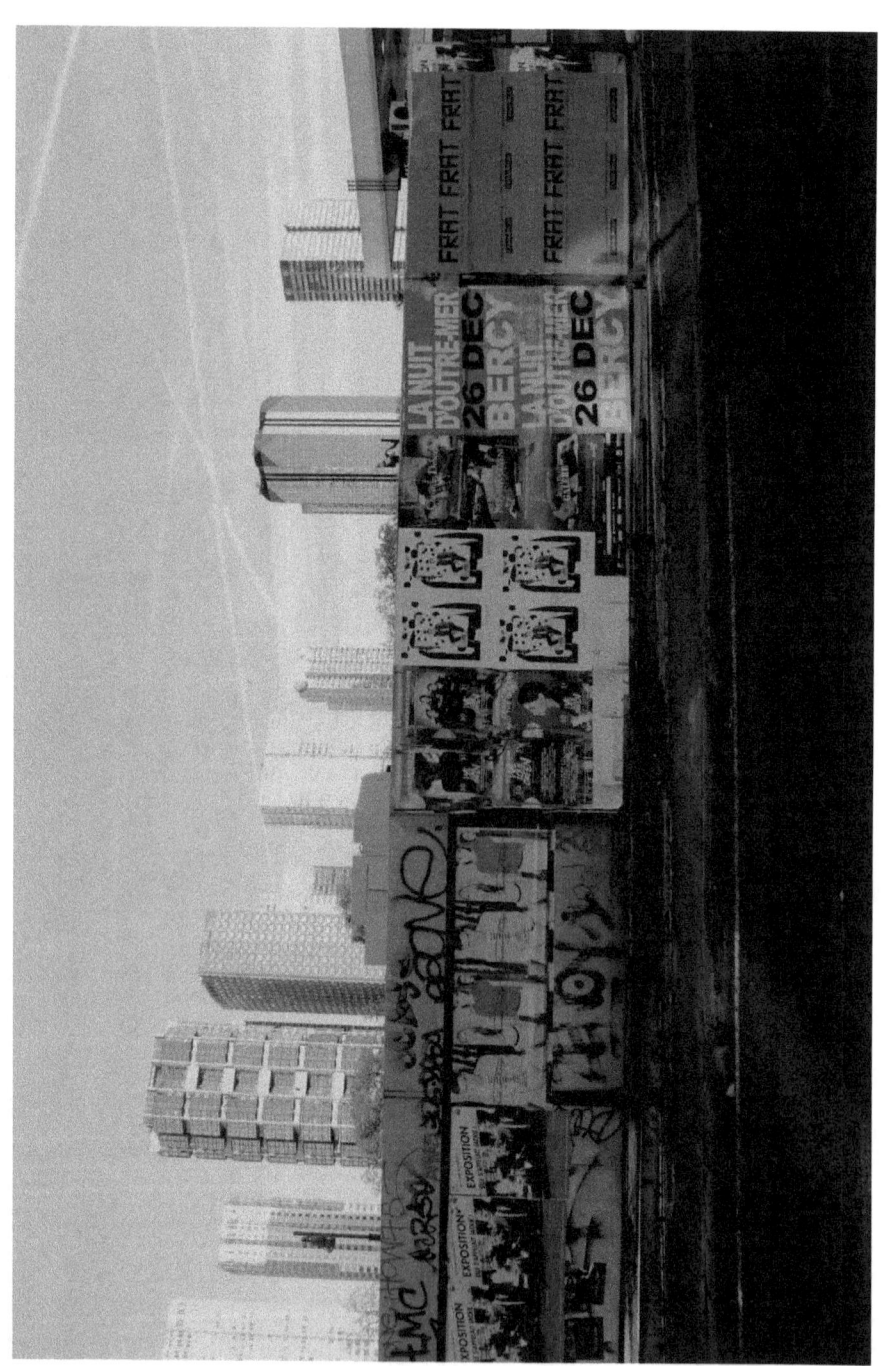

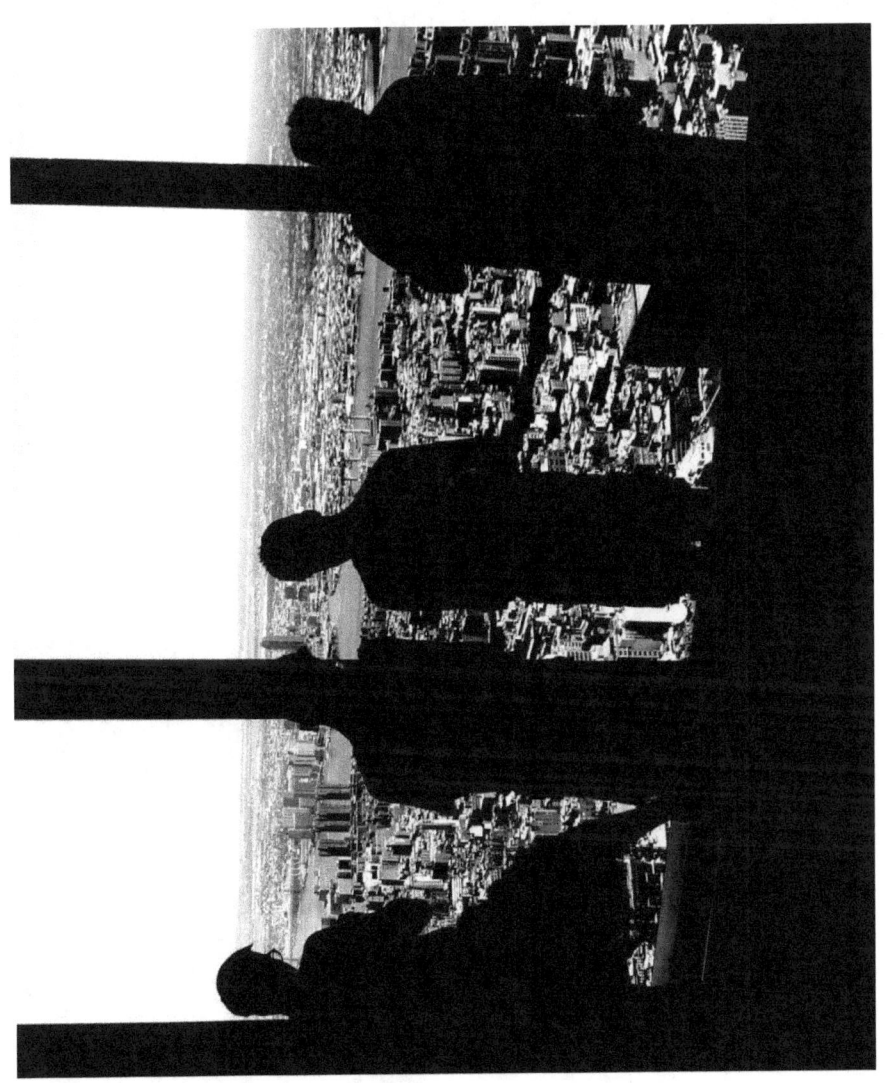

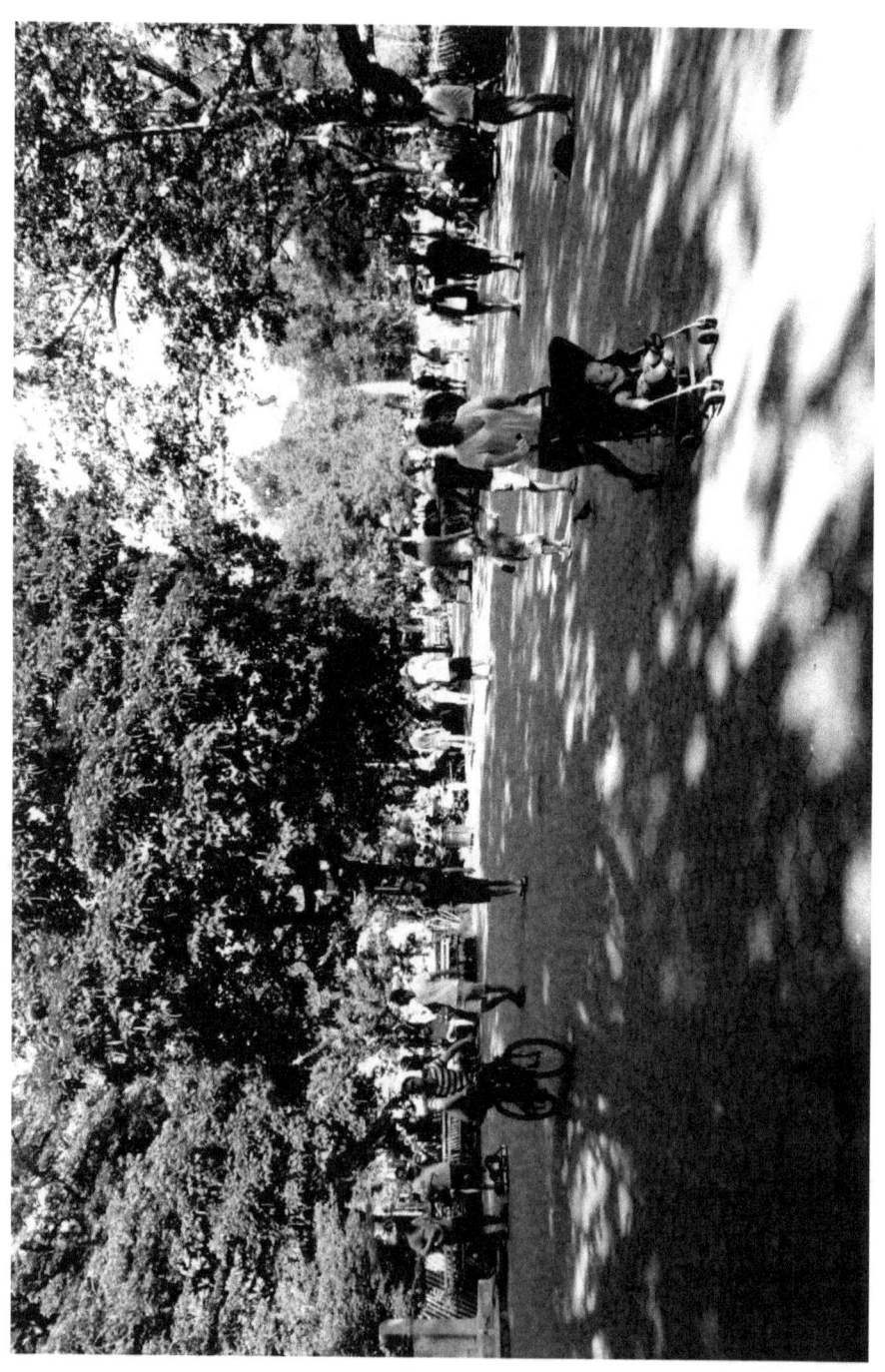

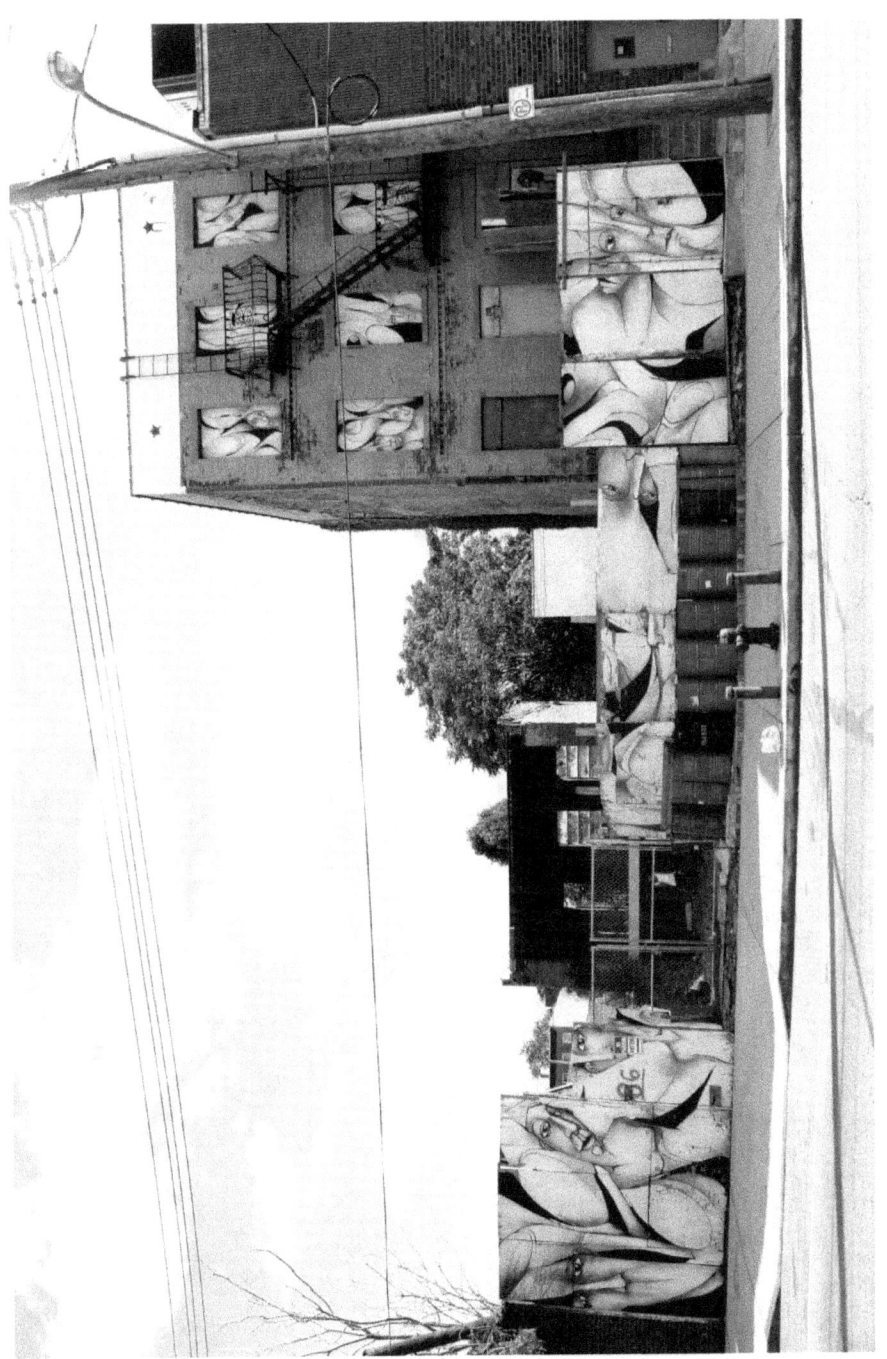

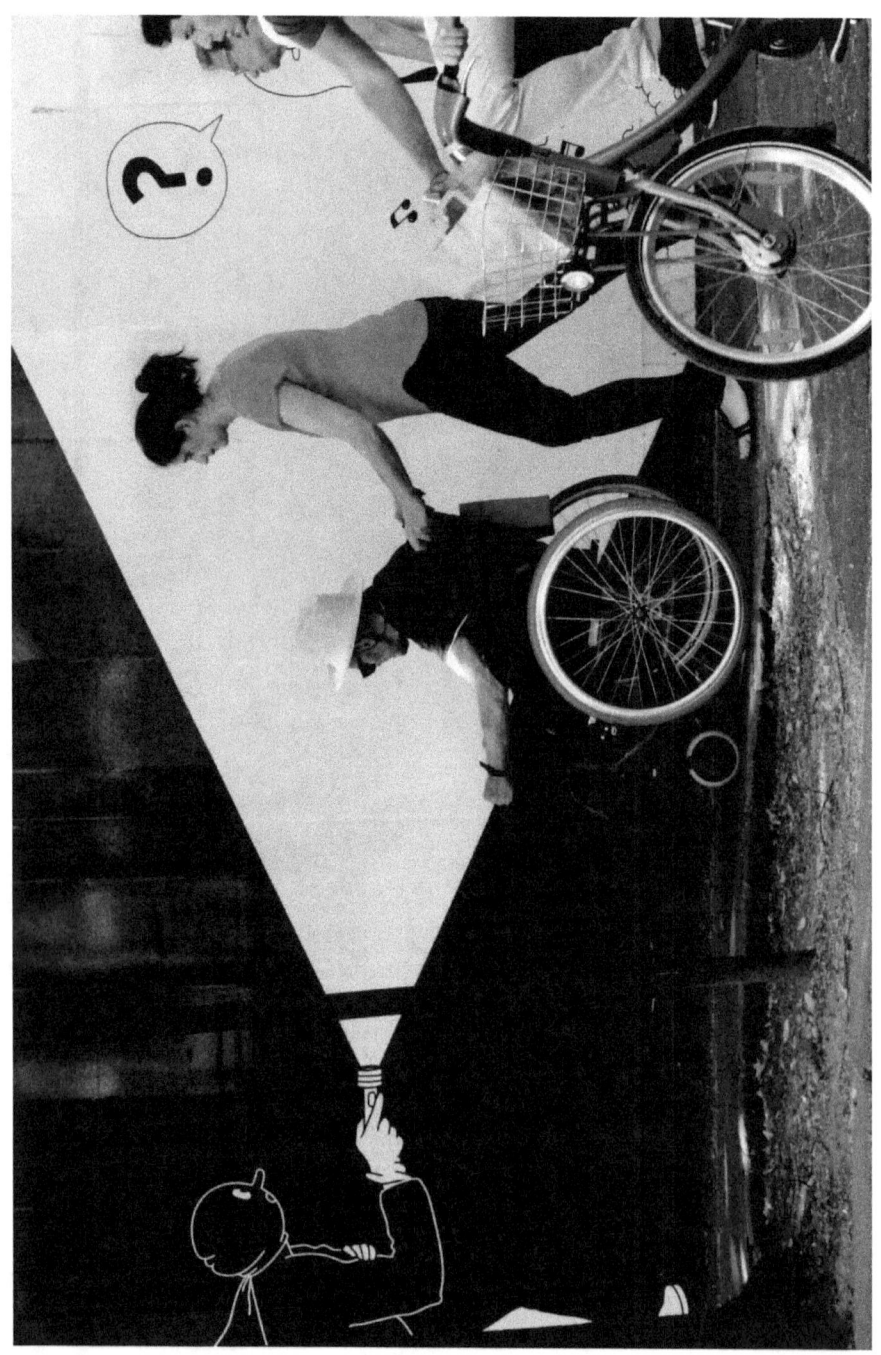

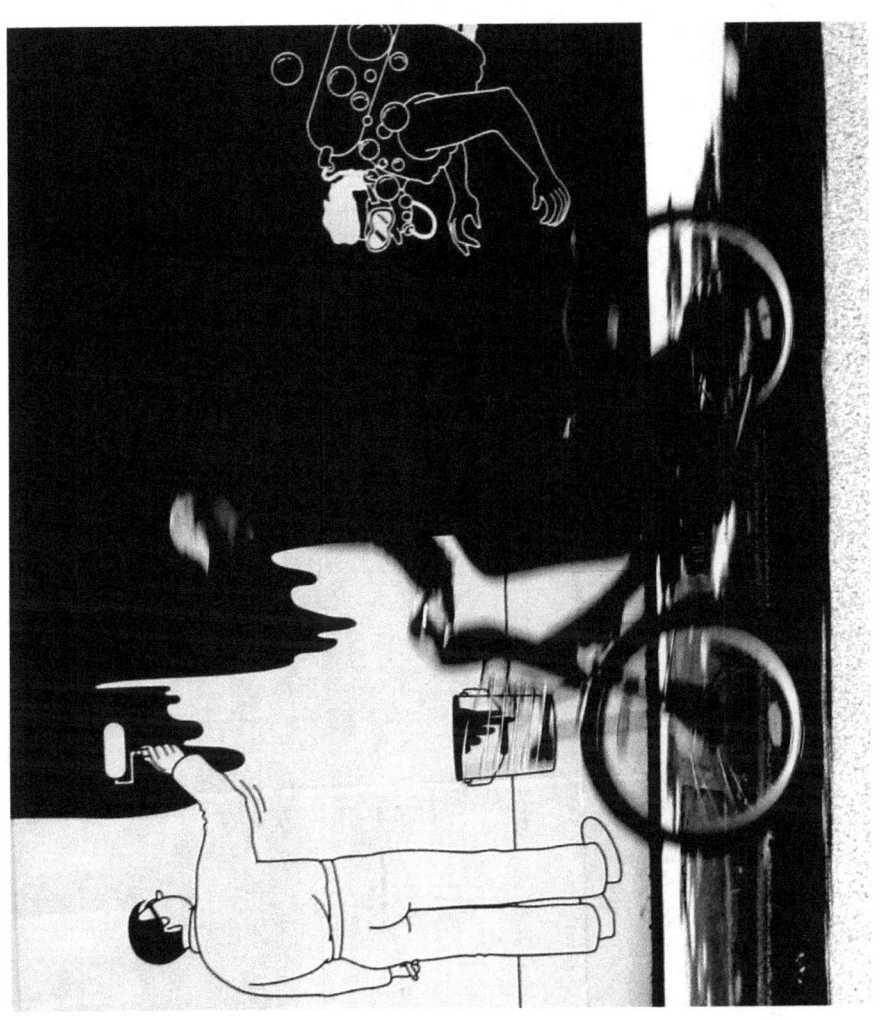

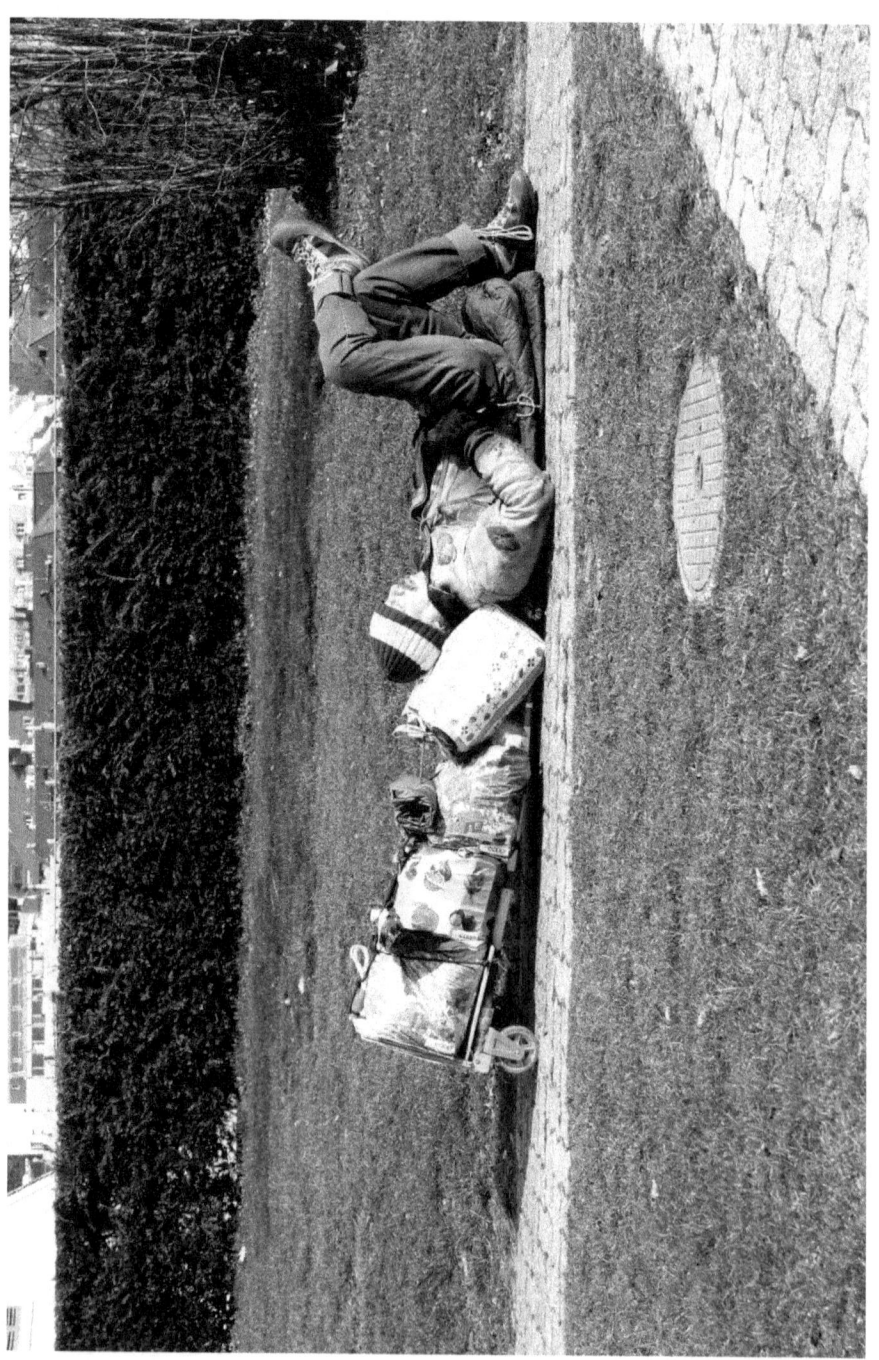

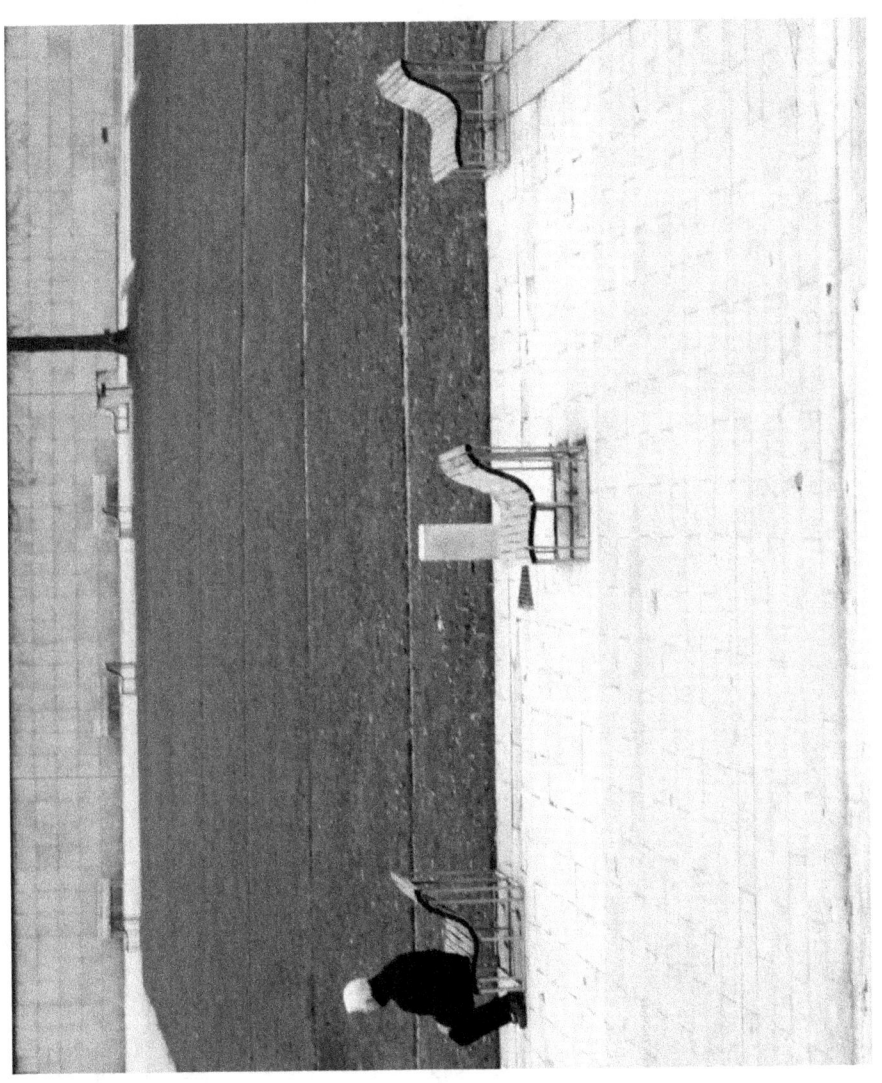

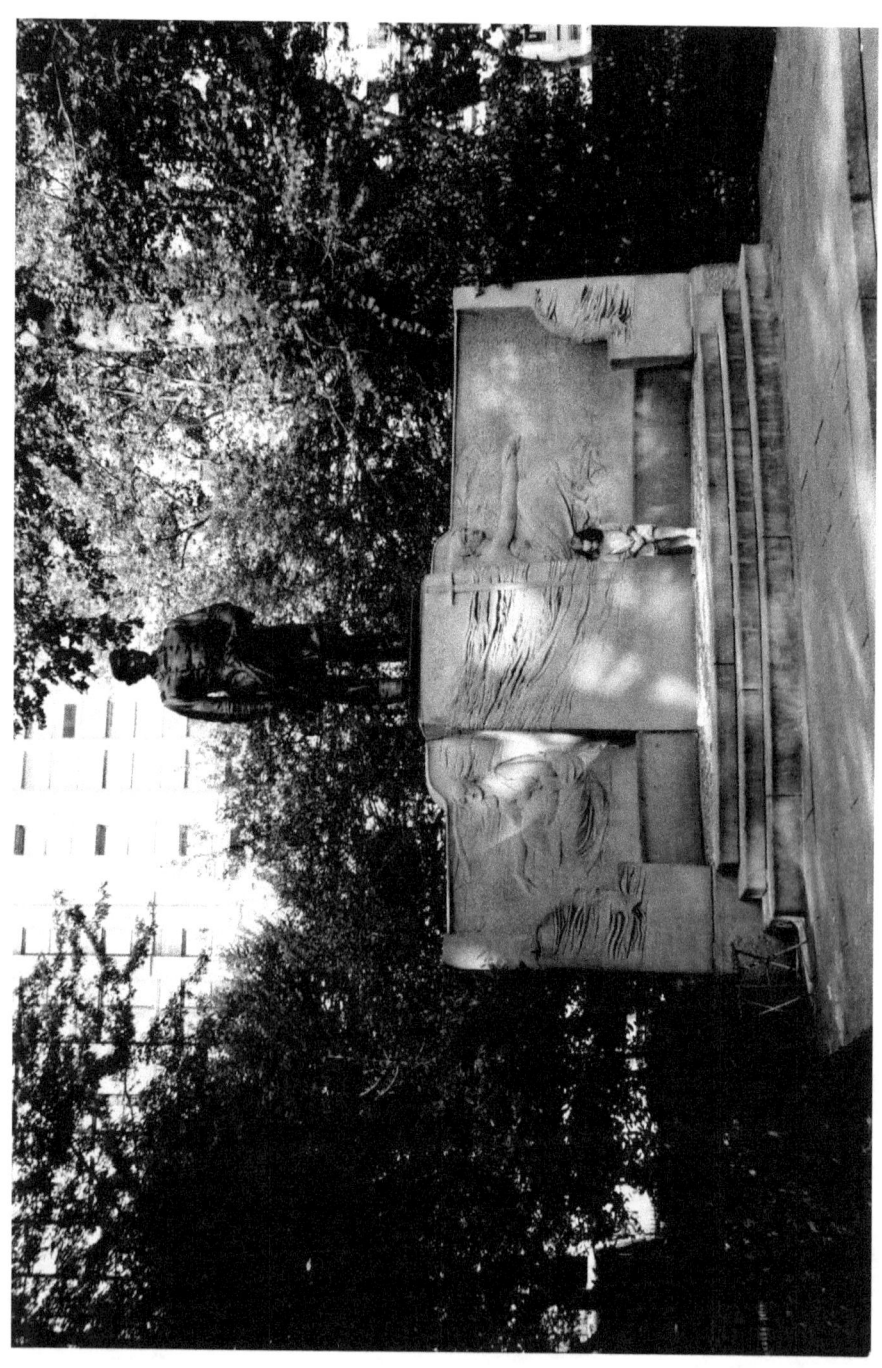

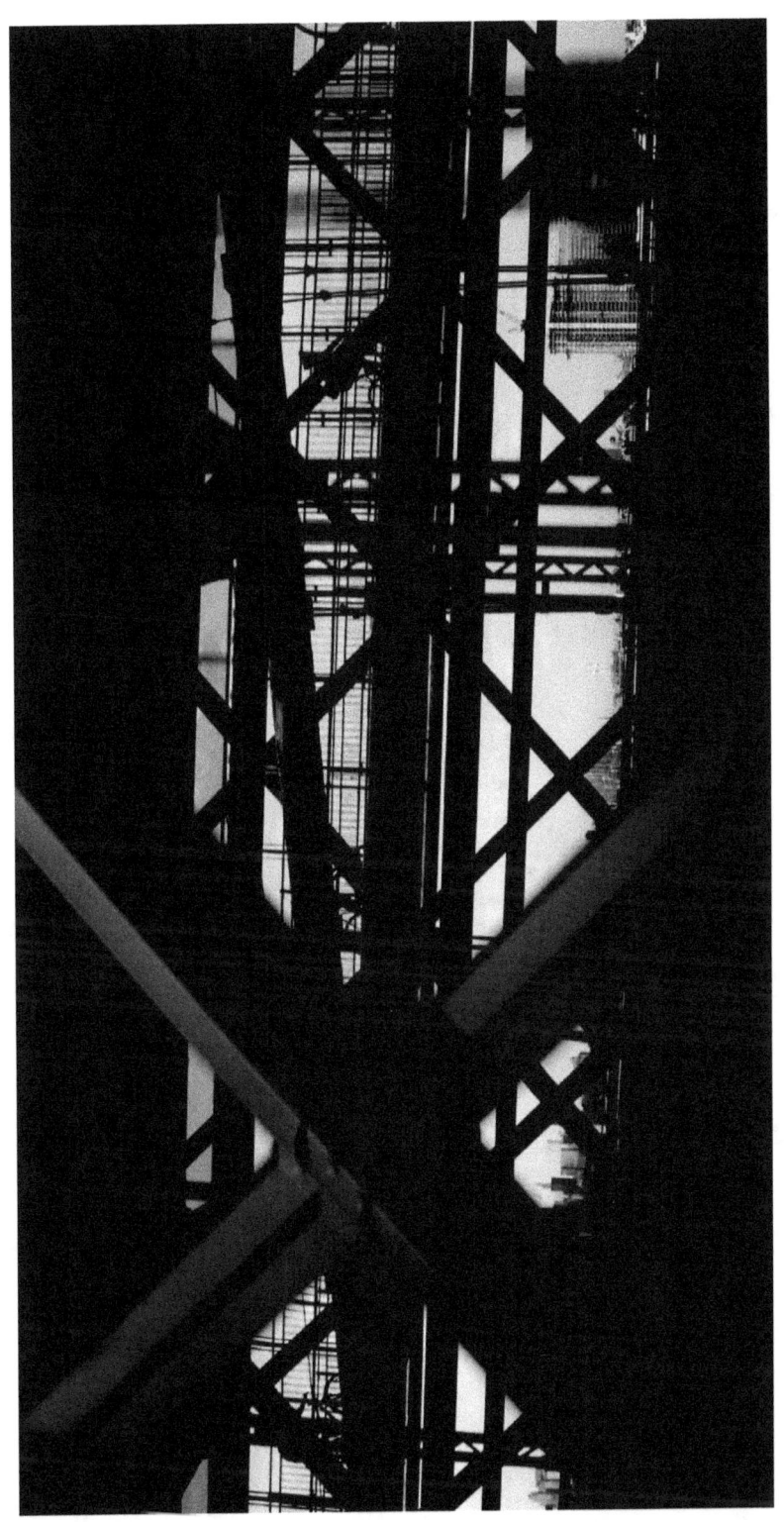

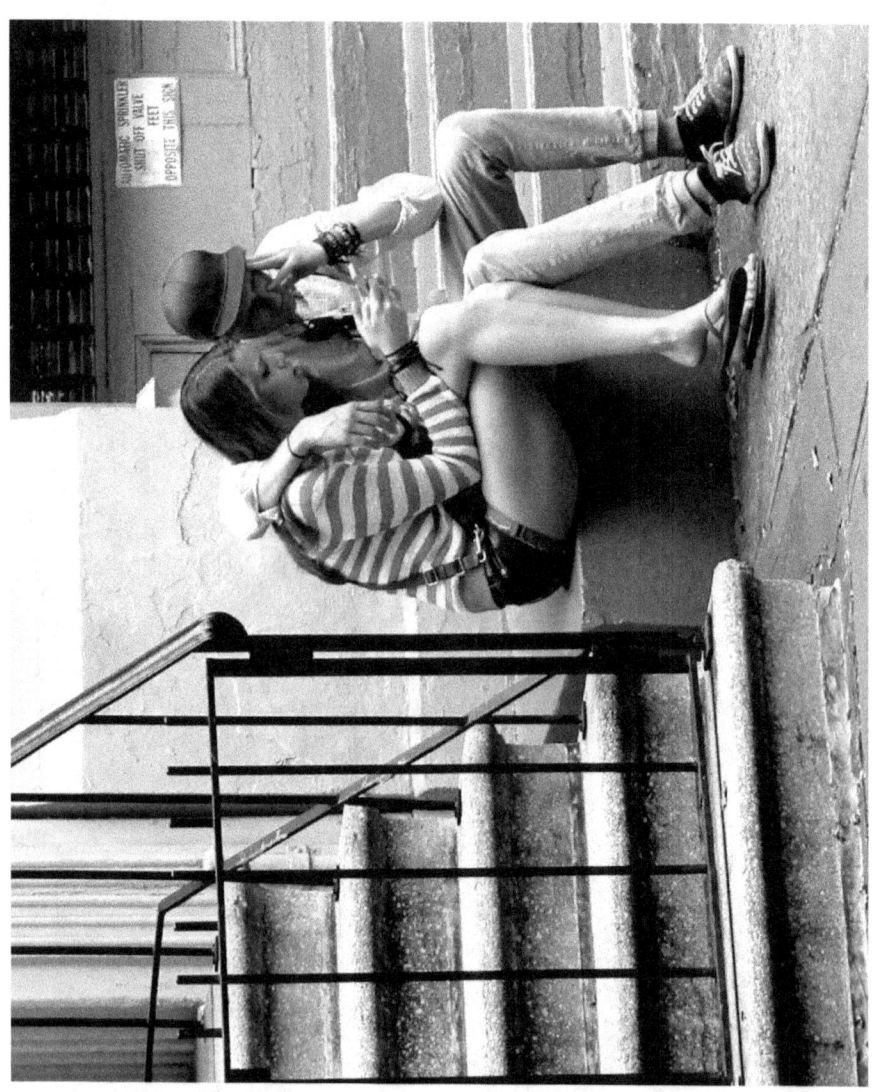

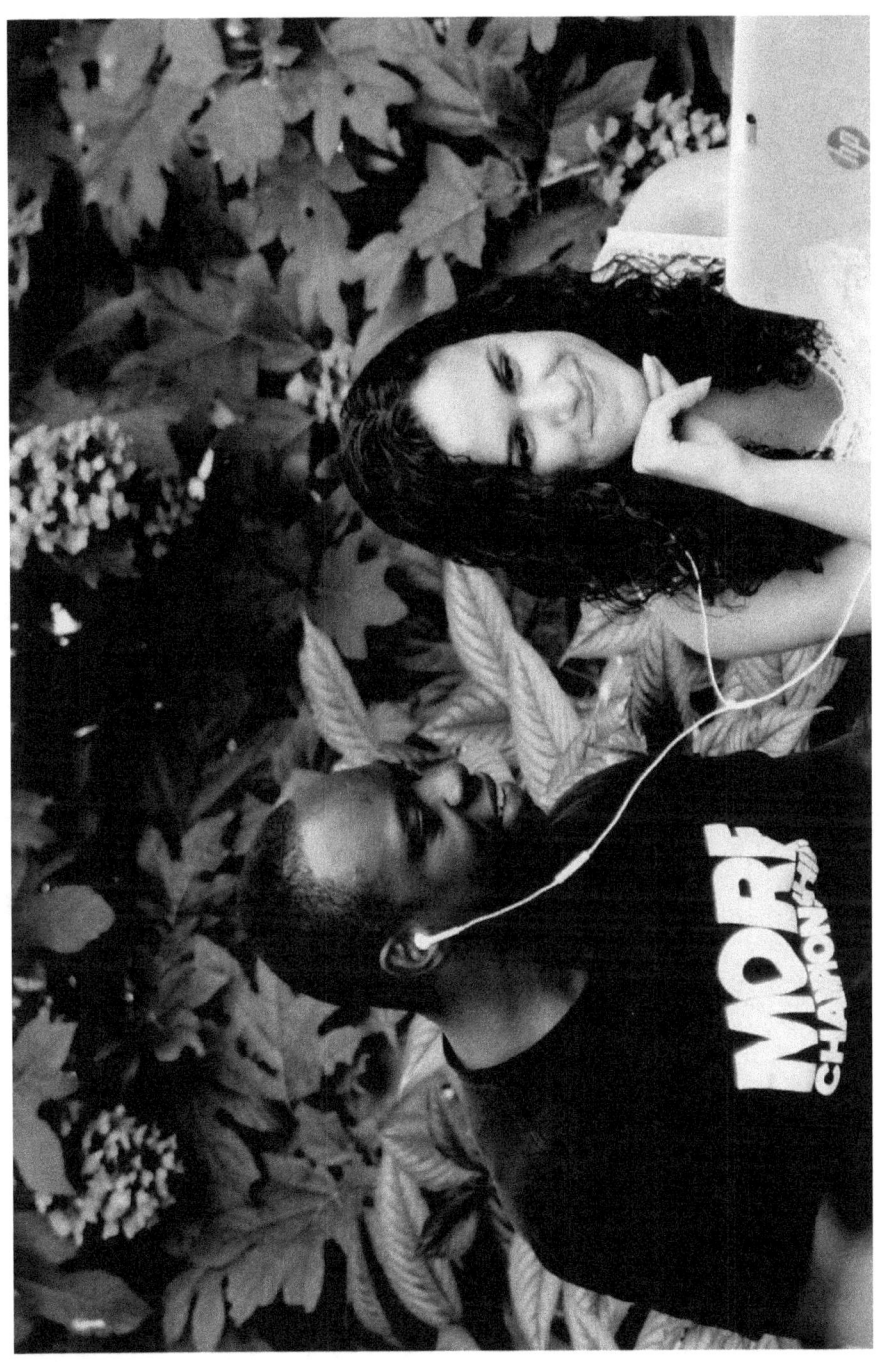

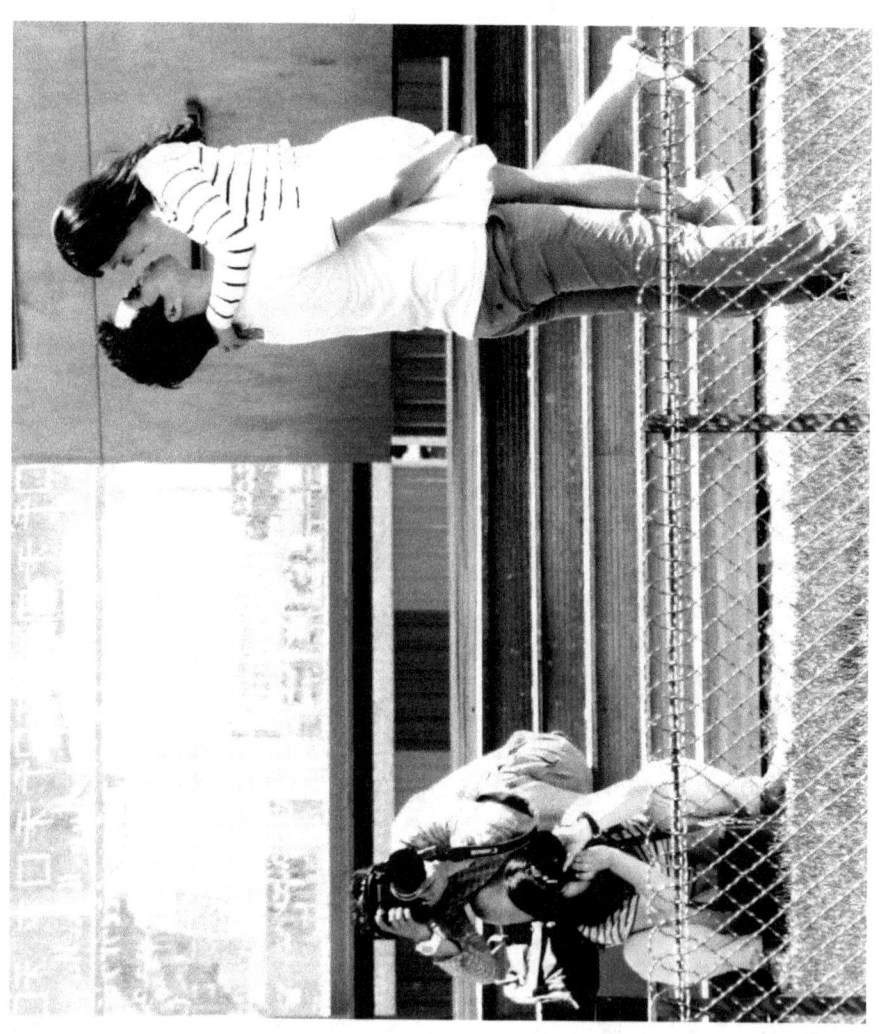

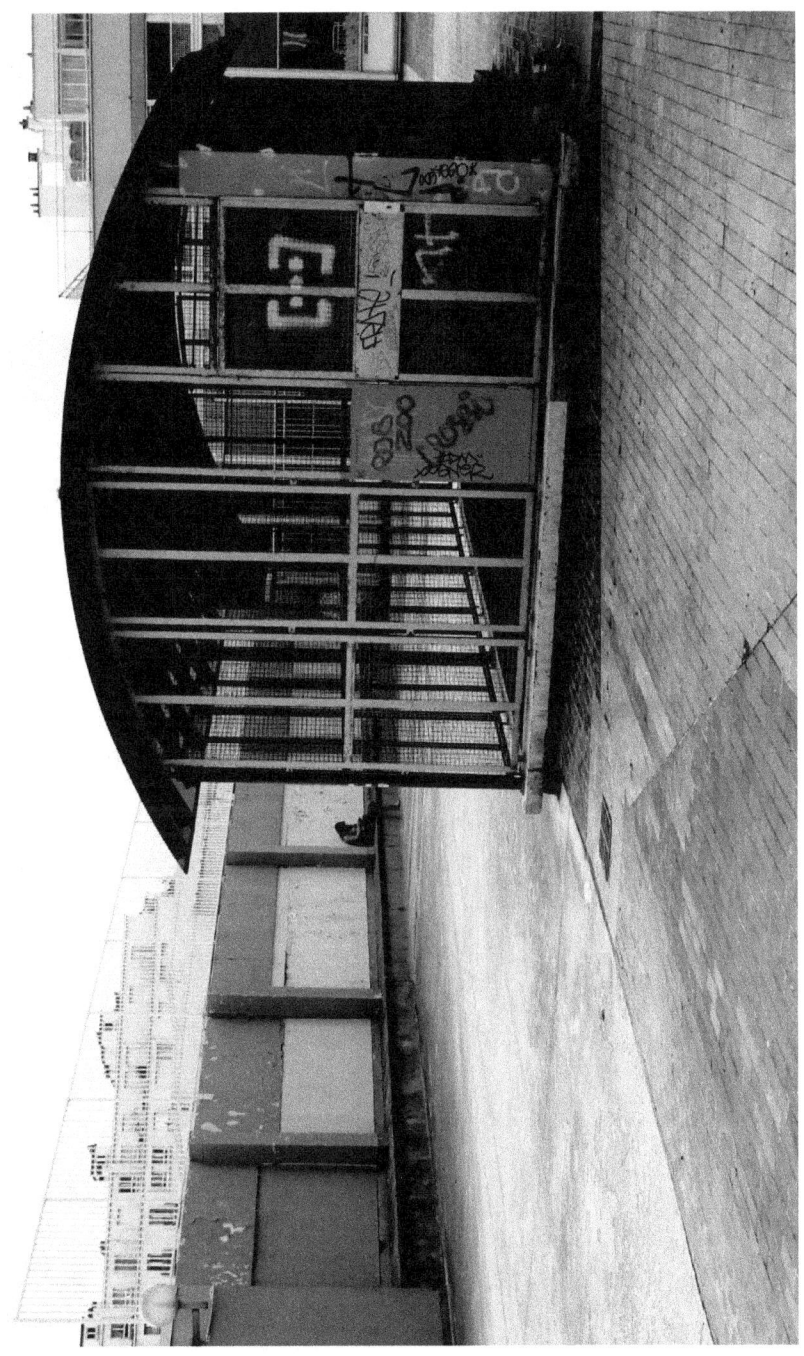

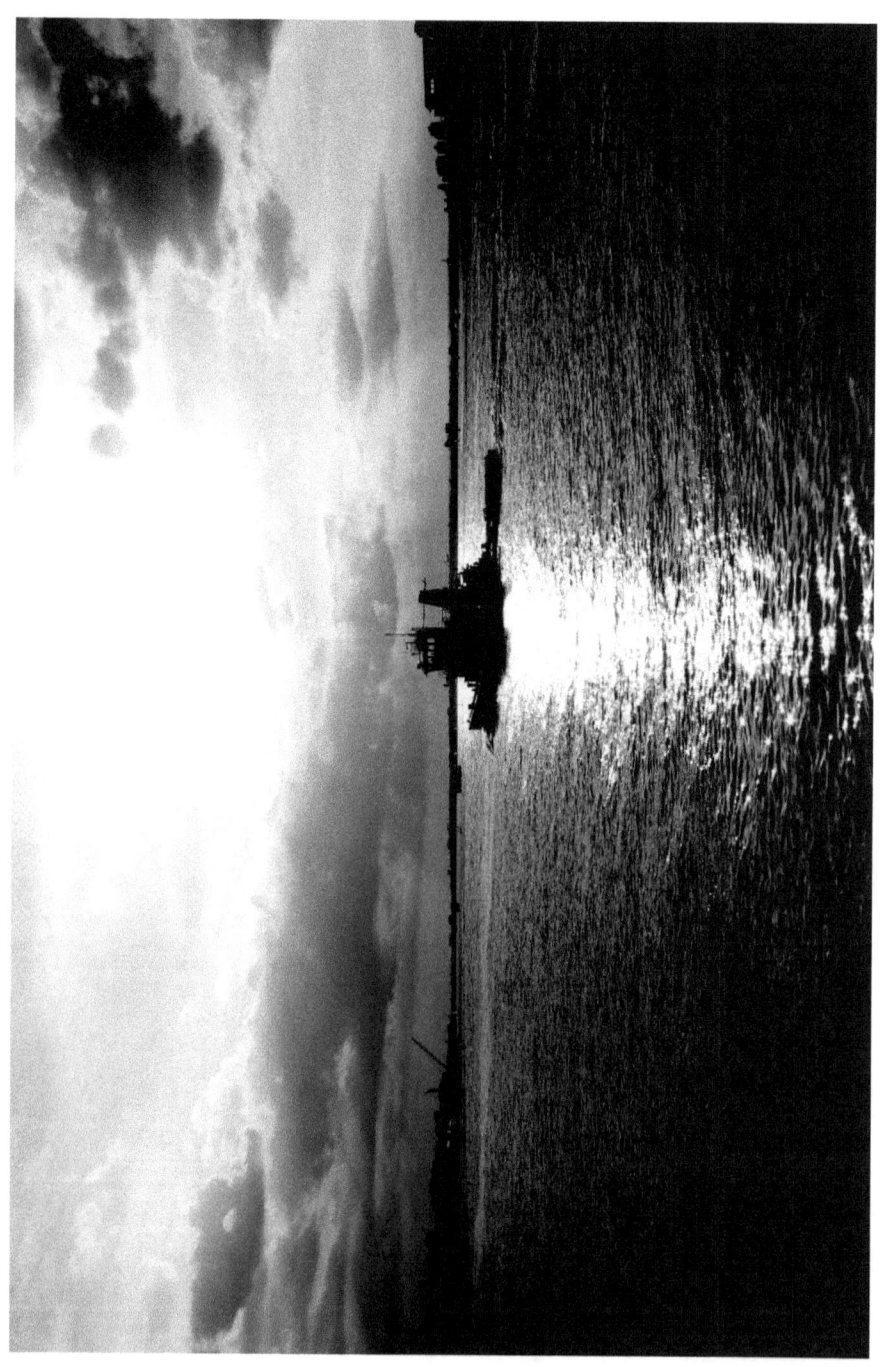

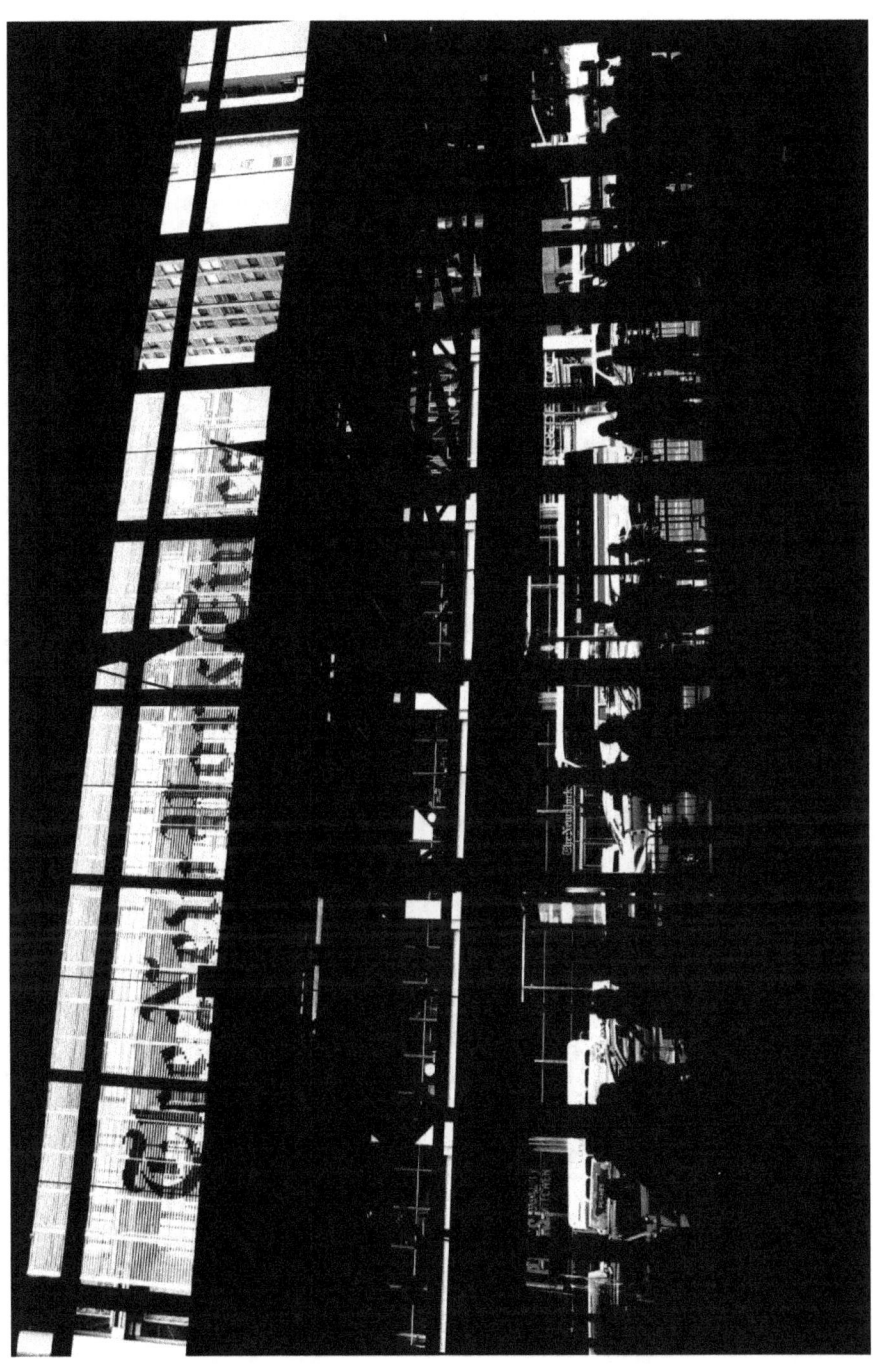

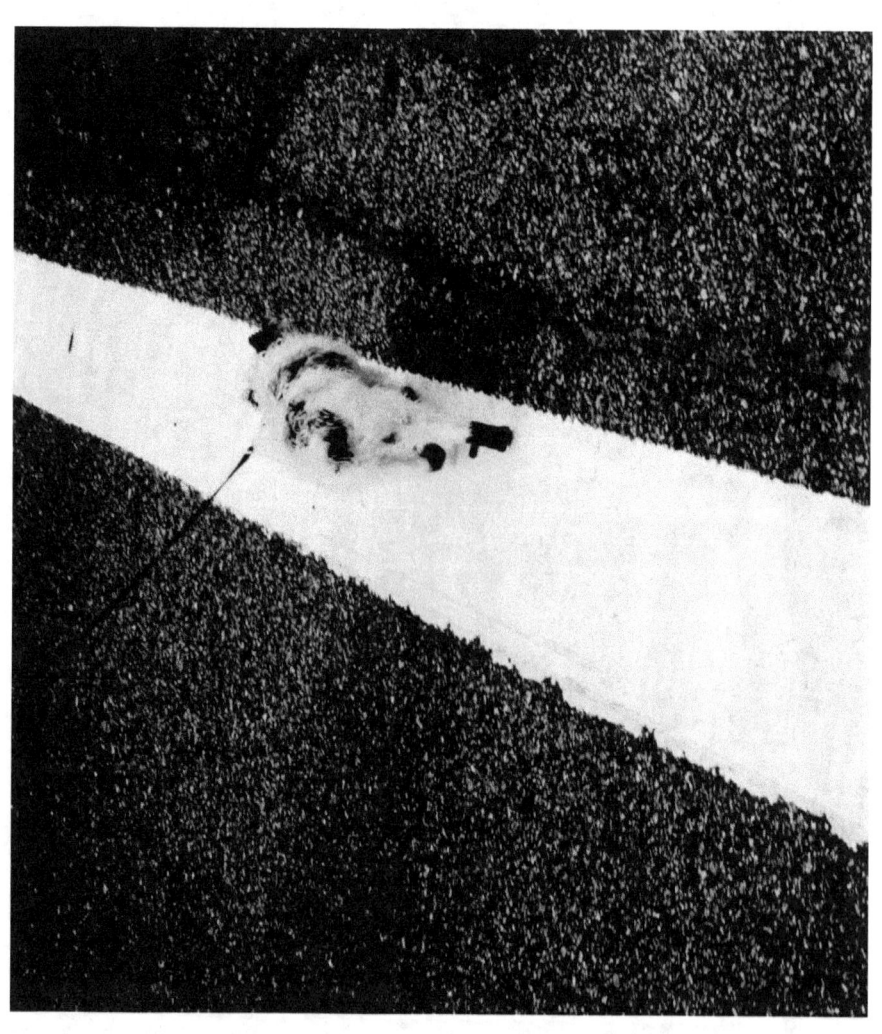

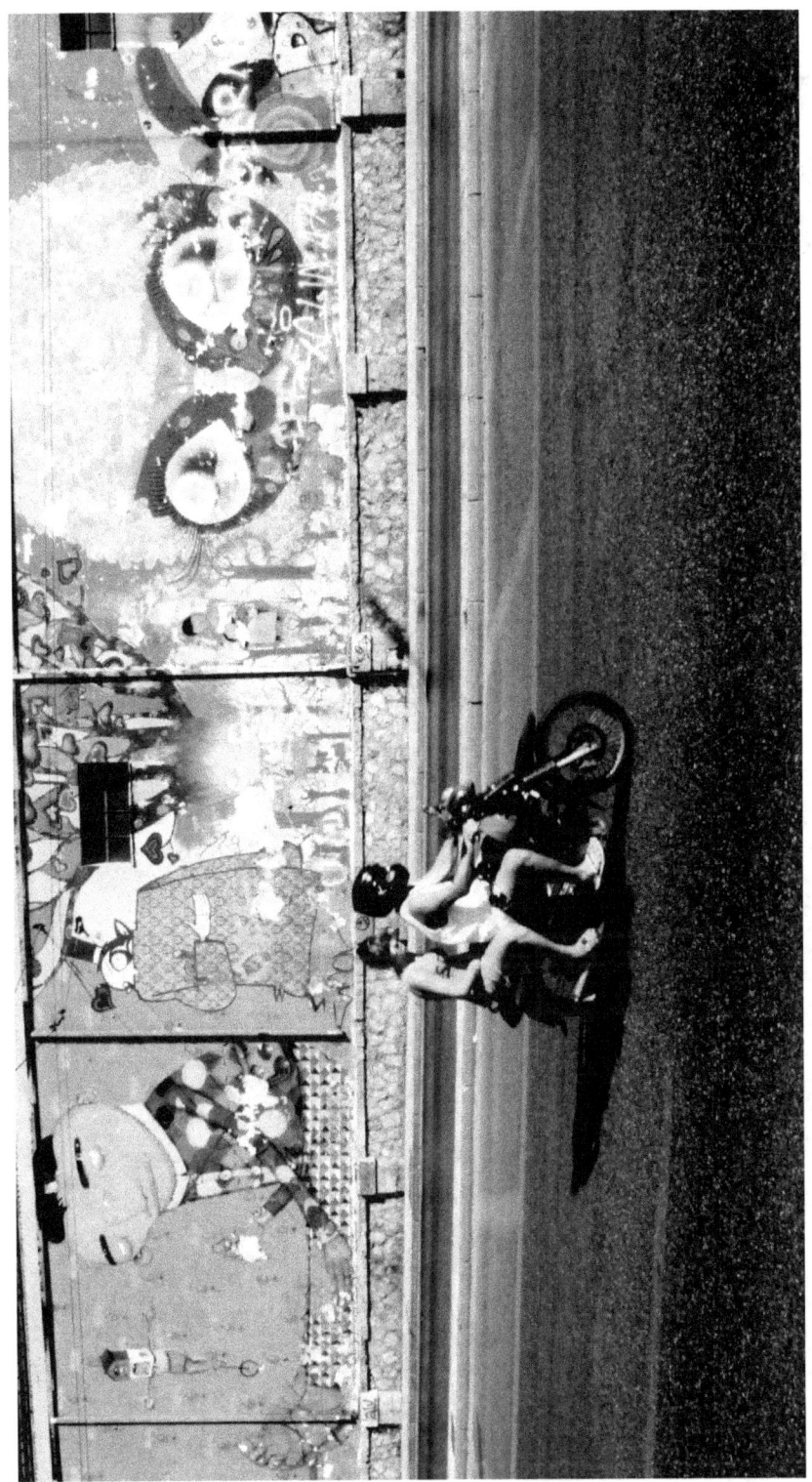

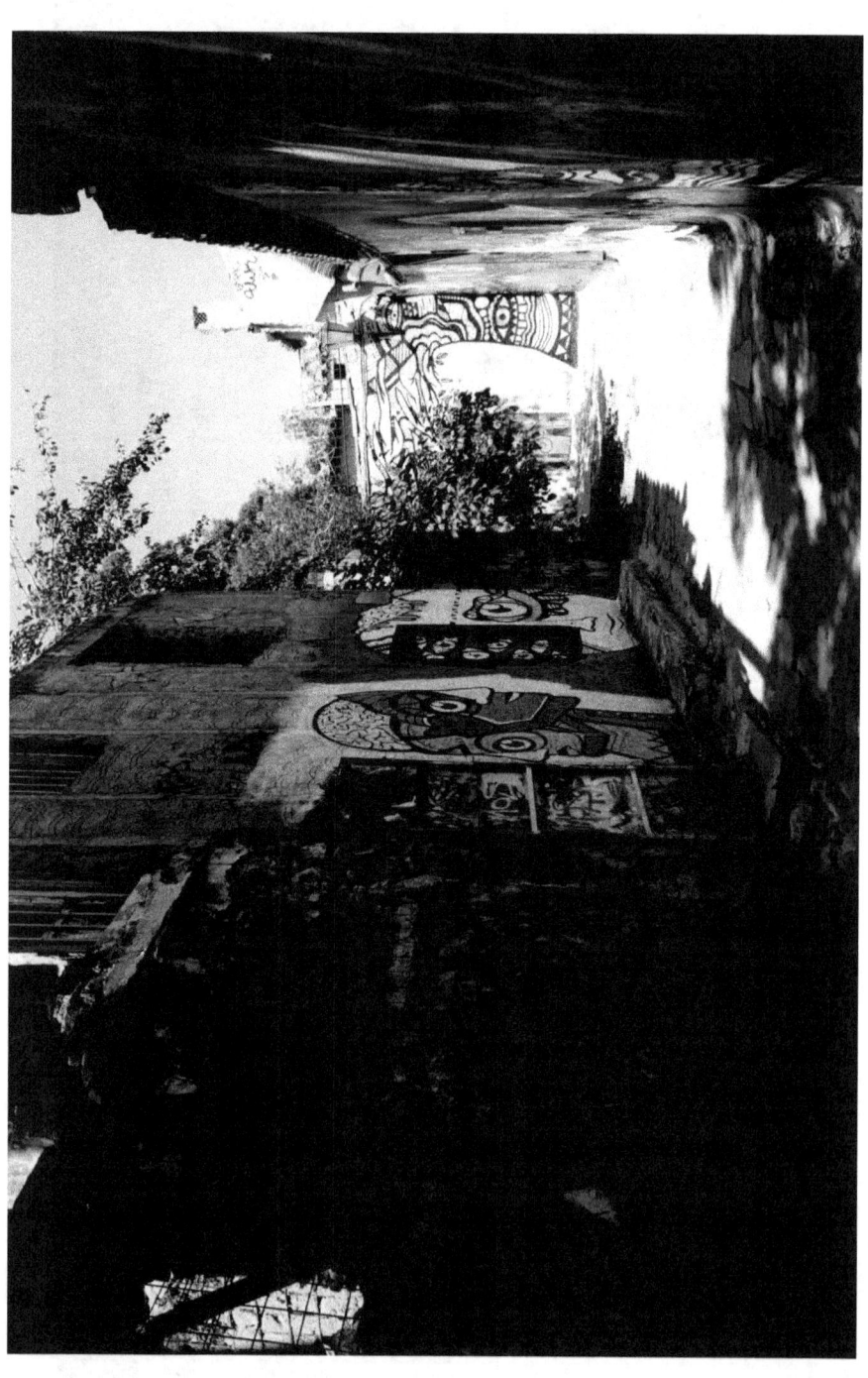

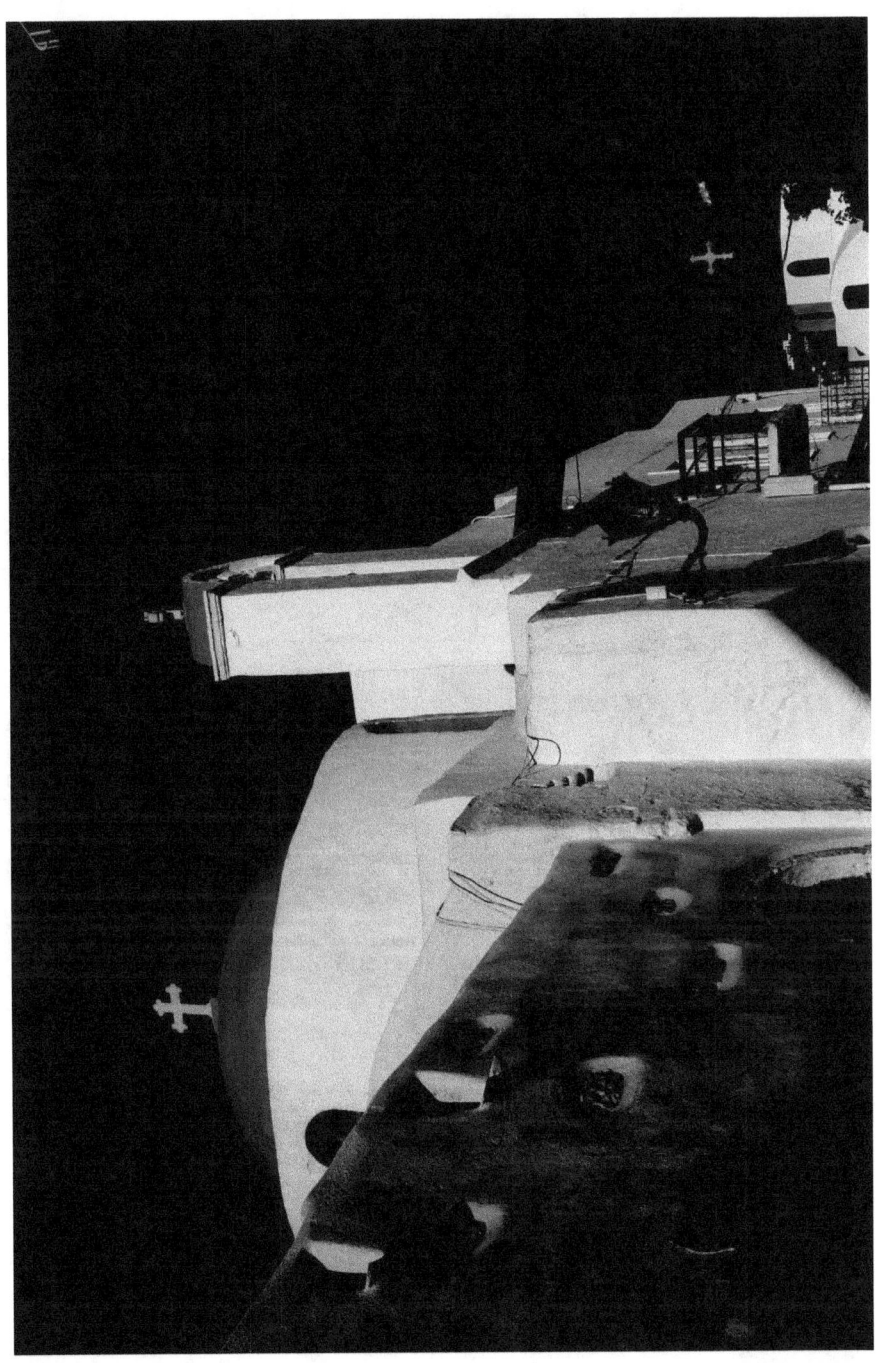

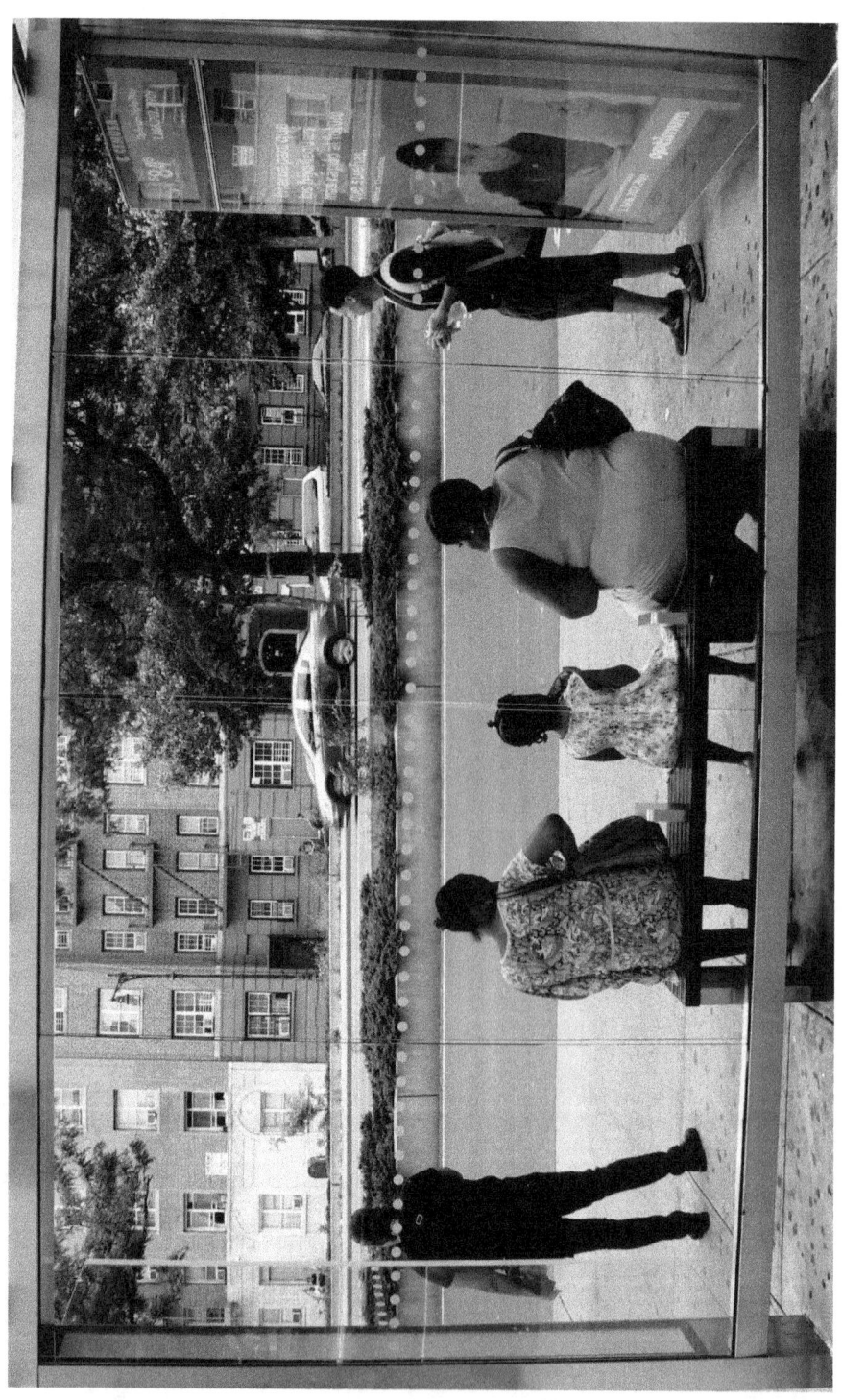

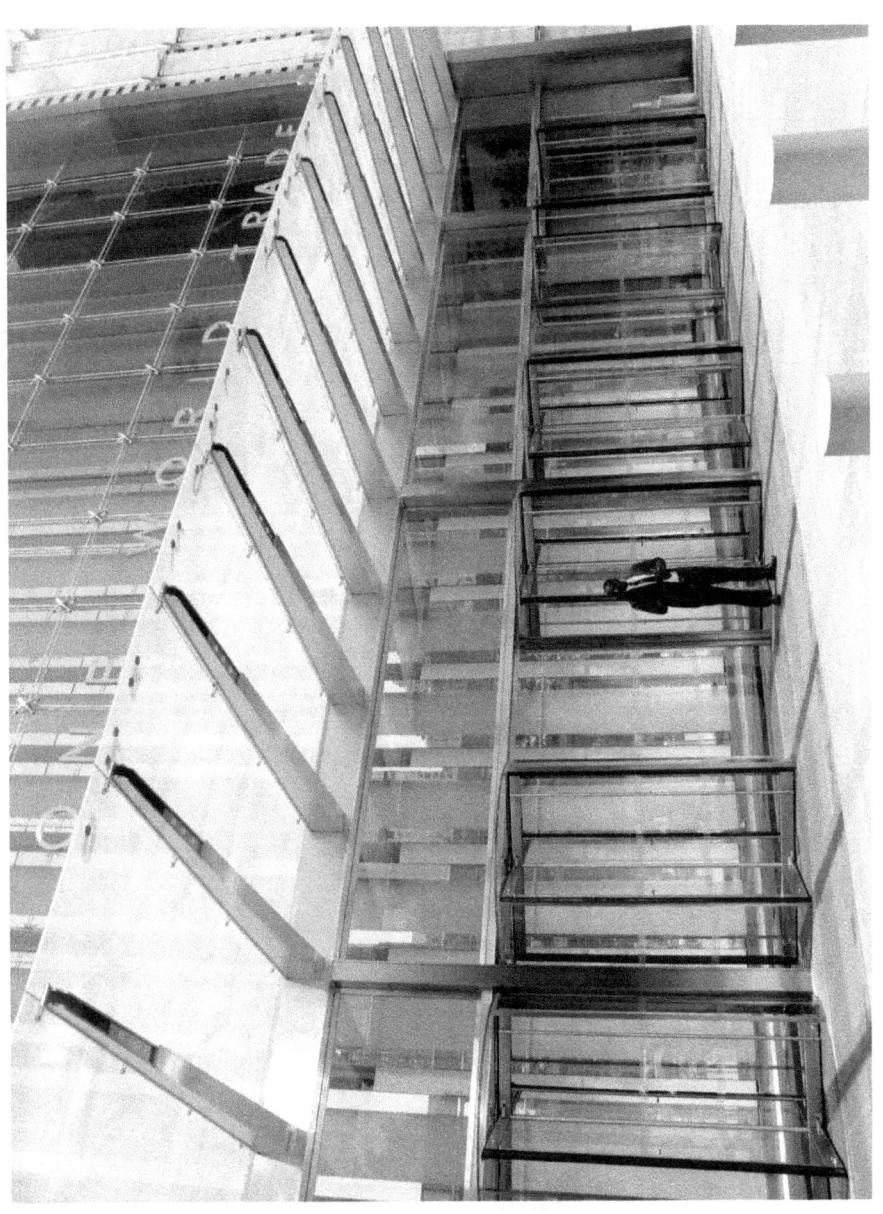

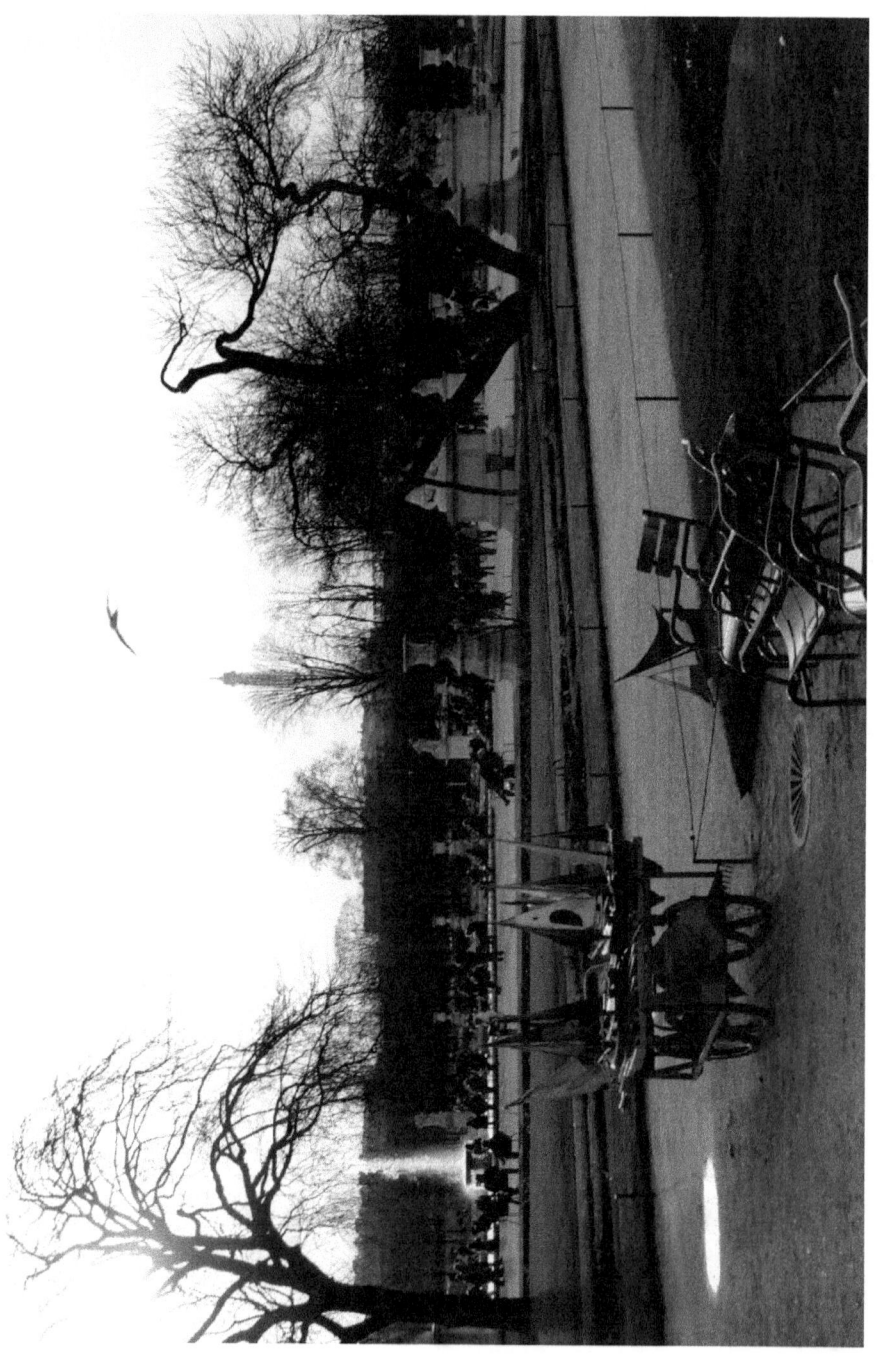

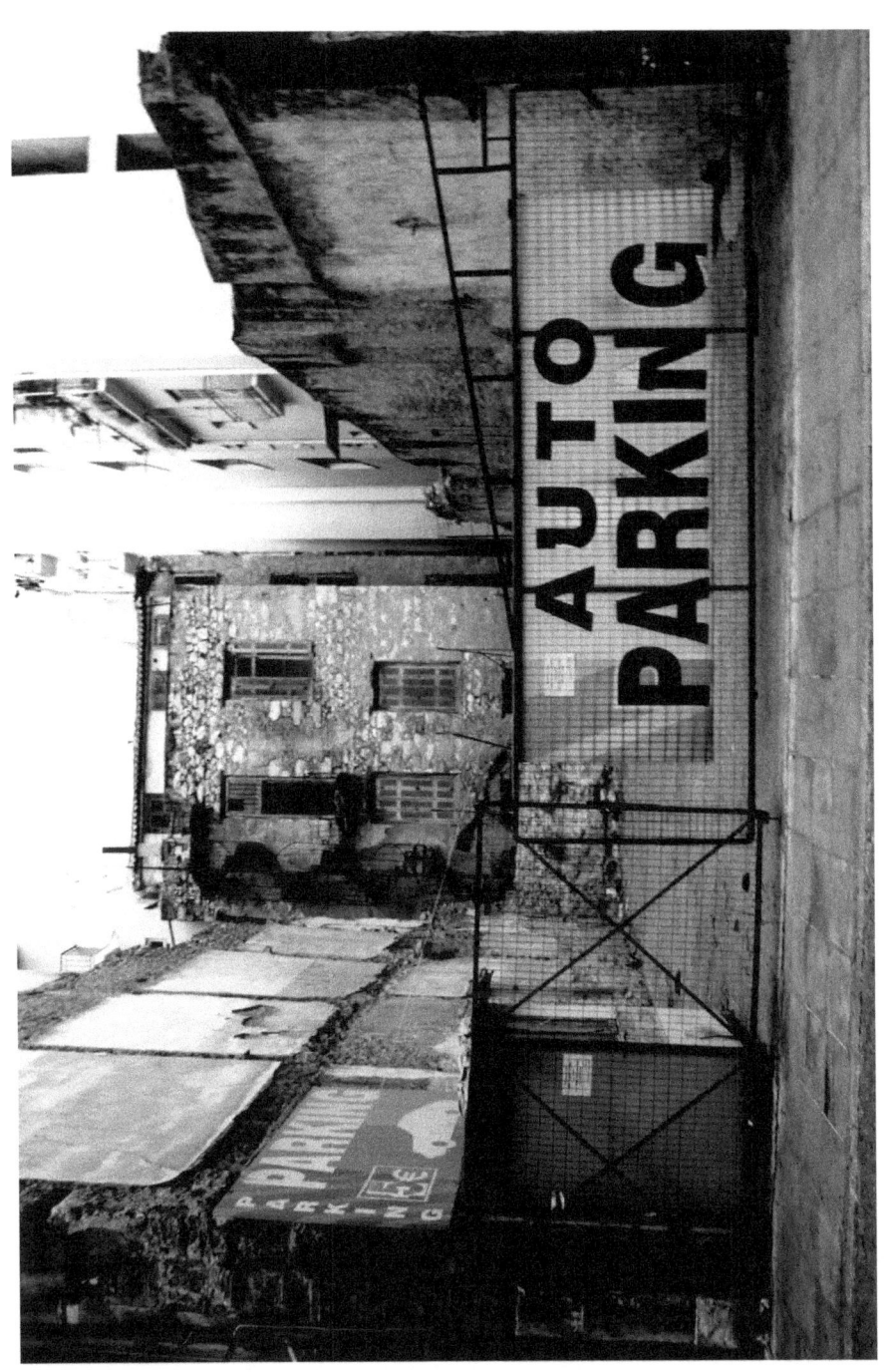

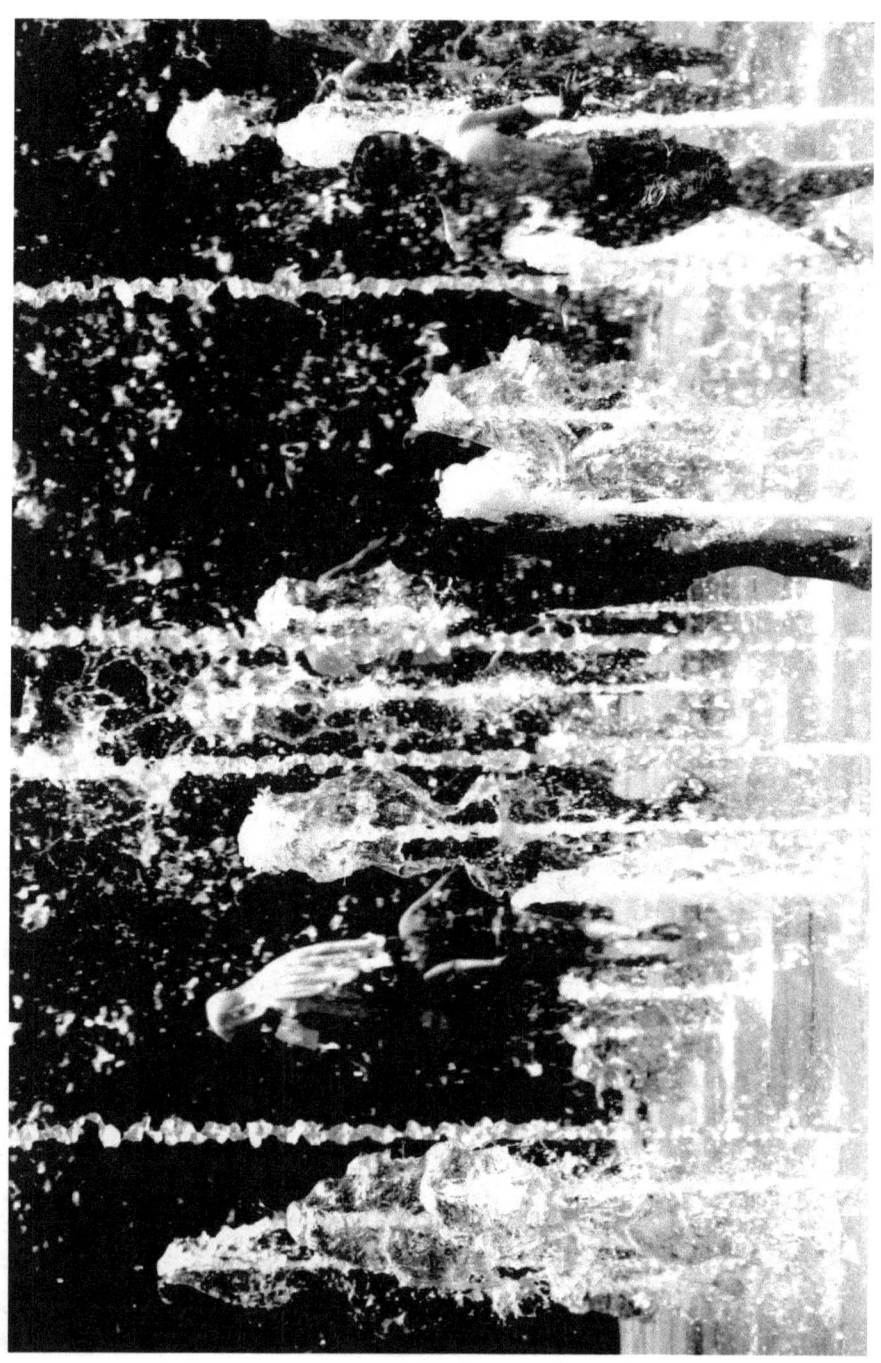

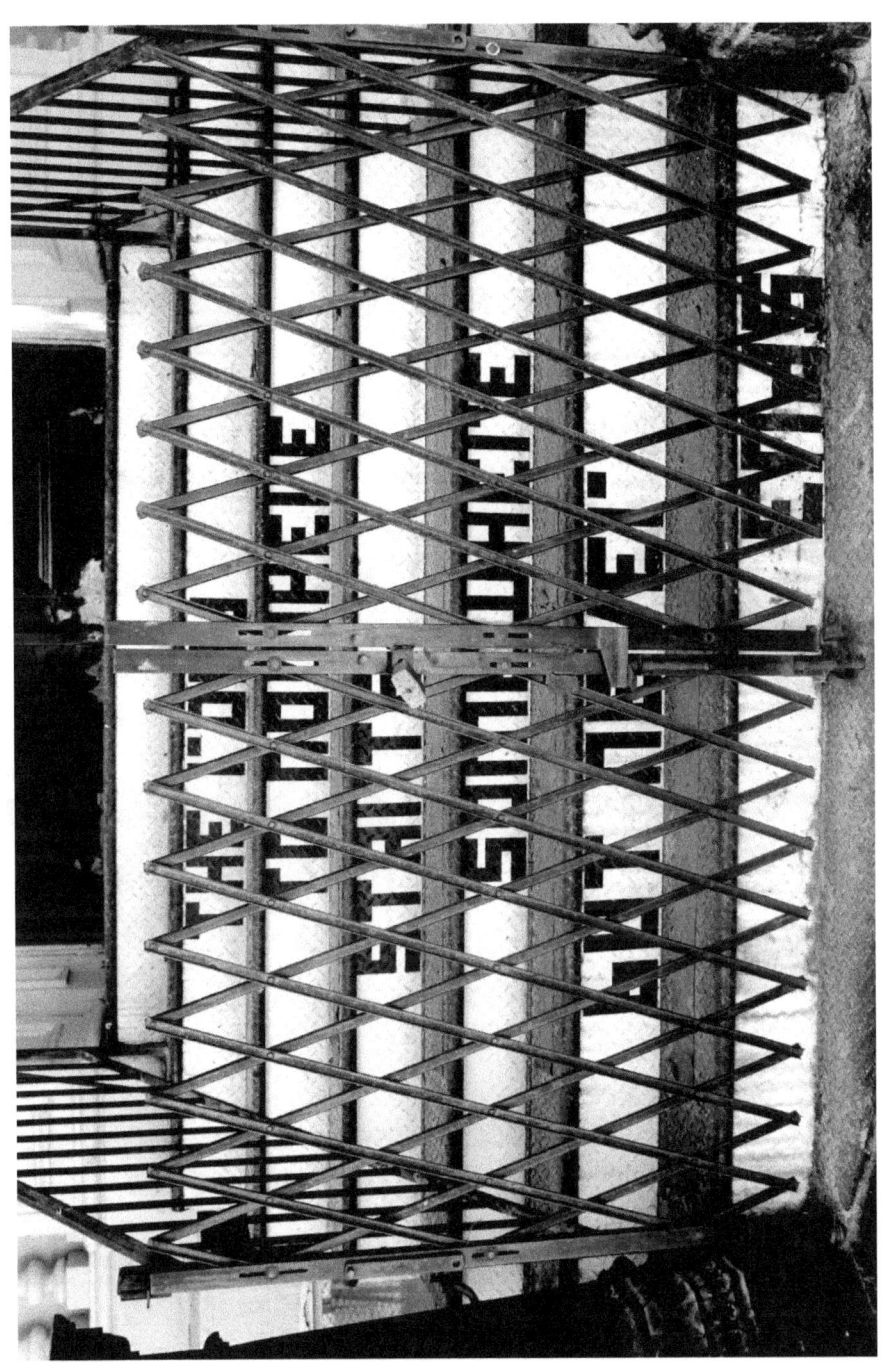

163

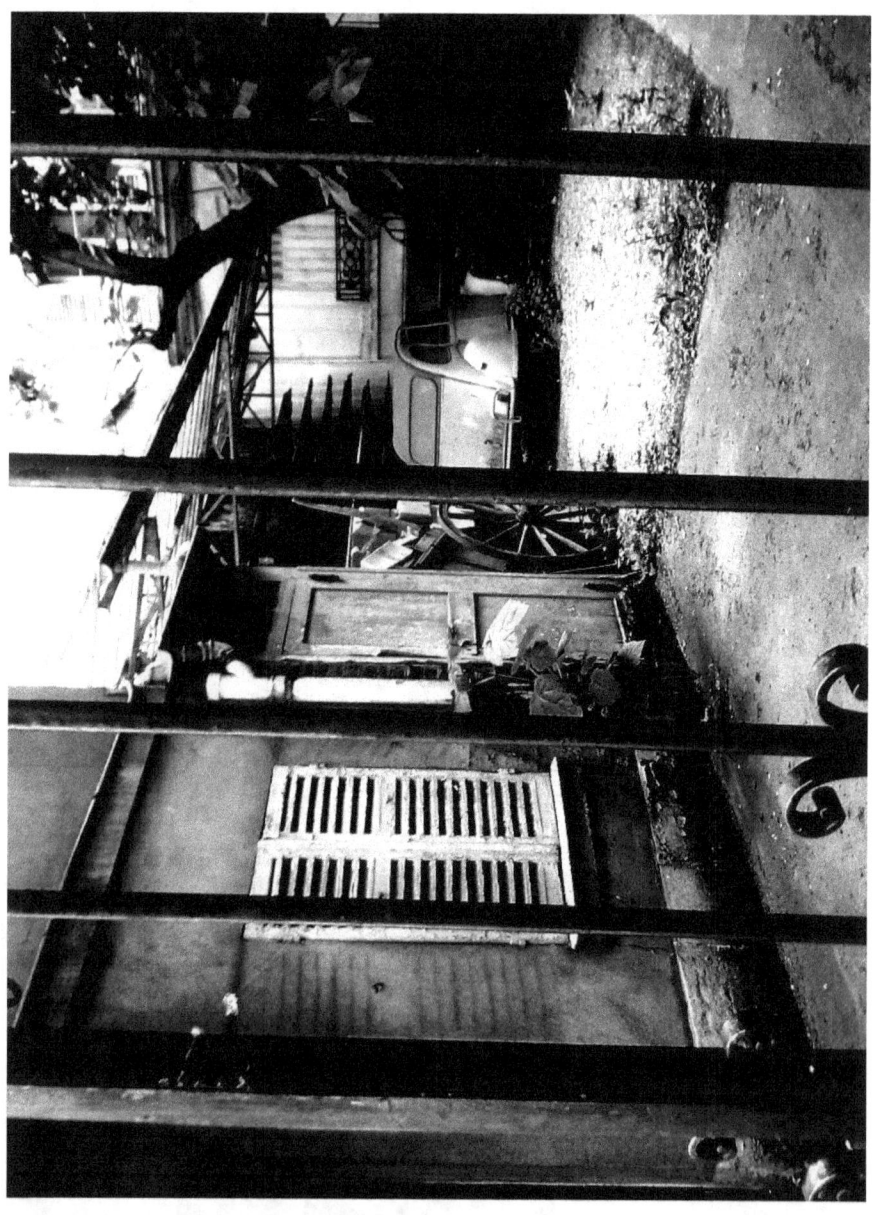

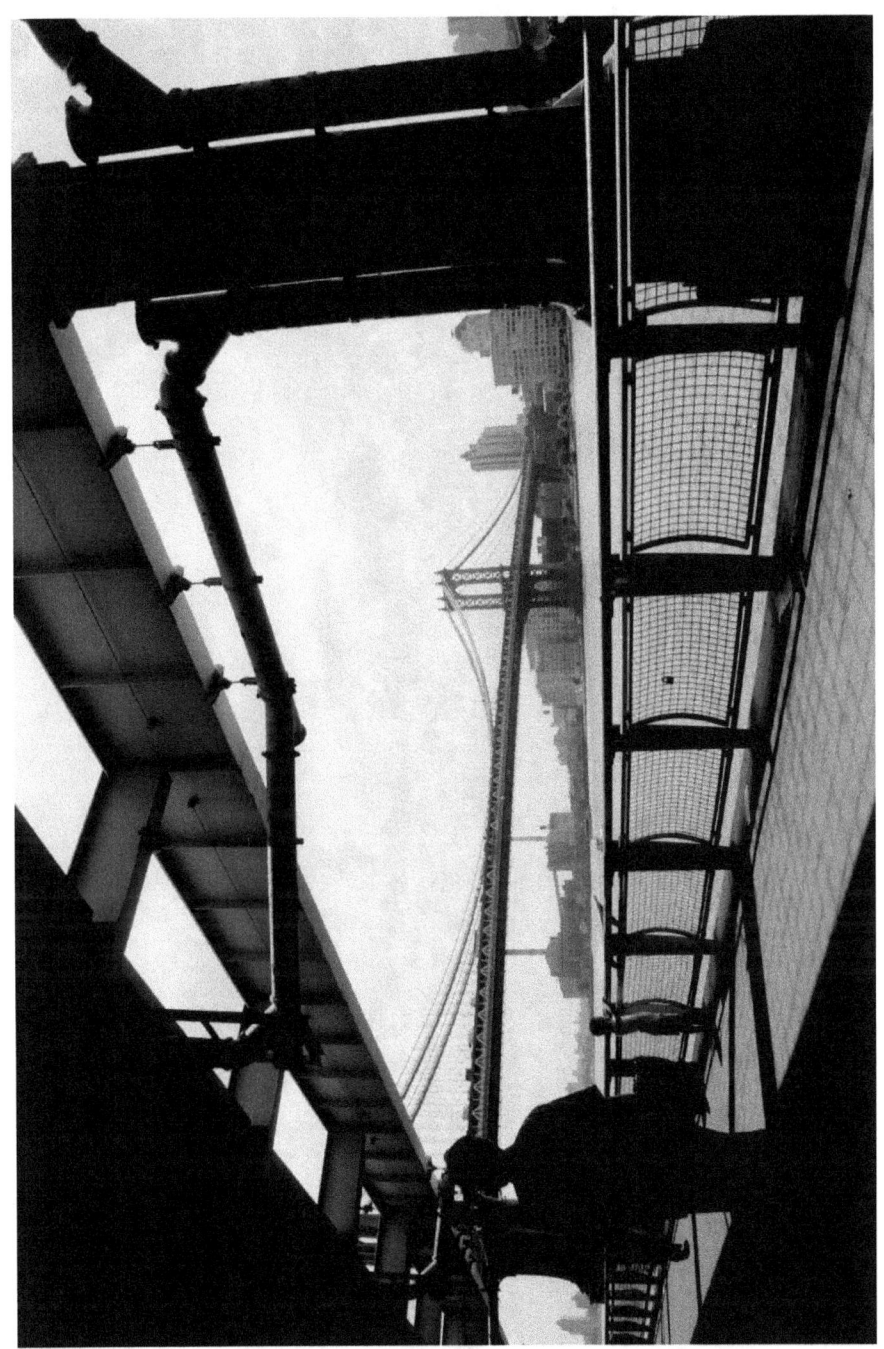

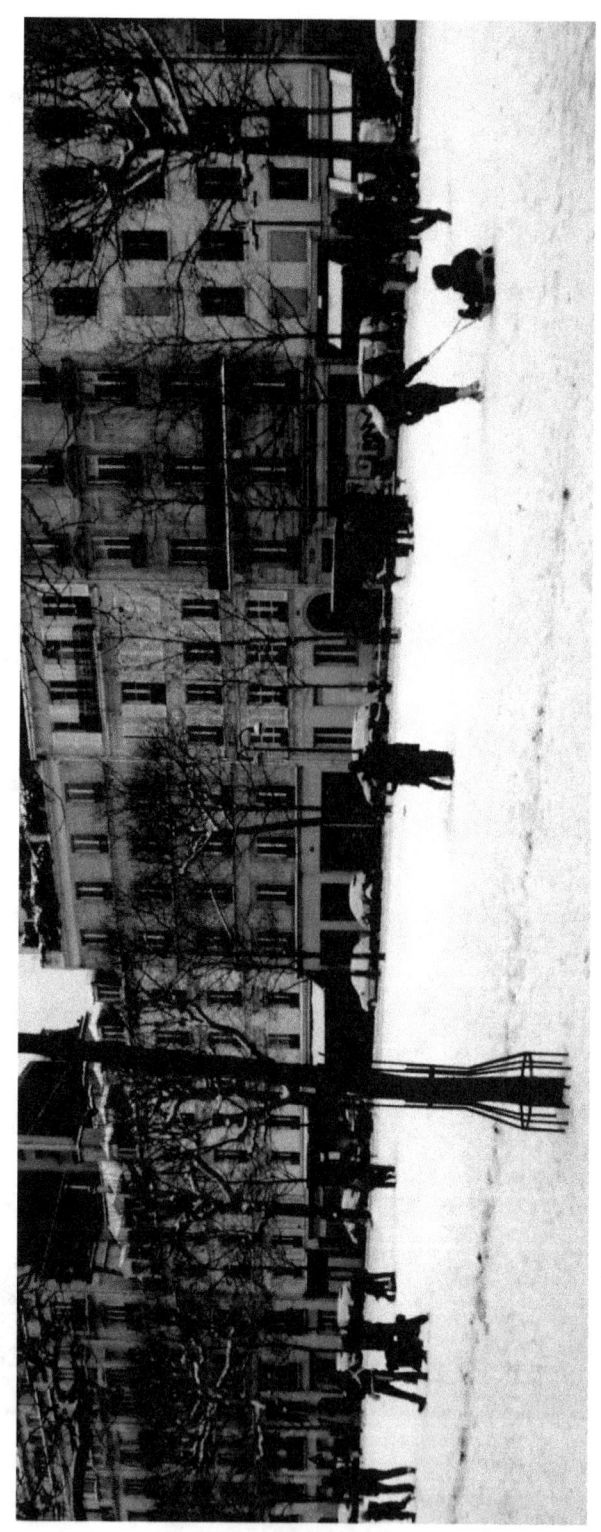

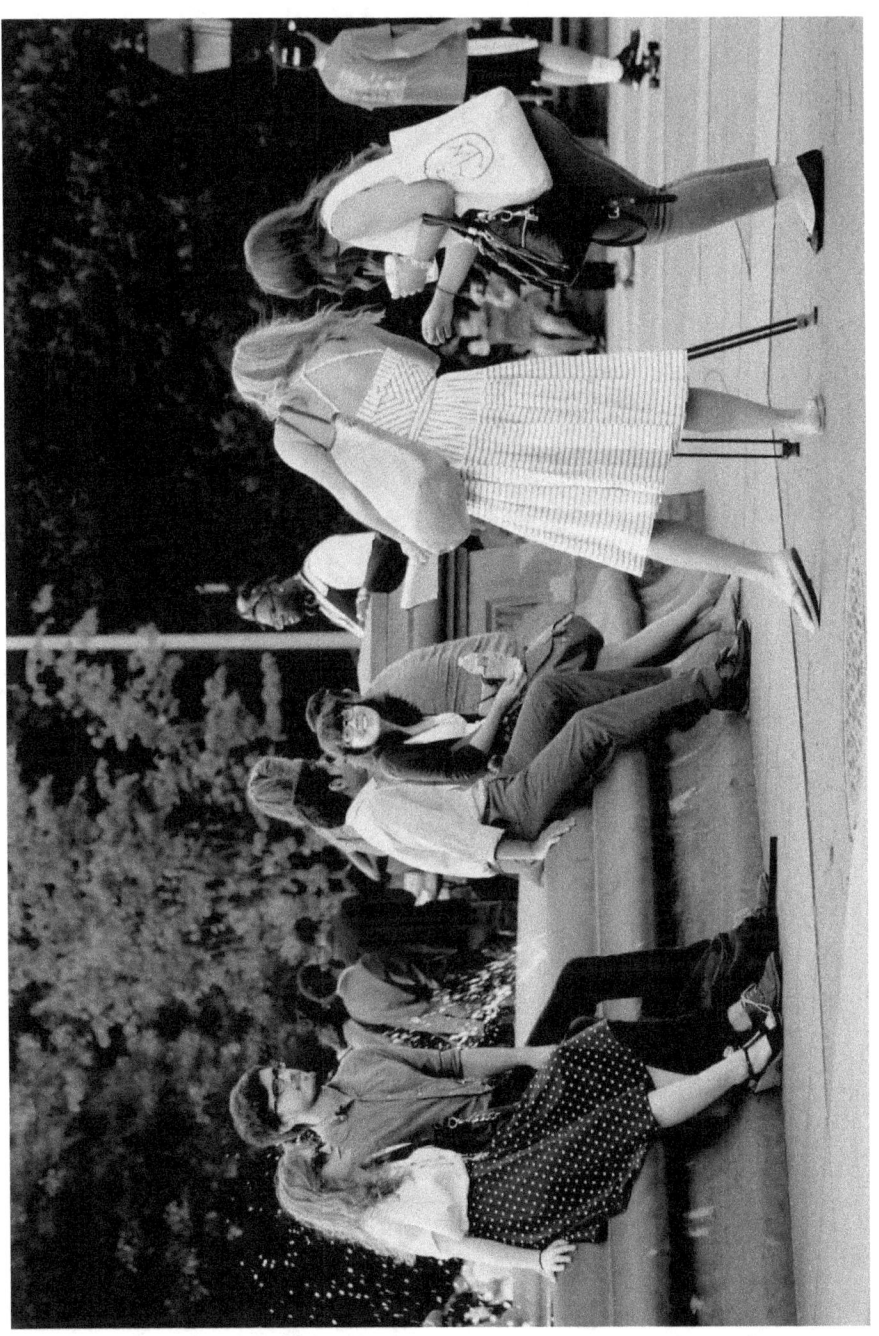

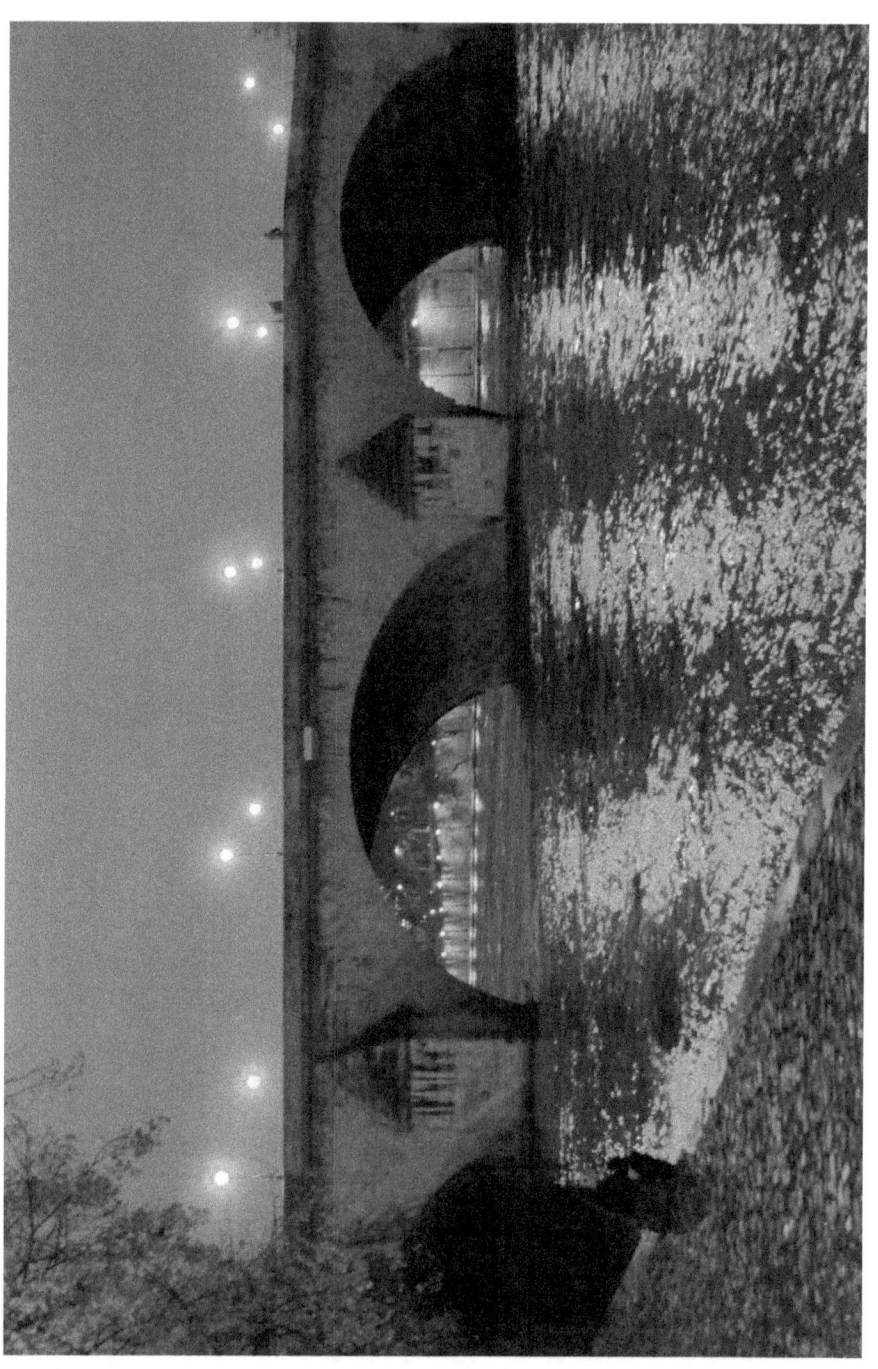

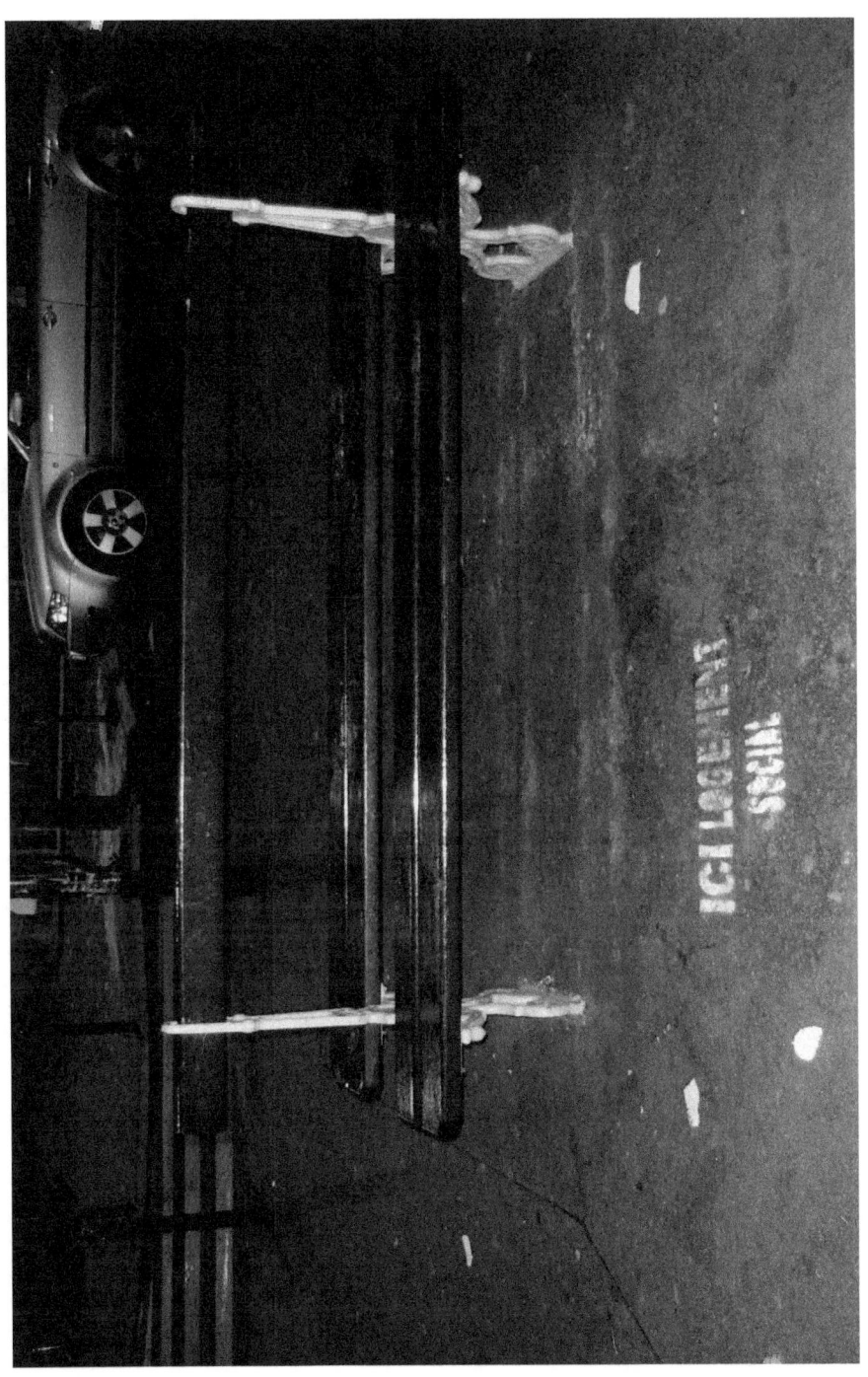

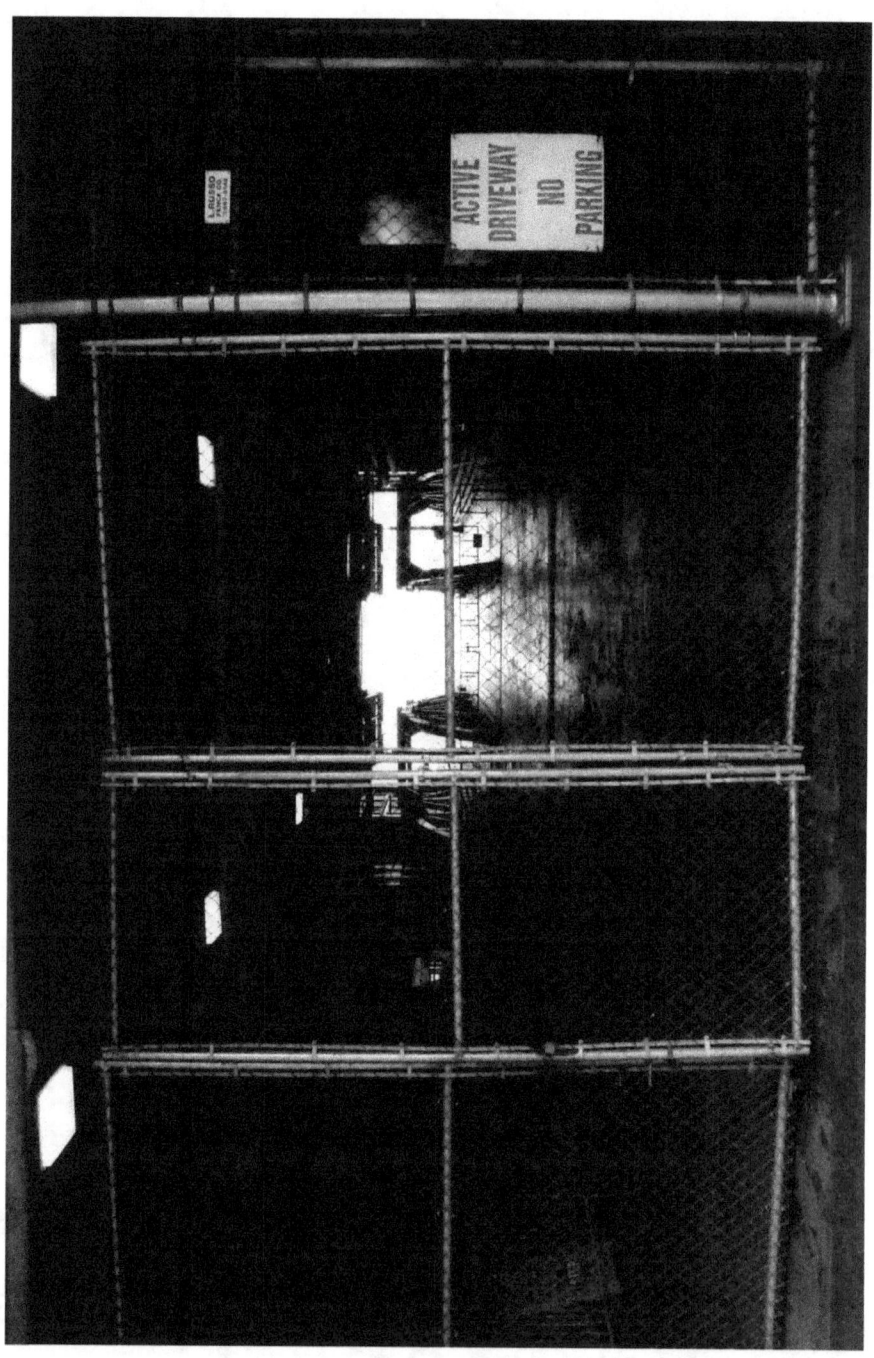

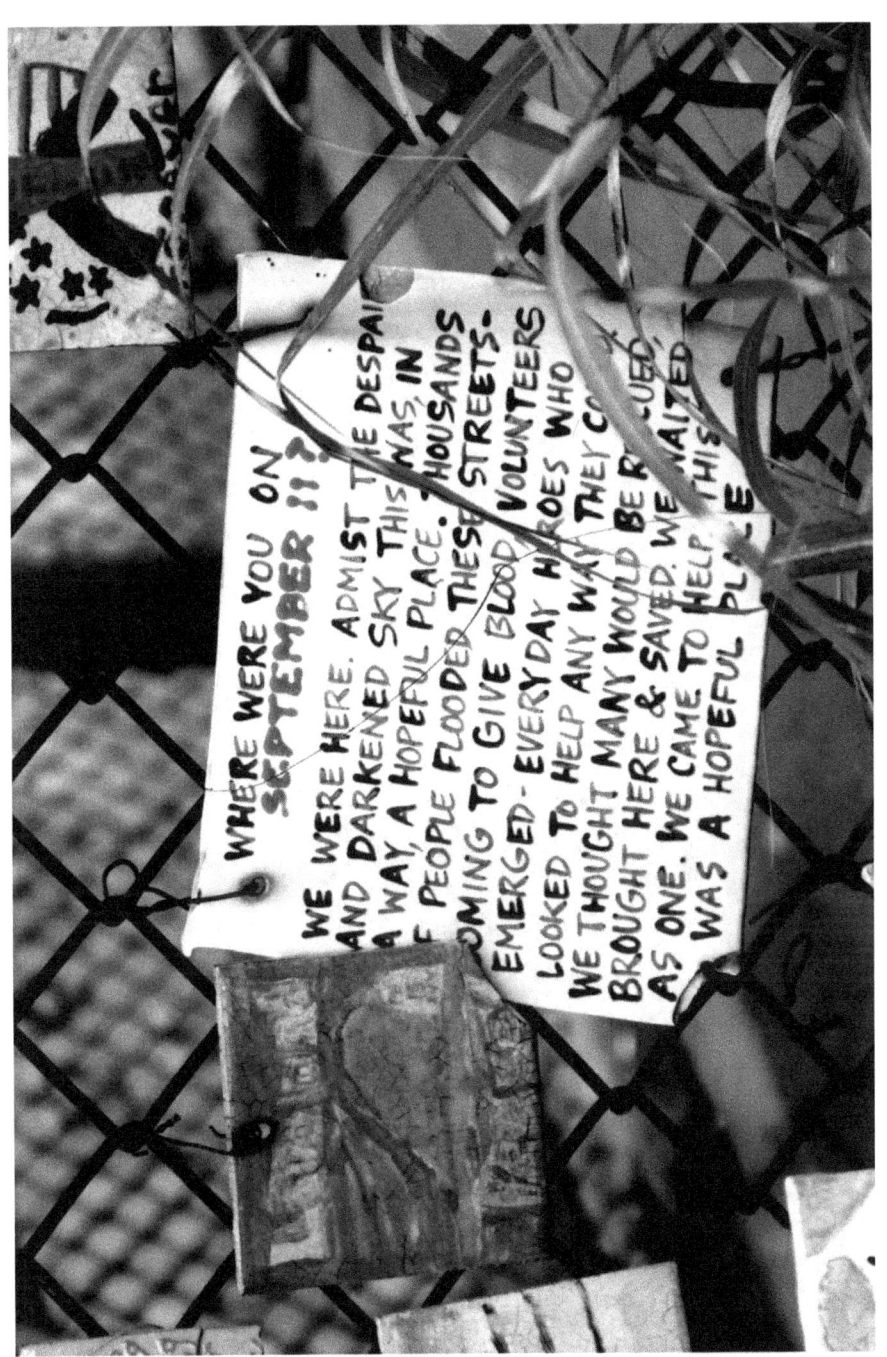

171

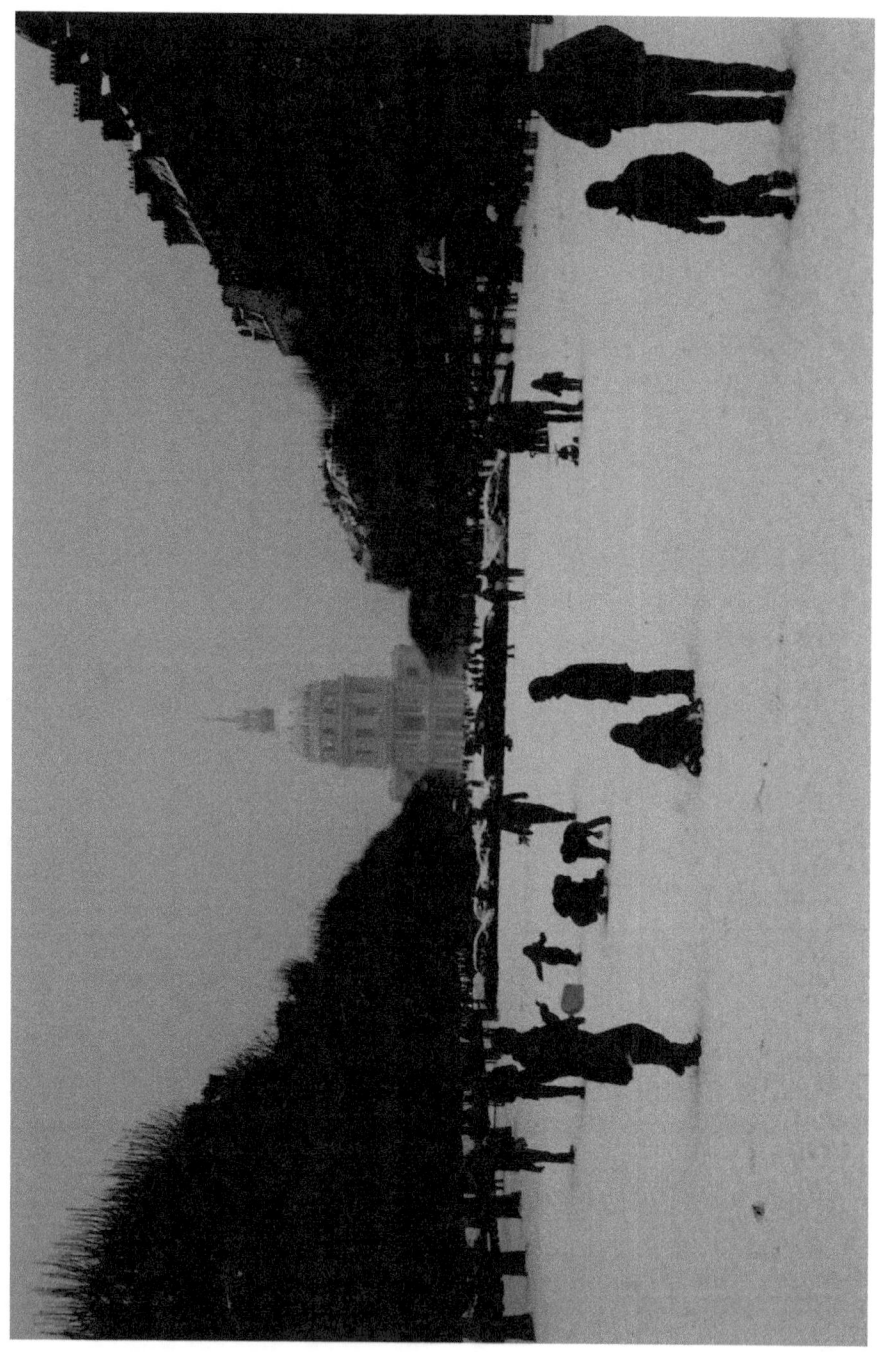

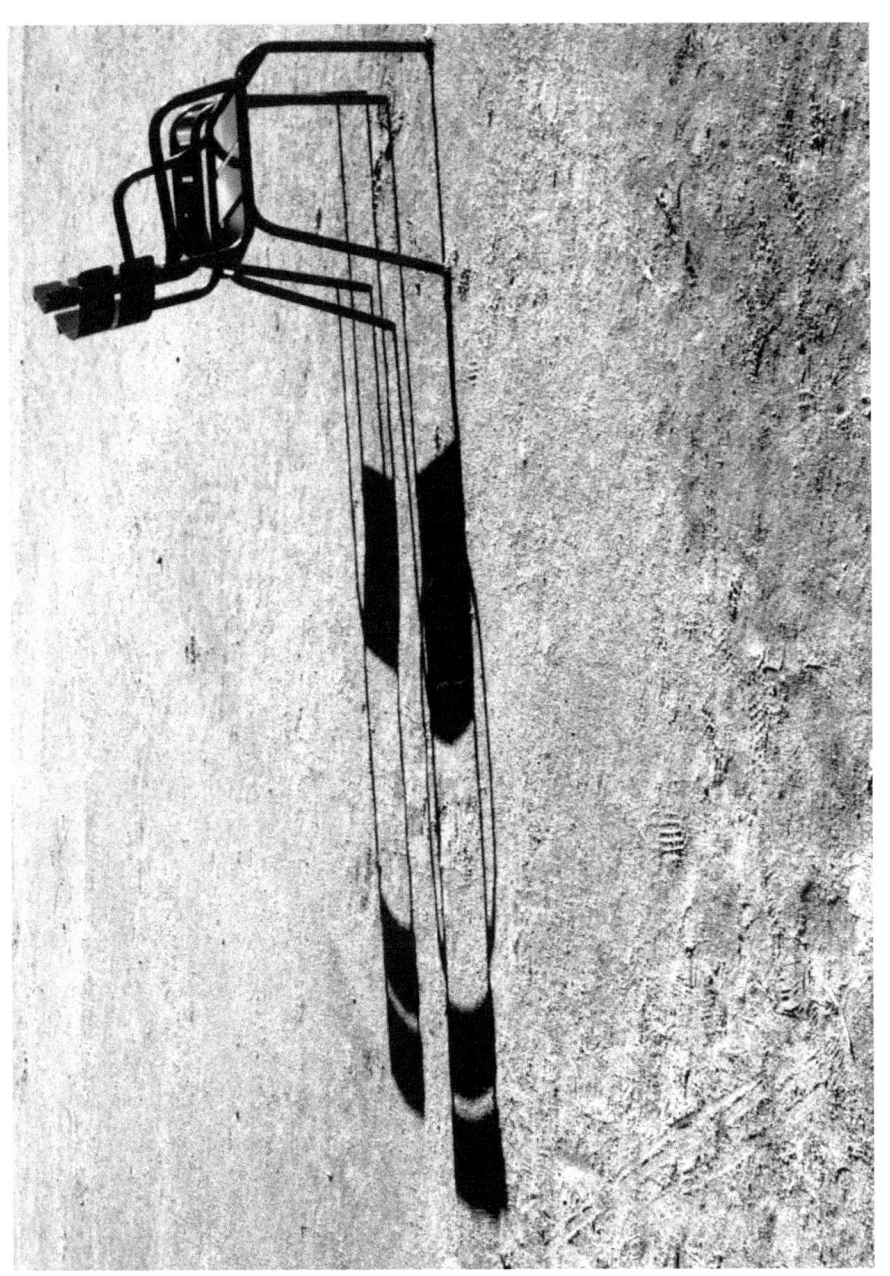

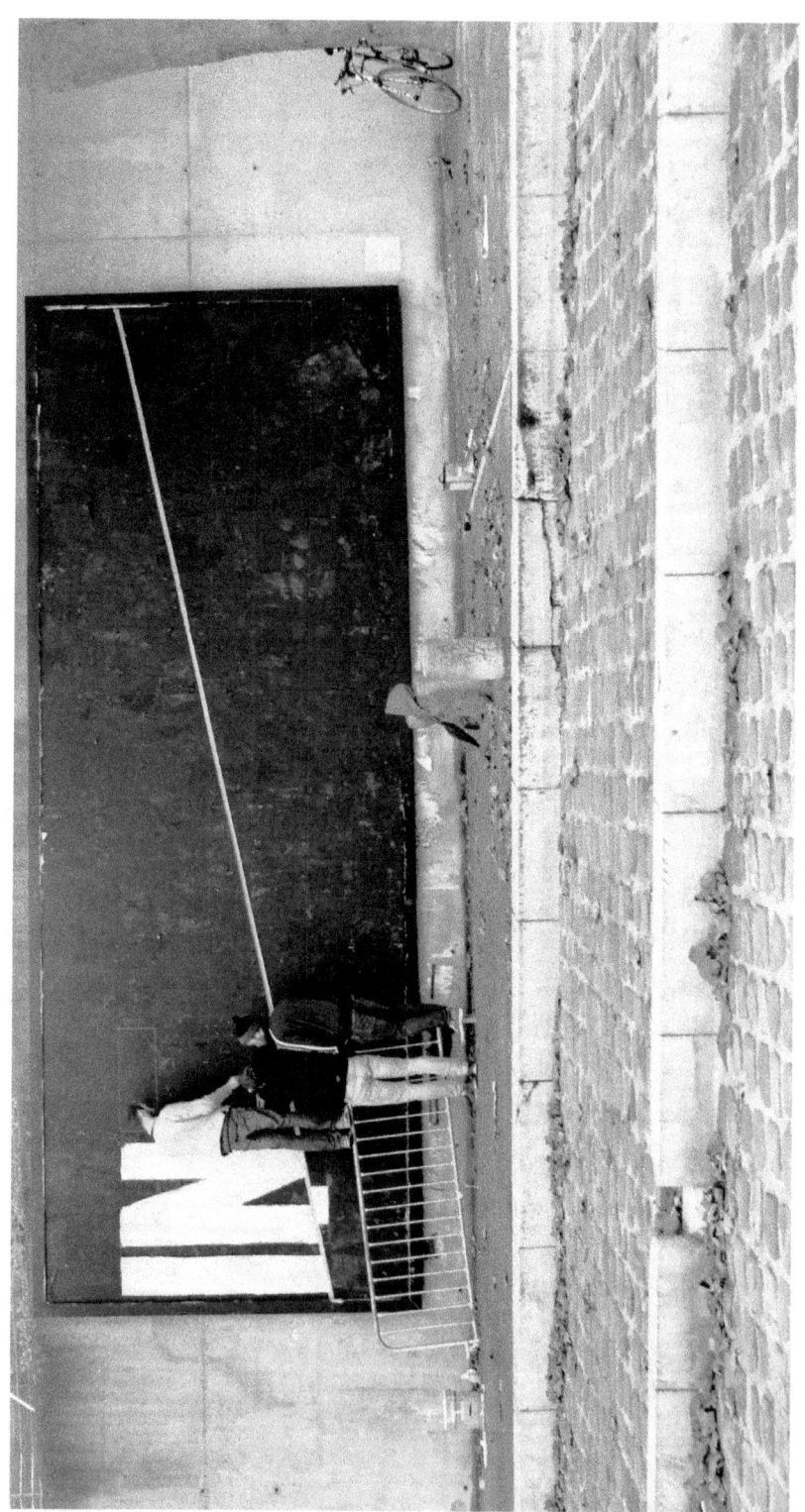

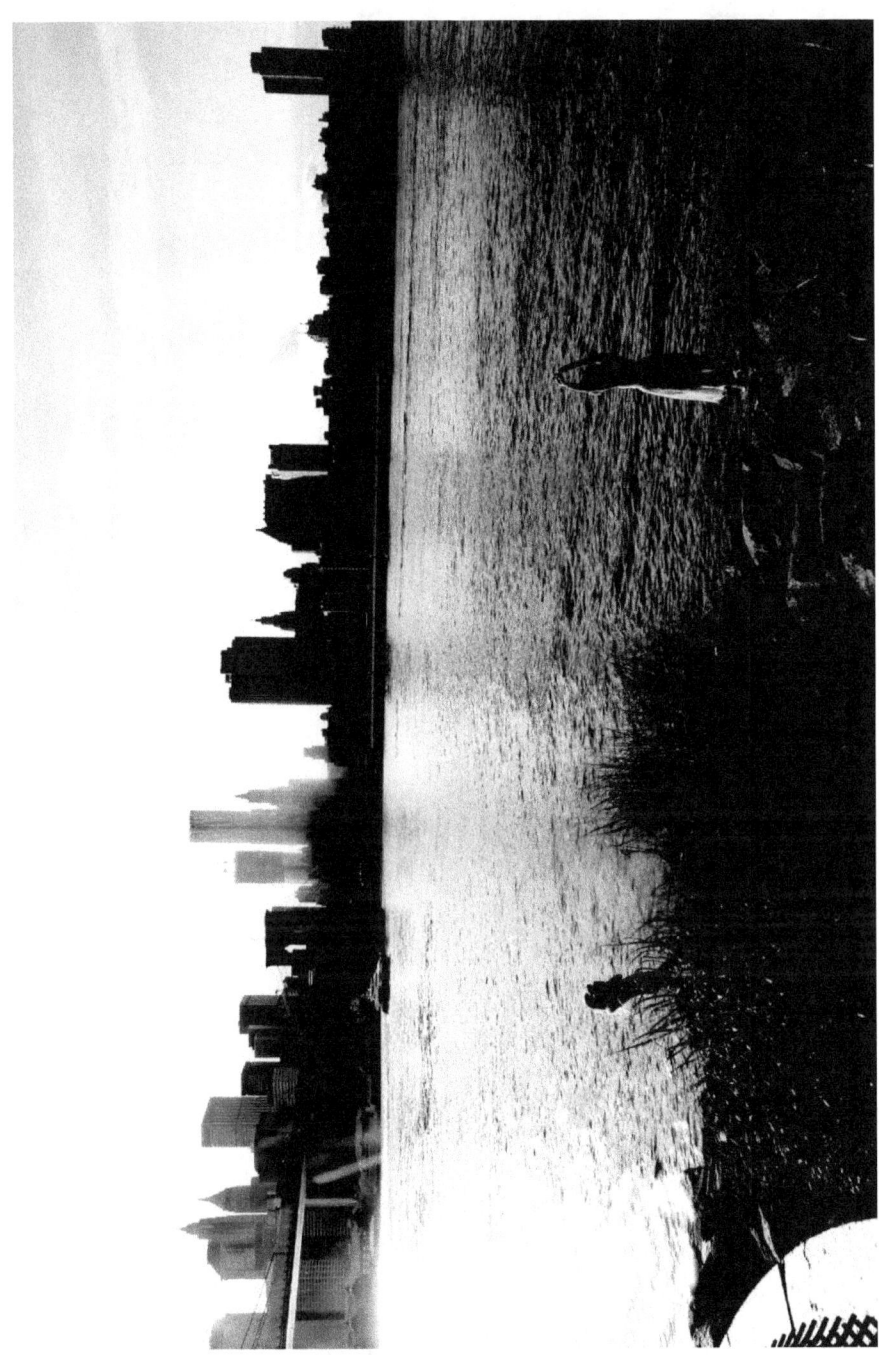

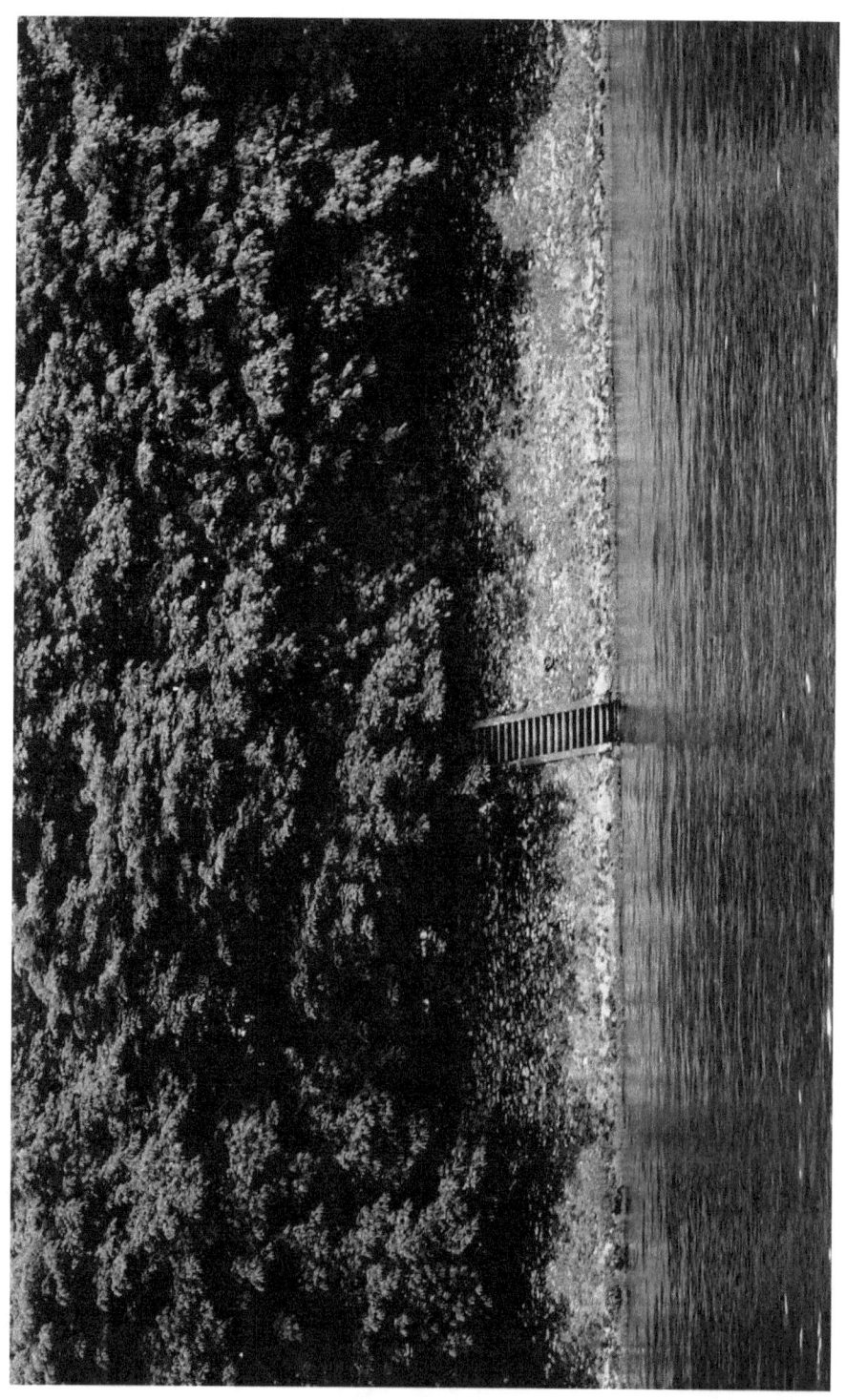

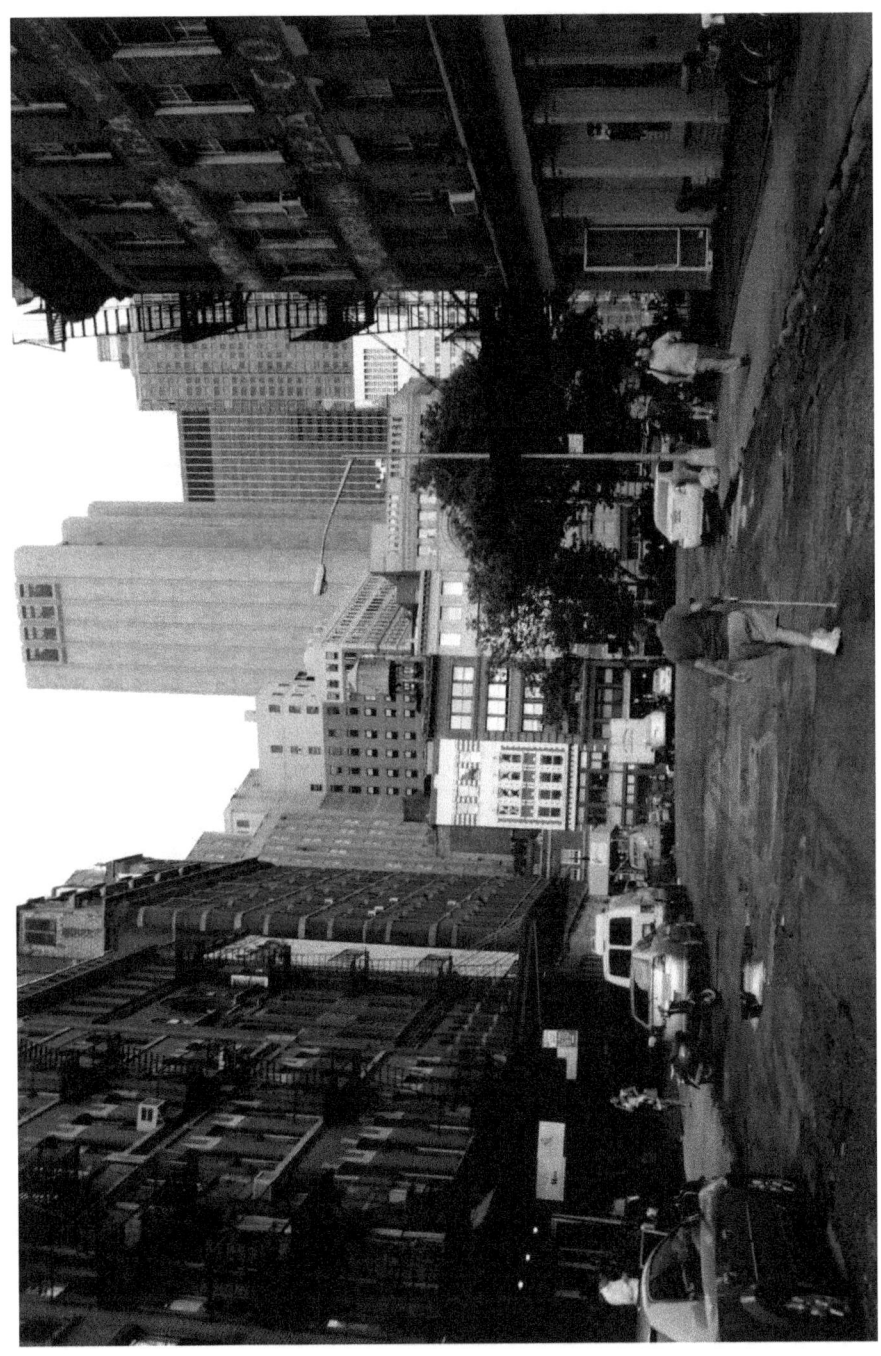

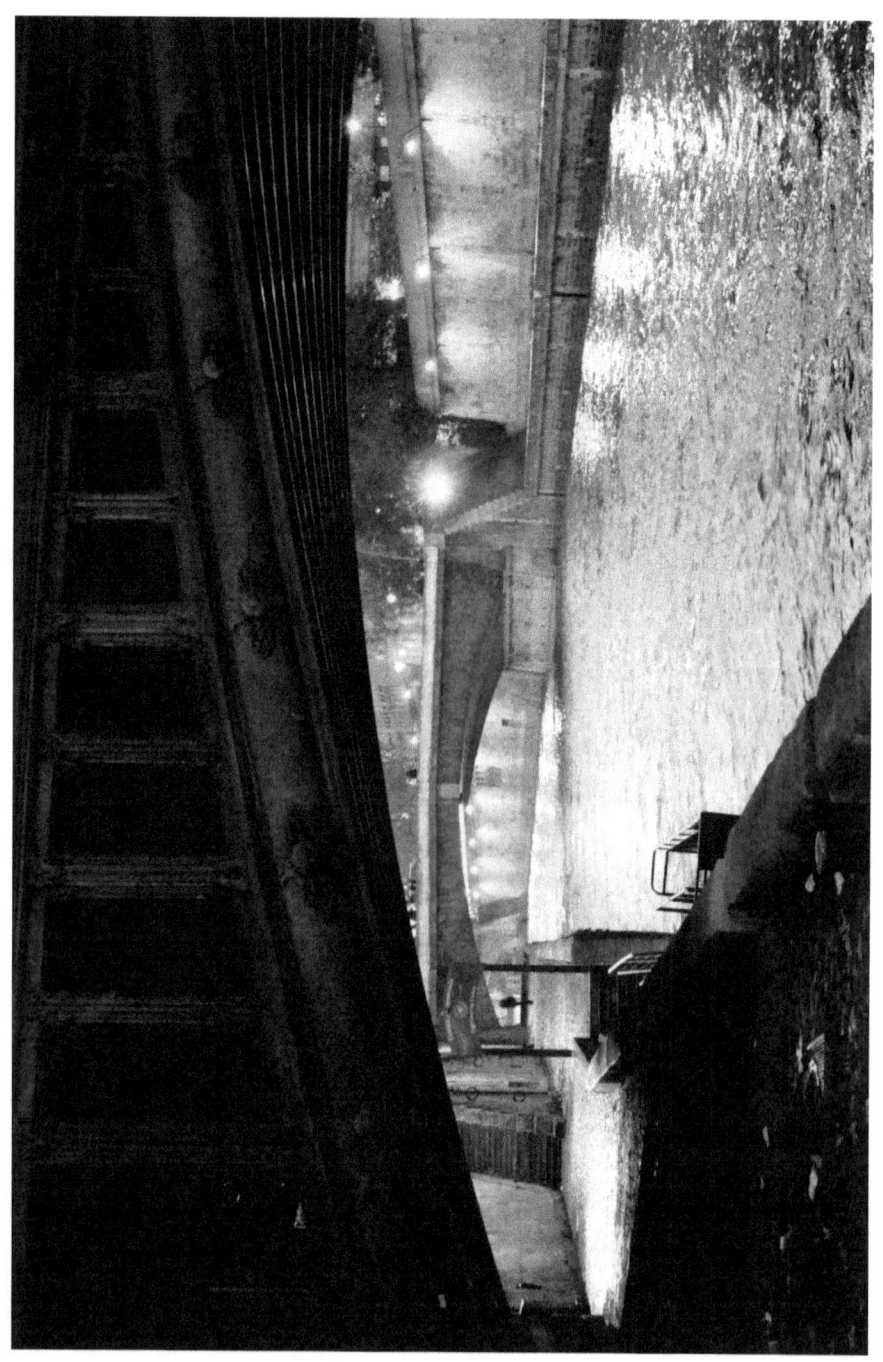

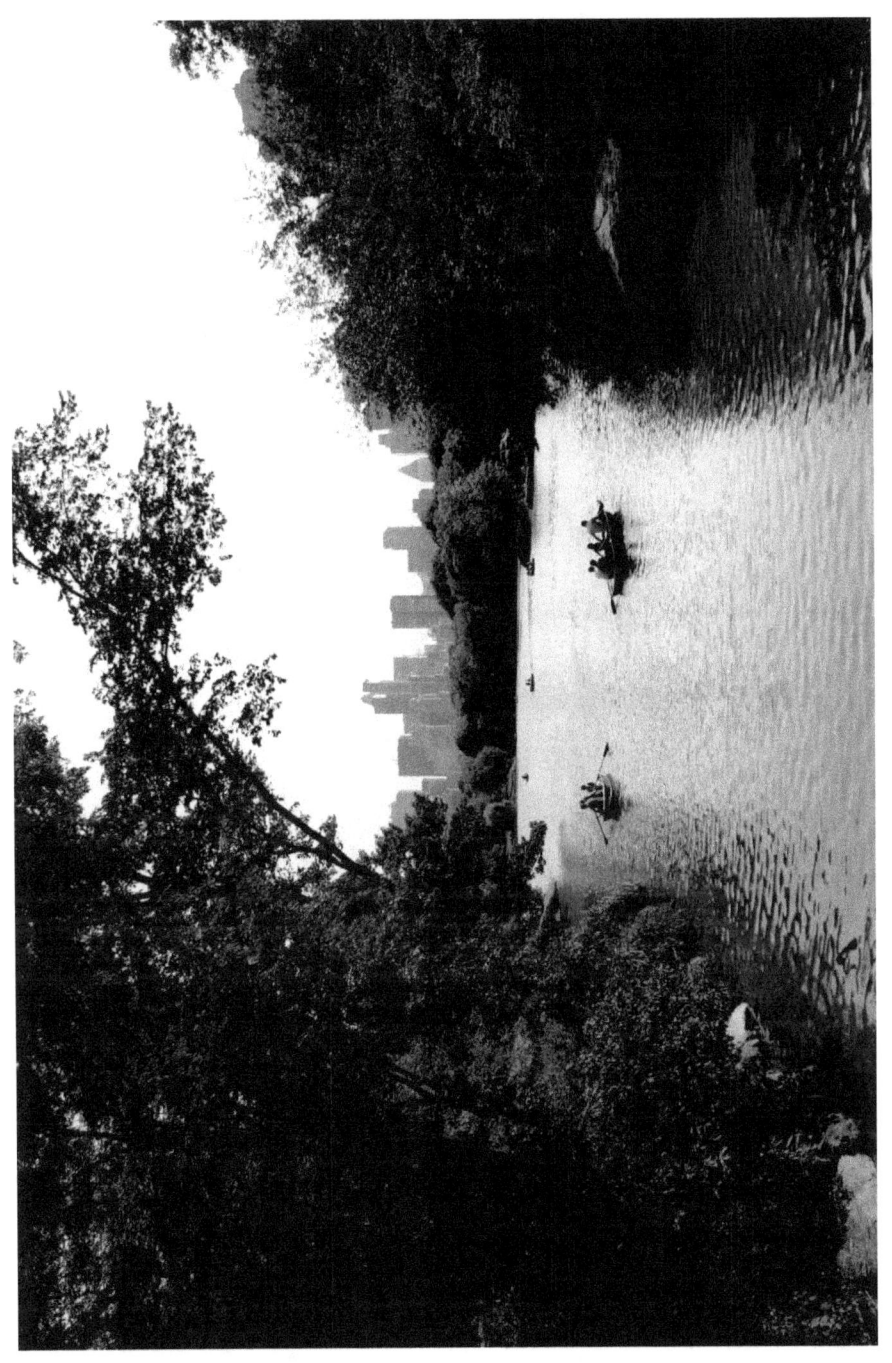

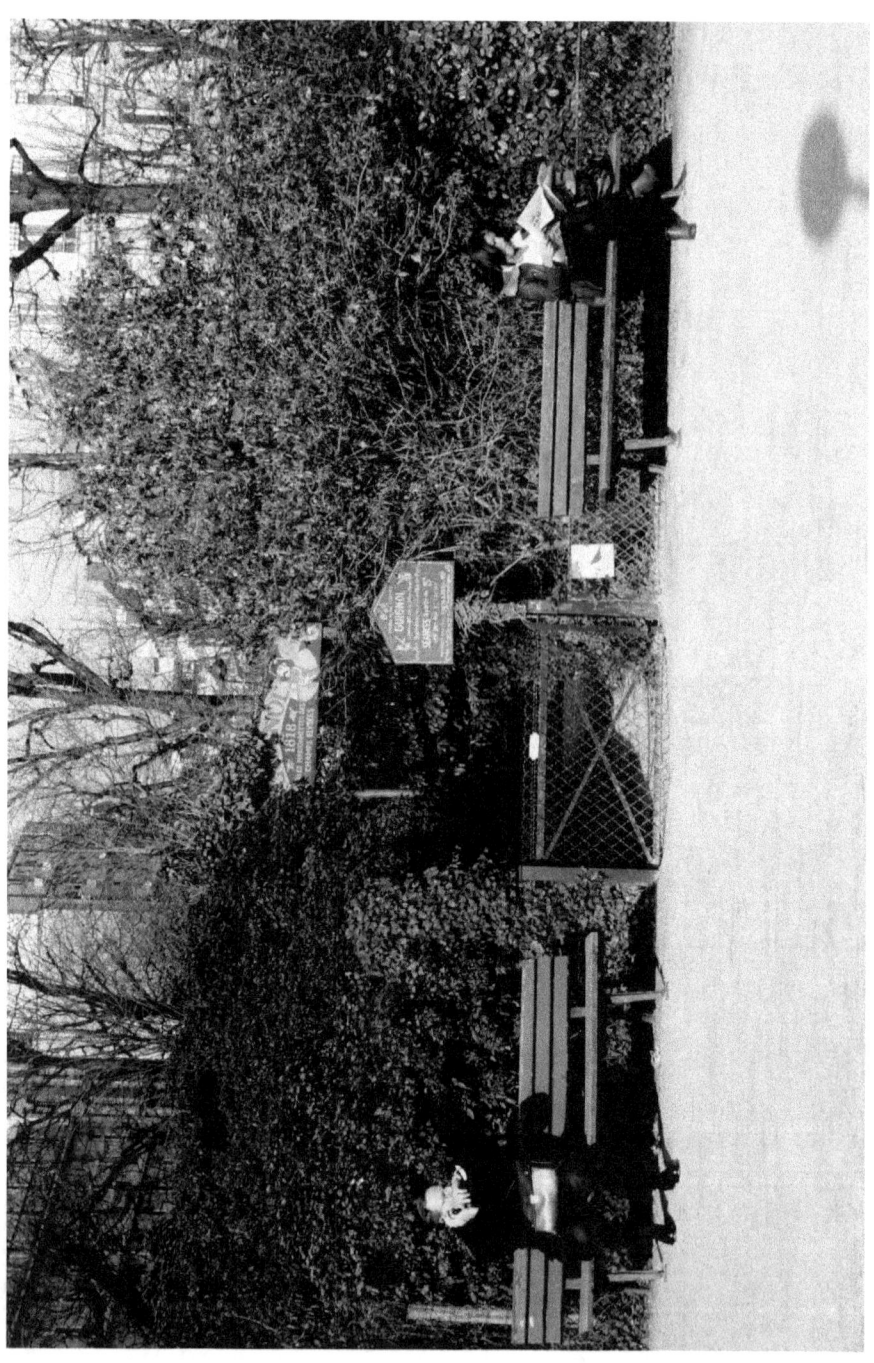

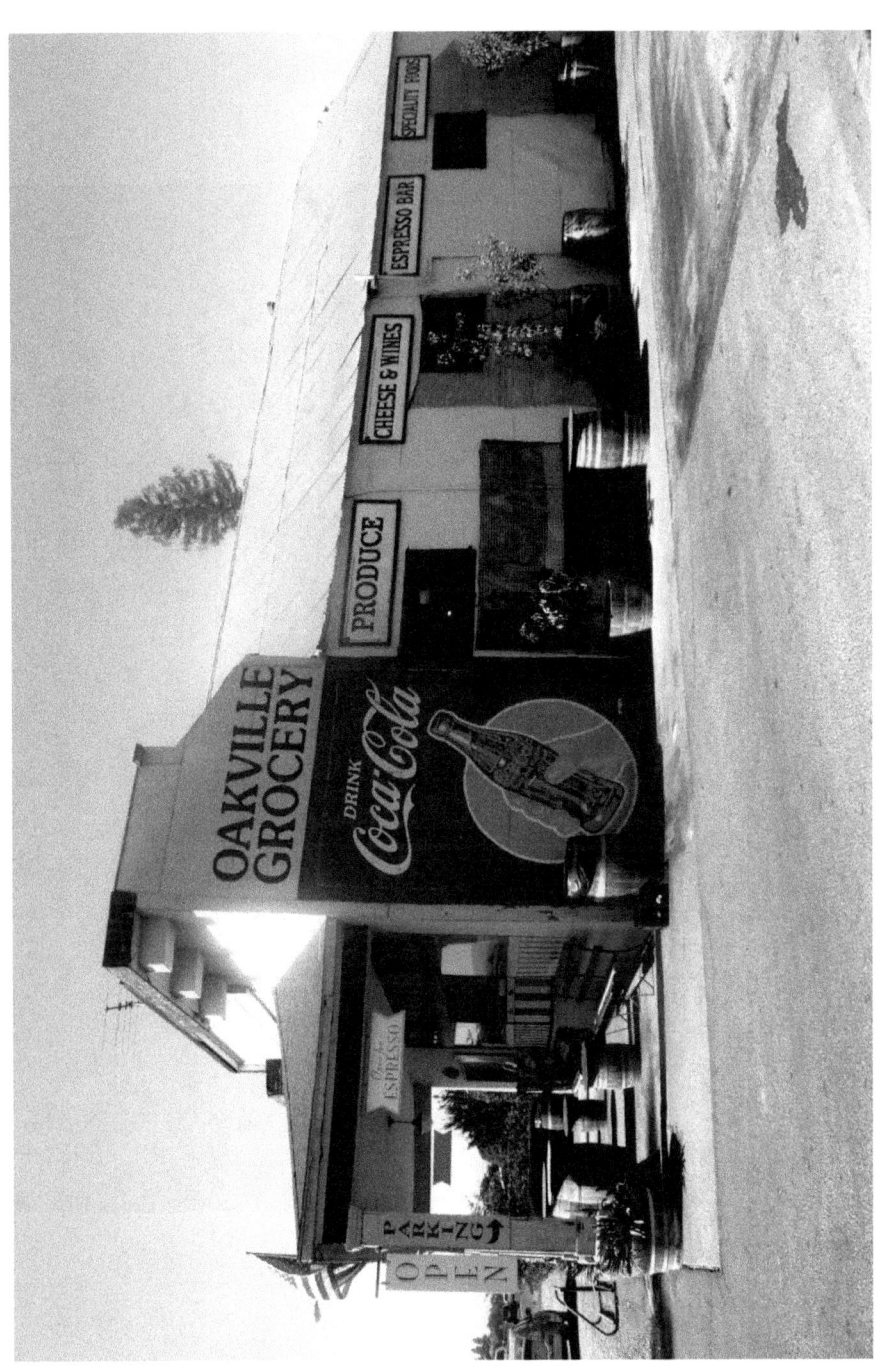

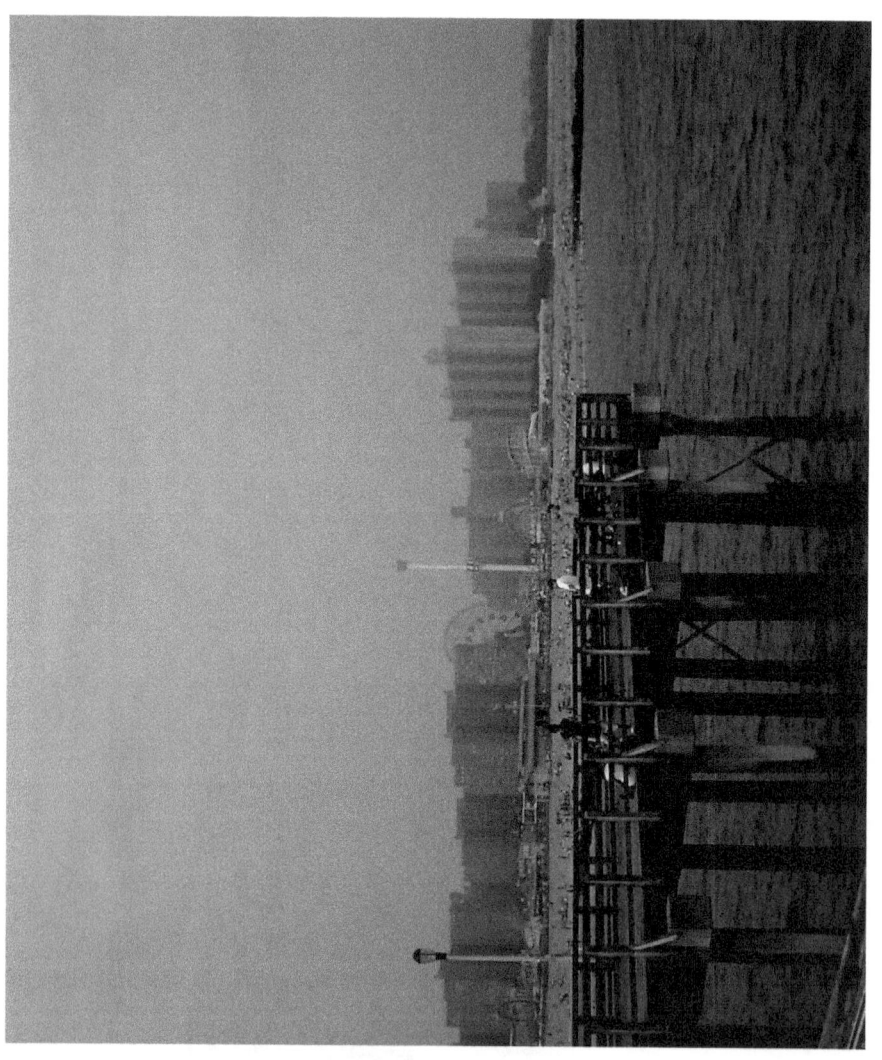

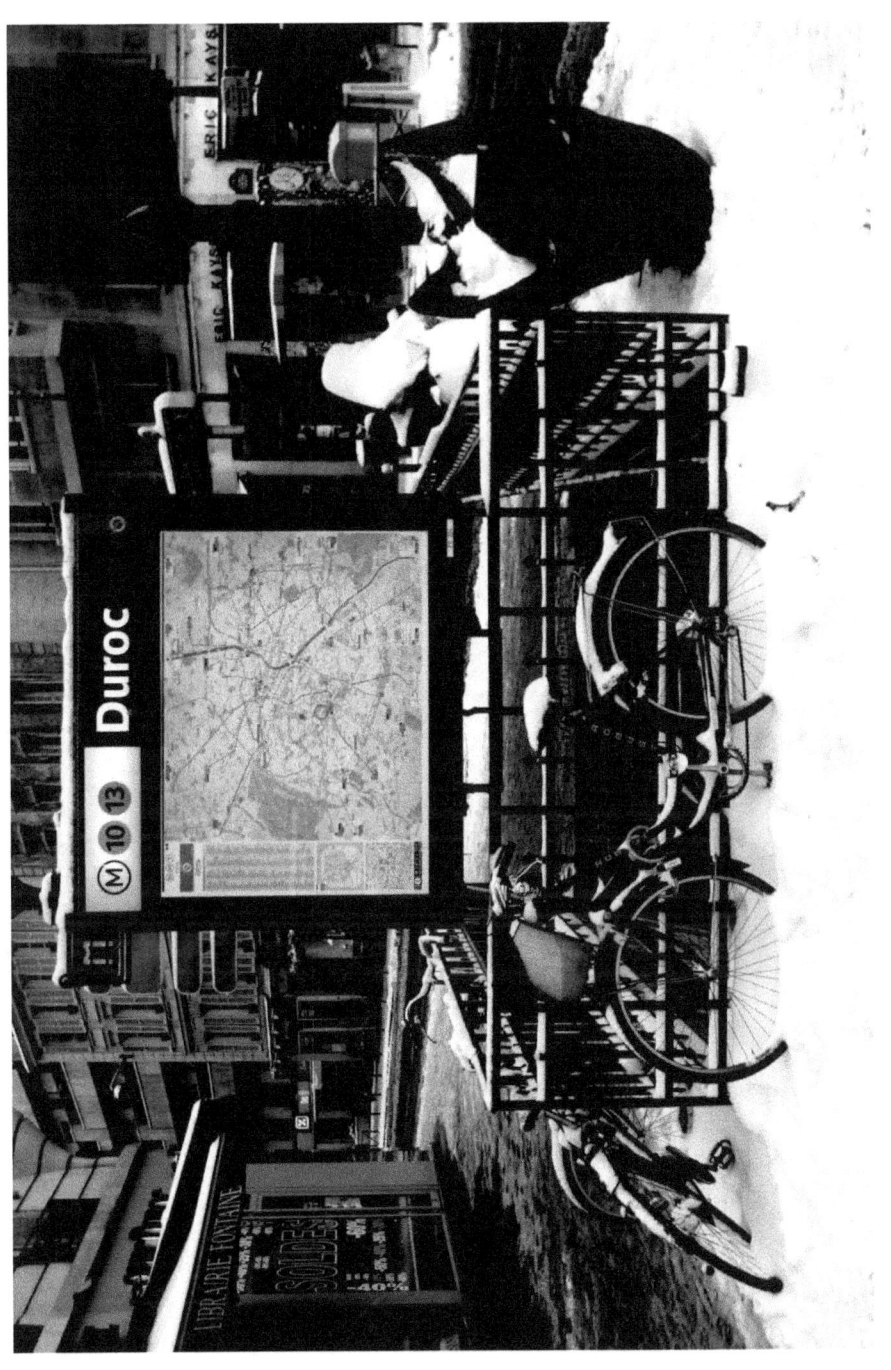

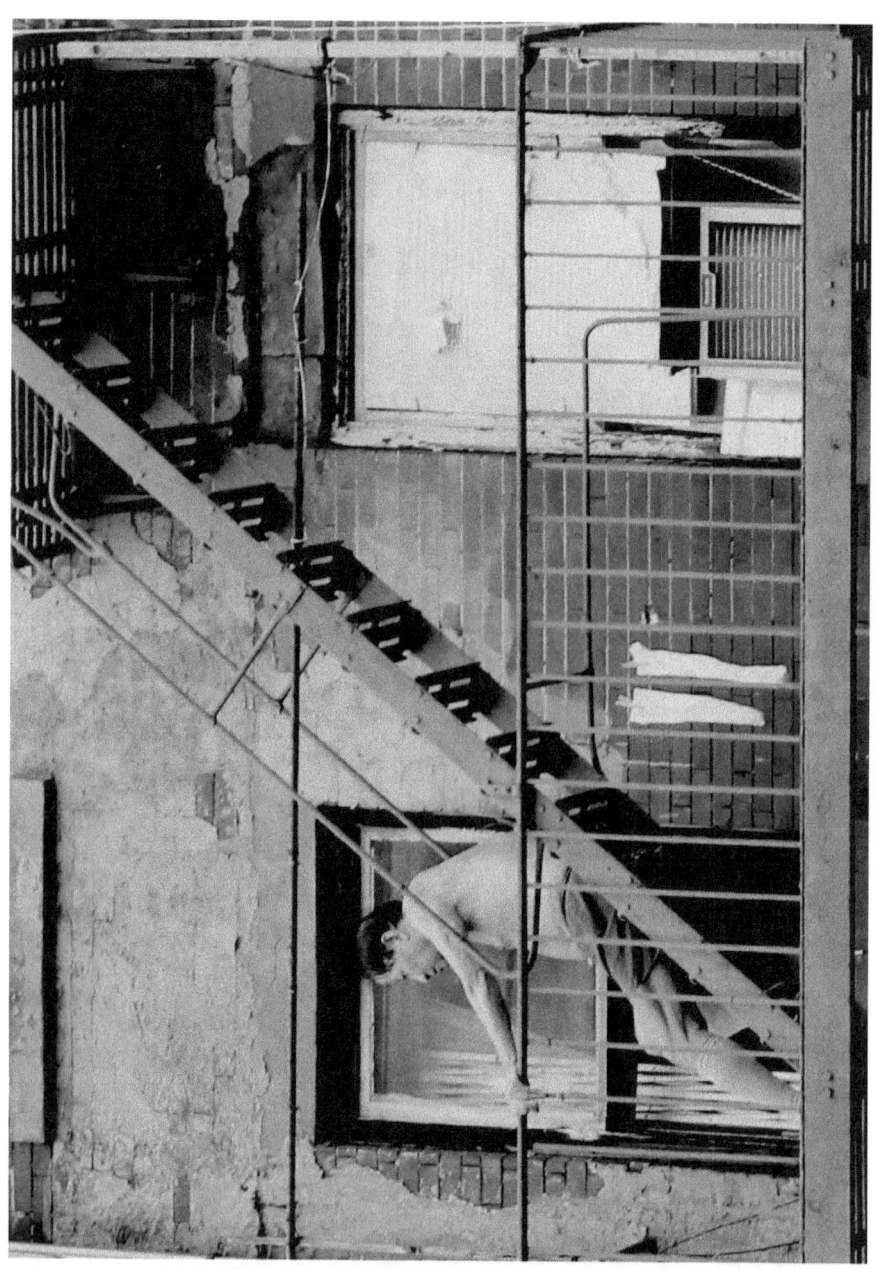

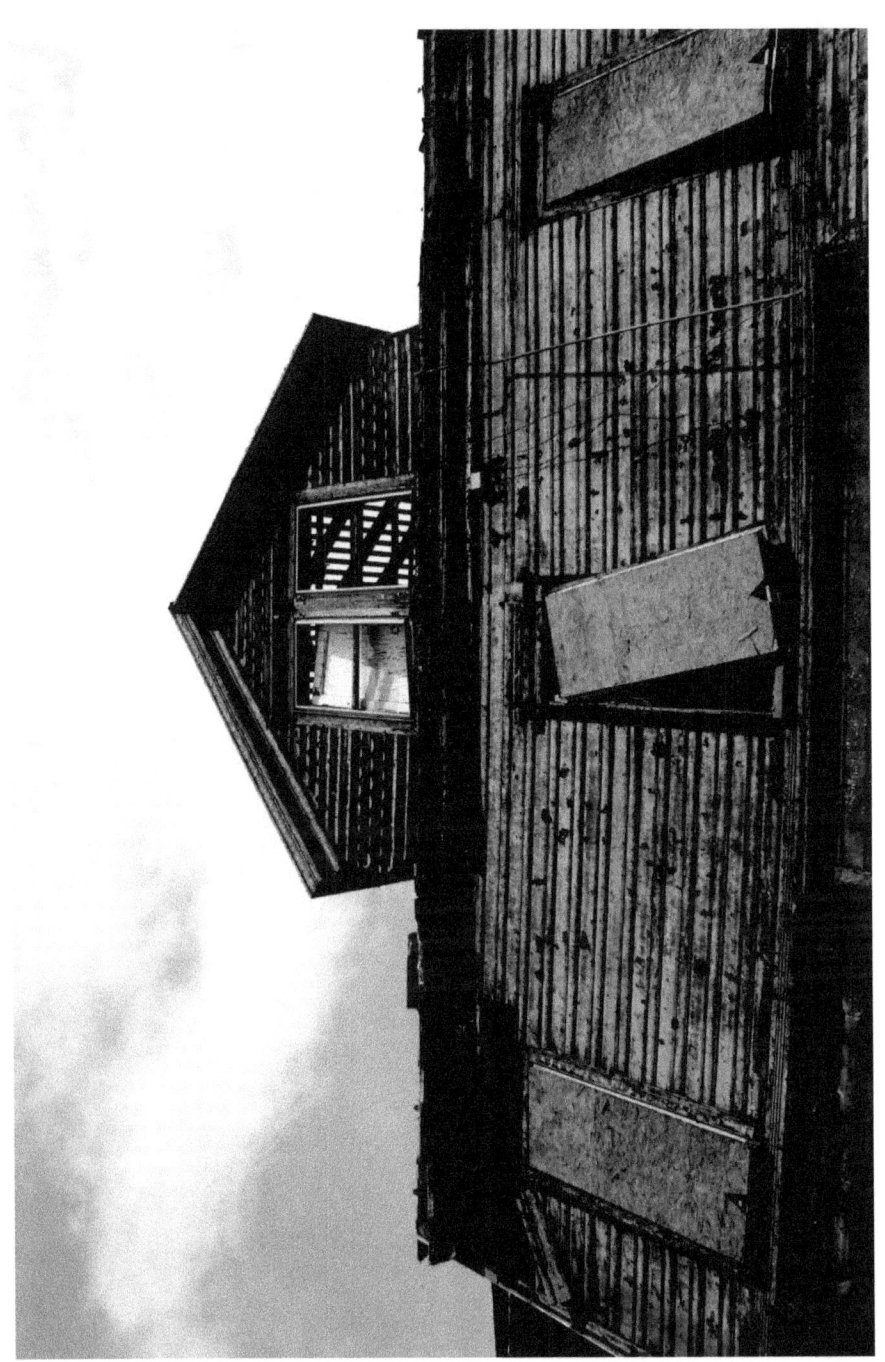

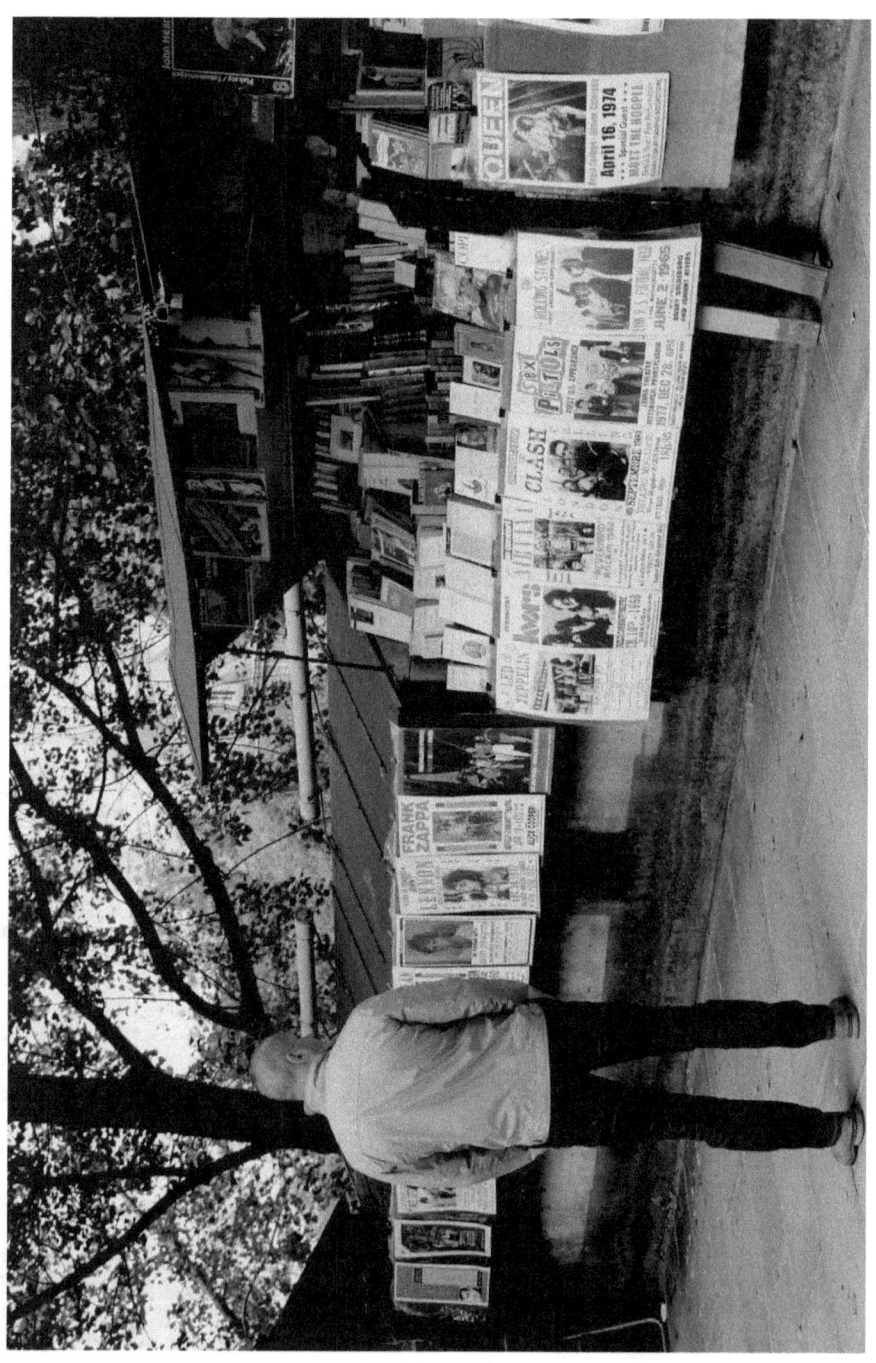

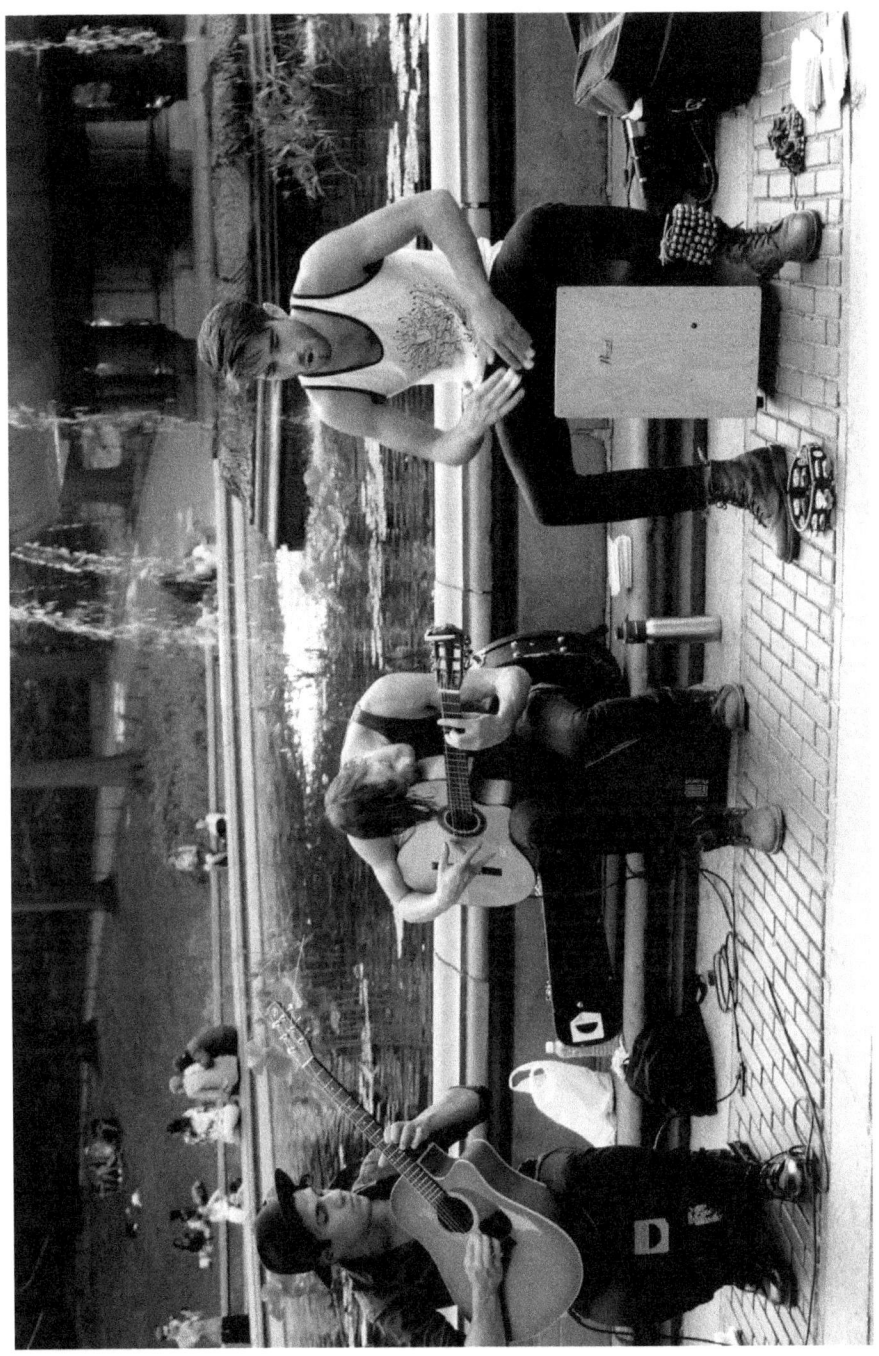

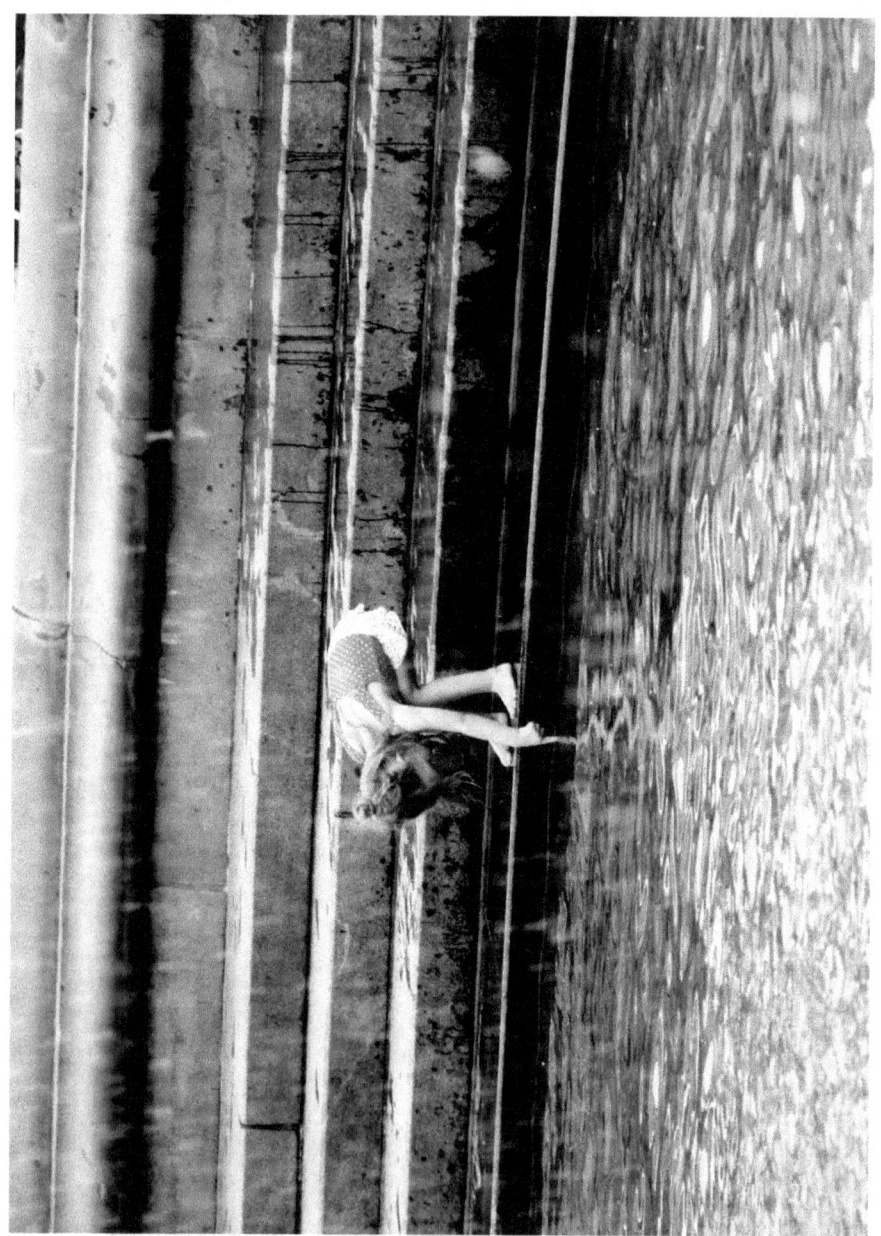

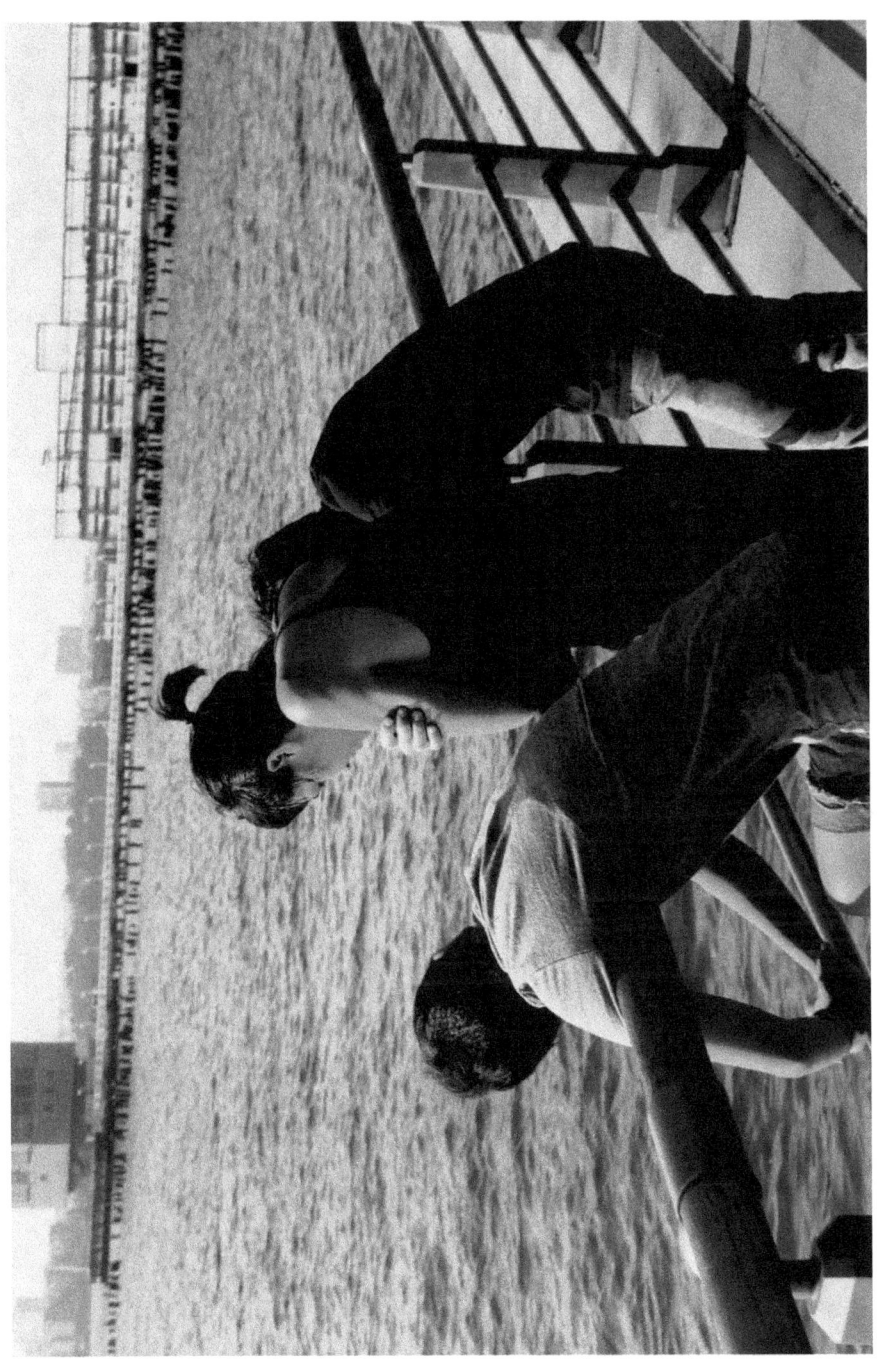

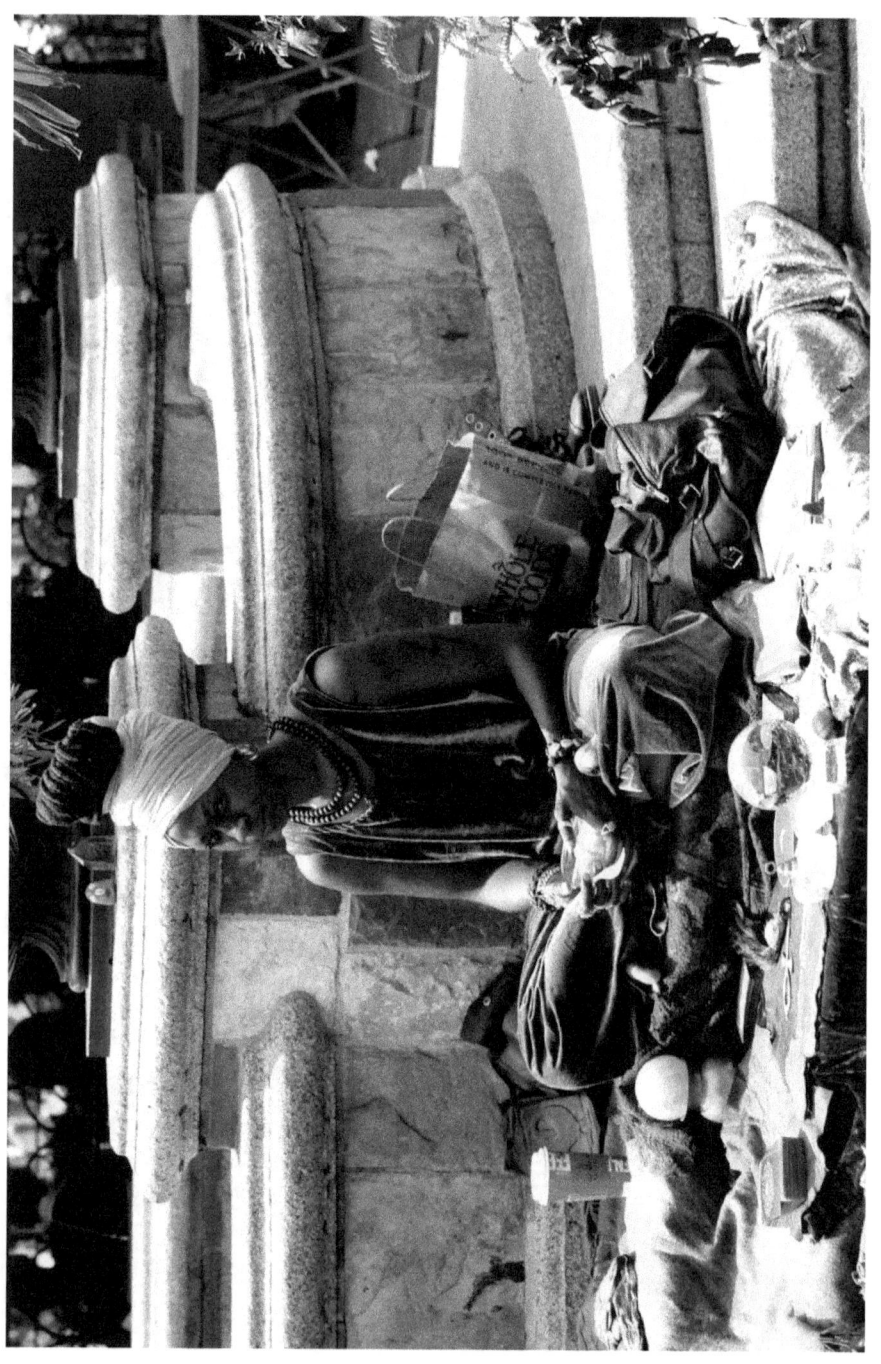

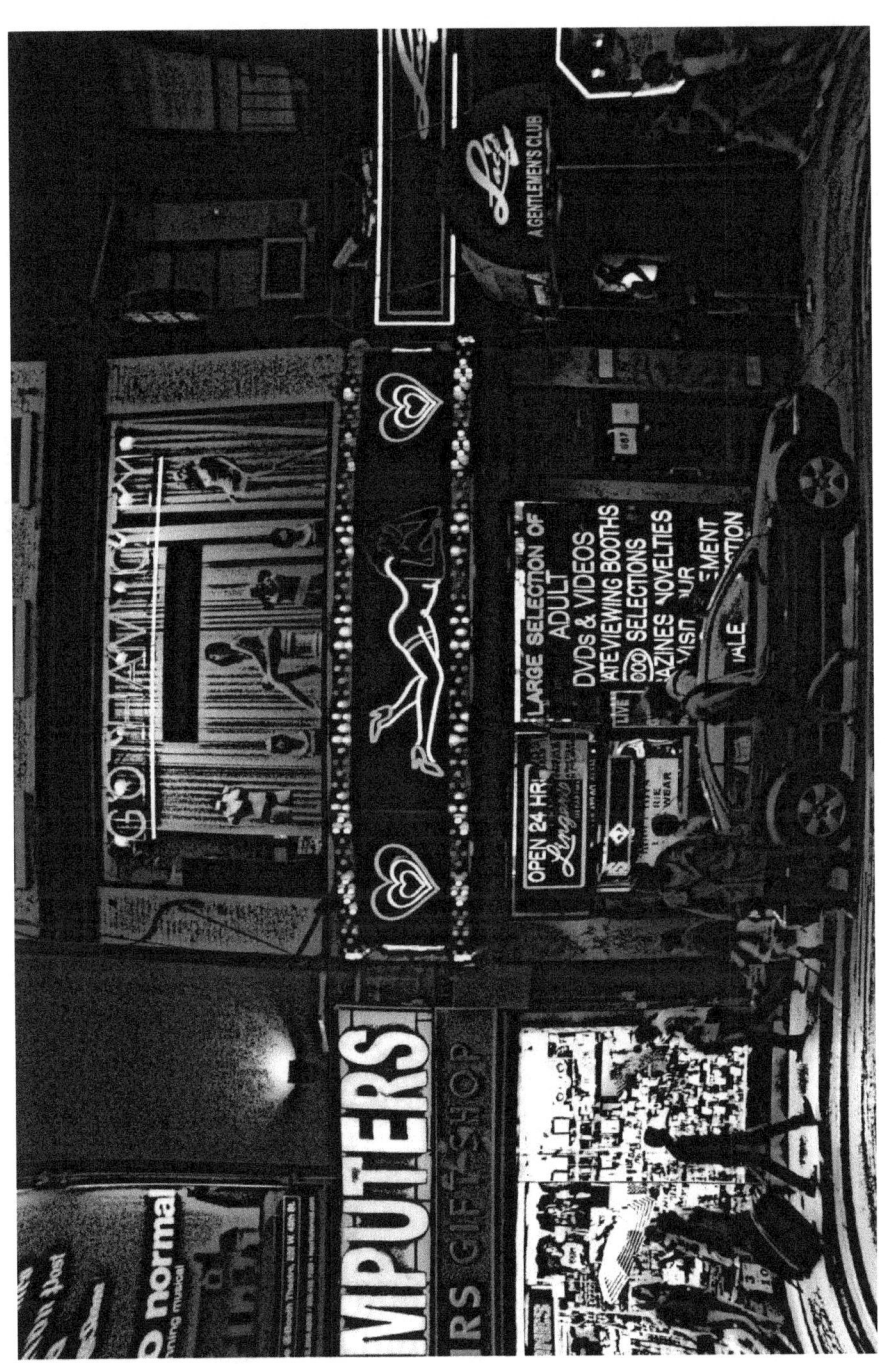

191

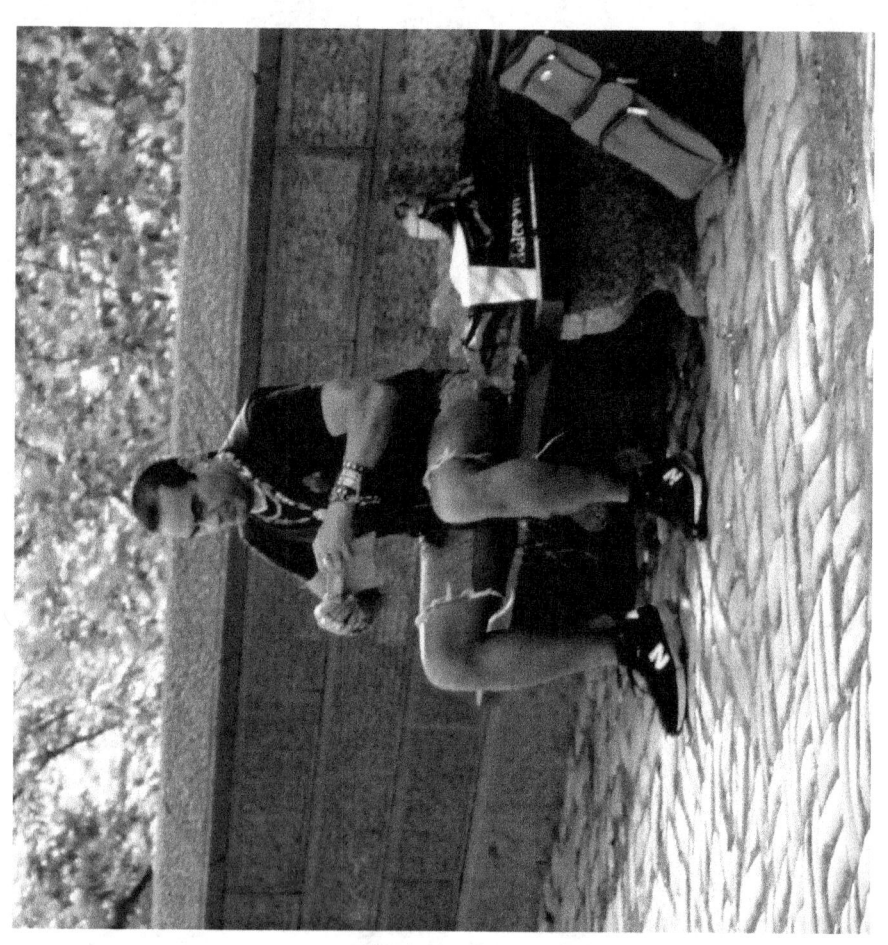

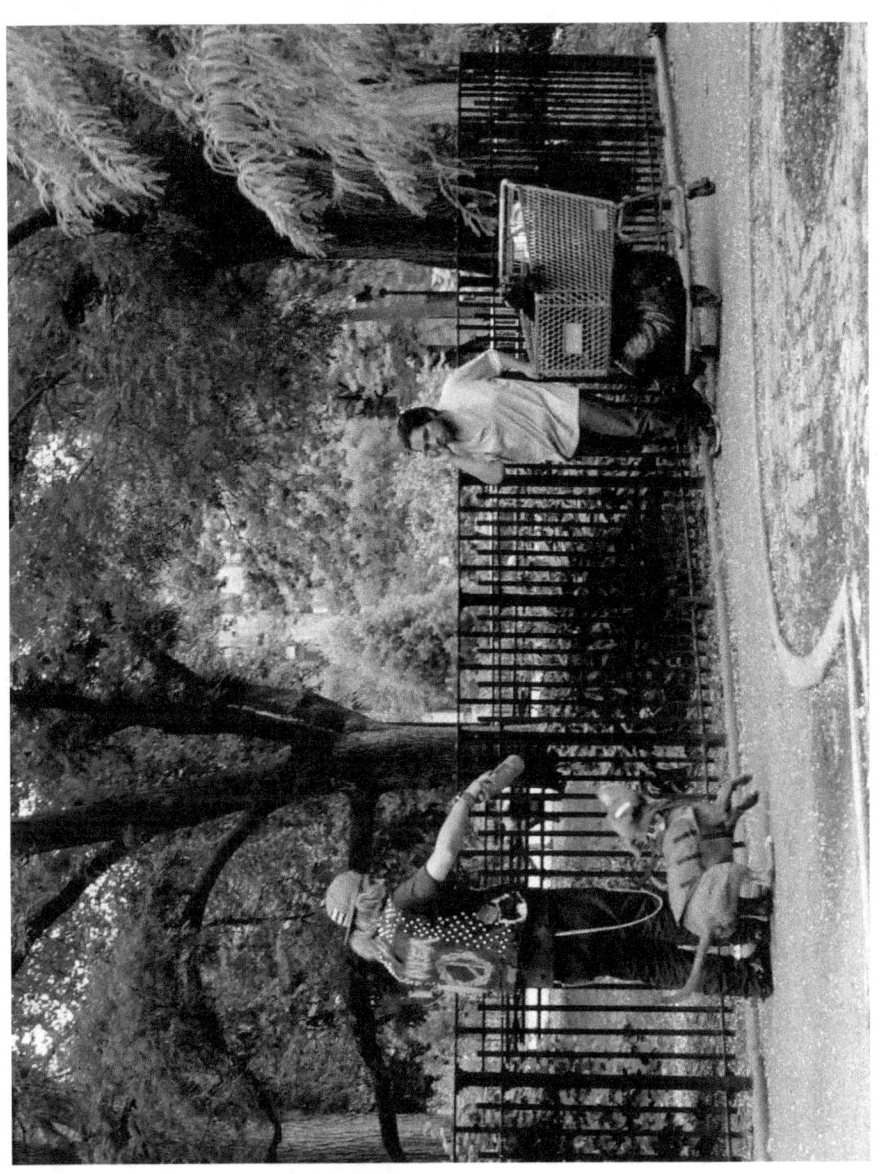

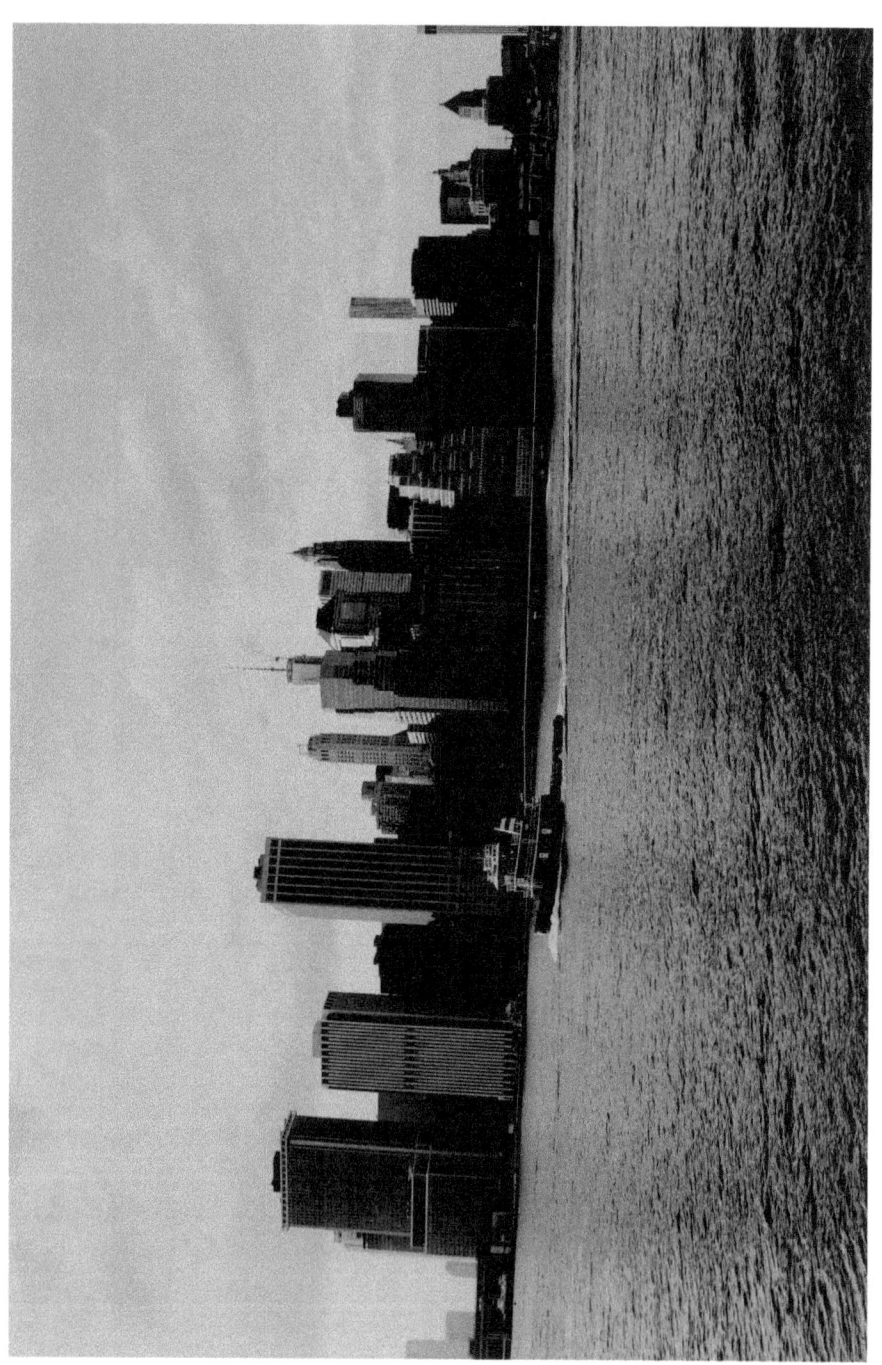

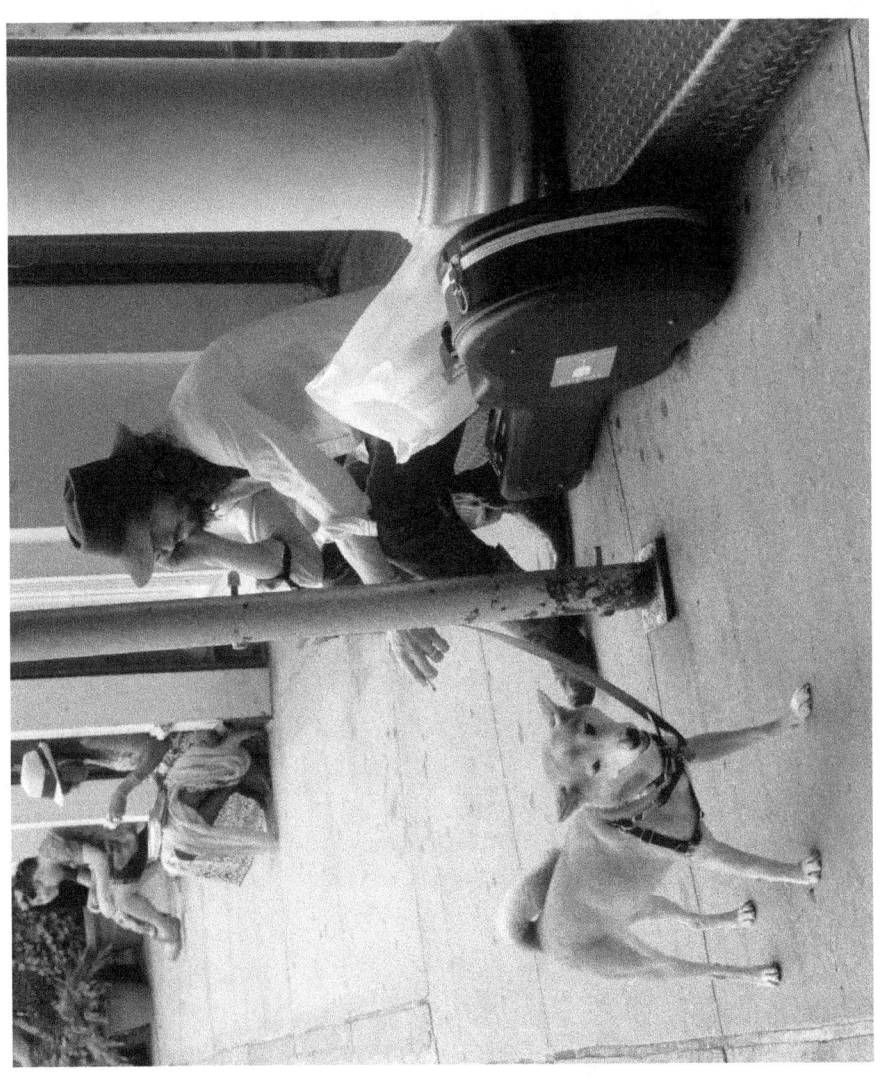

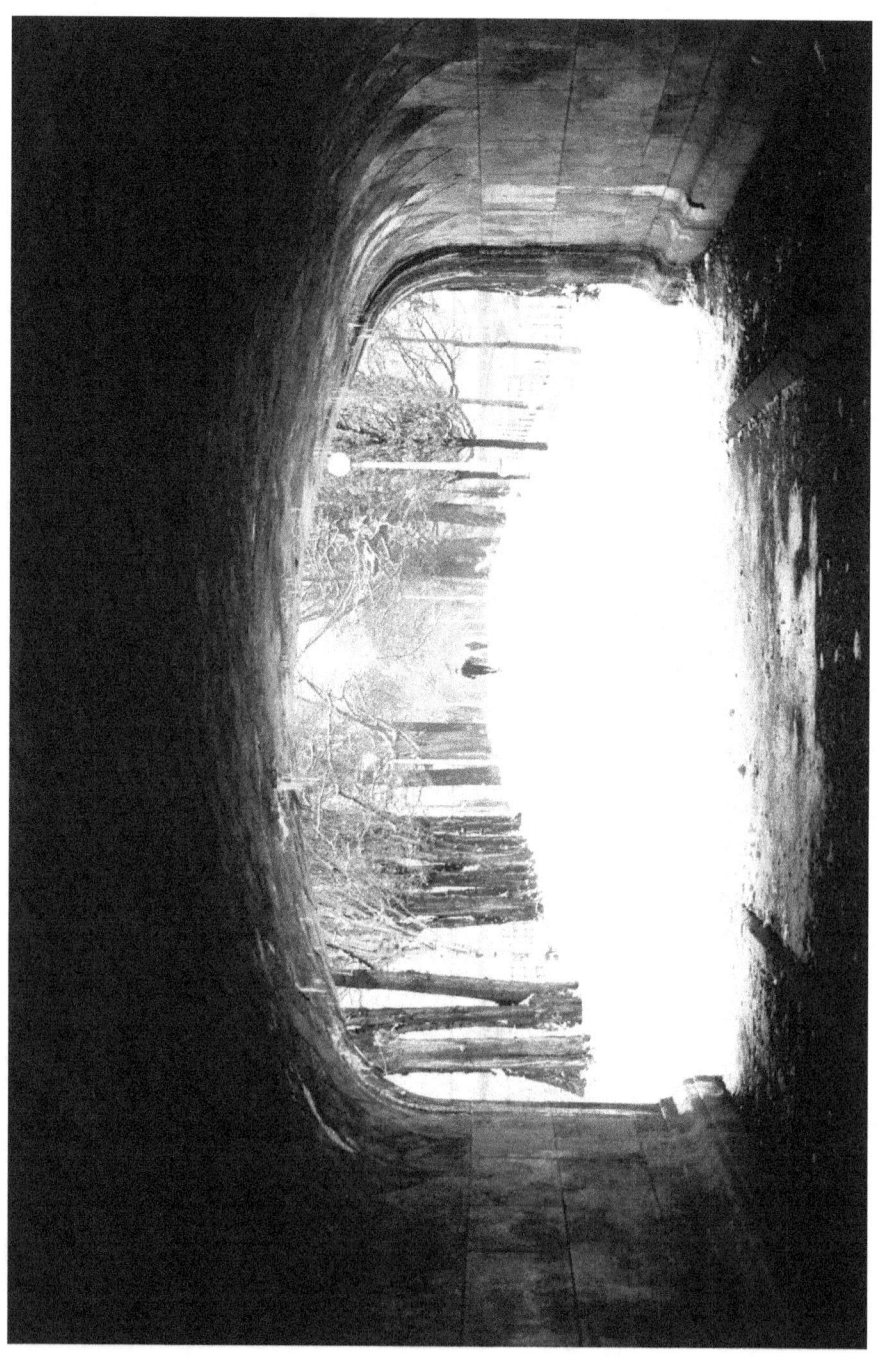

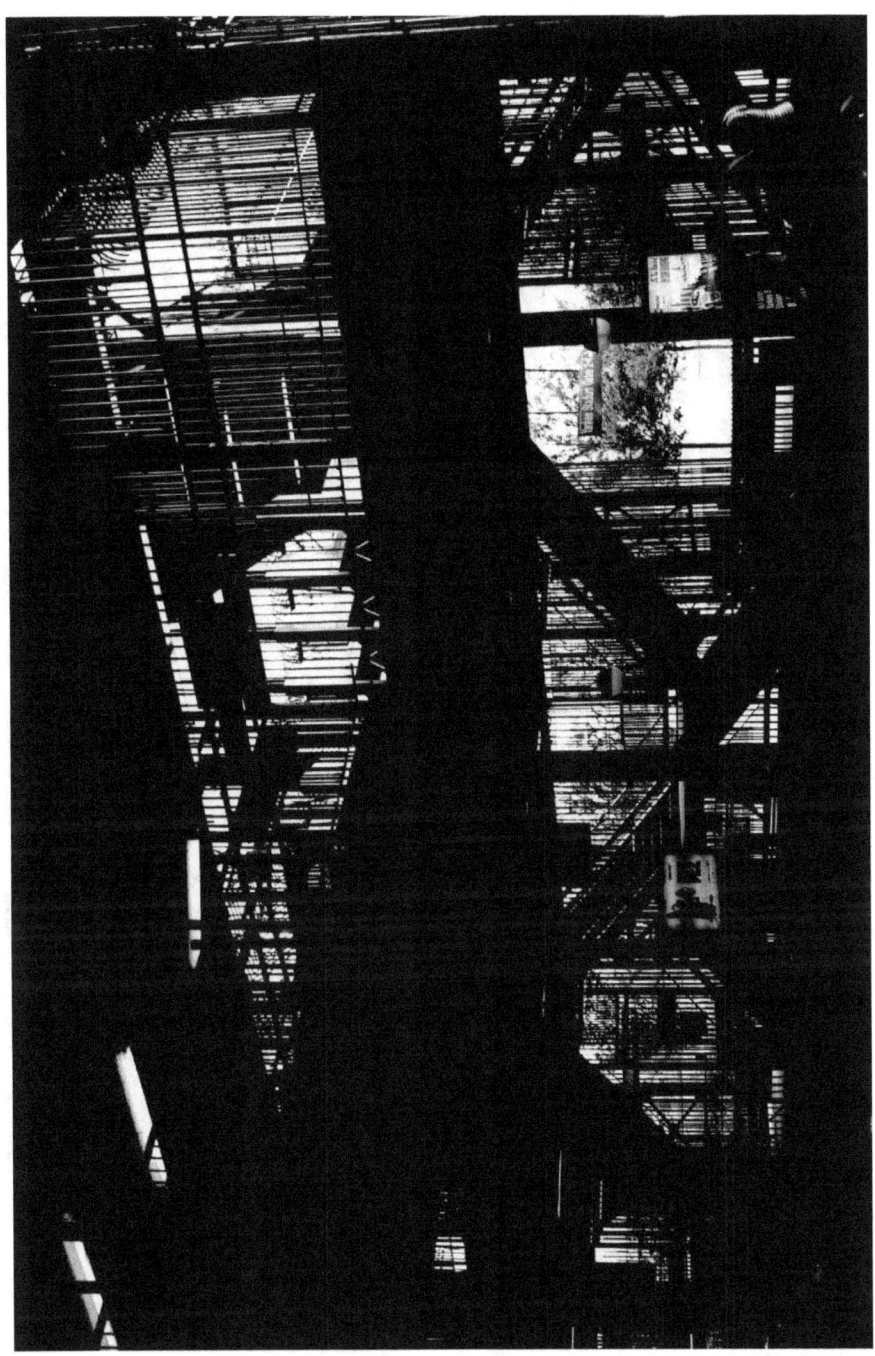

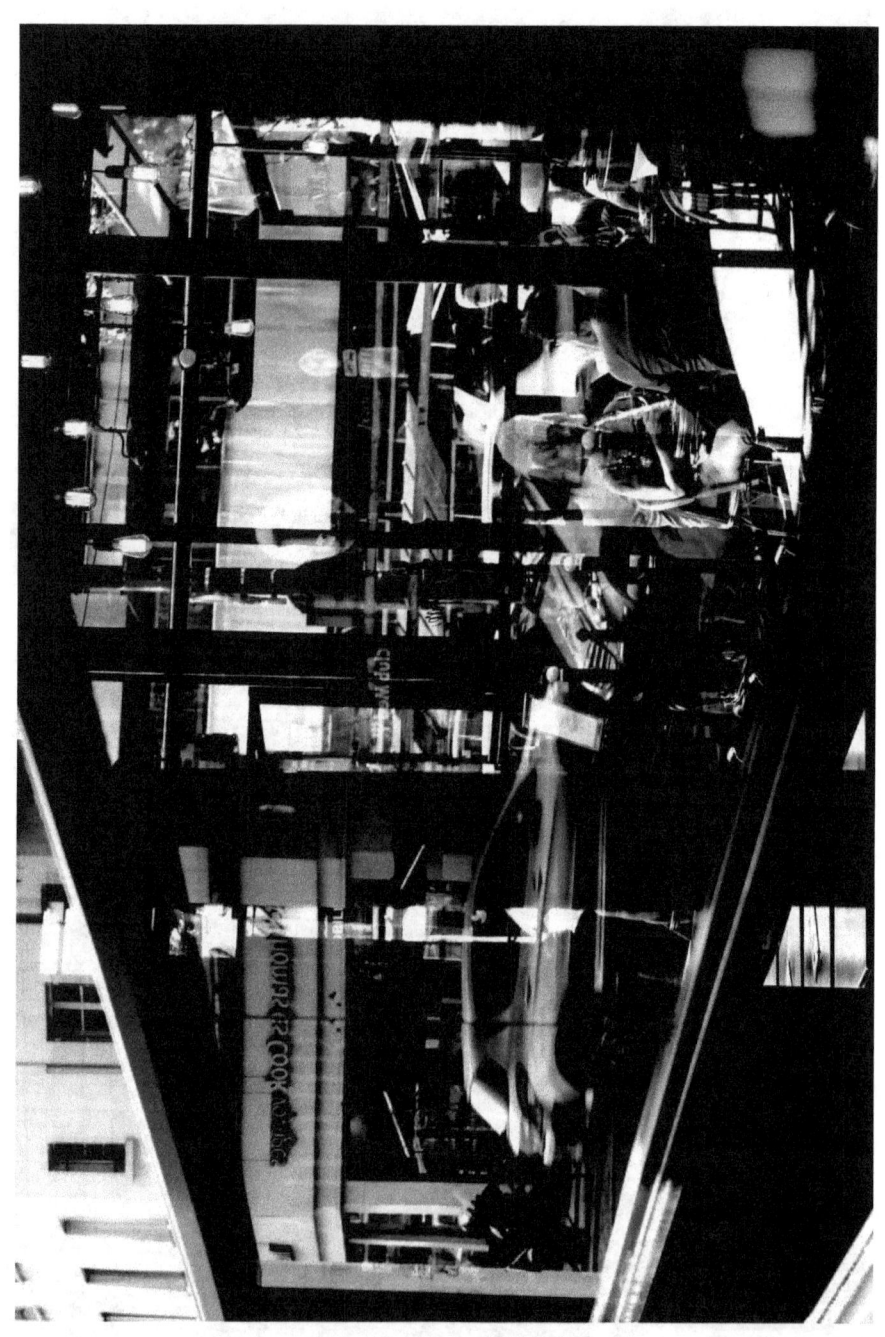

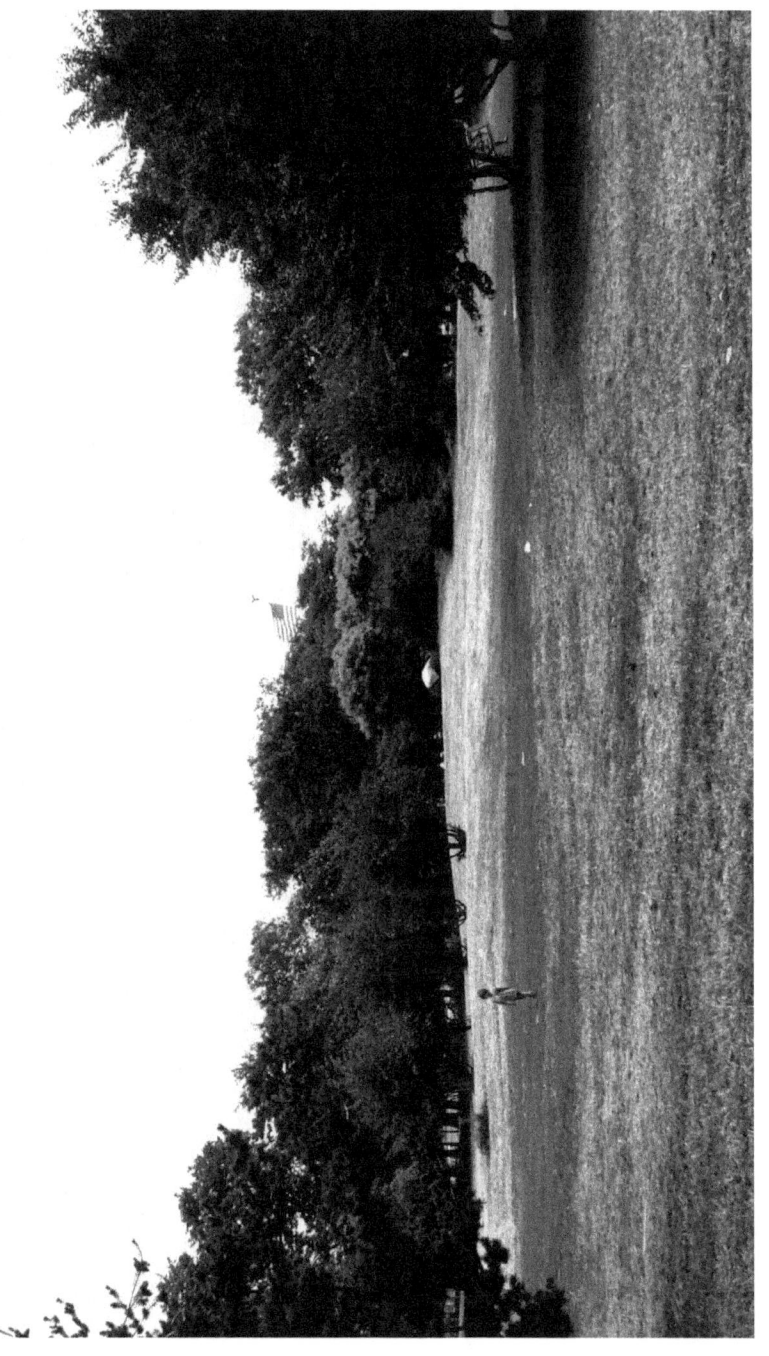

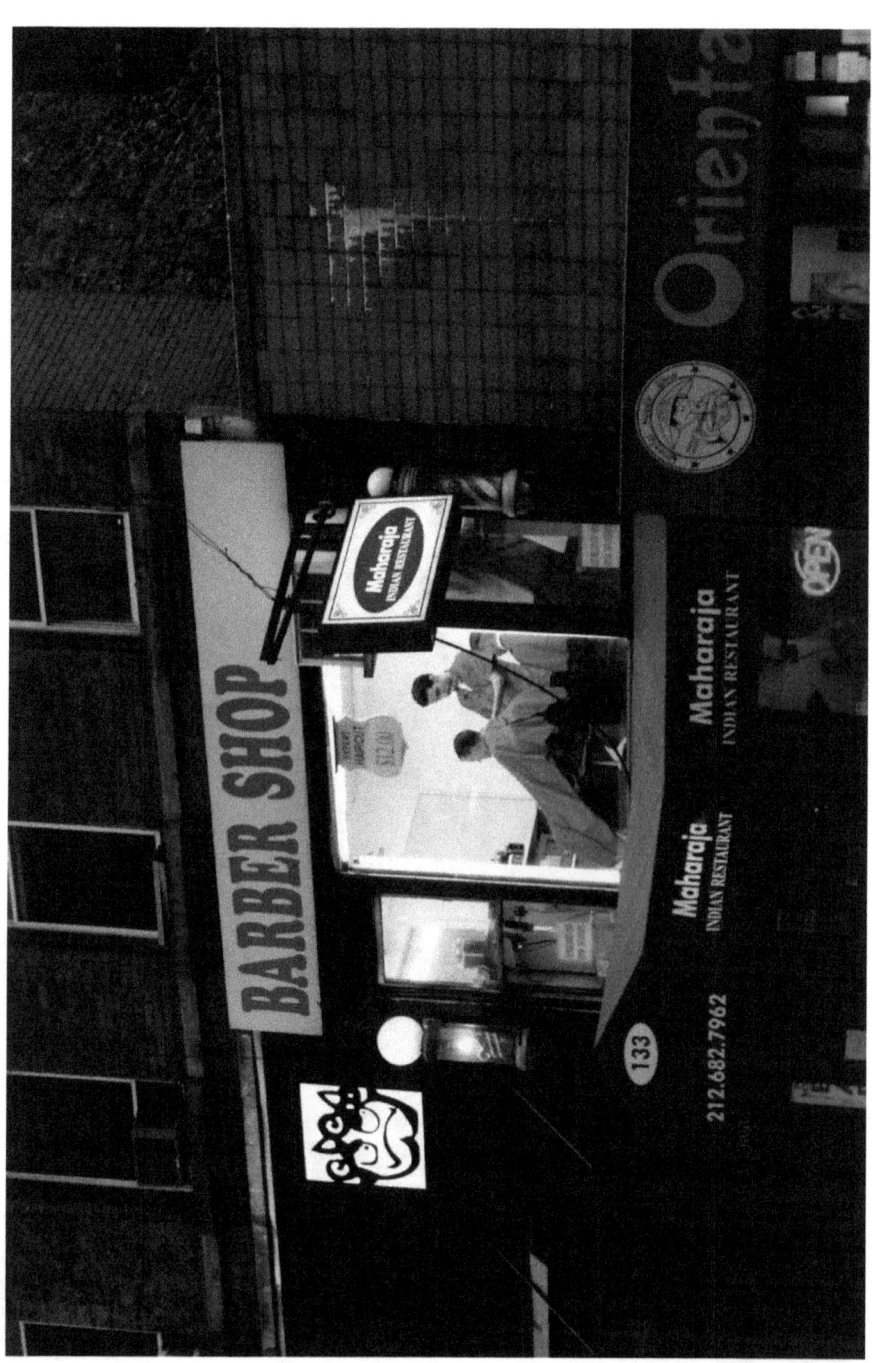

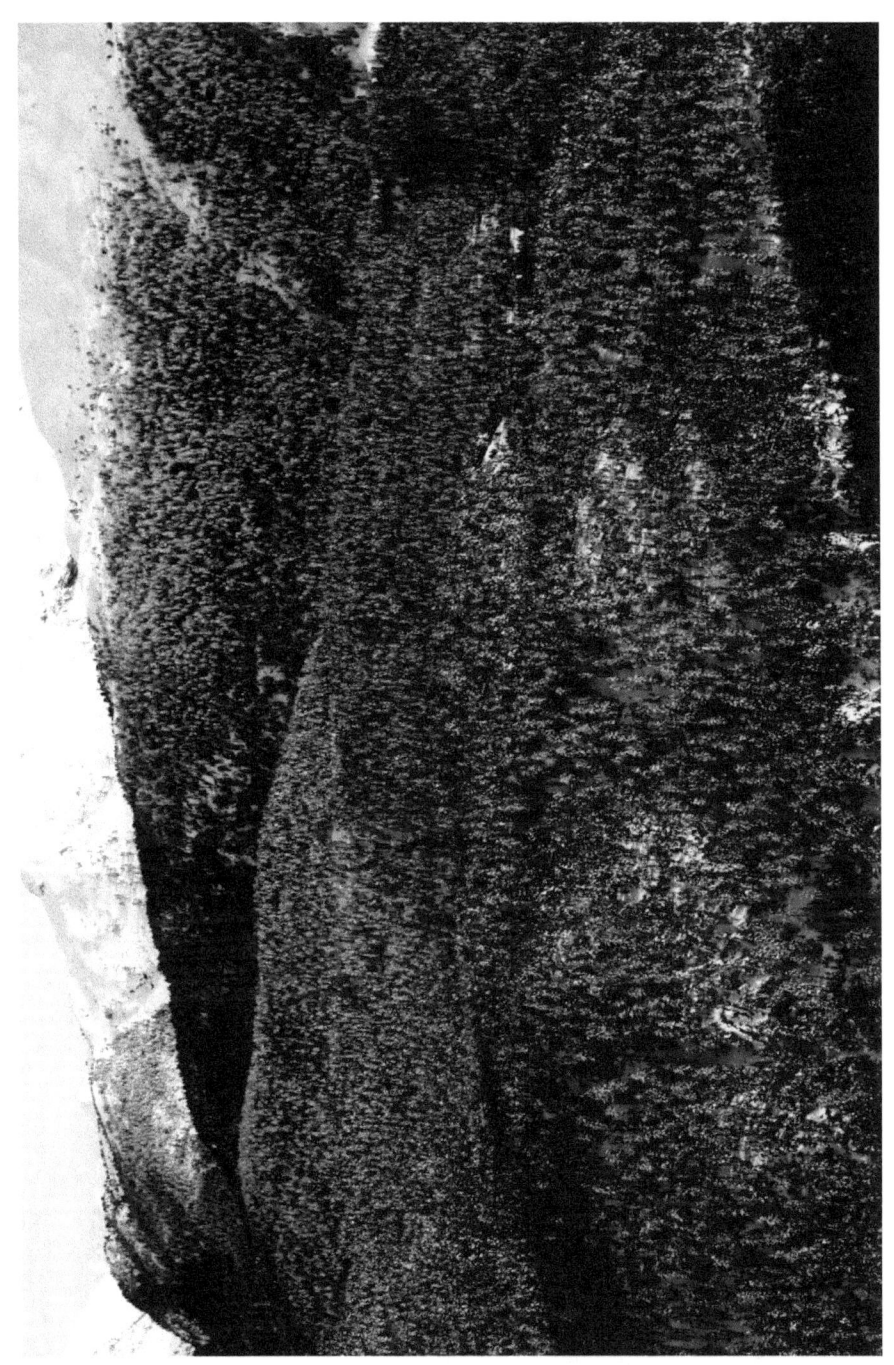

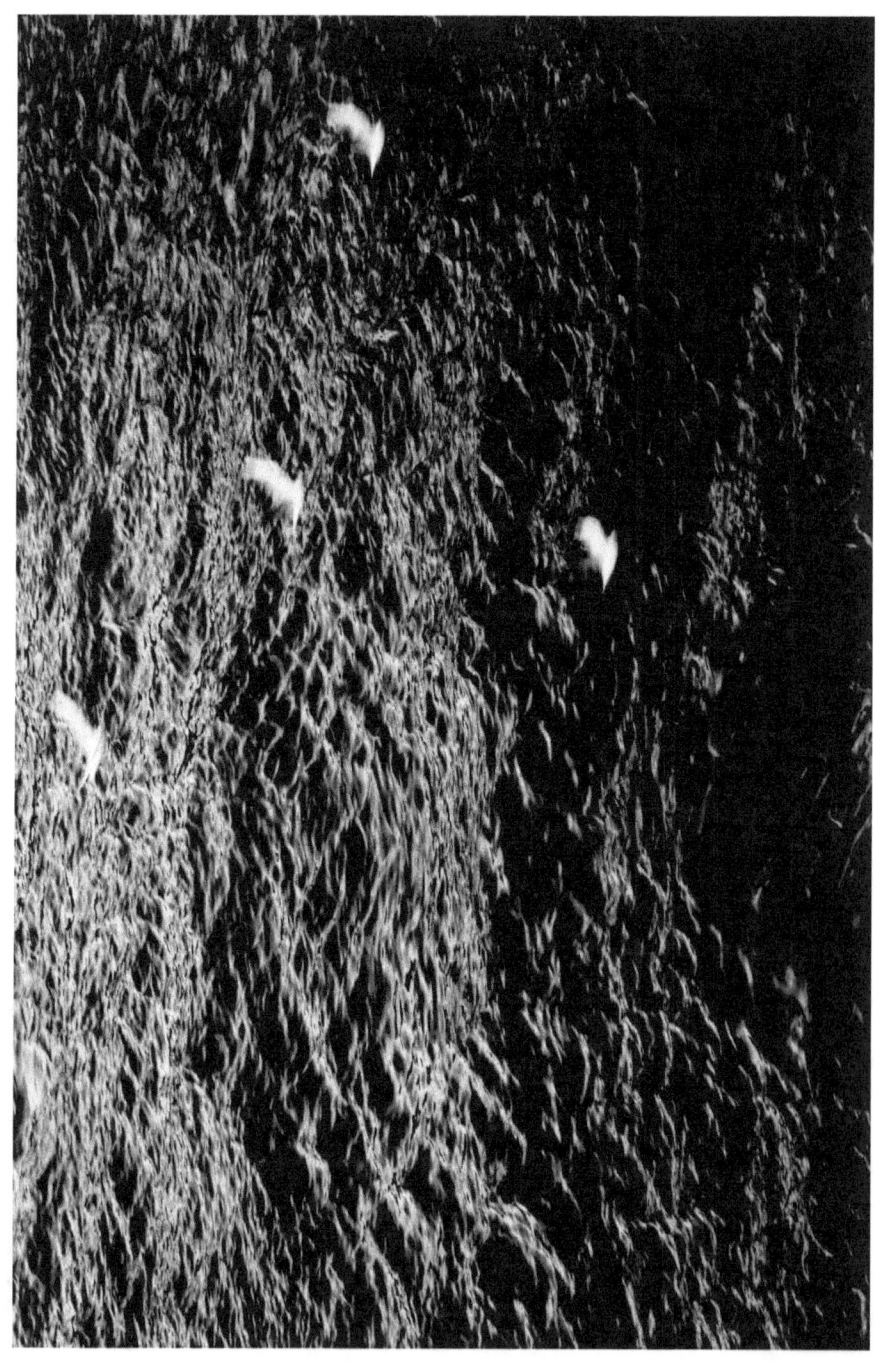

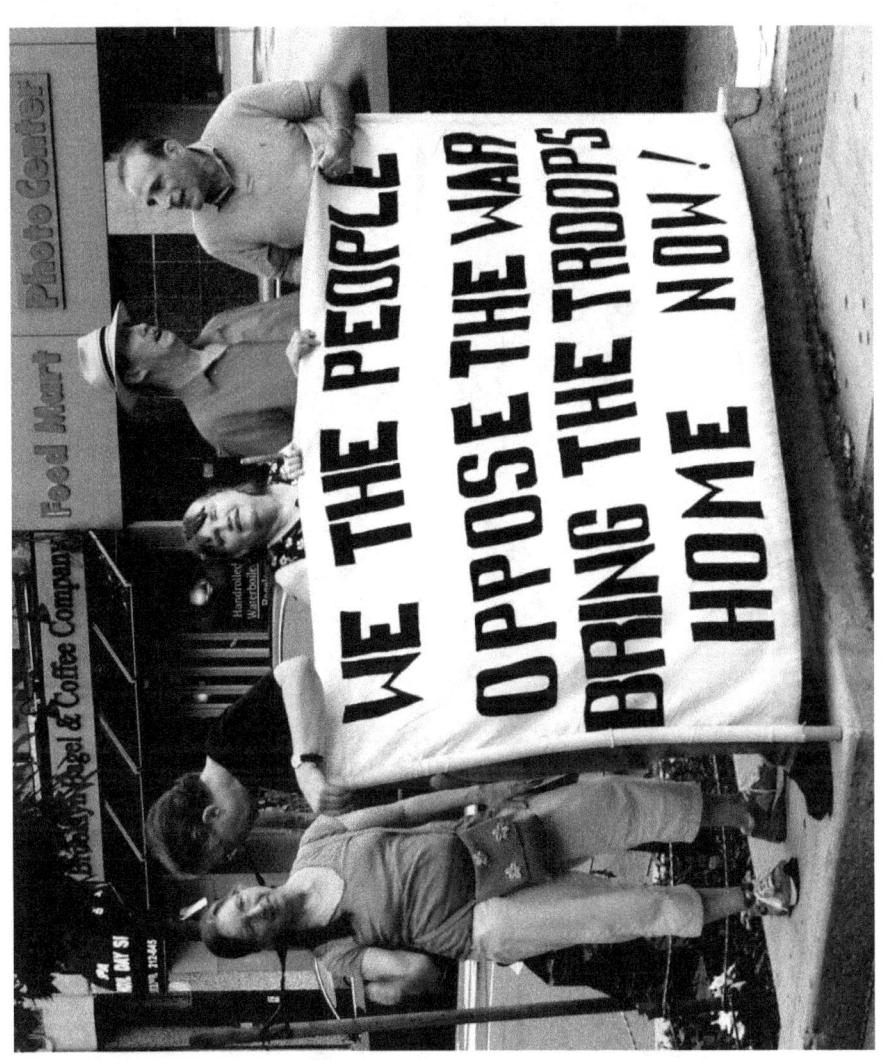

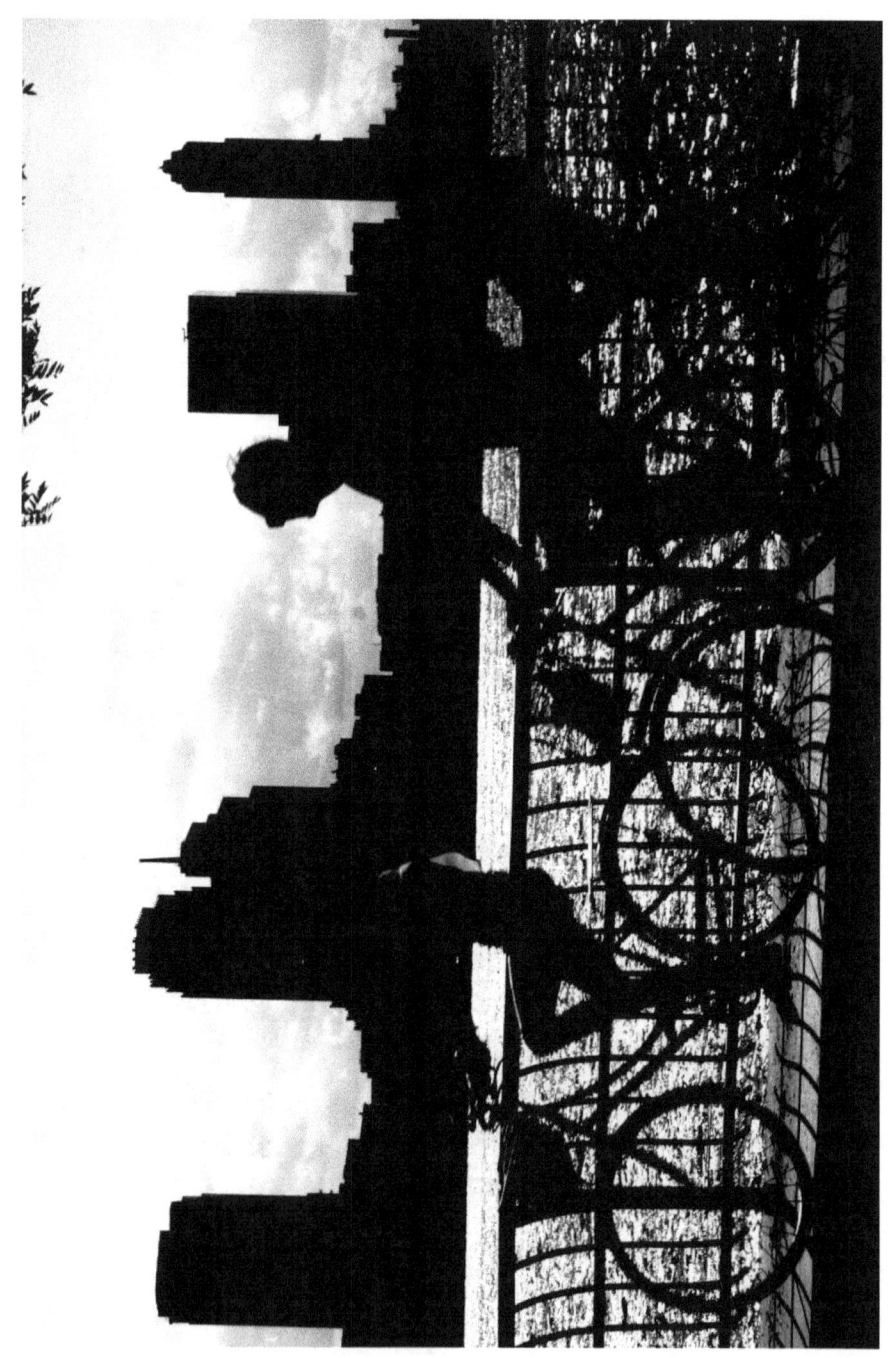

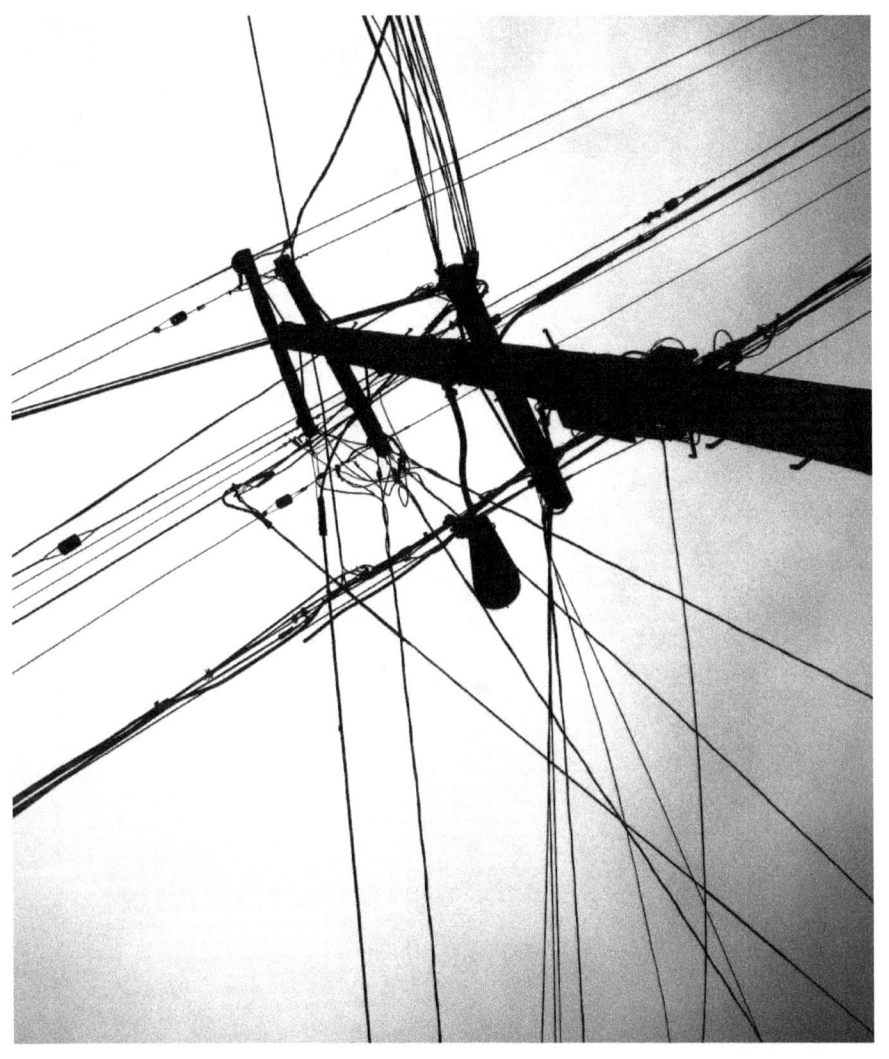

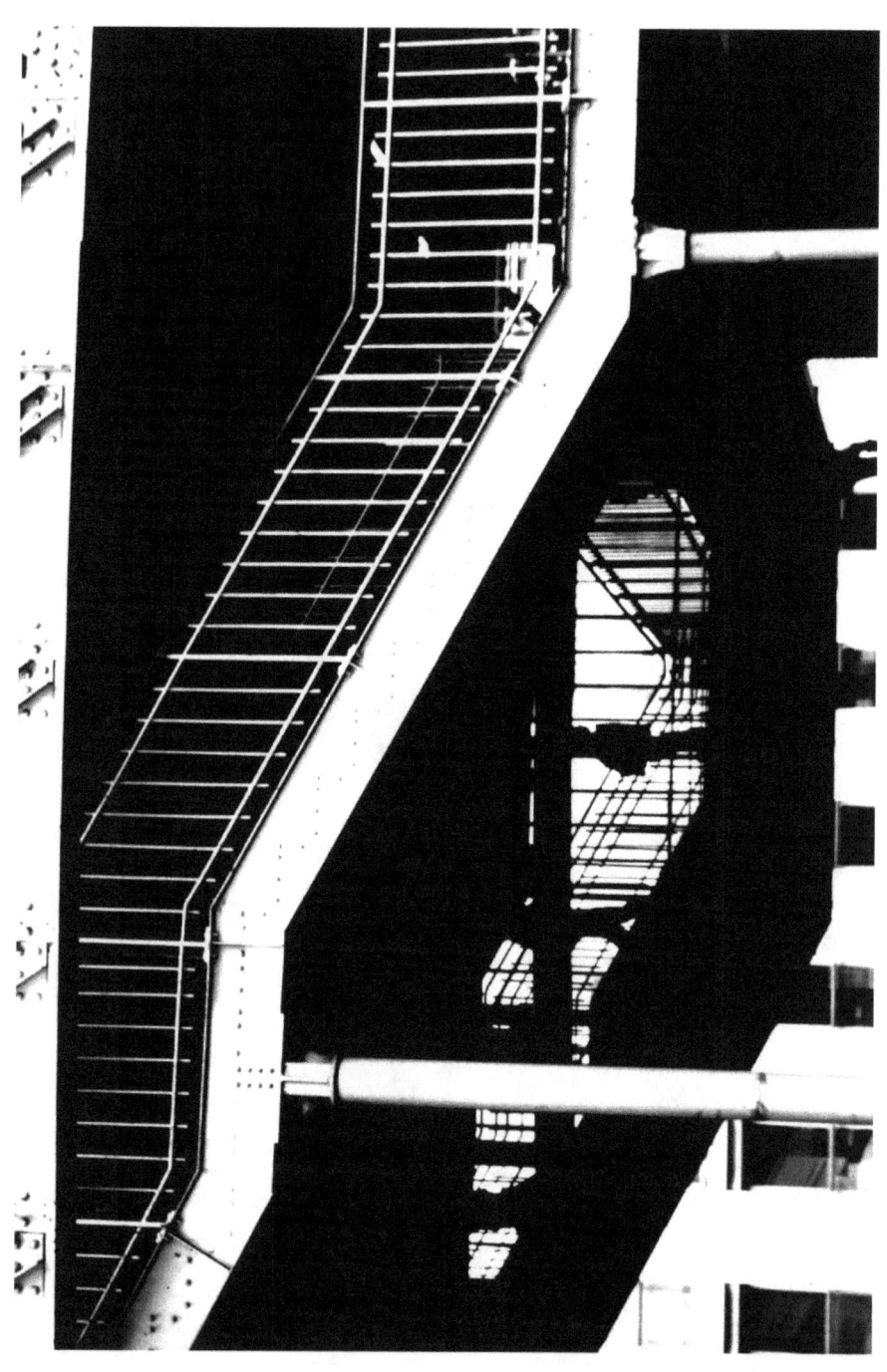

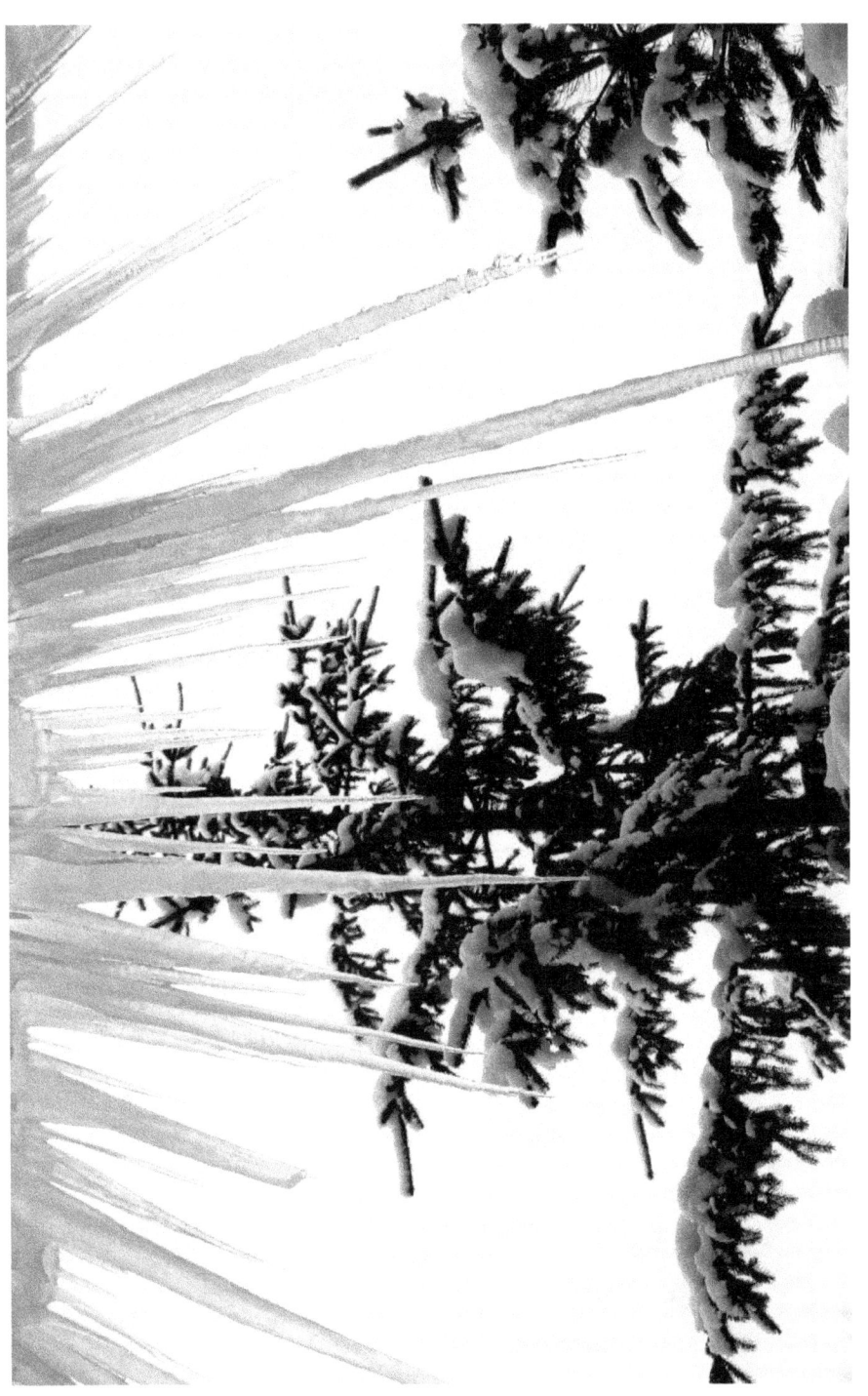

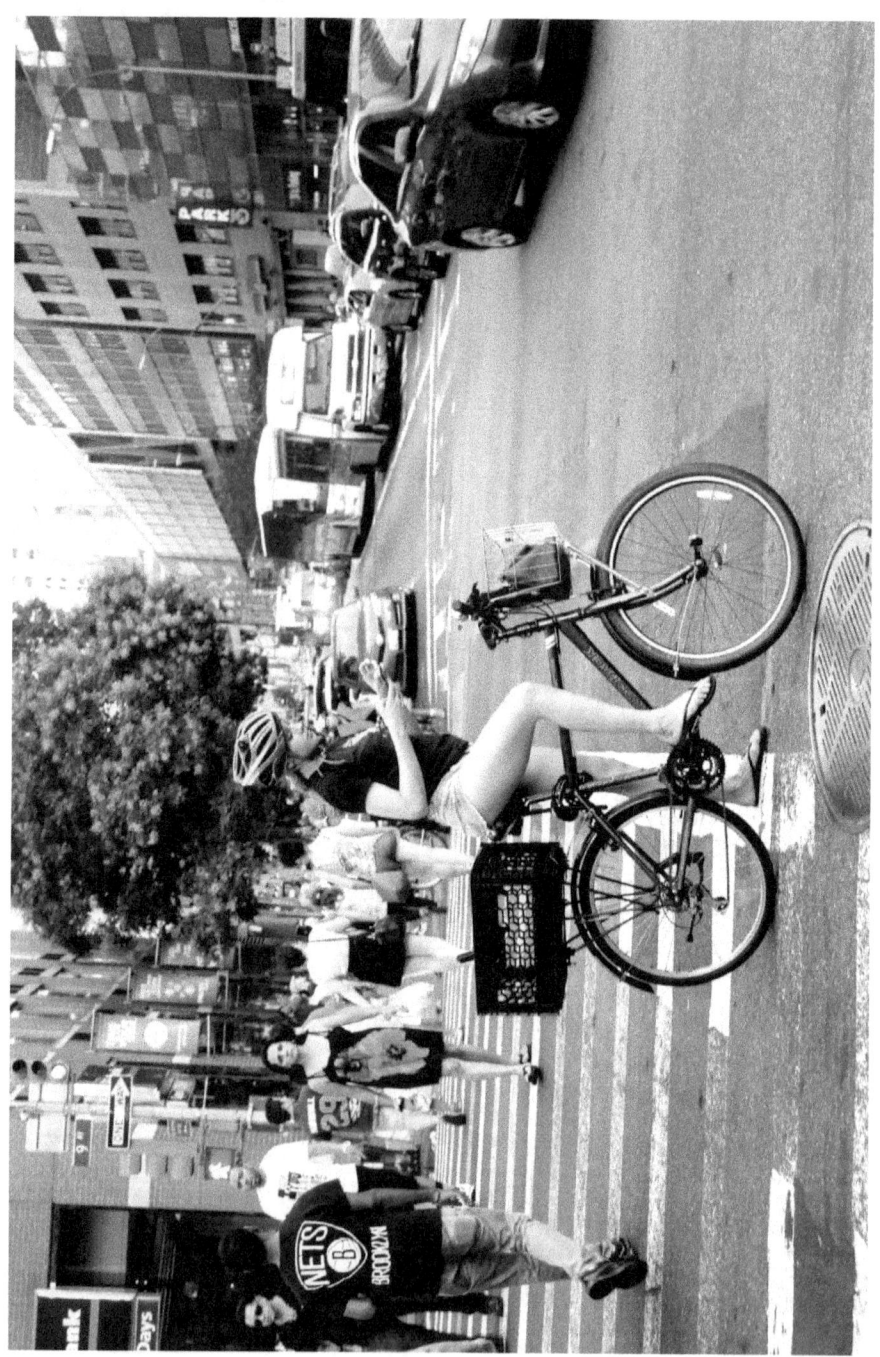

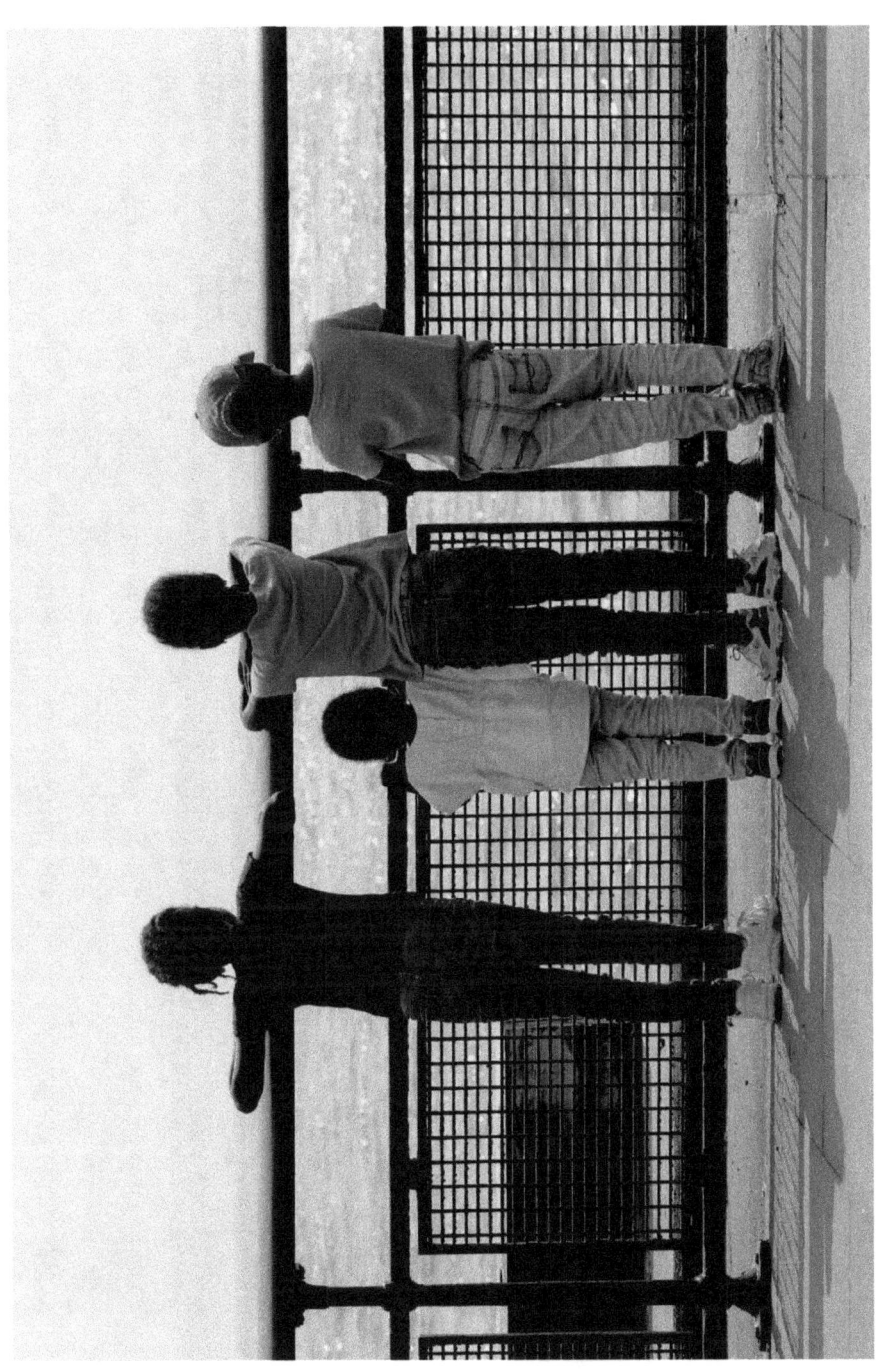

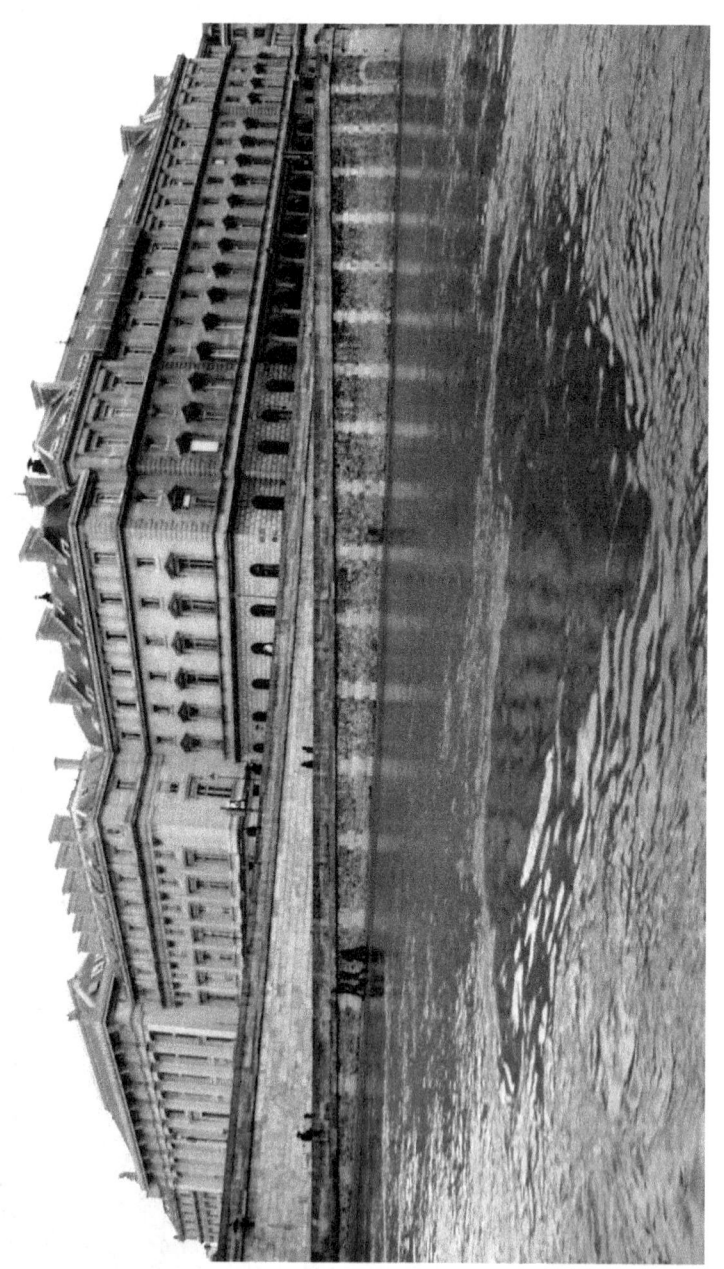

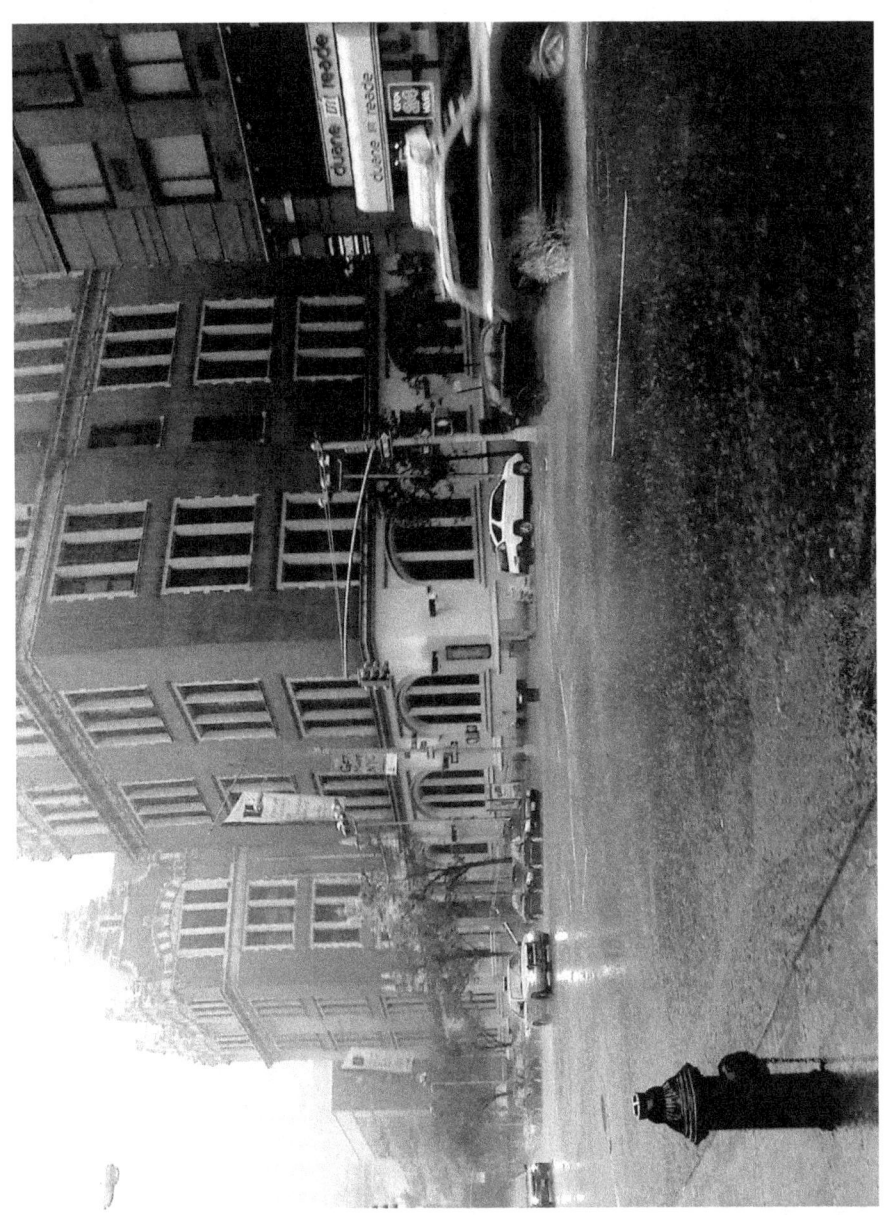

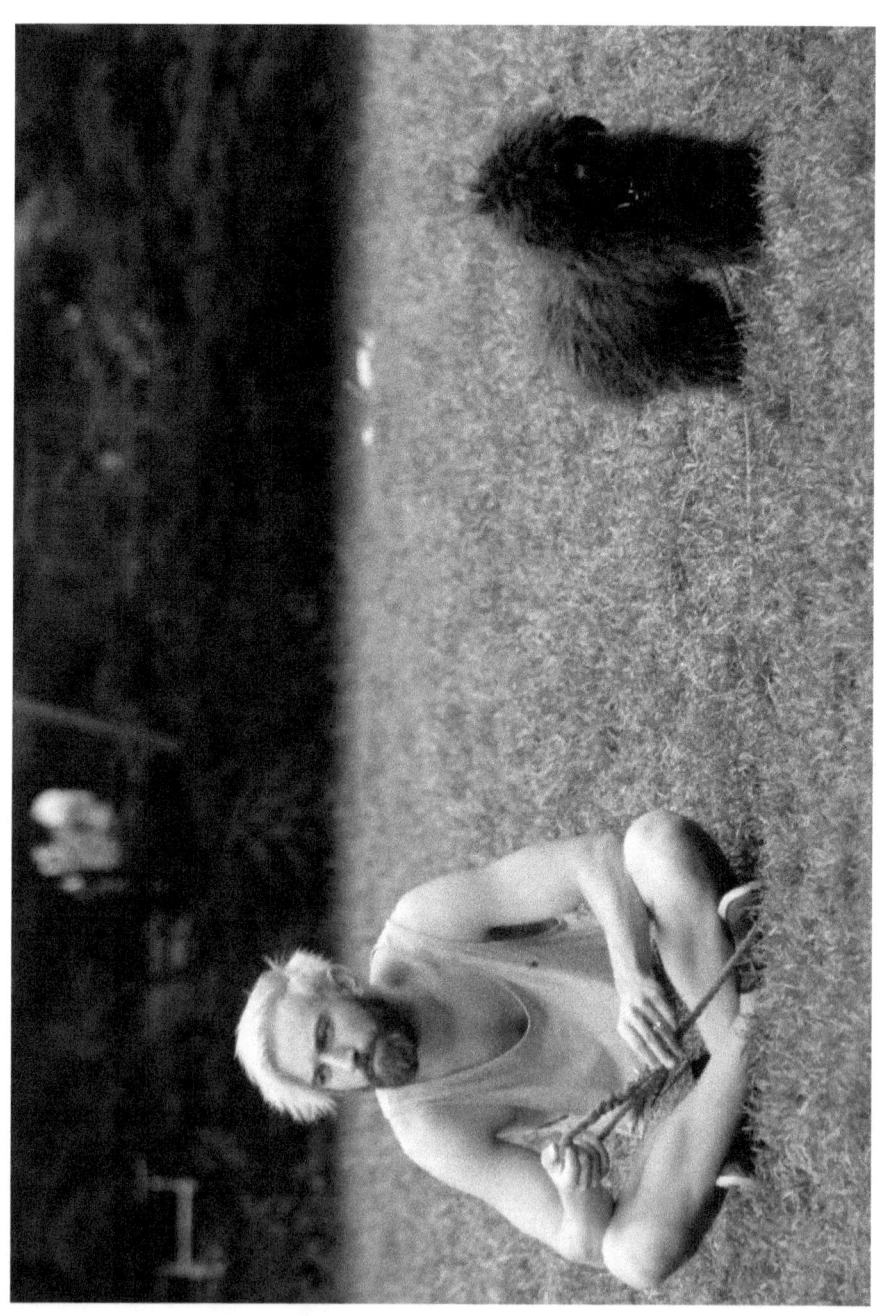

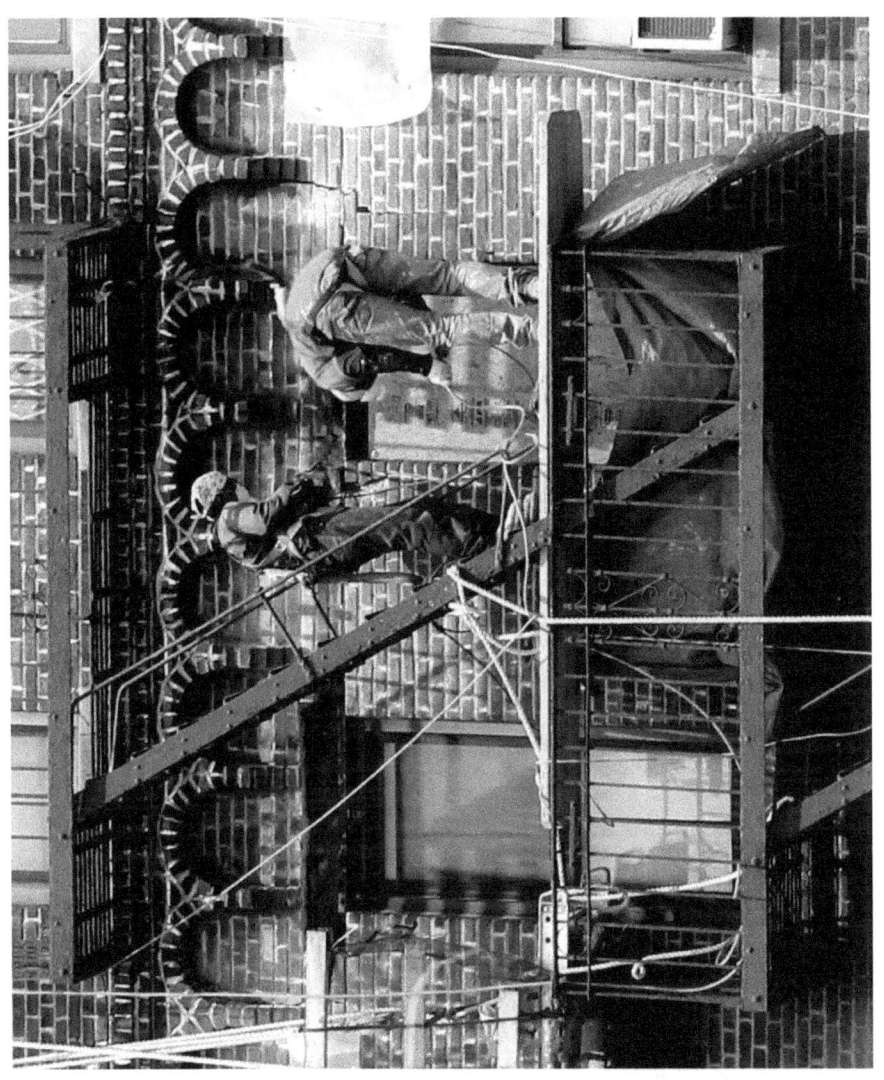

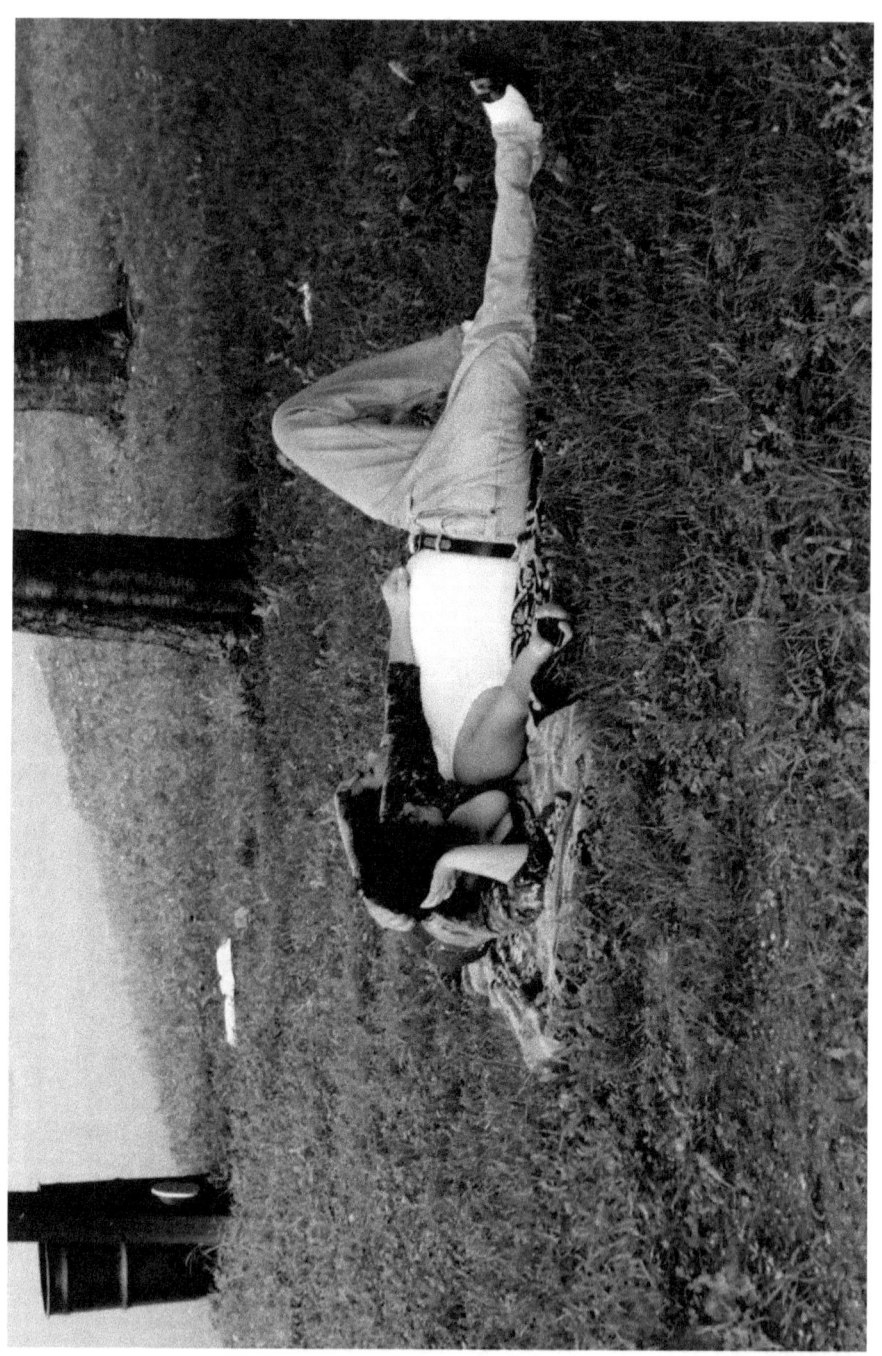

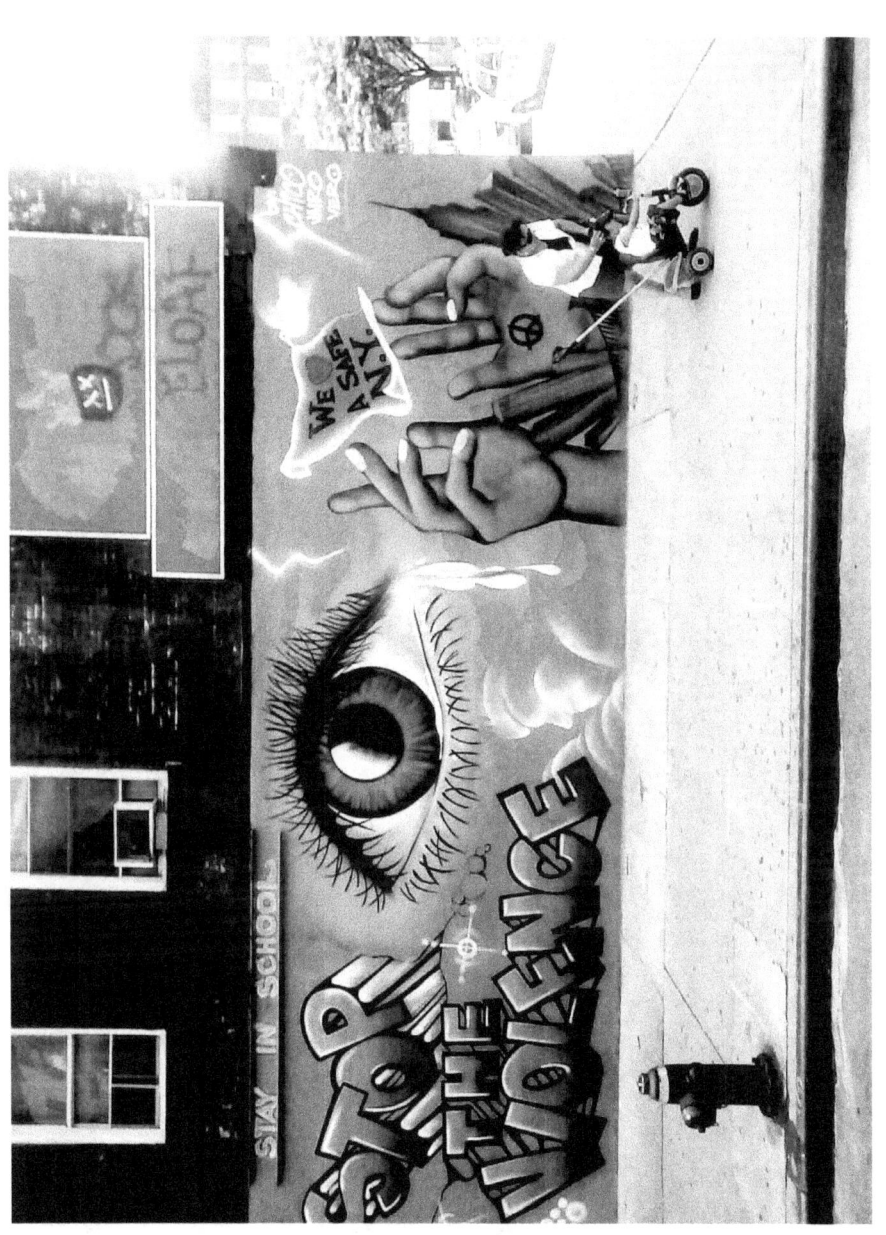

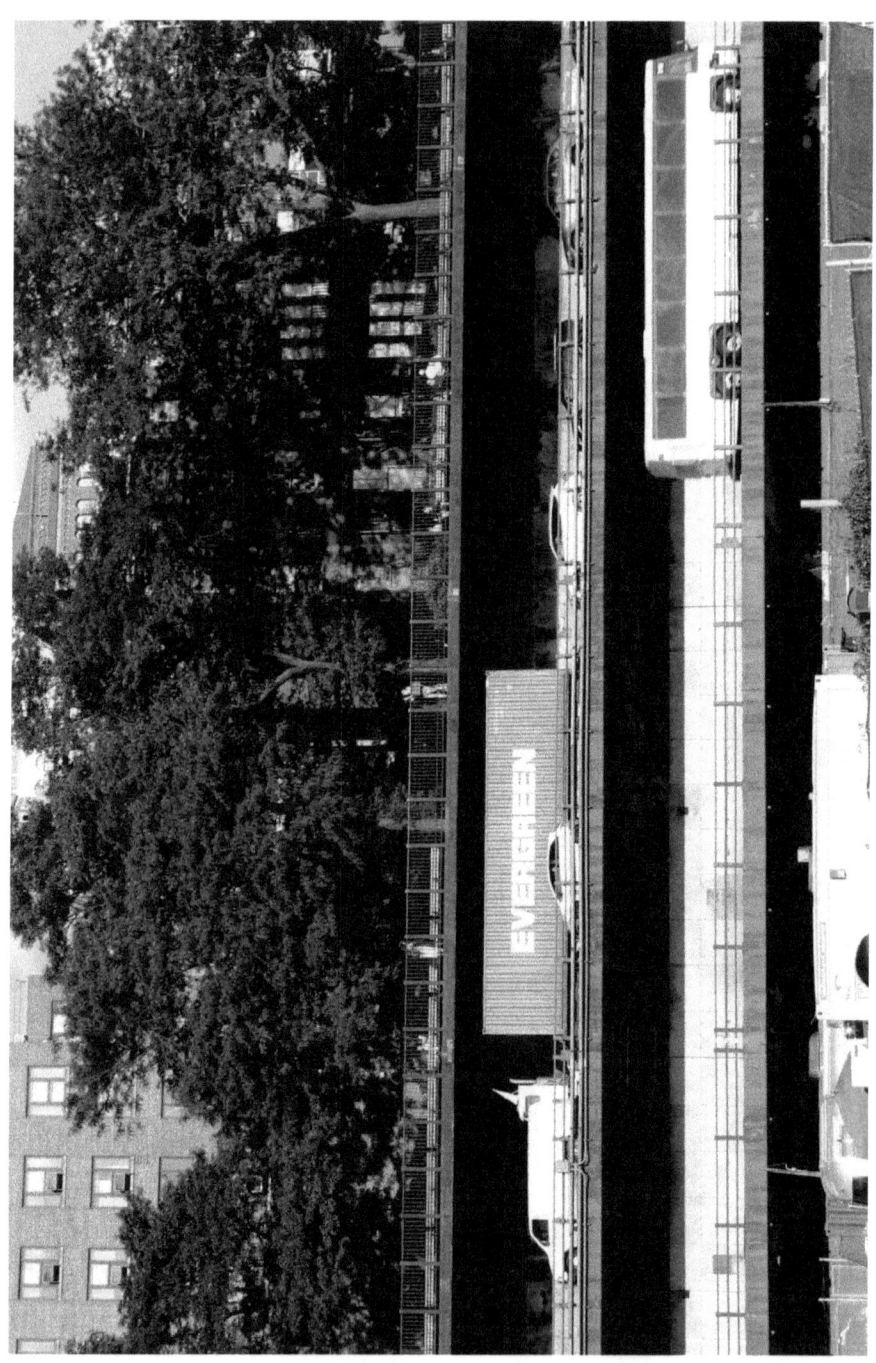

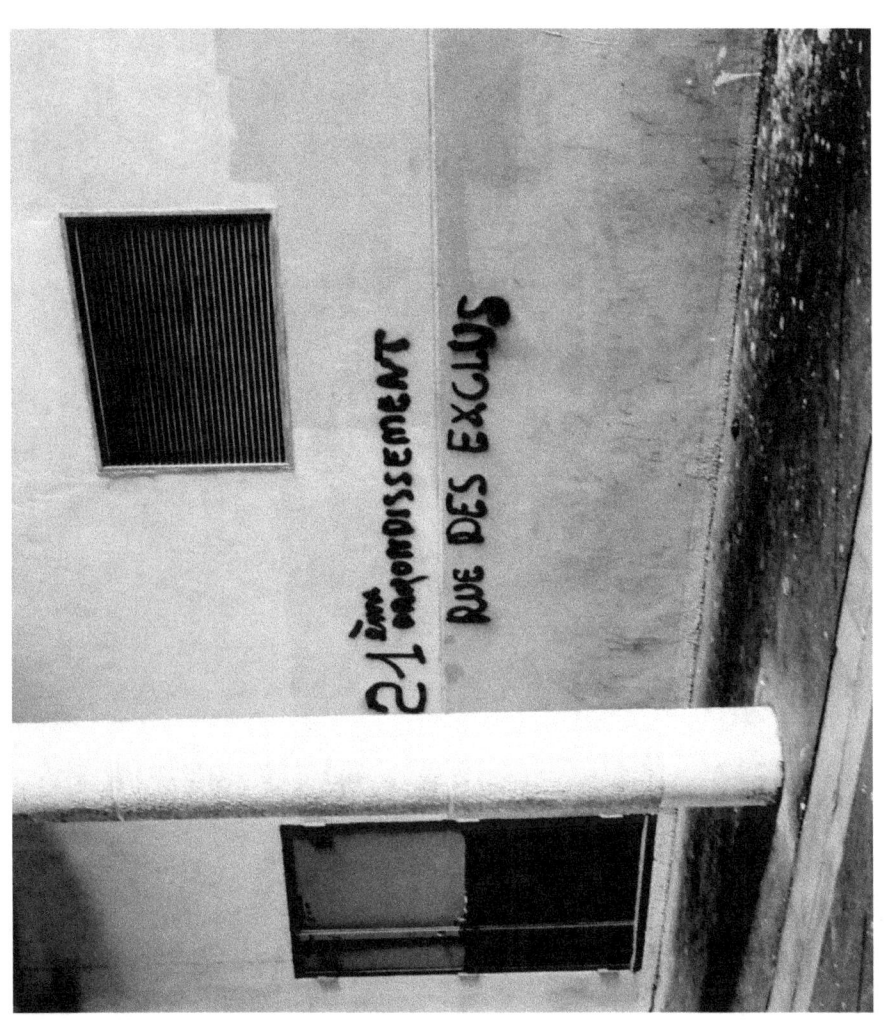

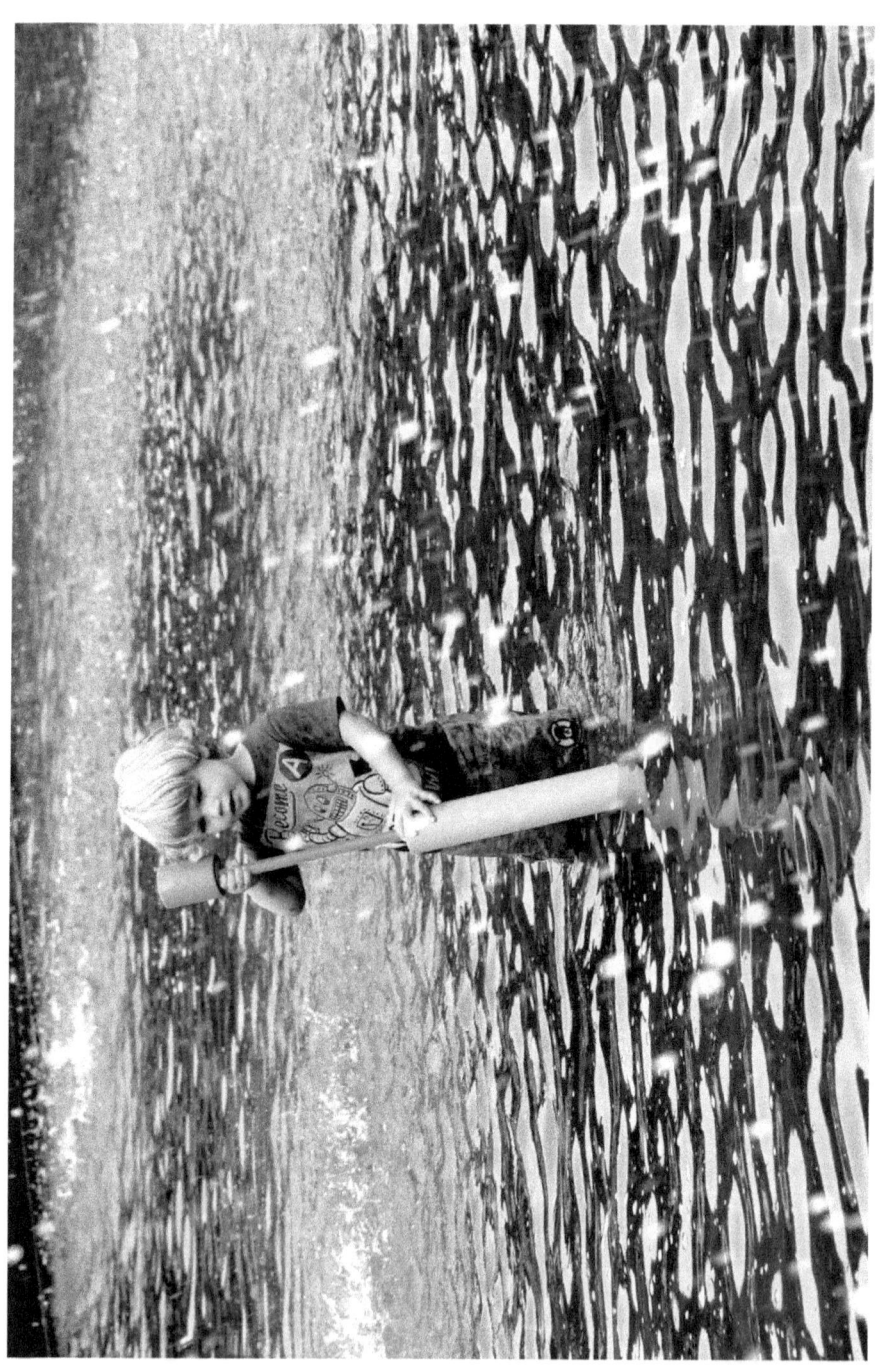

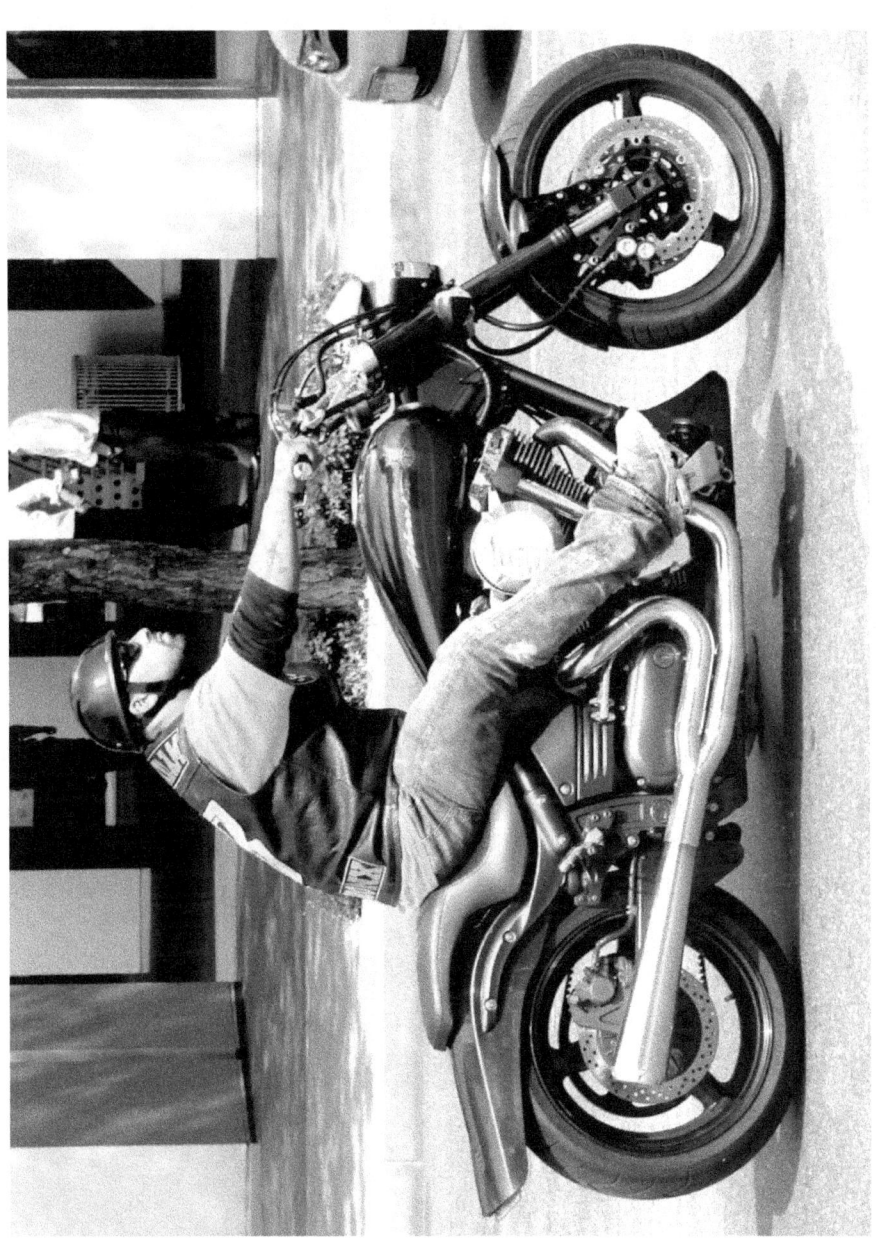

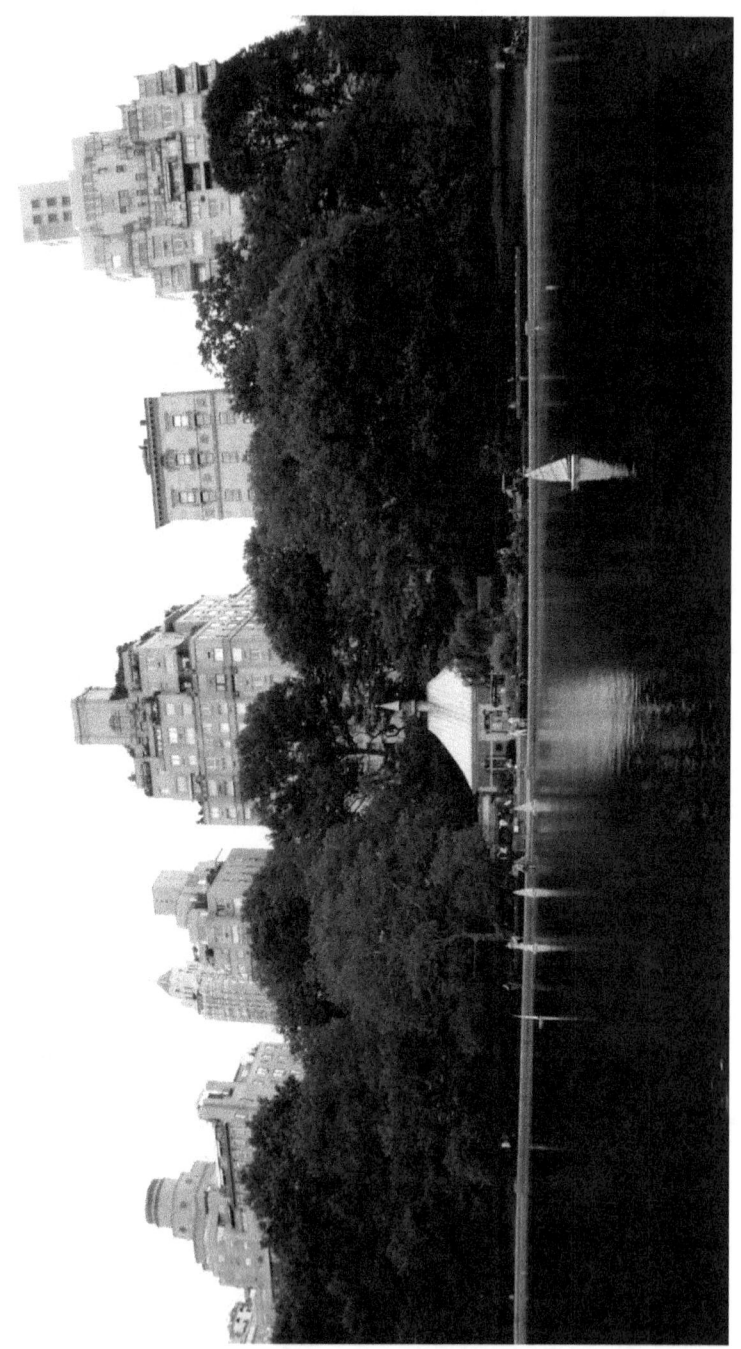

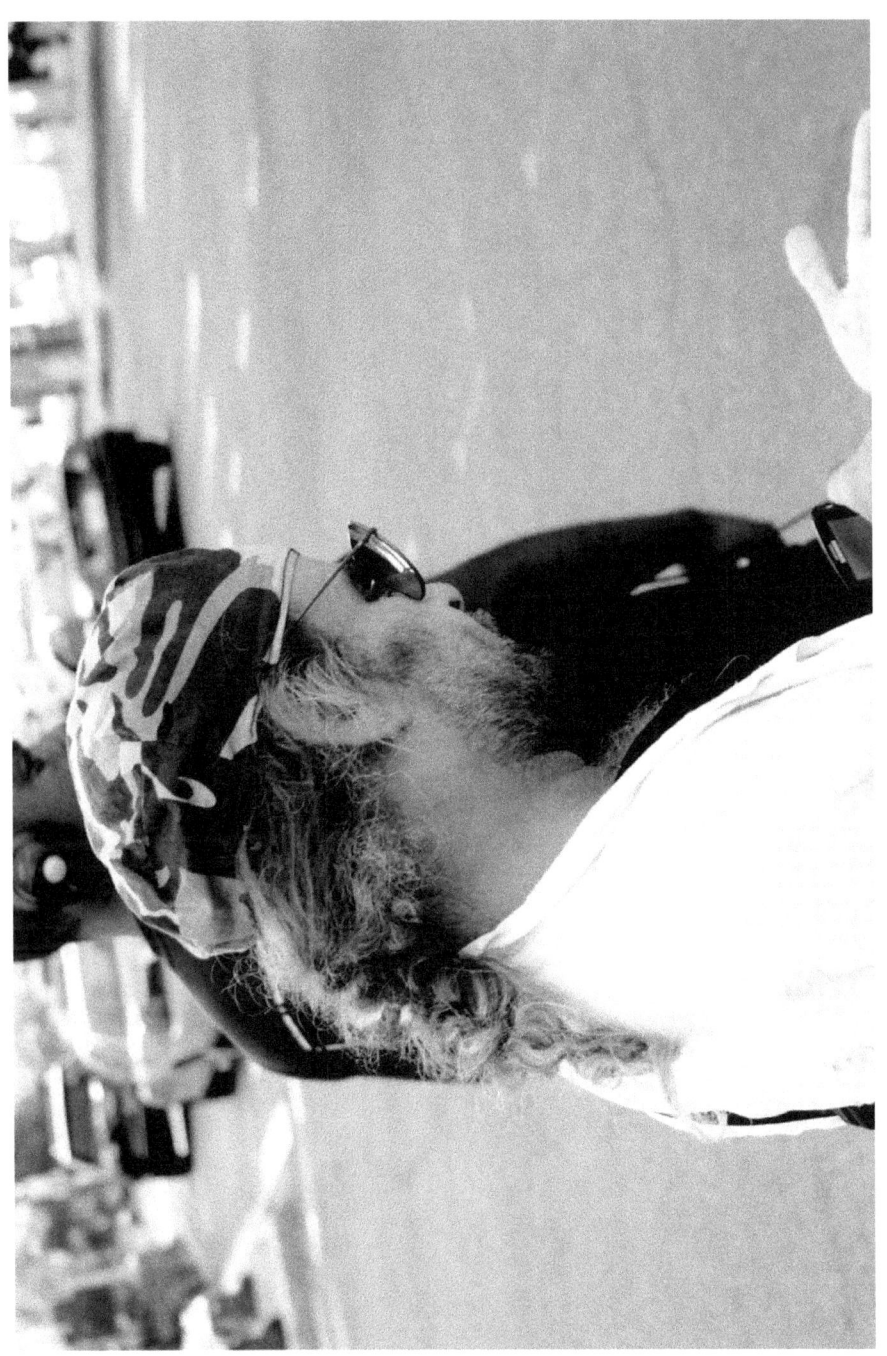

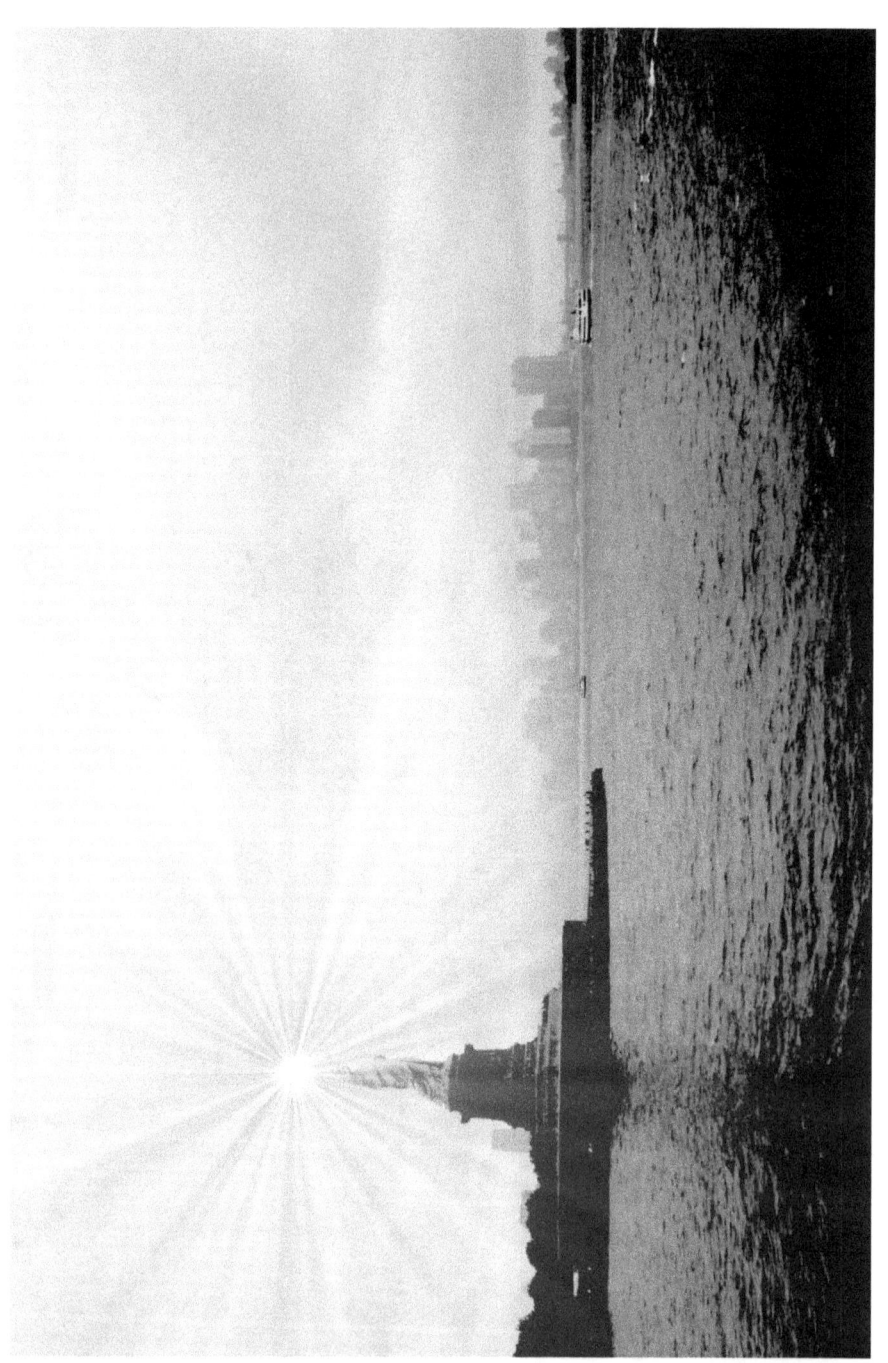

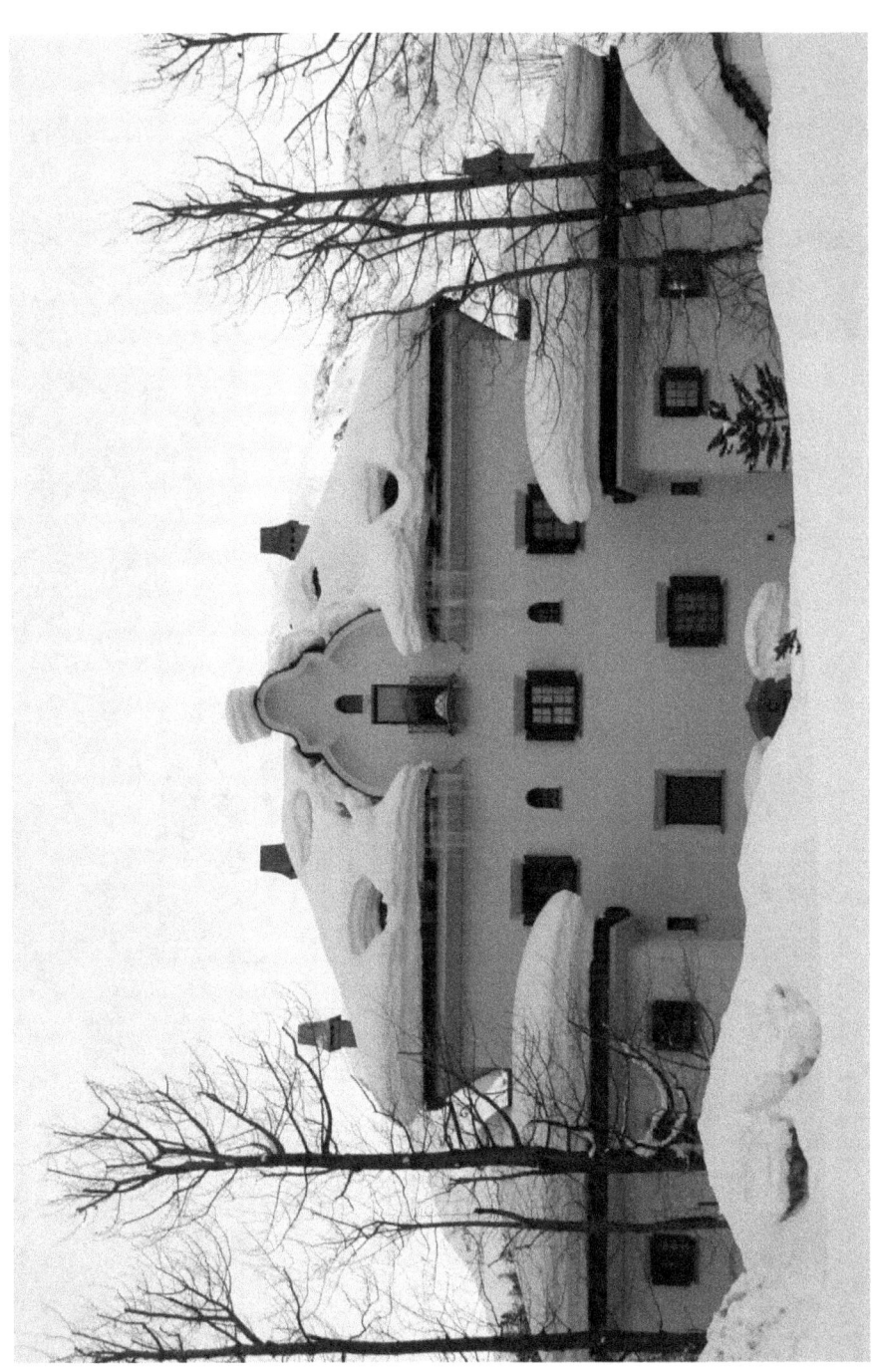

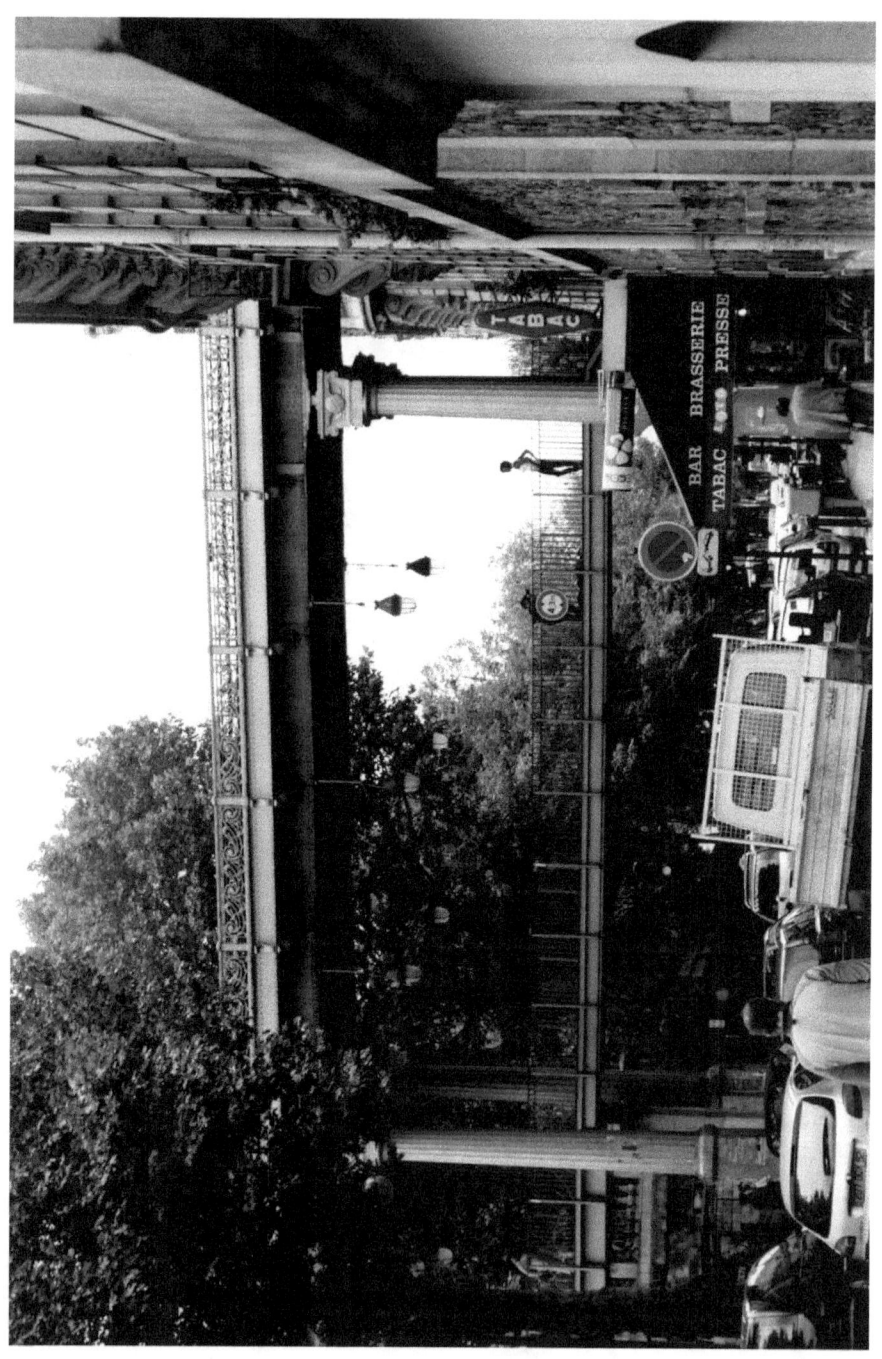

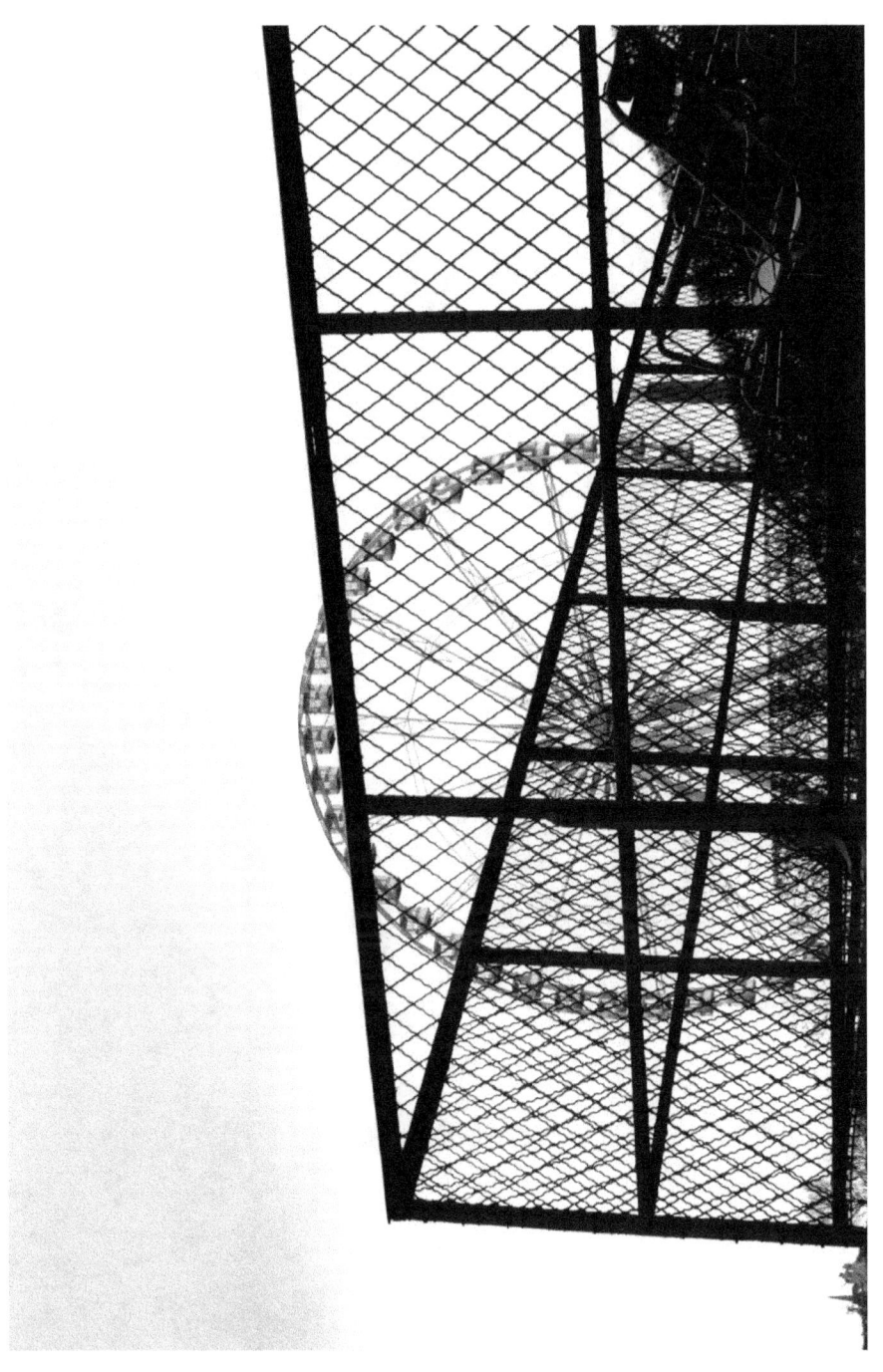

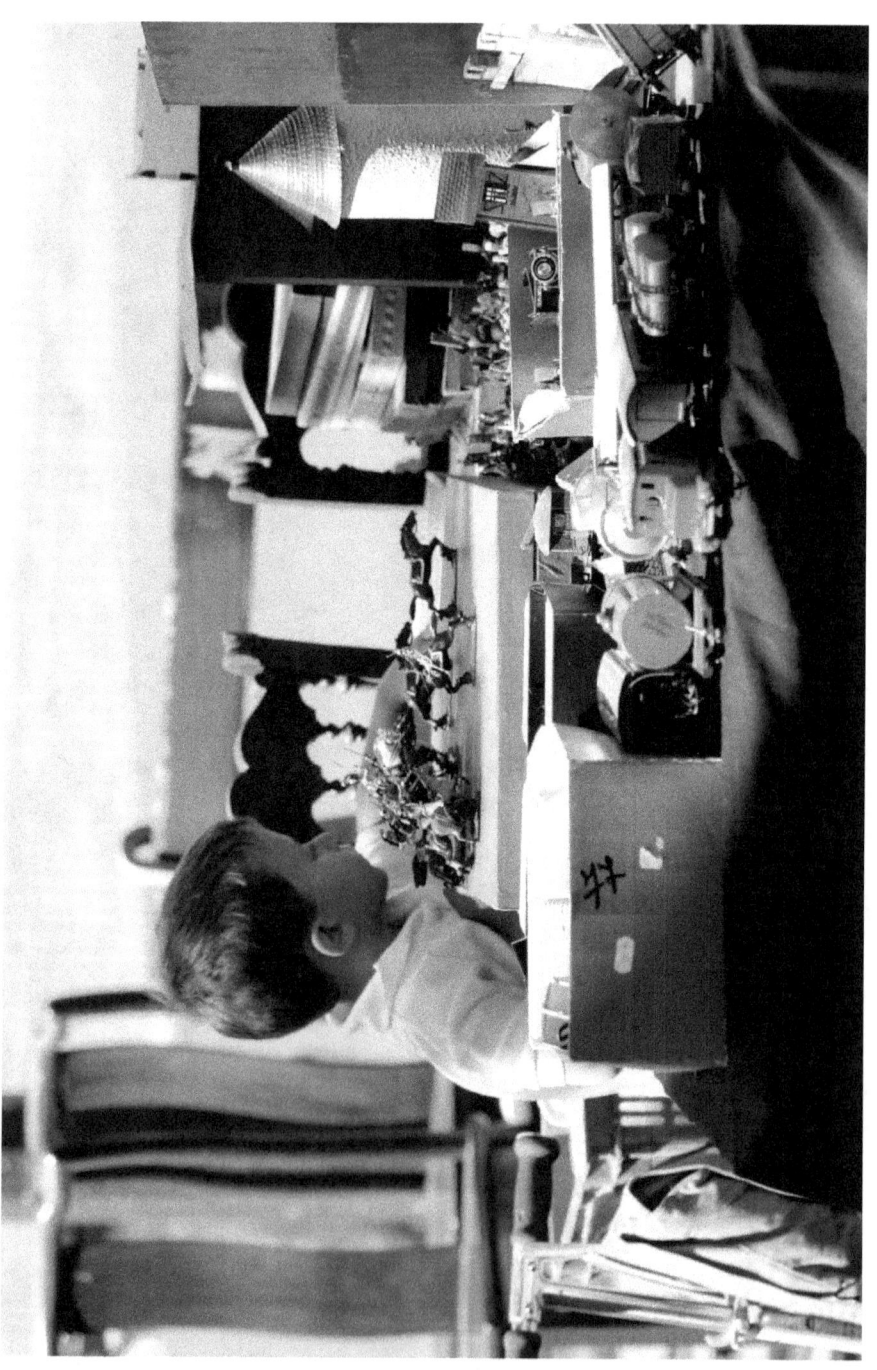

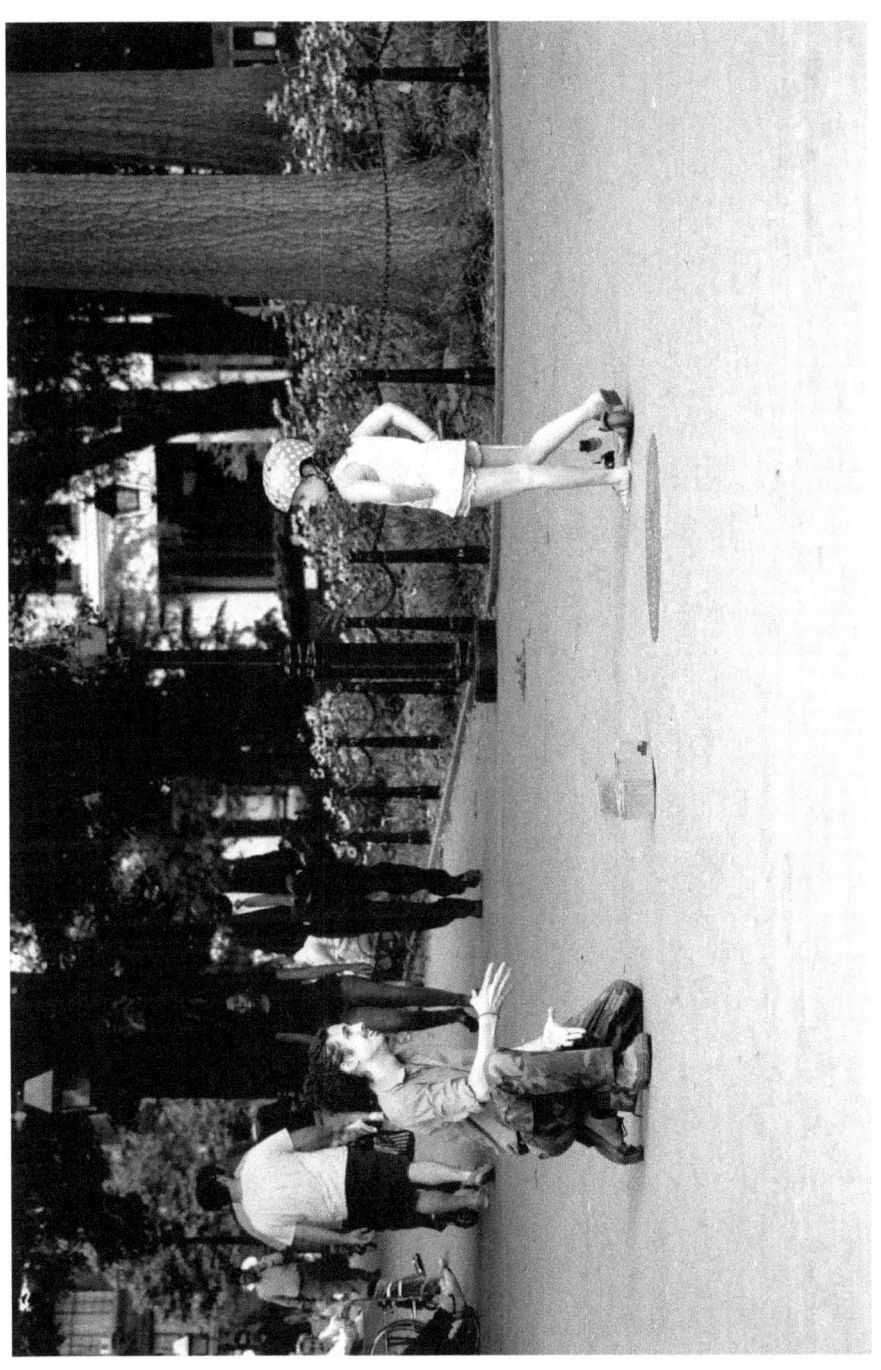

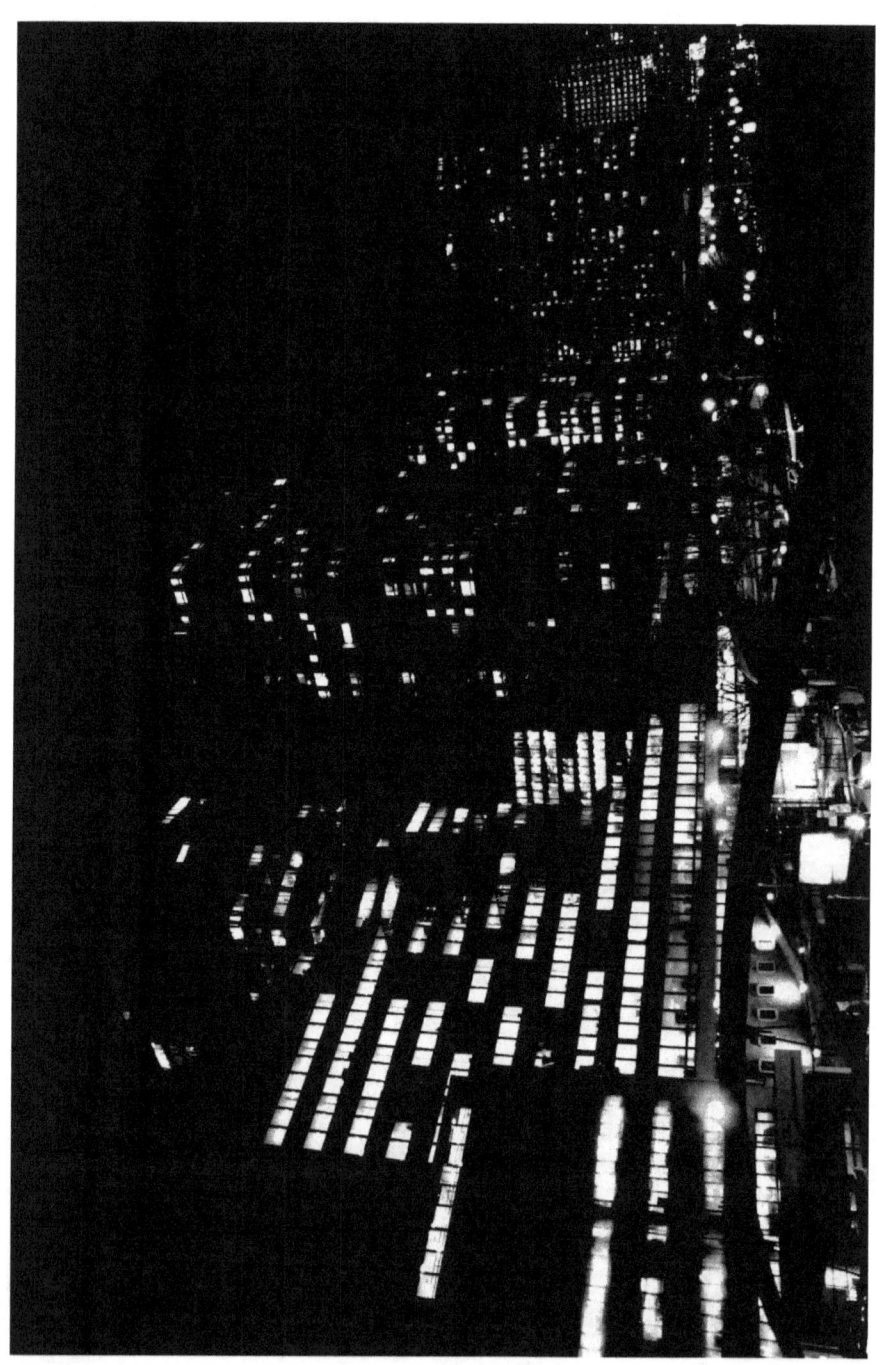

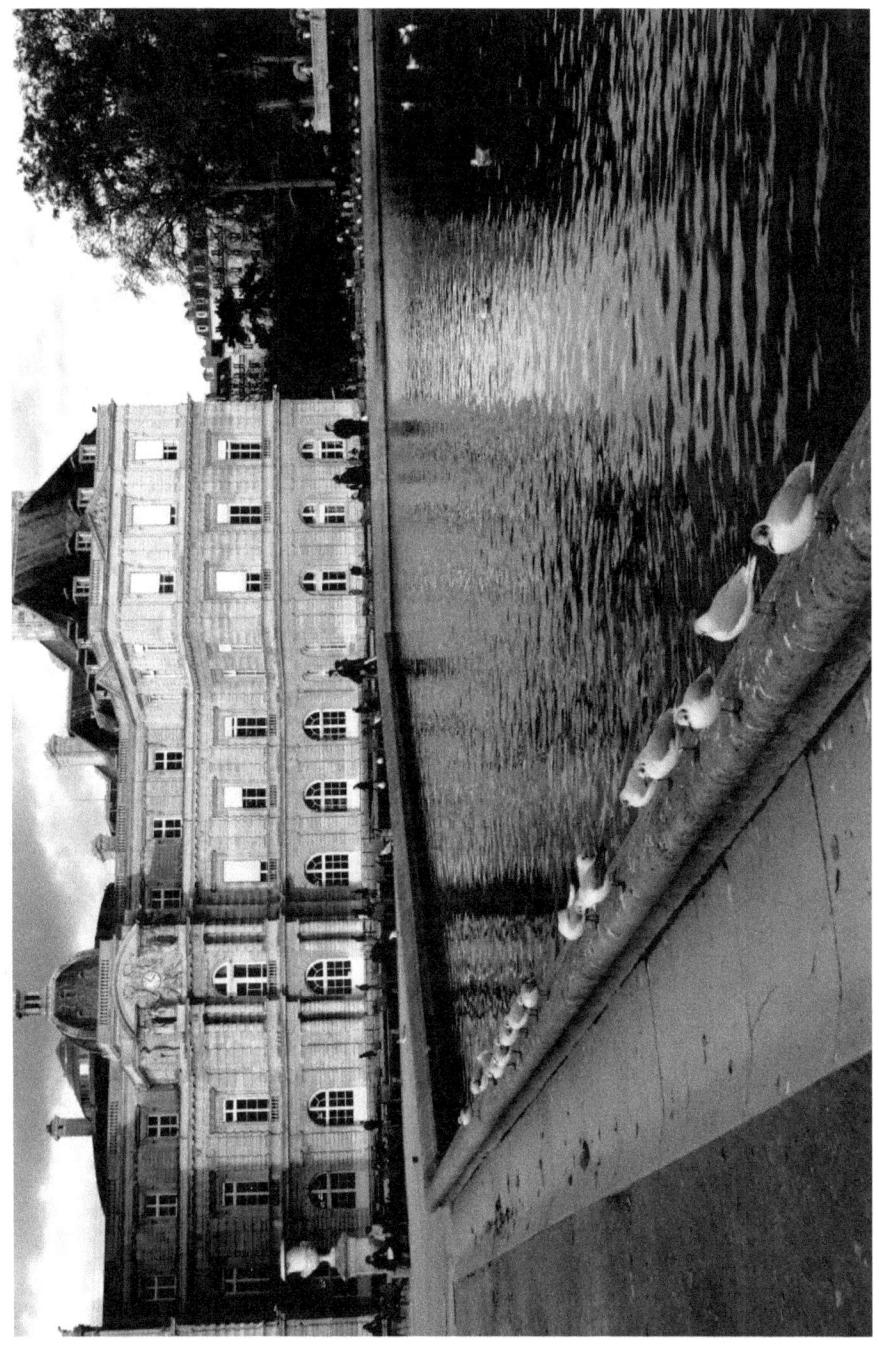

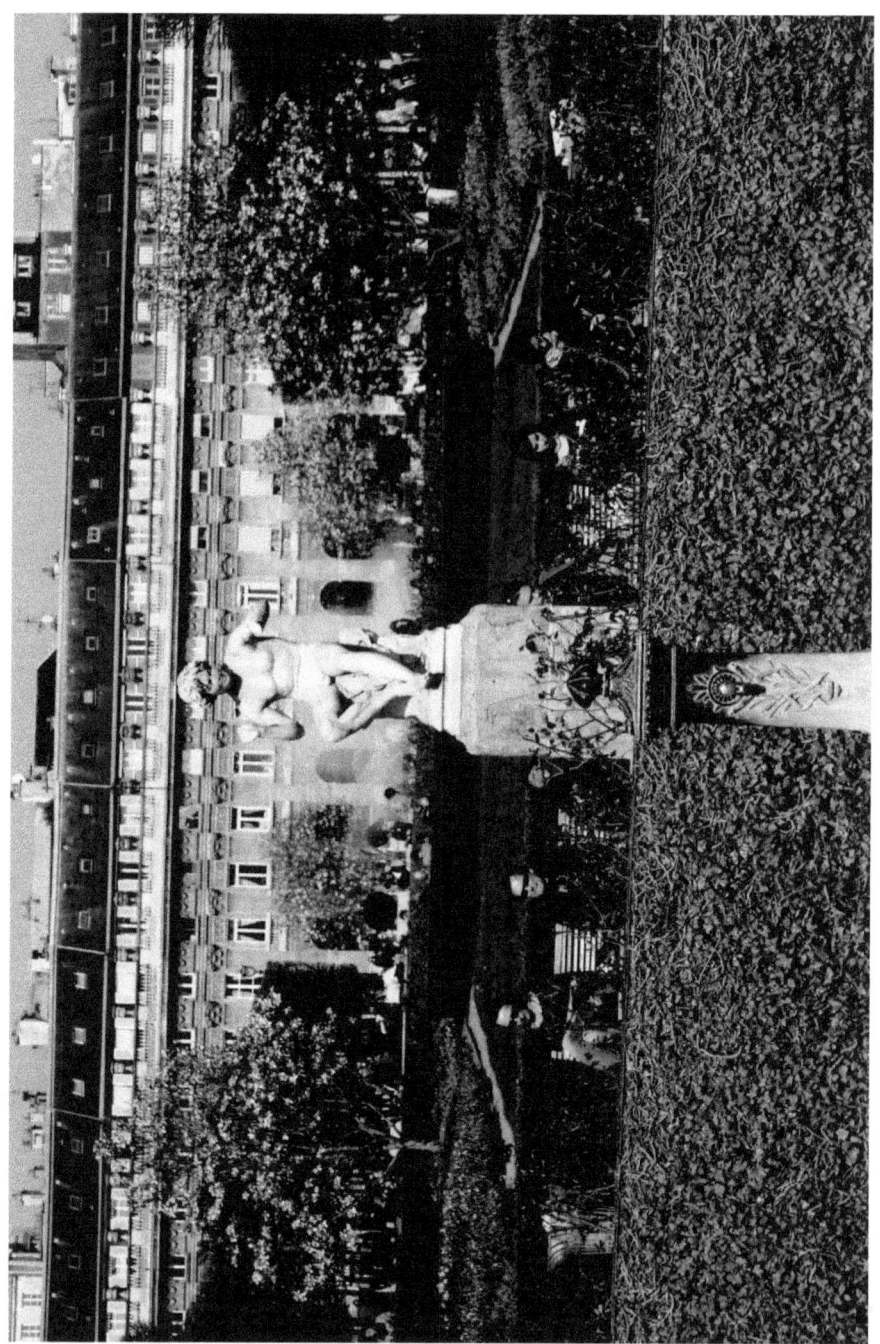

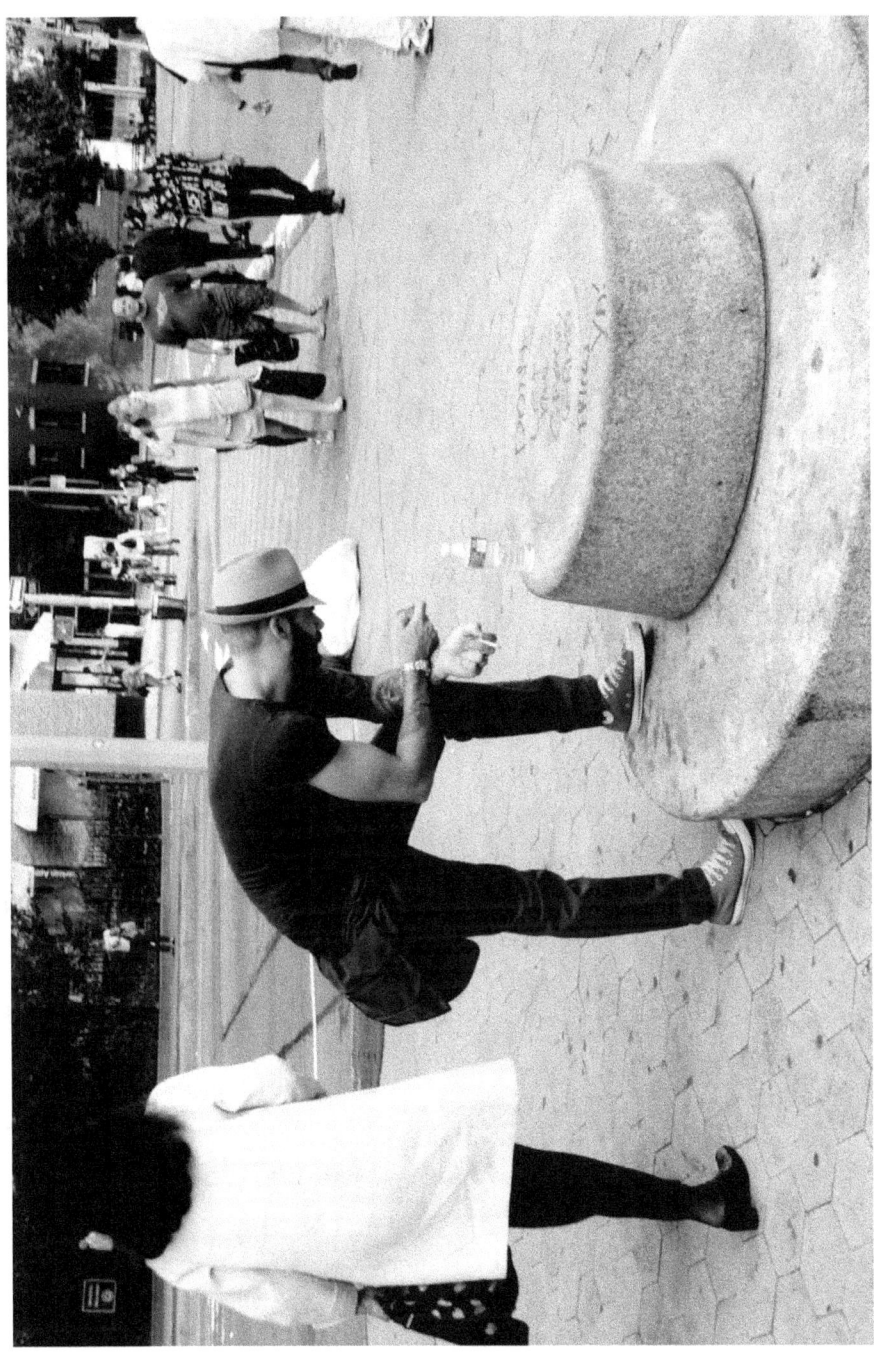

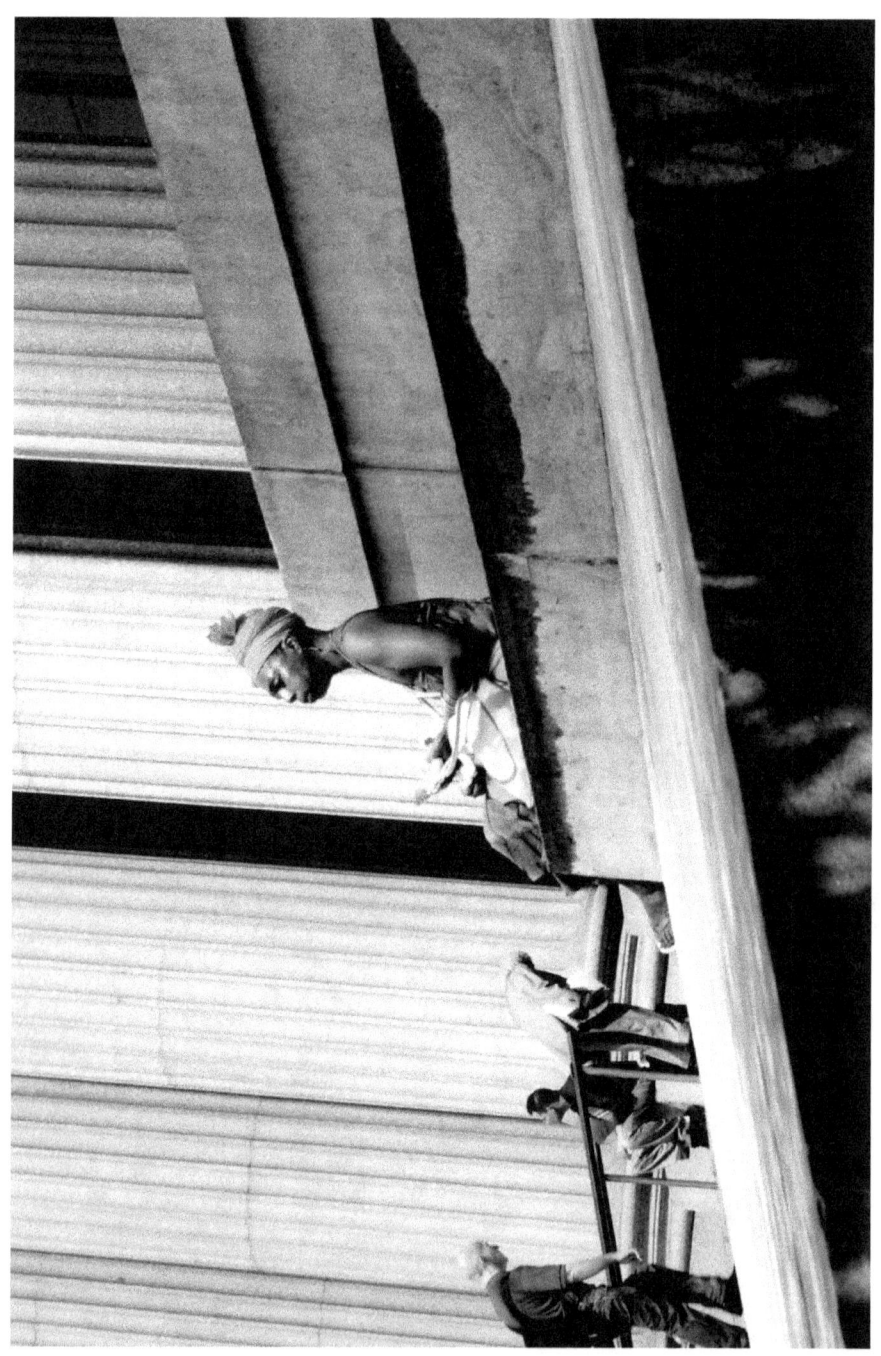

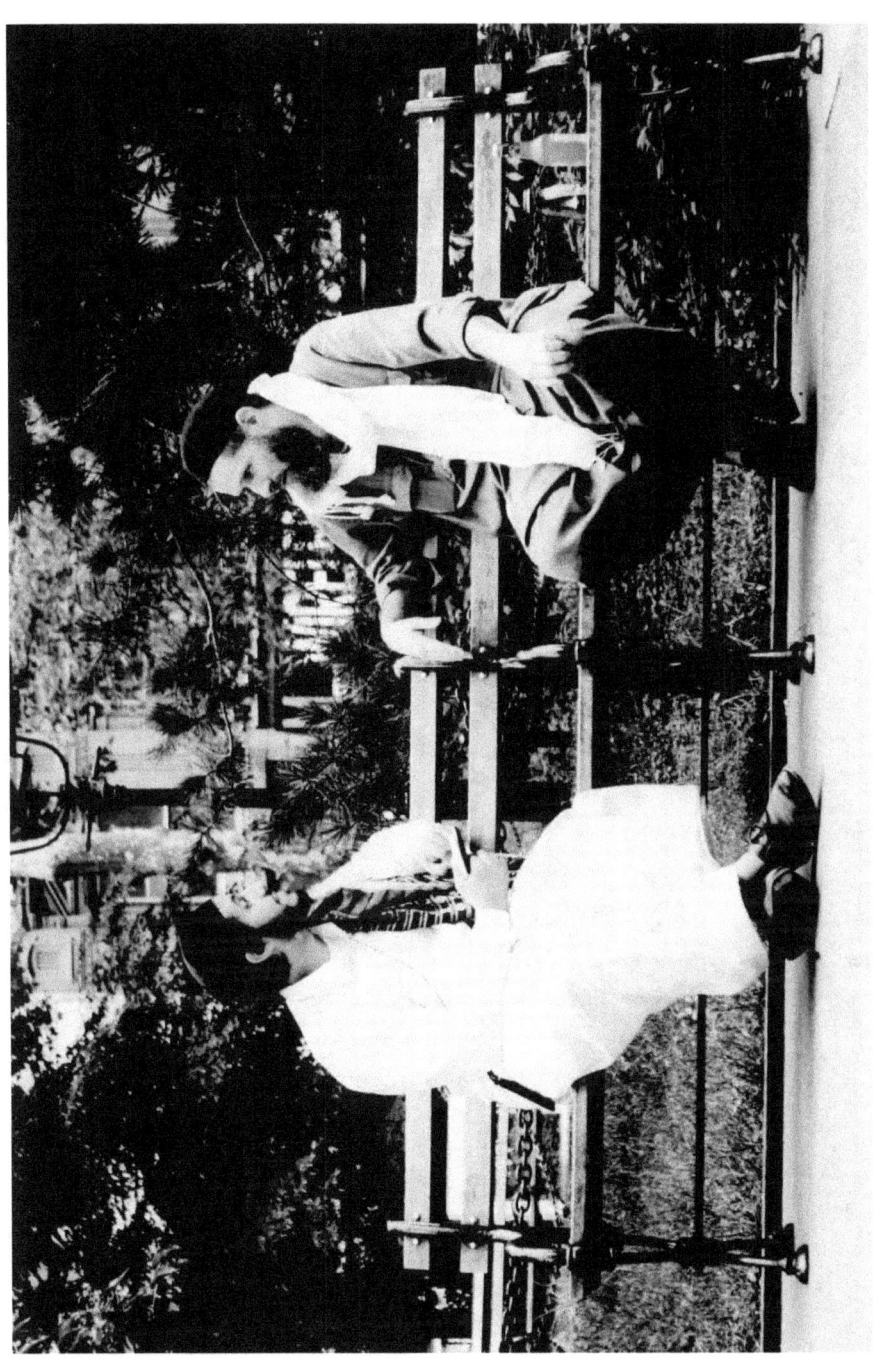

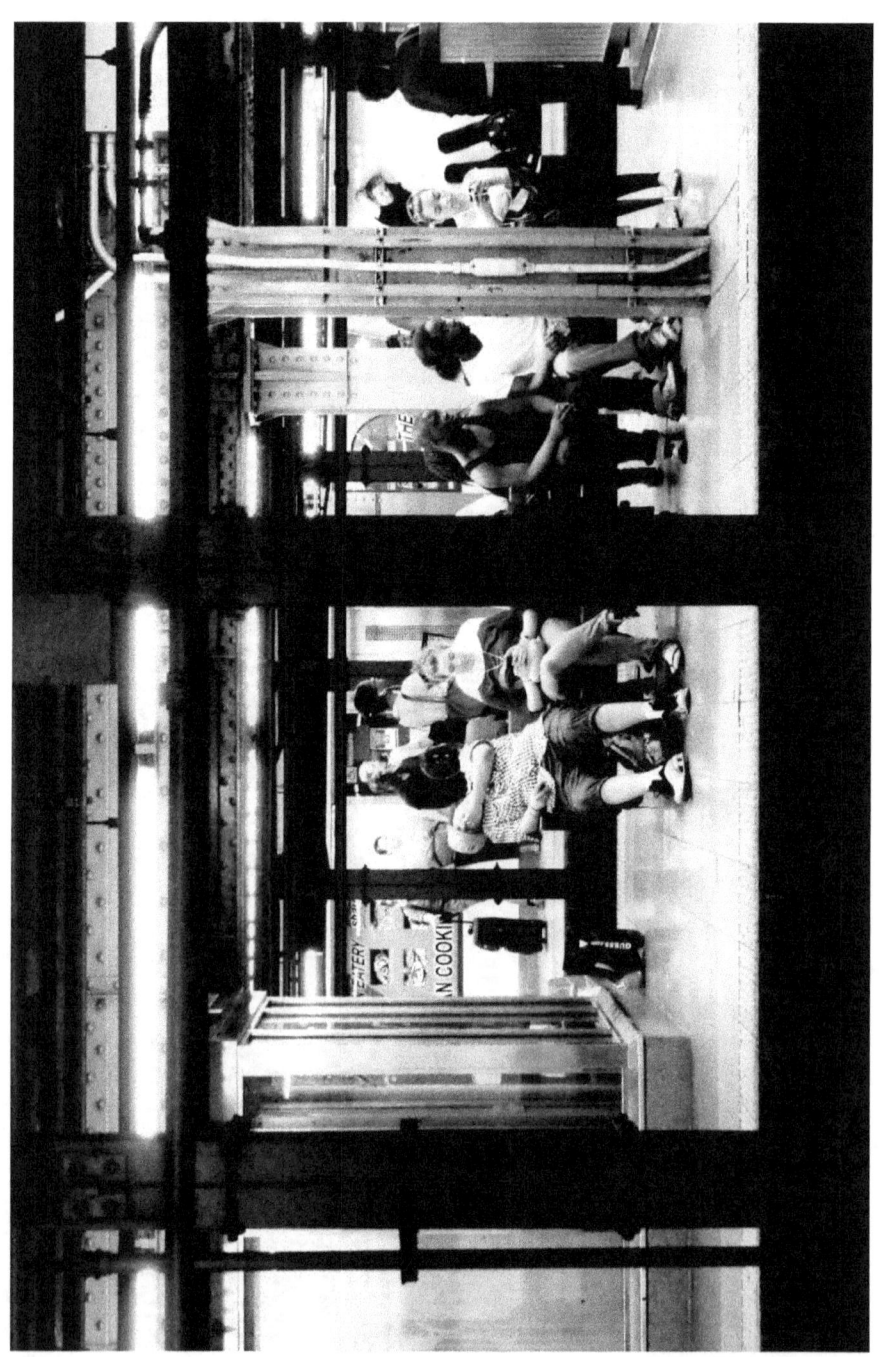

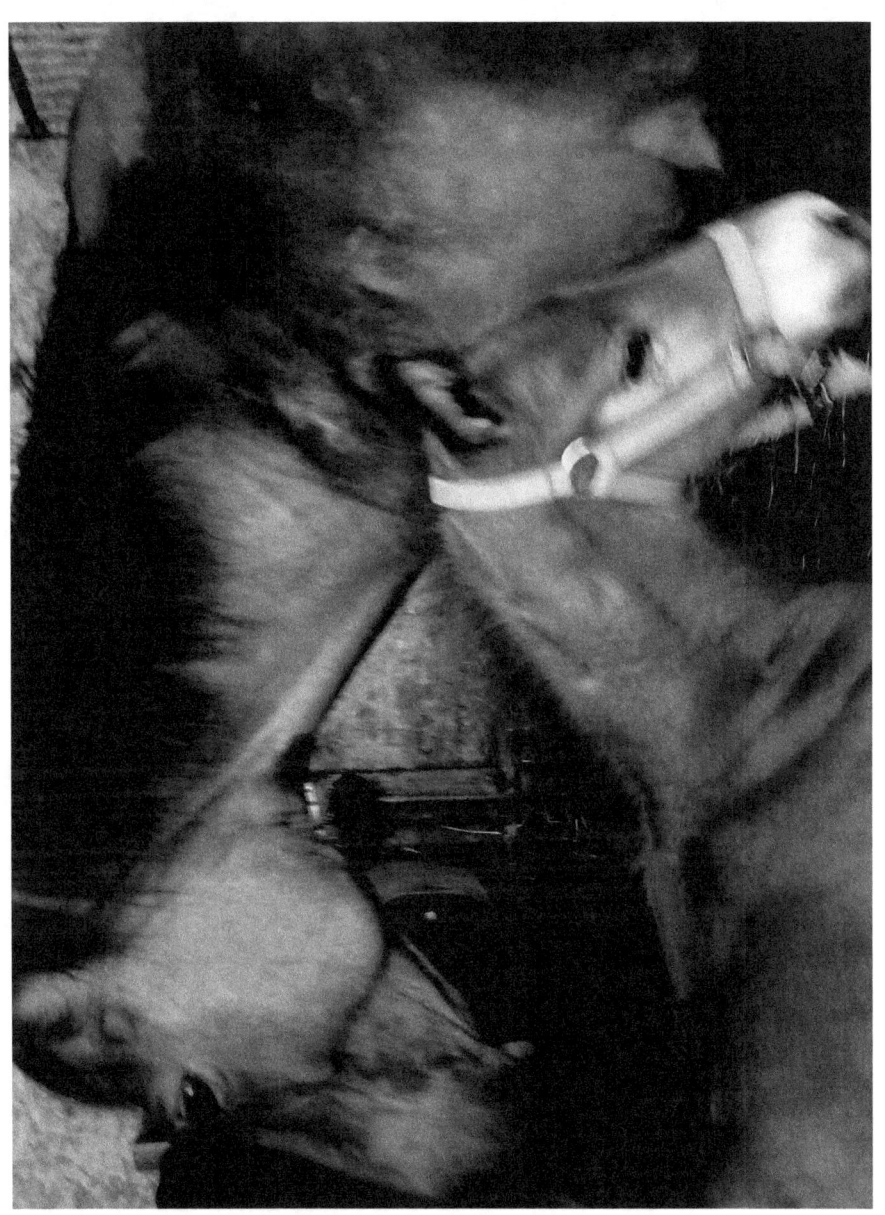

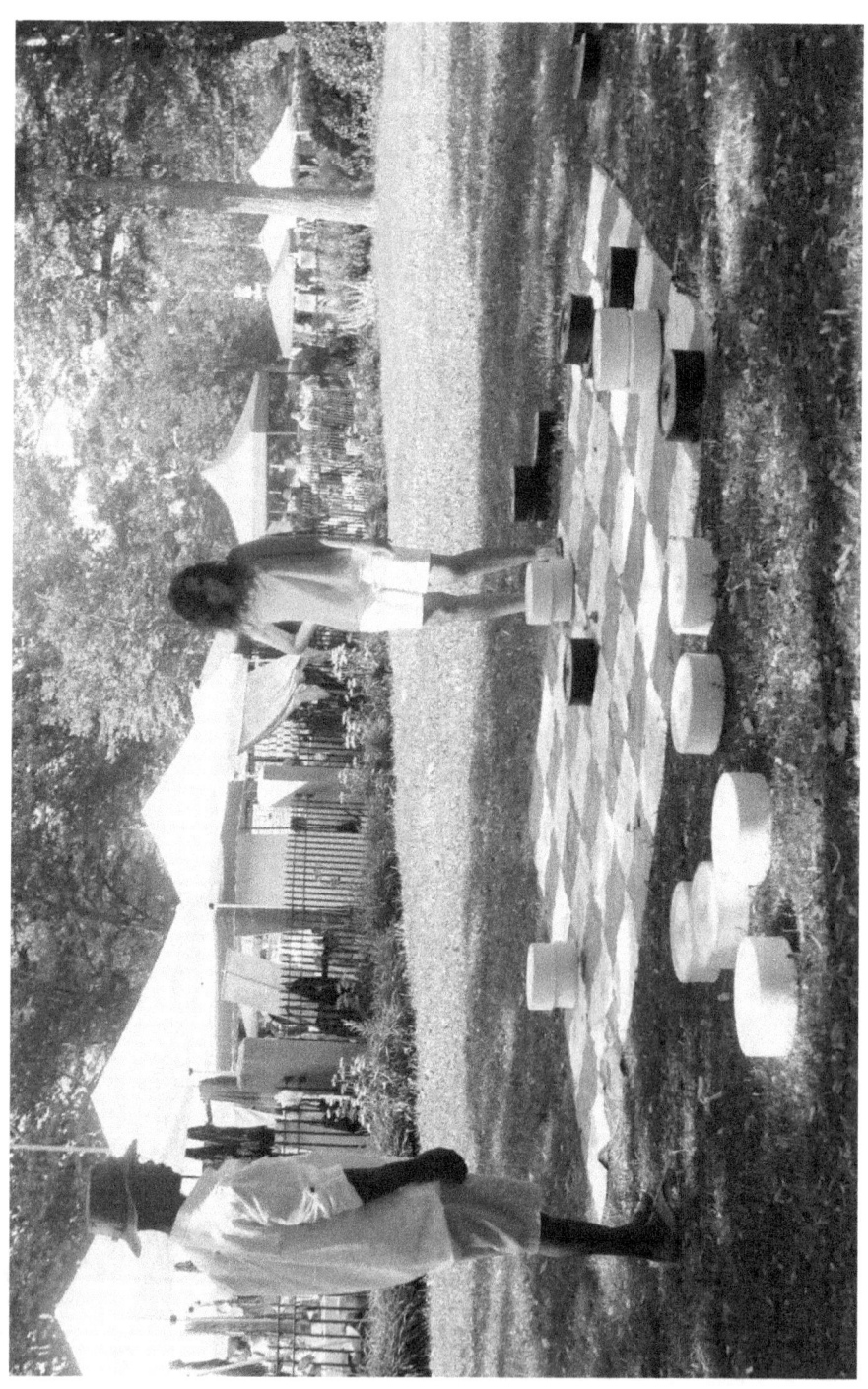

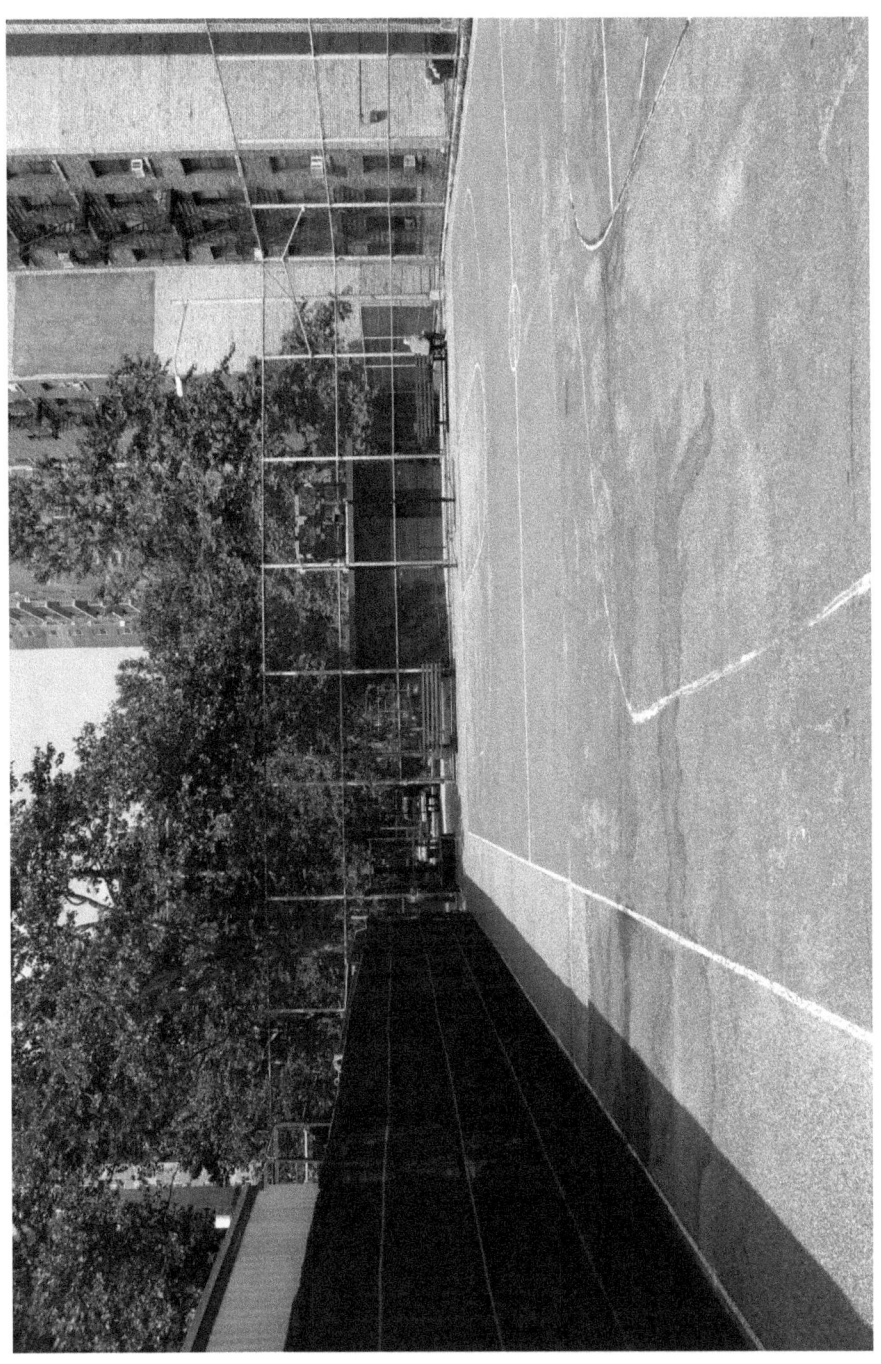

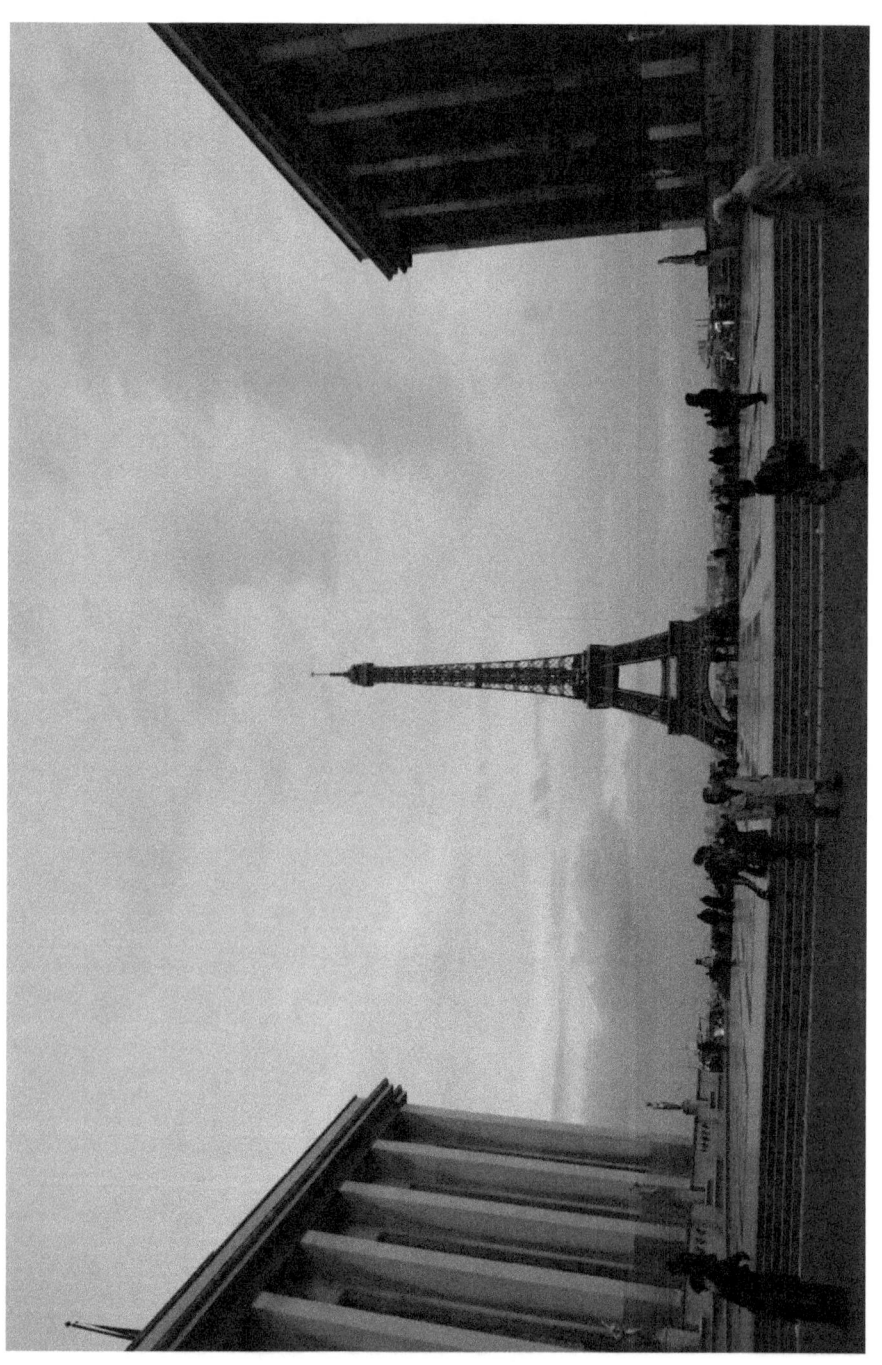

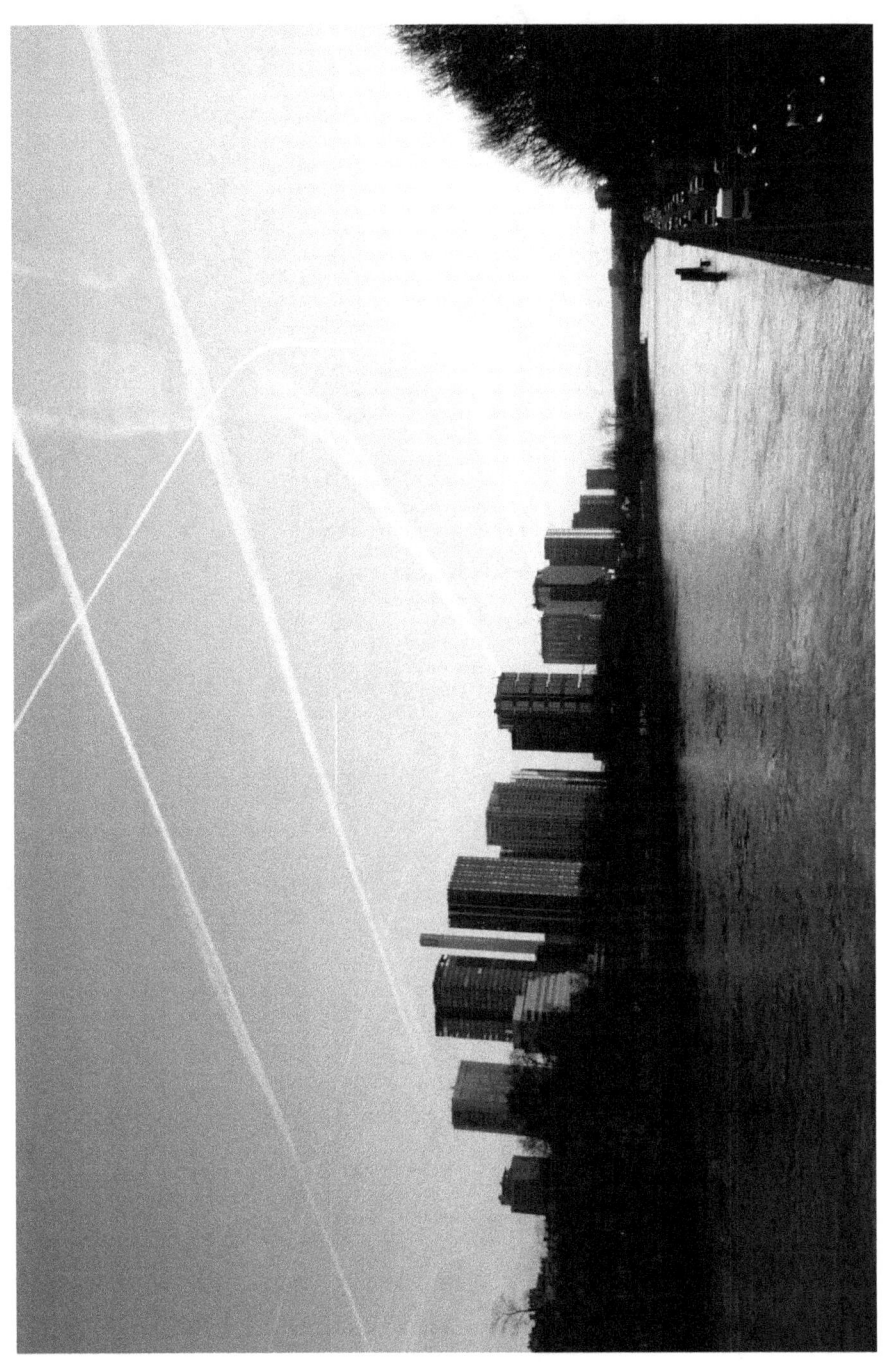

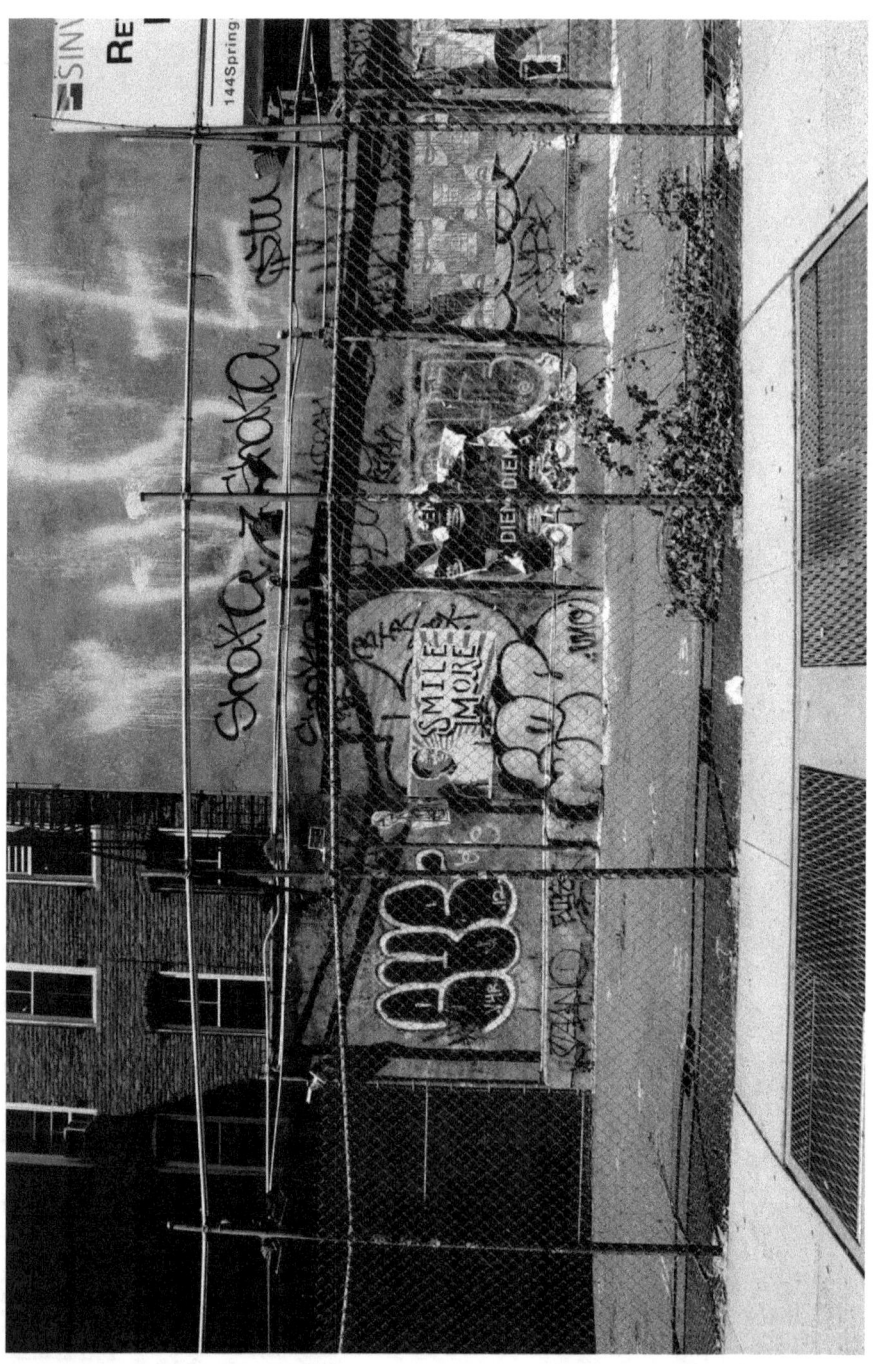

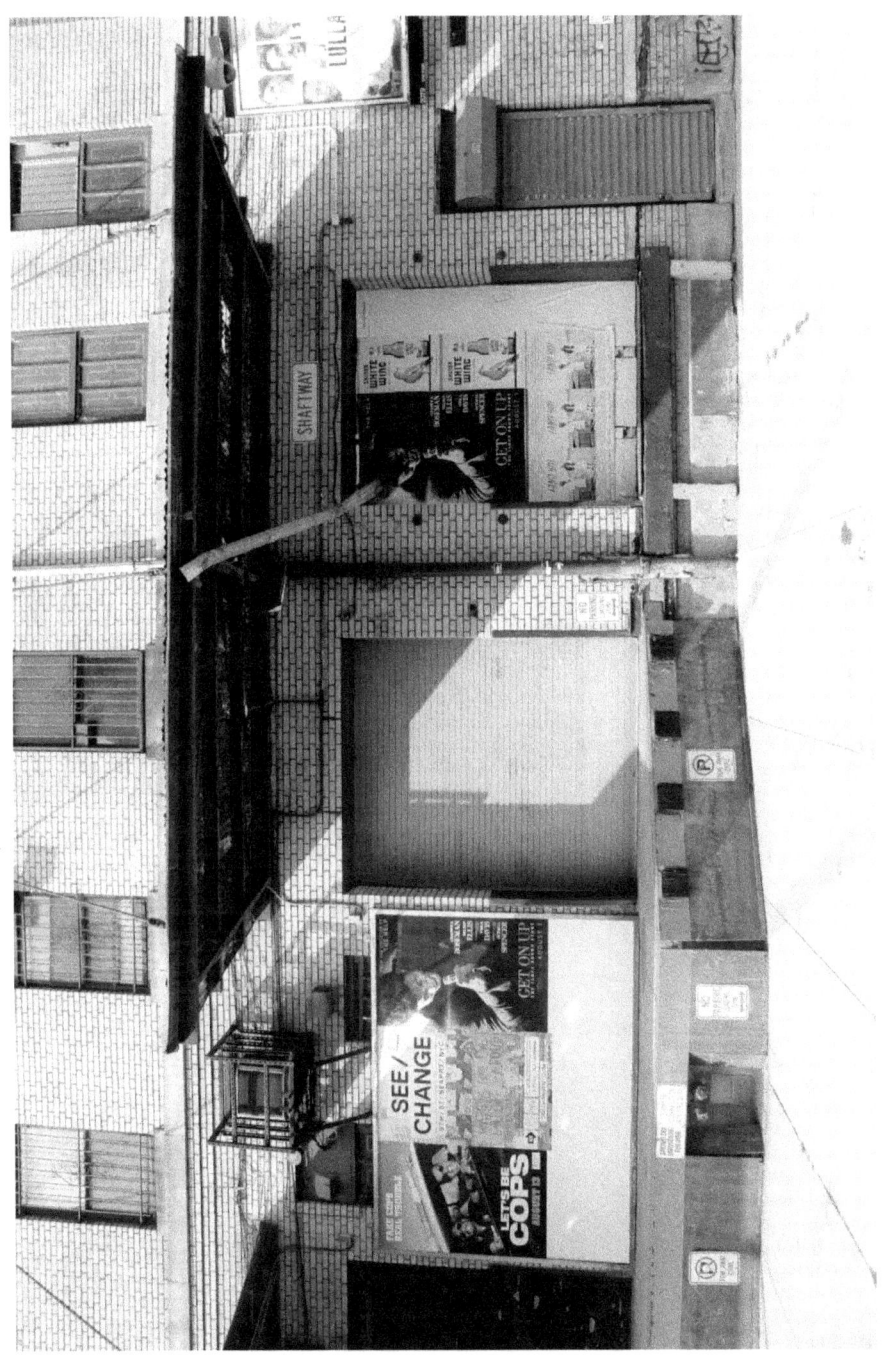

241

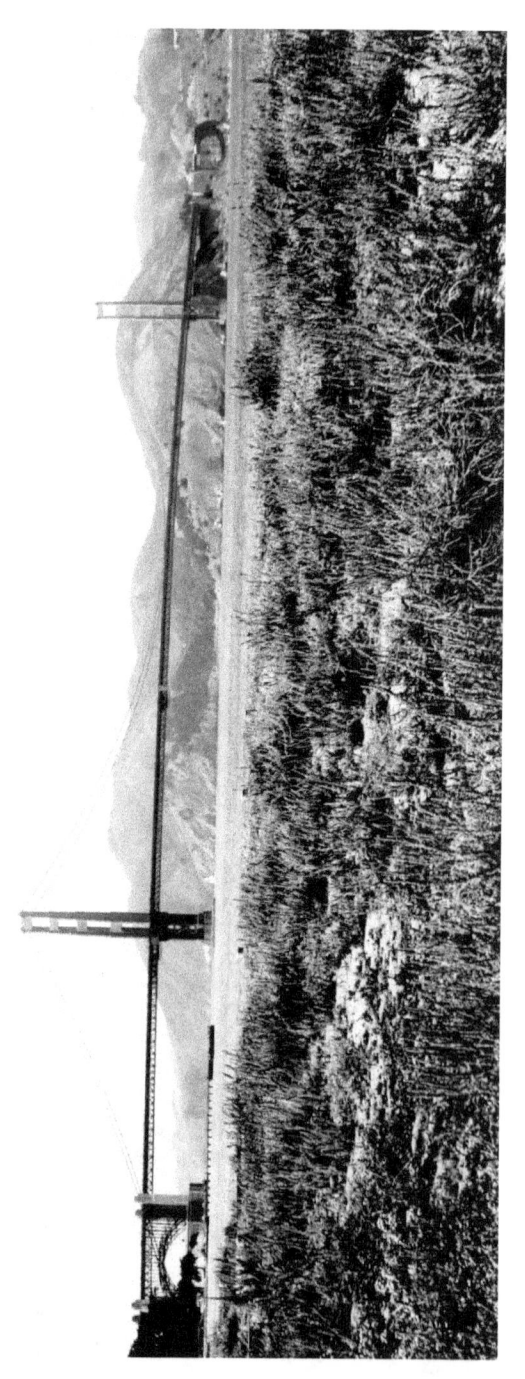

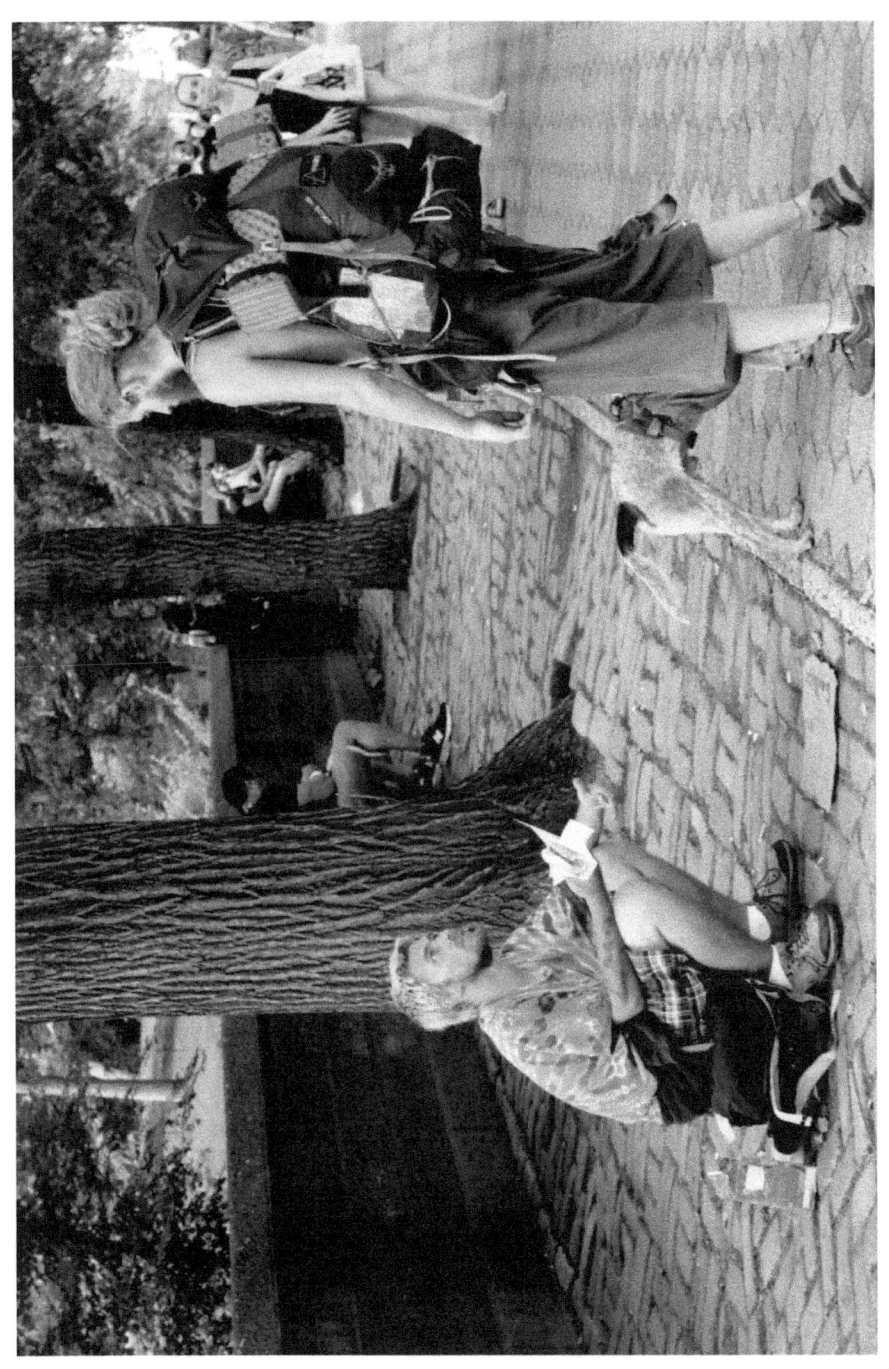

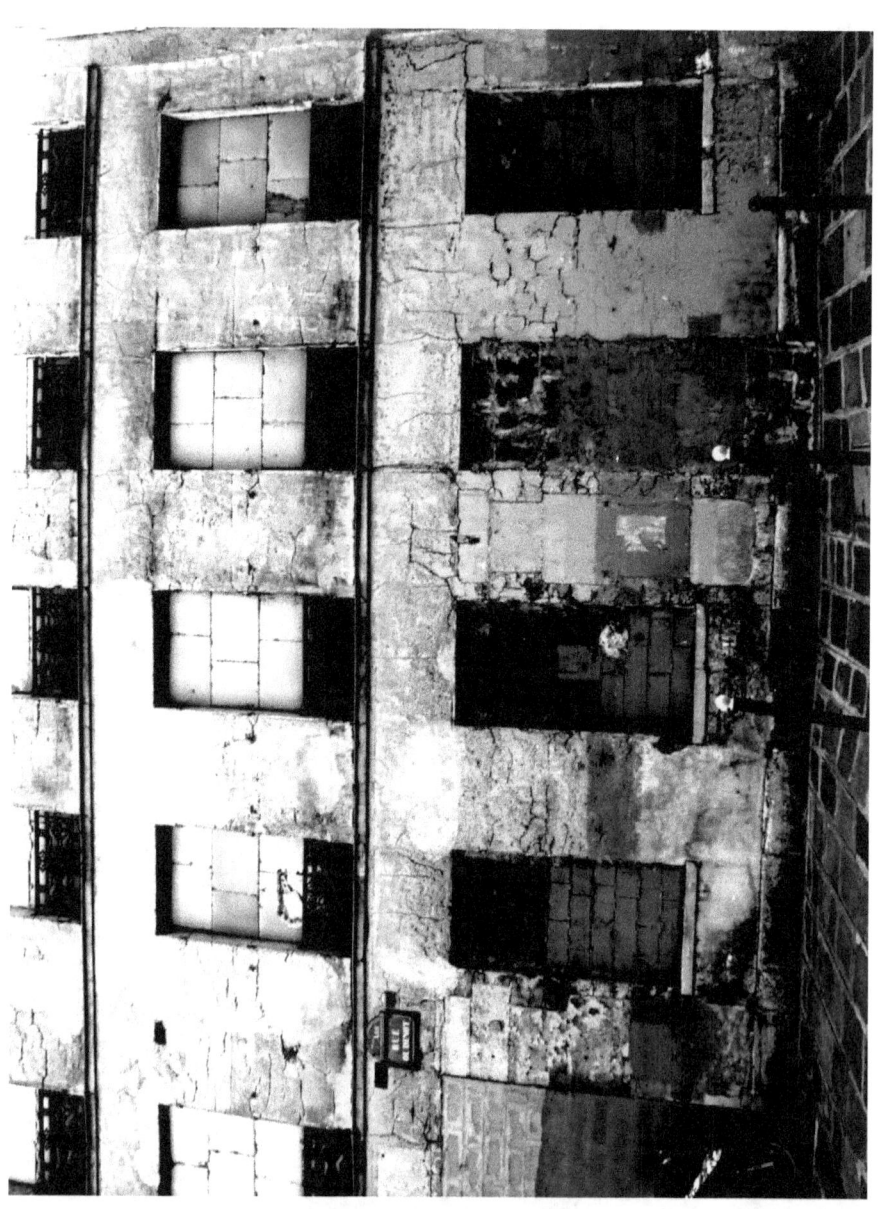

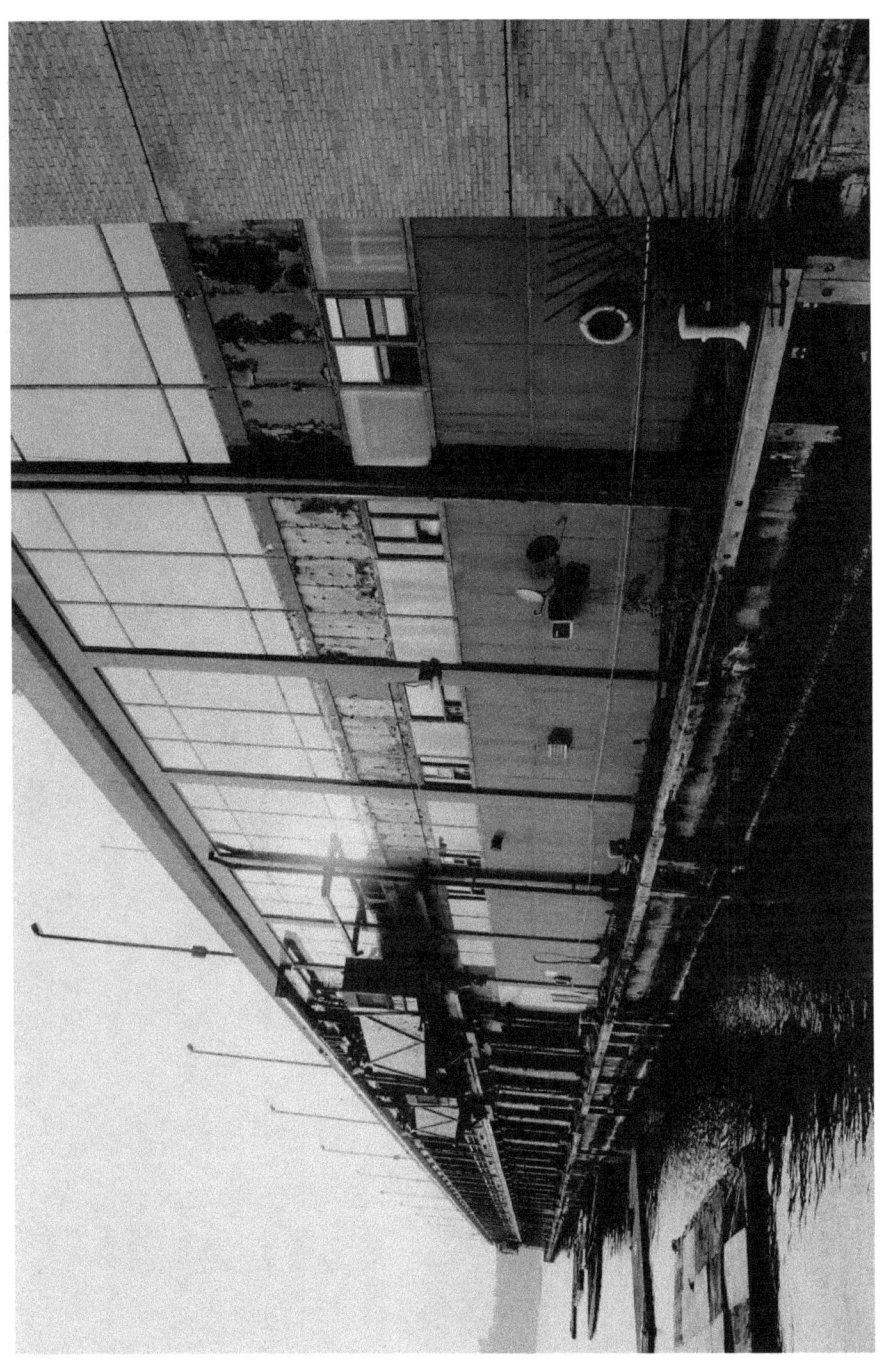

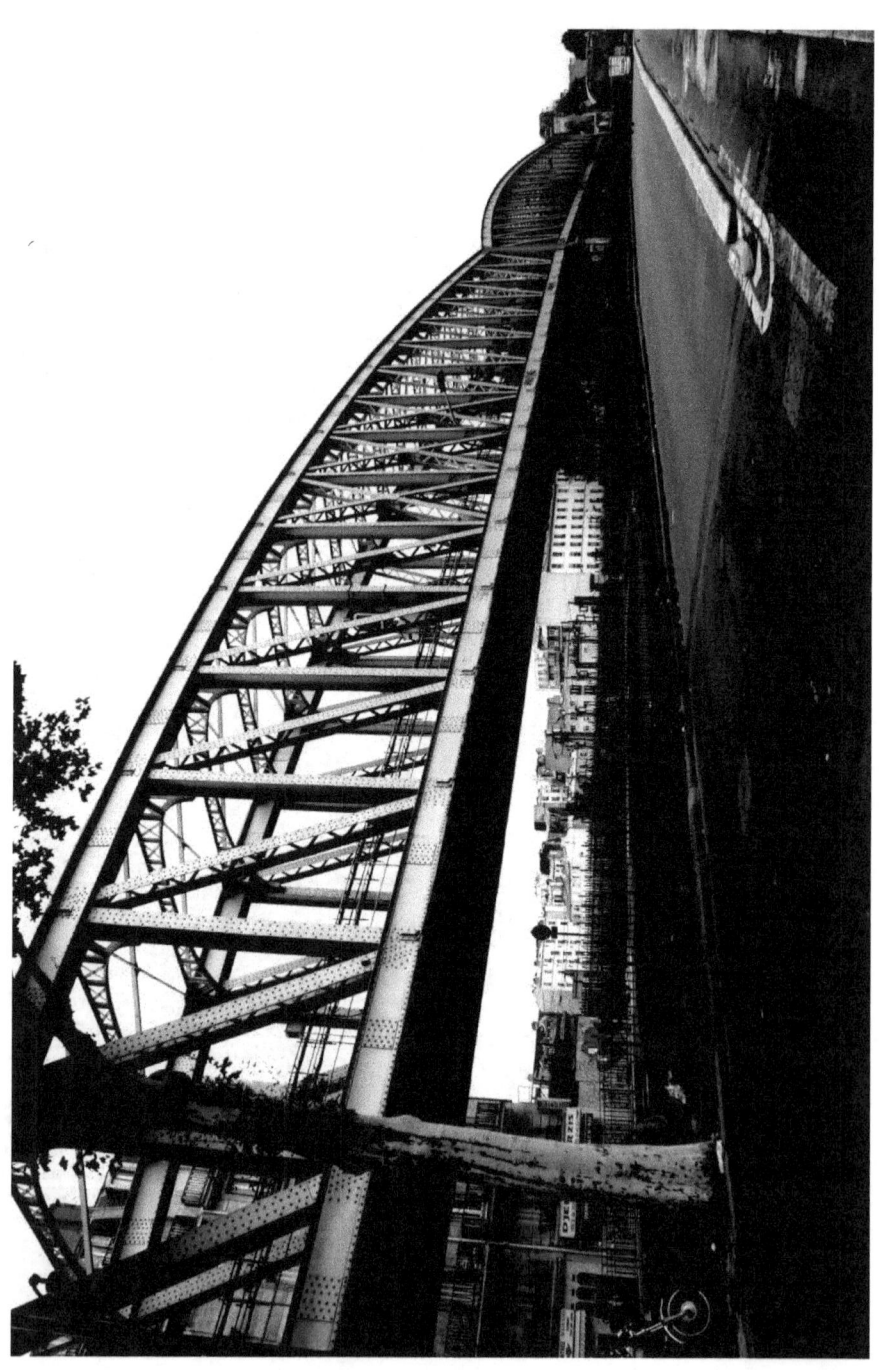

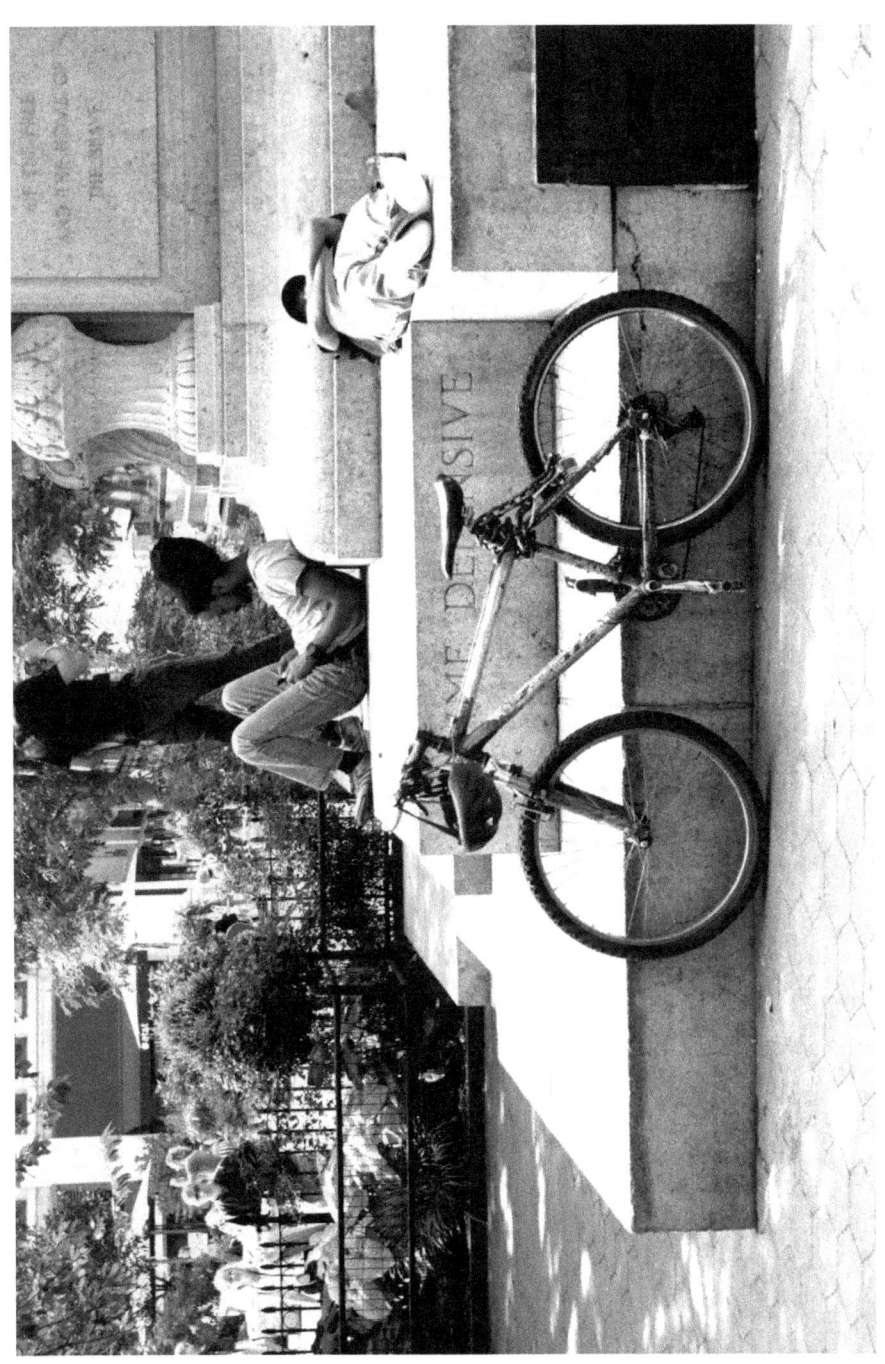

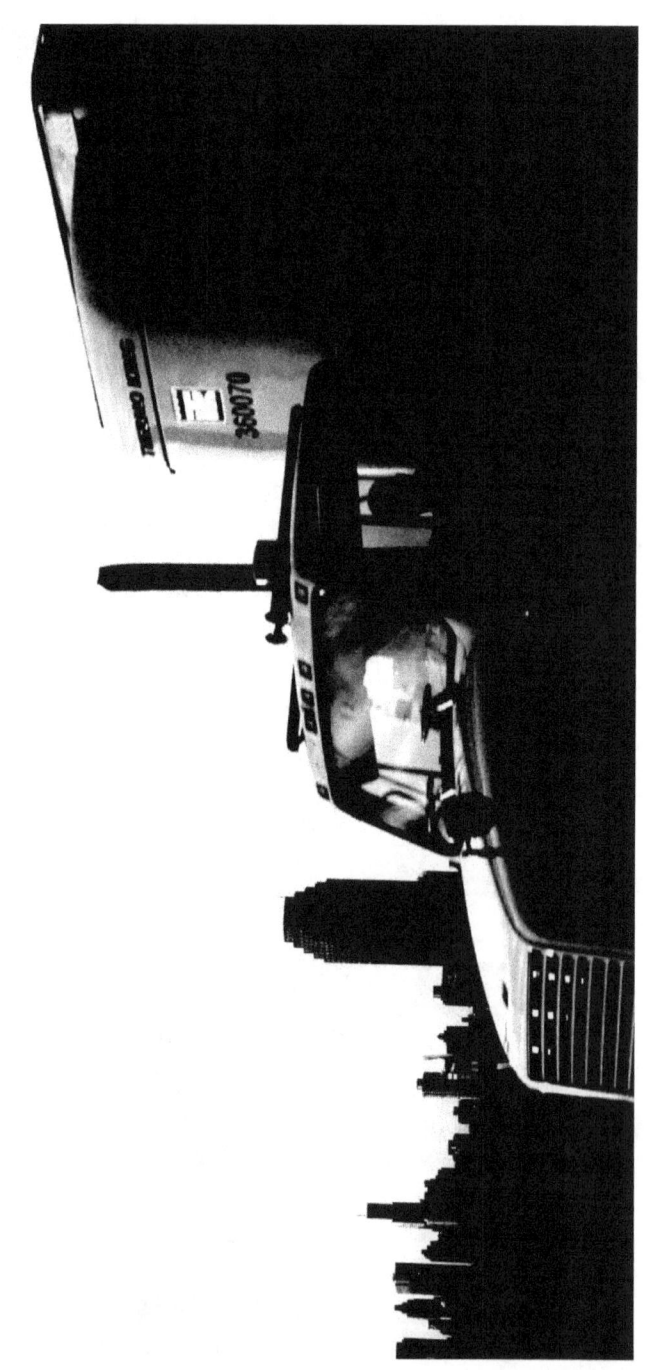

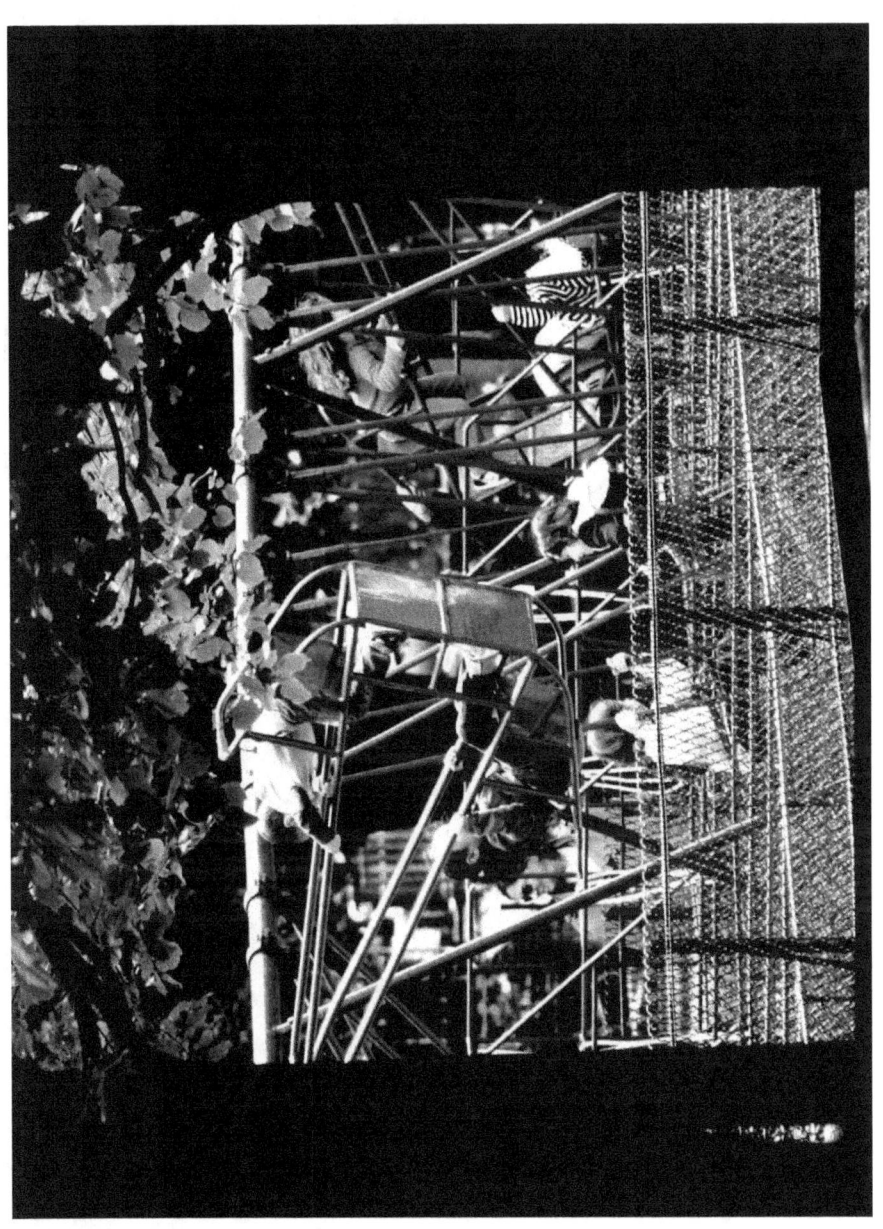

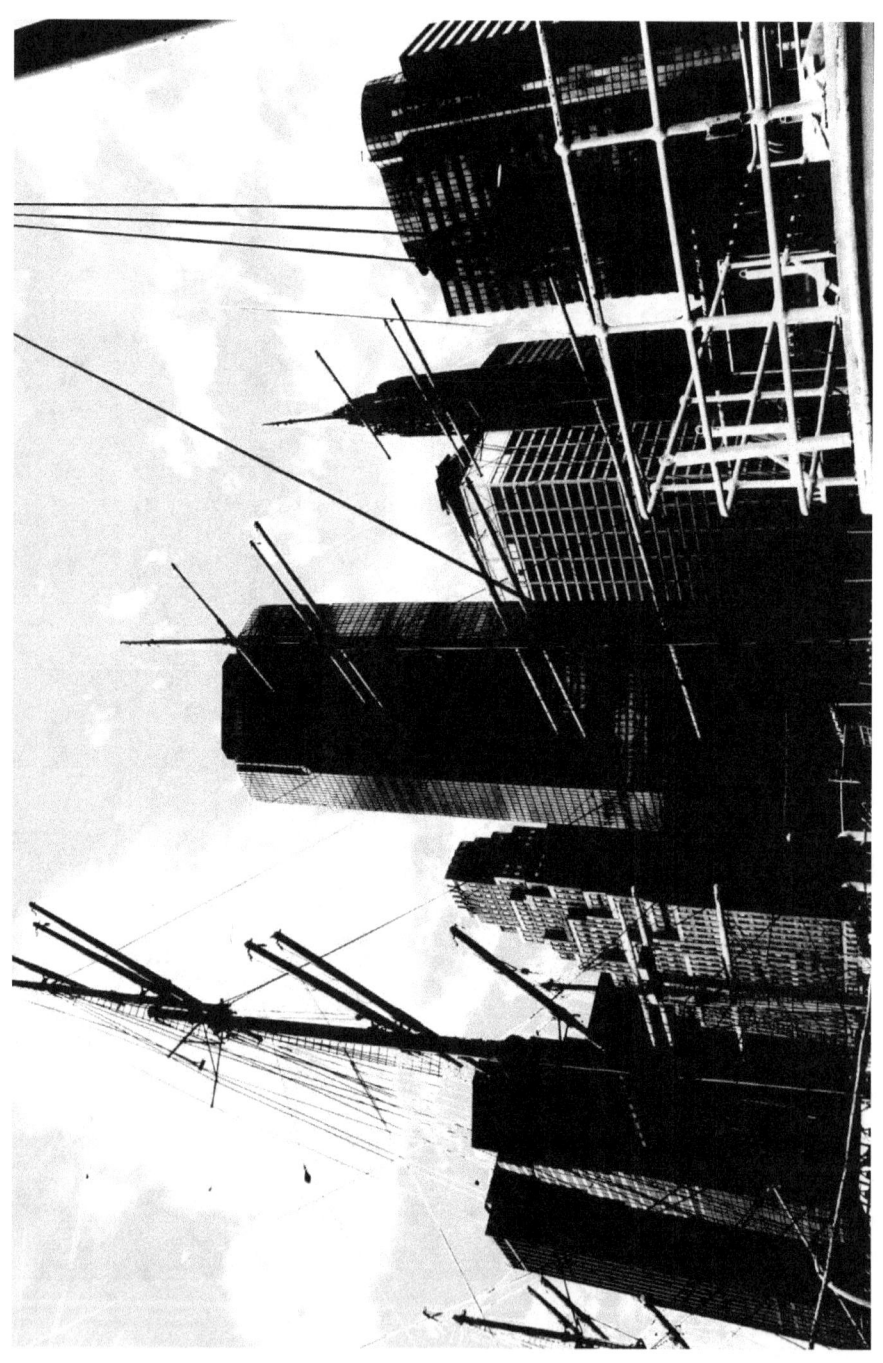

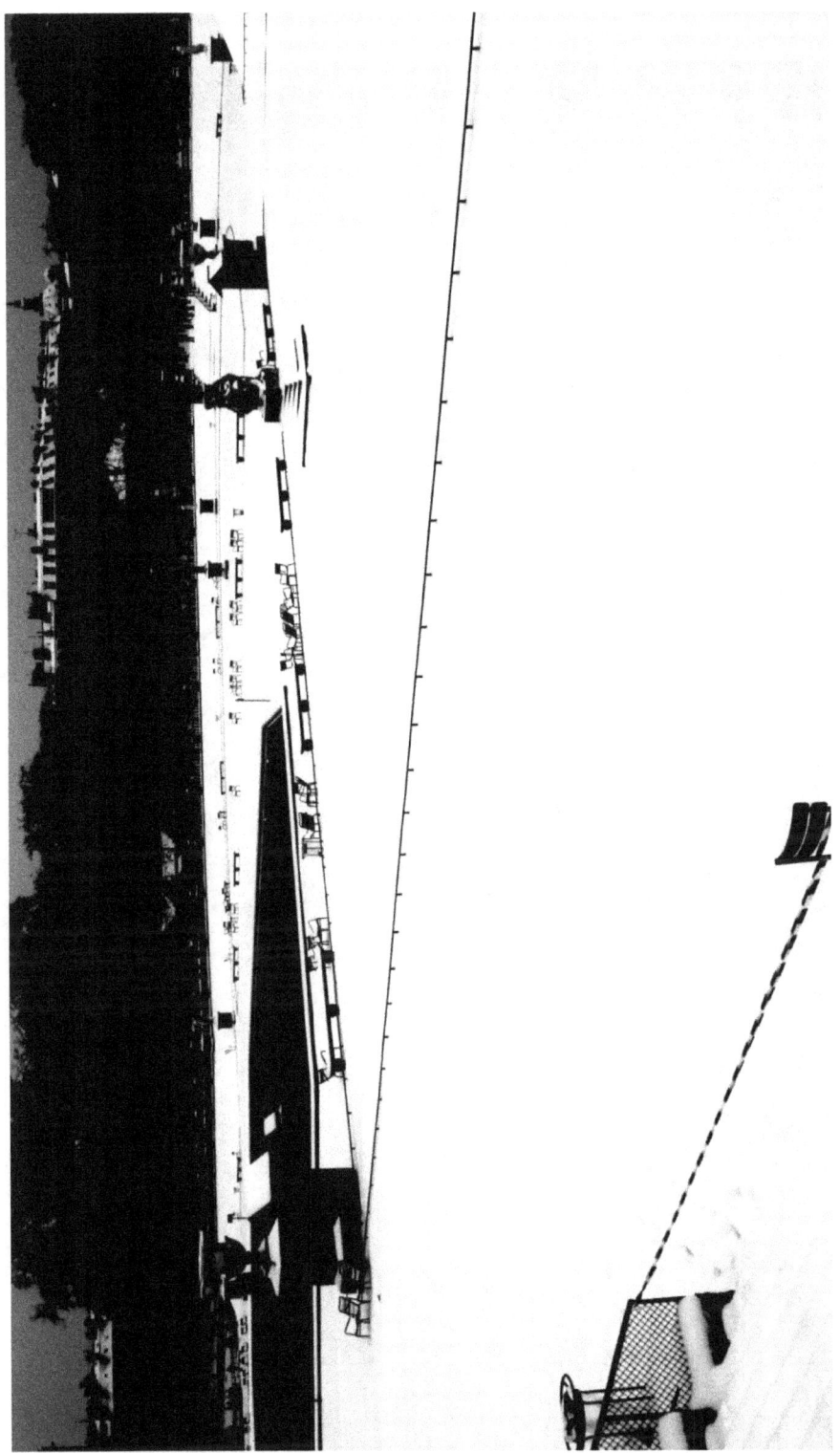

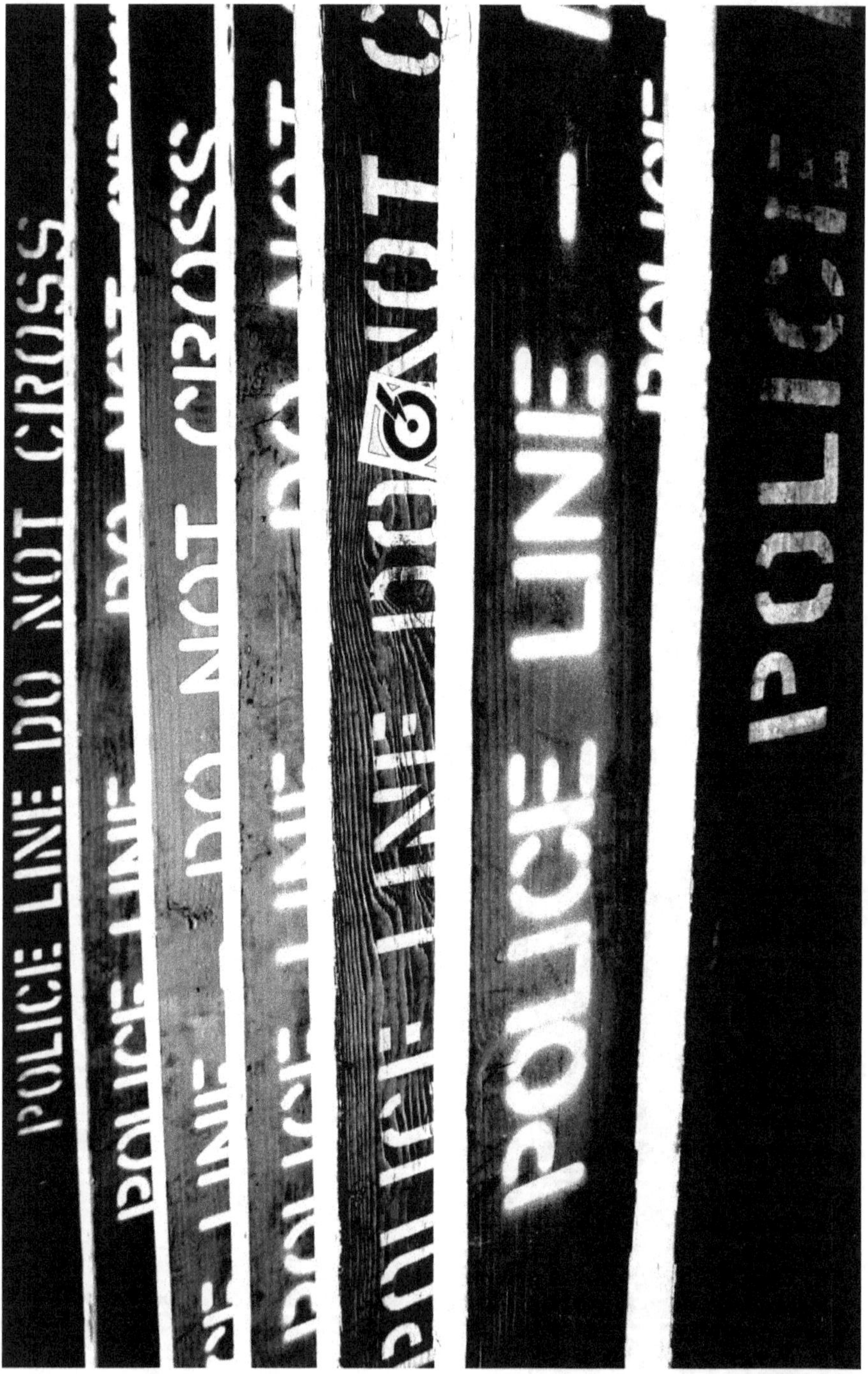
POLICE LINE DO NOT CROSS
POLICE LINE
POLICE

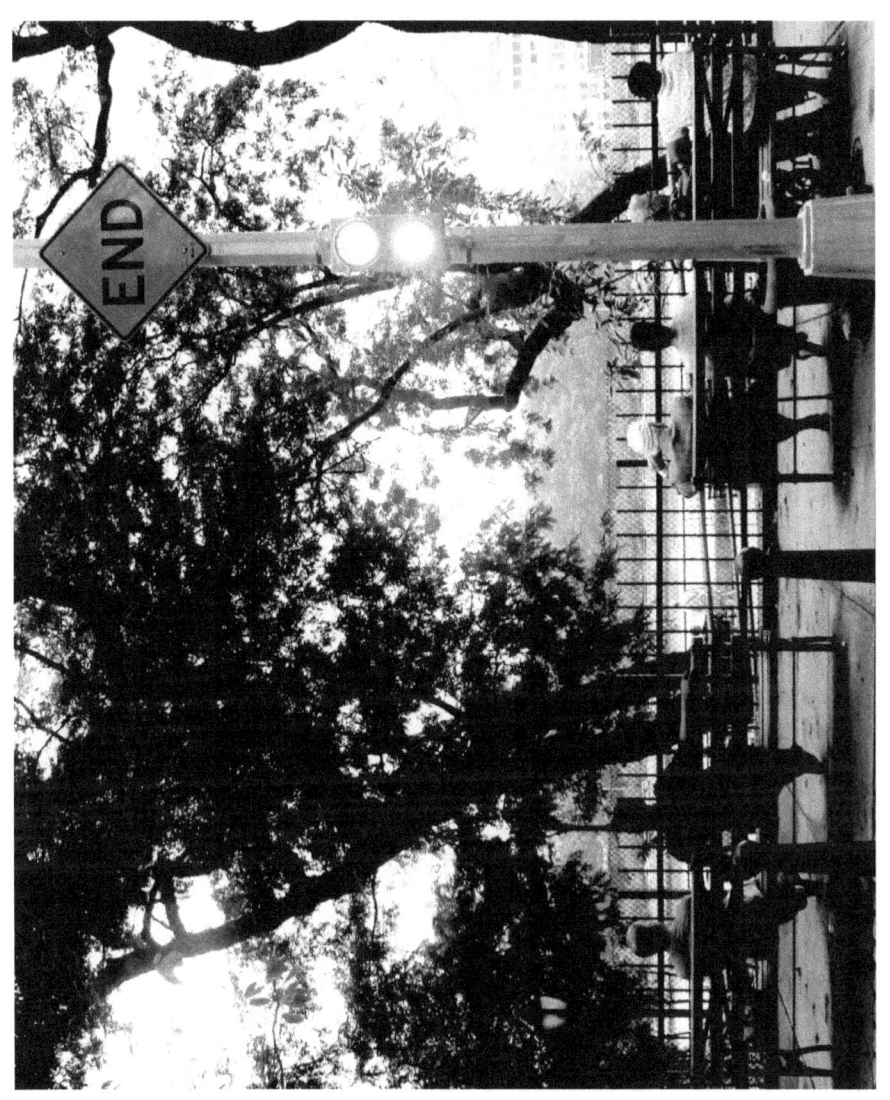

Photo captions – légendes photo

5 Teenager looking spyhole, New York City
Jeune fille regardant vasistas, New York

6 Young couple in the subway going to a Mets baseball game, Queens,
New York City
Jeune couple dans le métro se rendant à un match de baseball de l'équipe
des Mets, New York

7 Billboard, New York City
Panneau d'affichage New York

8 Running man under the rain, Varick Street, Soho, New York City
Homme courant sous la pluie, Varick Street, Soho, New York

9 Quai d'Orsay, Paris

10 Church & Cross, Dieppe, France
Eglise & Croix, Dieppe, France

11 Statue, Jardin du Luxembourg, Paris

12 Chimney & Eiffel Tower, Paris
Cheminée & Tour Eiffel, Paris

13. Window & Eiffel Tower, Paris
Fenêtre & Tour Eiffel, Paris

14 Be what you dream, New York City

15 Swings, Jardin du Ranelagh, Paris
Balançoires, Jardin du Ranelagh, Paris

16 Stairs & Bir Hakeim bridge, Paris
Escalier & Pont Bir Hakeim, Paris

17 Tattooed man at PS1, Queens, New York City
Homme tatoué au PS1, Queens, New York

18 Tattooed man, New York City
Homme tatoué, New York

19 Man sitting on a window, 14th Street, New York City
Homme assis sur une fenêtre, 14th Street, New York

20 Forbidden, East Village, New York City
Interdit, East Village, New York

21 Mother and daughter with an umbrella, Union Square Market, New York City
Mère et fille au parapluie, marché d'Union Square, New York

22 The big secret, Union Square, New York City

23 Poster Russell King, New York City
Affiche Russell King, New York

24 Cyclists, rue du Commerce, Paris
Cyclistes, rue du Commerce, Paris

25 Couple on telephone, Jardin des Tuilerie, Paris
Couple au téléphone, Jardin des Tuileries, Paris

26 Billboards on roof, Manhattan, New York City
Panneaux publicitaires sur les toits de Manhattan, New York

27 Eiffel Tower, Paris
Tour Eiffel, Paris

28 Seaport museum of NYC, Downtown, New York City
Musée de New York City à Seaport, Downtown, New York

29 Cranes, London
Grues, Londres

30 Begging musician child, rue Mouffetard, Paris
Enfant musicien mendiant, rue Mouffetard, Paris

31 Bird & statue of General de Gaulle, Champs Elysées, Paris
Oiseau & statue du Général de Gaulle, Champs Elysées, Paris

32 Tree in the street, Paris
Arbre dans la rue, Paris

33 Skateboarders, 14th street, New York City

34 View of the Empire State Building from Williamsburg, Brooklyn, New York City
Vue de l'Empire State Building de Williamsburg, Brooklyn, New York

35 Buildings & chimney, Brooklyn, New York City
Immeubles & cheminée, Brooklyn, New York

36 Station, Celerina, Switzerland
Gare, Celerina, Suisse

37 Man & warehouse, TriBeCa, New York City
Homme et entrepôts, TriBeCa, New York

38 Fire Station, Downtown, New York City
Caserne de pompiers, Downtown, New York

39 Woman & path, Zurich
Femme & passage, Zurich

40 Waste ground, Brooklyn, New York City
Terrain vague, Brooklyn, New York

41 Woman in burqa eating a cotton candy
Femme en burqa mangeant une barbe à papa

42 Child, Queens museum, Corona Park, New York City
Enfant, musée du Queens, Corona Park, New York

43 Building & chimney, Bastille district, Paris
Immeuble & cheminée, Quartier de la Bastille, Paris

44 Girls on scooters, Brooklyn, New York City
Filles faisant de la trottinette, Brooklyn, New York

45 Girl hiding behind a statue, Paris
Fille se cachant derrière une statue, Paris

46 Queens, New York City

47 Sailboat, Statue of Liberty & Battery Park, New York City
Voilier, Statue de la Liberté, Battery Park, New York

48 Violonist, Zurich lake, Zurich
Violoniste, lac de Zurich, Zurich

49 Stairs, Eiffel Tower, Paris
Escaliers, Tour Eiffel, Paris

50 Snow in Paris, Paris
Neige à Paris, Paris

51 Statues & reader, Jardin du Luxembourg, Quartier Latin, Paris
Statues & lectrice, Jardin du Luxembourg, Quartier Latin, Paris

52 Ellis Island, New York City

53 Man in disguise, Washington Square Park, New York City

Homme déguisé, Washington Square Park, New York

54 Dead end & theater, Montparnasse district, Paris
Impasse & théâtre, Quartier de Montparnasse, Paris

55 Lovers, banks of the Seine, Paris
Amoureux, quais de Seine, Paris

56 Electric transformer, New York City
Transformateur électrique, New York

57 Buildings, New York City
Immeubles, New York

58 Flags & building, New York City
Drapeaux & immeuble, East village, New York

59 Bastions park, Geneva
Parc des Bastions, Genève

60 Bicycle & art gallery, New York City
Bicyclette & gallerie d'art, New York

61 Death & Co, New York City

62 Face in the mirror, New York City
Visage dans miroir, New York

63 Chinese demonstrator in front on United Nations, New York City
Manifestante chinoise devant l'ONU, New York

64 Man & dog in a street of Athens
Homme & chien dans une rue, Athènes

65 Stony building in glass building, New York City
Immeuble de pierre dans immeuble de verre, New York

66 In a building, Chelsea, New York City
Dans un immeuble, Chelsea, New York

67 Saint-Michel Fountain
Fontaine Saint-Michel, Paris

68 Street of Zurich
Rue de Zurich

69 Church, Zurich
Eglise, Zurich

70 Eiffel Tower & tourist with an umbrella, Paris
Tour Eiffel & touriste au parapluie, Paris

71 The Pacific in San Francisco
Le Pacifique à San Francisco

72 Building & church, Avenue Marceau, Paris
Immeuble & église, Avenue Marceau, Paris

73 Lamppost & Eiffel Tower, Paris
Lampadaire & Tour Eiffel, Paris

74 Bicycle in a park, Paris
Bicyclette dans un parc, Paris

75 Looking for a wealthy lady, 5th Avenue, New York City

76 Alone in the skyscraper, Paris
Seul dans le gratte ciel, Paris

77 Snowy barges on the Seine, Paris
Péniches enneigées sur la Seine, Paris

78 Brooklyn & Manhattan Bridge, New York City
Brooklyn & Pont de Manhattan, New York

79 Inner courtyard, Paris
Cour intérieure, Paris

80 Nursery school, Paris
Jardin d'enfants, Paris

81 Eiffel Tower & Obelisk, Paris
Tour Eiffel & Obélisque, Paris

82 Stairs & skyscraper, Paris
Escalier et gratte ciel, Paris

83 Statue of Liberty seen from Red Hook, Brooklyn, New York City
Statue de la Liberté vue de Red Hook, Brooklyn, New York

84 Mother & child with balloon, Seine banks, Paris
Mère & enfant avec un ballon, quais de la Seine, Paris

85 Girls playing together in the street, Paris
Filles jouant ensemble dans la rue, Paris

86 Painter & Notre-Dame of Paris, Paris
Peintre & Notre-Dame de Paris, Paris

87 Punk, Union Square, New York City

88 Jogger crossing street, Downtown, New York City
Jogger traversant la rue, Downtown, New York

89 Teenagers, Midtown, New York City
Jeunes filles, Midtown, New York

90 Path, Bastille district, Paris
Passage, Quartier de la Bastille, Paris

91 Children, Bronx, New York City
Enfants, Bronx, New York

92 Hôtel de Bercy, Paris

93 Street, Parthenon, Athens
Rue, Parthénon, Athènes

94 Cranes & pier, New York City
Grues et quai, New York

95 Agora, Athens
Agora, Athènes

96 Pont Bir Hakeim, Paris

97 View of Broadway from a lingerie shop, New York City
Vue de Broadway d'un magasin de lingerie, New York

98 Road sign & bicycle, Paris
Panneau & bicyclette, Paris

99 Duck & Beaugrenelle, Paris
Canard & Beaugrenelle, Paris

100 Street poet, New York
Poète de rue, New York

101 Man with an US flag in the back, Brooklyn, New York City
Homme avec un drapeau des Etats-Unis dans le dos, Brooklyn, New York

102 Beaubourg, Paris

103 Reader, New York City

Lectrice, New York

104 Bar chairs, Paris
Chaises de bar, Paris

105 Quartier Latin scene, Paris
Scène du Quartier Latin, Paris

106 Is it the wind, Paris
Est-ce le vent, Paris

107 Love date, Paris
Rencontre amoureuse, Paris

108 Brooklyn bridge, New York City
Pont de Brooklyn, New York

109 Pantheon University, Paris
Université Panthéon, Paris

110 Church 1, Paros, Greece
Eglise 1, Paros, Grèce

111 Church 2, Paros, Greece
Eglise 2, Paros, Grèce

112 Painter copying picture, Art modern museum, Paris
Peintre copiant un tableau, Musée d'Art moderne, Paris

113 Parikia, Paros, Greece / Grèce

114 Sèvres-Babylone metro station, Paris
Métro Sèvres-Babylone, Paris

115 Chess players and watchers, Jardin du Luxembourg, Quartier Latin, Paris
Joueurs d'échecs et spectateurs, Jardin du Luxembourg, Quartier Latin, Paris

116 Musician & young woman, Washington Square Park, Greenwich Village, New York City
Musicien & jeune femme, Washington Square Park, Greenwich Village, New York

117 Cyclists, 6th Avenue, Greenwich Village, New York City
Cyclistes, 6th Avenue, Greenwich Village, New York

118 Children playing, Invalides, Paris

Enfants jouant, Invalides, Paris

119 Man with a sandwich board New York Dolls, Downtown, New York City
Homme-sandwich New York Dolls, Downtown; New York

120 Blond teenager looking at Brigitte Bardot photo & photo of Serge Gainsbourg and Jane Birkin, Paris
Jeune fille blonde regardant une photo de Brigitte Bardot & photo de Serge Gainsbourg en compagnie de Jane Birkin, Paris

121 Parc André Citroën, Paris

122 The Immigrant, East Side, New York City

123 One World Trade Center seen from Red Hook, Brooklyn, New York City
World Trade Center vu de Red Hook, Brooklyn, New York

124 Teenager singing, New York City
Jeune fille chantant, New York

125 Made for New York, New York City

126 Skyline from Brooklyn, New York City
Skyline vue de Brooklyn, New York

127 Sun bath, André Citroën park, Paris
Bain de soleil, Parc André Citroën, Paris

128 Vanneau metro station & rue de Sèvres, Paris
Métro Vanneau & rue de Sèvres, Paris

129 Musicians, Ile aux Cygnes, Paris
Musiciens, Ile aux Cygnes, Paris

130 Saxophonist, Bercy, Paris
Saxophoniste, Bercy, Paris

131 Smoker sunbathing, Paris
Fumeuse prenant un bain de soleil, Paris

132 Cemetery & photo exhibition about the war in Syria, Paris
Cimetière & expo photo de la guerre en Syrie, Paris

133 Chelsea New York City

134 Drôle de Drame, Quartier Latin, Paris

135 Fire escape, New York City
Escaliers de secours, New York

136 Man sitting in a park, Paris
Homme assis dans un parc, Paris

137 No age to play, Zurich
Pas d'âge pour jouer, Zurich

138 Beaugrenelle & poster, Paris
Beaugrenelle & affiches, Paris

139 New York from the World Trade Center, New York City
New York vu du World Trade Center, New York

140 Washington Square Park, Greenwich Village, New York City

141 House in Brooklyn, New York City
Maison Brooklyn, New York

142 Scene 1, Avenue du Président Kennedy, Paris
Scène 1, Avenue du Président Kennedy 1, Paris

143 Scène Scene 2, Avenue du Président Kennedy, Paris
Scène 2, Avenue du Président Kennedy 1, Paris

144 Rest, Zurich
Repos, Zurich

145 Man in the André Citroën park, Paris
Homme au Parc André Citroën, Paris

146 Little Girl, Madison Square Park, New York City
Petite fille, Madison Square Park, New York

147 Cyclists, Manhattan Bridge, New York City
Cyclistes, Pont de Manhattan, New York

148 Couple, SoHo, New York City
Couple, SoHo, New York

149 Man & woman, Bryant Park, New York City
Homme et femme, Bryant Park, New York

150 Couple & photographs, Paris
Couple & photographes, Paris

151 Esplanade Paris 15°, Paris

152 Dugboat on the Atlantic, New York City
Remorqueur dans l'Atlantique, New York

153 New York Times seen from bus terminal, Midtown, New York City
New York Times vu du Terminal Bus, Midtown, New York

154 Dog, New York City
Chien, New York

155 Motorbike & graph, Athens
Moto & graffiti, Athènes

156 Tags, Athens
Tags, Athènes

157 Churches & houses, Paros, Greece
Eglises & maisons, Paros, Grèce

158 People waiting for a bus, Bronx, New York City
Gens attendant l'autobus, Bronx, New York City

159 One World Trade Center, New York City

160 Little boats, Jardin des Tuileries, Paris
Petits bateaux, Jardin des Tuileries, Paris

161 View of Omonia district, Athens
Vue du quartier Omonia, Athènes

162 Children playing with water jets, Parc André Citroën, Paris
Enfants jouant avec jets d'eau, Parc André Citroën, Paris

163 Stairs, East Village, New York City
Escaliers, East Village, New York

164 House & courtyard, Grenelle district, Paris
Maison et cour, Quartier de Grenelle, Paris

165 Child looking at the East River, New York City
Enfant regardant l'East River, New York

166 Children playing in the snow covered lawn, avenue de Breteuil, Paris
Enfants jouant sur une pelouse recouverte de neige, avenue de Breteuil,
Paris

167 Couple being photographed in Washington Square Park, Greenwich Village, New York City
Couple se faisant photographier dans le Washington Square Park, Greenwich Village, New York

168 Young Woman, banks of the Seine, Paris
Jeune femme, quais de Seine, Paris

169 Bench, Paris
Banc, Paris

170 Governors Island Terminal, Manhattan, New York City
Embarcadère pour Governors Island, Manhattan, New York

171 9/11 Memorial, Greenwich Village, New York City
Mémorial du 11 septembre, Greenwich Village, New York

172 The Invalides under snow, Paris
Les Invalides sous la neige, Paris

173 Chairs, Jardin des Tuileries, Paris
Chaises, Jardin des Tuileries, Paris

174 Men painting a billboard, banks of the Seine, Paris
Hommes peignant un panneau, quais de Seine, Paris

175 Women, East River, New York City
Femmes, East River, New York

176 Ile aux Cygnes, Paris

177 Downtown, New York City

178 Quai Saint-Michel, Quartier Latin, Paris

179 Boats at Central Park, New York City
Barques à Central Park, New York

180 Puppet theater, Champs Elysées, Paris
Guignol, Champs Elysées, Paris

181 Gorcery Store, Oakville, California

182 Cosney Island, New York City

183 Duroc metro station under snow, Paris
Le métro Duroc sous la neige, Paris

184 Man on an emergency stair, Chinatown, New York City
Homme sur un escalier de secours, Chinatown, New York

185 Old wooden house disused, Queens, New York City
Vieille maison en bois désaffectée, Queens, New York

186 Man looking at the posters of concerts at a bouquiniste, Quai de Montebello, Paris
Homme regardant les affiches d'un bouquiniste, Quai de Montebello, Paris

187 Musicians, Central Park, New York City
Musiciens, Central Park, New York

188 Little girl & the Washington Square Park Fountain, Greenwich Village, New York City
Petite fille & la Fontaine du Washington Square Park, Greenwich Village, New York

189 Teenagers, Hudson River park, New York City
Jeunes, Hudson River Park, New York

190 Fortuneteller, Union square, New York City
Diseuse de bonnes aventures, Union Square, New York

191 Sex shop, 8th avenue, Midtown, New York City
Sex shop, 8° avenue, Midtown, New York

192 Native American craftsman, 5th avenue in front of Central Park, New York City
Artisan amérindien, 5° avenue devant Central Park, New York

193 Homeless men, Tompkins Square, East Village, New York City
Sans abris, Tompkins Square, East Village, New York

194 Tugboat, East River, New York City
Remorqueur, East River, New York

195 Musician & dog, Bowery, New York City
Musicien & chien, Bowery, New York

196 Joggeur à l'Ile aux Cygnes sous la neige, Paris

197 Subway Bronx, New York City
Métro Bronx, New York

198 Avenue de la Motte Picquet, Paris

199 Child in Corona Park, Queens, New York City

Enfant dans Corona Park, Queens, New York

200 Barber Shop, Midtown, New York City
Coiffeur, Midtown, New York

201 Mountains Engadine, Grisons, Switzerland
Montagnes Engadine, Grisons, Suisse

202 Seagulls flying over the Seine, Paris
Mouettes volant au-dessus de la Seine, Paris

203 Demonstrators, Chelsea, New York City
Manifestants, Chelsea, New York

204 Cyclists, Battery Park, New York City
Cyclistes, Battery Park, New York

205 Electric pole, San Francisco
Poteau électrique, Sans Francisco

206 Metro station, Paris
Station de métro, Paris

207 Fir & ice, Celerina, Switzerland
Sapin & glace, Celerina, Suisse

208 Cyclist in the streets of New York City
Cycliste dans les rues de New York

209 Children looking at the sea, Battery Park, New York City
Enfants regardant la mer, Battery Park, New York

210 Ile de la Cité & Seine, Paris

211 Rainy day, New York City
Jour pluvieux à New York

212 Man & dog, Washington Square Park, Greenwich Village, New York City
Homme & chien, Washington Square Park, Greenwich Village, New York

213 Building workers, Brooklyn, New York City
Ouvriers du bâtiment, Brooklyn, New York

214 Lovers, Corona Park, Queens, New York City
Amoureux, Corona Park, Queens, New York

215 Mother & child, Lower East Side, New York City

Mère et enfant, Lower East Side, New York

216 Expressway, Brooklyn Heights, New York City
Voie rapide, Brooklyn Heights, New York

217 Graffiti on building wall, Paris
Graffiti sur un mur d'immeuble, Paris

218 Child playing, Washington Square Park Fountain, Greenwich Village,
New York City
Enfant jouant, Fontaine du Washington Square Park, Greenwich Village,
New York

219 Biker in the streets of New York City
Motard dans les rues de New York

220 Central Park, New York City
Central Park, New York

221 Man in the streets of New York City
Homme dans les rues de New York

222 Statue of Liberty, New York City
Statue de la Liberté, New York

223 House & snow, Celerina, Switzerland
Maison & neige, Celerina, Suisse

224 Photograph & model, Pont de Bir Hakeim, Paris
Photographe & modèle, Pont de Bir Hakeim, Paris

225 Ferris wheel, place de la Concorde, Paris
Grande roue, place de la Concorde, Paris

226 Boy playing with little soldiers at a flea market, Paris
Garçon jouant avec des petits soldats à une brocante, Paris

227 Young man playing Shakespeare in front of a little girl on a scooter,
Washington Square Park, Greenwich Village, New York City
Jeune home jouant du Shakespeare devant une petite fille en trottinette,
Washington Square Park, Greenwich Village, New York

228 Beaugrenelle district at night, Paris
Quartier de Beaugrenelle la nuit, Paris

229 Palais du Luxembourg, Paris

230 Jardin du Palais Royal, Paris

231 Man looking at his mobile phone, 6th avenue, Greenwich Village, New York City
Homme regardant son téléphone mobile, 6° avenue, Greenwich Village, New York

232 Woman in front of the tribunal, Downtown, New York City
Femme devant le tribunal, Downtown, New York

233 Men talking, City Hall Square, New York City
Hommes discutant, City Hall Square, New York

234 People waiting for a train in a subway station, New York City
Personnes attendant une rame de métro, New York

235 Horses, La Chapelle aux Pots, France
Chevaux, La Chapelle-aux-Pots, France

236 Chekers players, Riverside Park, Harlem, New York City
Joueurs de Dames, Riverside Park, Harlem, New York

237 Basketball ground, East Village, New York City
Terrain de basket-ball, East Village, New York

238 Trocadéro & Eiffel Tower, Paris
Le Trocadéro & la Tour Eiffel

239 Beaugrenelle, Ile aux Cygnes & Seine, Paris
Beaugrenelle, l'Ile-aux-Cygnes & la Seine, Paris

240 Street of New York City, New York City
Rue de New York, New York

241 Warehouse, Chelsea, New York City
Entrepôt, Chelsea, New York

242 Golden Gate Bridge, San Francisco

243 5th Avenue in front of Central Park, New York City
5th Avenue devant Central Park, New York

244 Walled up building, Cher Midi Street, Paris
Immeuble muré, rue du Cherche Midi, Paris

245 Pier on Hudson River, New York City
Quai sur la rivière Hudson, New York

246 Aerial metro, Paris

Métro aérien Paris

247 Resting cyclist, Madison Square Park, New York City
Cycliste au repos, Madison Square Park, New York

248 Truck, Expressway, Queens, New York City
Camion, Expressway, Queens, New York

249 Children on swings, Jardin du Luxembourg, Quartier Latin, Paris
Enfants sur des balançoires, Jardin du Luxembourg, Quartier Latin, Paris

250 Sailboat in New York harbor, New York City
Voiliers dans le port de New York

251 Snowy Jardin du Luxembourg, Paris
Jardin du Luxembourg enneigé, Paris

252 Do not cross the line, New York City

253 The end, New York City

DYLIC – VATIMBELLA
© 2016

www.ingramcontent.com/pod-product-compliance
Lightning Source LLC
Chambersburg PA
CBHW051856170526
45168CB00001B/134